THE
WHY
OF THE
BUY

CONSUMER BEHAVIOR AND FASHION MARKETING

Patricia Mink Rath
Marketing Education Consultant—Winnetka, IL

Stefani Bay
The Illinois Institute of Art—Chicago

Richard Petrizzi
The Illinois Institute of Art—Chicago

Penny Gill
PWG Communications Inc.—White Plains, NY

**FAIRCHILD BOOKS
AN IMPRINT OF BLOOMSBURY
PUBLISHING INC.**

Fairchild Books
An imprint of Bloomsbury Publishing Inc.

1385 Broadway
New York
NY 10018
USA

50 Bedford Square
London
WC1B 3DP
UK

www.bloomsbury.com

First published in 2015

Library of Congress Cataloging-in-Publication Data
Rath, Patricia Mink.
The why of the buy : consumer behavior and fashion marketing / Patricia Mink Rath, International Academy of Design and Technology, Chicago, Stefani Bay, The Illinois Institute of Art, Chicago, Richard Petrizzi, The Illinois Institute of Art, Chicago, Penny Gill, PWG Communications Inc., White Plains, NY. -- Second Edition.
pages cm
Includes bibliographical references and index.
ISBN 978-1-60901-898-6 (alk. paper)
1. Fashion merchandising--United States. 2. Consumer behavior--United States. I. Title.
HD9940.U4R38 2014
746.9'20688--dc23
2014008262

ISBN: 978-1-60901-898-6

Typeset by Precision Graphics
Cover Design by Paul Burgess
Text Design by Cara David Design
Printed and bound in China

Contents

Extended Contents

PART II

Internal Factors Influence Fashion Consumers

PART III

External Factors Influence Fashion Consumers 152

Preface

How do people decide what to buy for their wardrobes and their homes? What makes them select a particular item or brand instead of another? Consumer behavior can appear to be a mysterious set of activities, sometimes not even recognized by consumers themselves as they make up their minds for or against purchasing a new outfit, pair of shoes, set of towels, or sofa. There are, however, certain internal and external influences and patterns of decision making that shed some light on that enigma. Exploring what those influences and patterns are, and how they are interwoven in the fashion consumer's decision-making process, is the purpose of this text.

This book was originally developed because no previous work existed to meet the needs of college students as they explore the consumer buying process specifically as it relates to the fashion industries; it has been updated in this new edition to reflect the dramatic impact that social media and mobile computing, among other current trends, now exert on many aspects of consumer behavior and fashion marketing. The text begins with an overview of why the study of consumer behavior is important and the relationship between consumers and marketers. It continues by explaining the internal and external factors that influence fashion consumers, describes how fashion marketers communicate their messages and how fashion consumers make their decisions, and concludes with a discussion of fashion consumers, ethics, and responsible citizenship. To provide relevant industry examples of fashion interest to consumers, each chapter contains related Point of View and Case in Point sidebars as well as Key Terms, Questions for Review, Activities, and Mini-Projects.

Organization of The Text

Part I: We Are All Consumers

Chapter 1 explains why consumer behavior is important, and Chapter 2 elucidates the relationship between consumers and fashion marketers.

Part II: Internal Factors Influence Fashion Consumers

Chapter 3 describes how consumers perceive, learn, and remember; Chapter 4 explains motivation in relation to consuming fashion goods. In Chapter 5 consumer attitudes are explored; while personality and the consumer are the topics of Chapter 6.

Part III: External Factors Influence Fashion Consumers

In Chapter 7, age, family, and life cycle influences are covered; Chapter 8 deals with the topic of social influences on consumers; while demographics and psychographics important in understanding consumer behavior in fashion are found in Chapter 9.

Part IV: How Fashion Marketers Communicate and Consumers Decide

Chapter 10 is concerned with marketing research, how marketers obtain and use consumer information; Chapter 11 delves into the impact and importance of social media to fashion consumers and marketers. Chapter 12 details how consumers reach their buying decisions; while Chapter 13 explores when, where, and how consumers purchase fashion goods. The global aspects of fashion design and consumption are the topic of Chapter 14.

Part V: Fashion Consumers and Responsible Citizenship

Chapter 15 explains how ethics and social responsibility influence consumer behavior; and Chapter 16 describes the role of government and how laws and regulations, as well as consumer advocacy groups, play a role in consumers' decisions to purchase fashion goods.

Text Features

In addition to its enthusiastic and engaging writing style, *The Why of the Buy* contains a number of features concerning consumer behavior and marketing strategies that arouse student attention and maintain interest. They are useful for further investigation, class discussion, individual reports, and team projects.

WHAT DO I NEED TO KNOW ABOUT . . . ?

Each chapter opens with a list of major concepts that students will find covered within that chapter, providing a roadmap for their study and an easy reference to ensure they have met the objectives upon completing the chapter.

CASE IN POINT

Each chapter contains one or more Case in Point sidebars that put a spotlight on current examples of consumer behavior or consumer-driven marketing concepts in real-life situations or activities. These features add timeliness and interest to the chapter content and make the material more meaningful to the student. Following are some examples:

- Why Millennials don't shop online
- How Dove celebrates diversity in its advertising
- The changing face of the American family
- Macy's use of YouTube personalities to promote its fashions
- Burberry's multimedia store design that replicates the online experience for customers

POINT OF VIEW

The chapters also feature one or more Point of View sidebars that offer fresh, timely insights or current viewpoints on relevant consumer behavior and marketing topics. These segments, too, add a slice of reality and add to students' understanding of the fashion world in an intriguing way. Examples include the following:

- The "buttons" that help generate buzz
- How emotions influence what consumers buy
- How Millennials are creating their own circles of fashion influence
- The issues involved when social media sites monetize user reviews
- How consumer advocates have taken on the cosmetics industry over unsafe ingredients

LET'S TALK

Also contained within each chapter are several Let's Talk questions relating to the content just presented. These questions enable instructors and students to discuss, react to, and perhaps elaborate on the topics explained. Following are some examples:

- How do you decide what to buy? Do you base your decisions on trends, practicality, brand name, or the suggestions of friends?
- For each of the last three fashion purchases you made, which of the three elements of the hierarchy of attitude was the greatest influence? Explain.
- Why do you think consumers might tend to leave more positive feedback than negative comments about a brand on social media? Have you ever offered your feedback to a brand? Was it positive or negative? Did you get a reply?
- What products would you consider purchasing online? Are there any items you'd prefer to buy in a physical store? Why or why not?

SUMMARY AND REVIEW

At the end of each of the 16 chapters, the following features are designed to reinforce and strengthen student comprehension of that chapter's consumer behavior concepts in an interesting way:

- The Summary reviews the major chapter topics in a succinct, step-by-step manner.
- A Key Terms list recaps the most useful words in comprehending consumer behavior and in grasping the chapter emphasis. (Each term is fully

defined both in the chapter and in the Glossary at the end of the text.)

- Review Questions cover the major points brought out in the chapter, while Activities provide an opportunity for students to connect the study of consumer behavior to fashion marketing in a realistic setting.

MINI-PROJECTS

Rounding off the end-of-chapter materials are one or two Mini-Projects that offer an opportunity to apply, in a realistic fashion setting, some of the concepts presented in the chapter. Examples include the following:

- Creating a consumer profile and a corresponding brand personality
- Recalling a recent fashion purchase and identifying the decision-making process
- Teaming with other class members and identifying a product or service each team member recently purchased using either routine, limited, or extensive decision making
- Selecting an entry on a fashion-oriented blog and analyzing how it might (or might not) influence readers to purchase a particular product

GLOSSARY

The Glossary at the end of the text contains all the key terms from each of the 16 chapters, plus their definitions. These terms enable students to understand communication within the consumer behavior and fashion communities and to put their words to use.

INSTRUCTOR'S MANUAL

An Instructor's Manual accompanying *The Why of the Buy* is available and contains chapter outlines, answers to review and discussion questions and mini-projects, plus a test bank and answers.

POWERPOINT SLIDES

A PowerPoint program presents the text's major concepts by chapter, facilitating instructor lectures and class discussion.

Acknowledgments

The fresh outlook and updated content the authors crafted into this revision edition of *The Why of the Buy* would not have been possible without the support and assistance of many people, among them representatives of the publisher, experts in the fashion and academic fields, and our families.

The authors extend special appreciation to Olga T. Kontzias, Executive Editor Emerita of Fairchild Books, who recognized the need in the market for a fashion-focused consumer behavior text and enlisted us to tackle the topic, and whose vision contributed greatly to the book's first edition. Her encouragement to undertake an updated edition remained an inspiration for our enthusiasm throughout the revision process. To the many other dedicated professionals in the Editorial, Art, Production, and Marketing departments at Fairchild who helped make this work possible, the authors also offer our thanks.

Among those in the fashion and academic fields, the authors deeply appreciate the efforts of the following people for providing information and suggestions for the text, and, on occasion, for reading portions of the manuscript:

Eric Rath, Ph.D., Professor of History, University of Kansas, Lawrence

Margot Wallace, Professor of Marketing Communication, School of Media Arts, Columbia College, Chicago

Students and valued friends who continue to inform and inspire: Michelle Balsamo, Columbia College, Chicago; Maria Demetriades, Ph.D.; Nicholas Braggo; Gina Gesmond; and Inese Apale

Colleagues (and valued friends) whose expertise and encouragement in wide-ranging collaborations have provided great knowledge as well as inspiration

The reviewers whom Fairchild Books enlisted to peer review the manuscript: Leo Z. Archambault, Mount Ida College; Susan Creasey, Western Illinois University; Wanda Dooley, Wood Tobe-Coburn; Deborah Fowler, Texas Tech University; Jasmin Kwon, Middle Tennessee State University; Keunyoung Oh, Buffalo State University (SUNY); Carol Salusso, Washington State University; and Patricia Warrington, Texas Christian University.

Last but not least, this book is dedicated to our lives' best critics and warmest sources of encouragement: Phil, Eric, Kiyomi, and Dana; Dorothy, Kai, Avery, Joshua, Nathan, Justin P., and Jillian; and Justin G. and Phoebe/Mom.

Introduction

Wherever we live, whatever our age, occupation, and background, we are all alike in that we are all consumers of fashion—but at the same time, we all have different reasons for buying. Maybe we just want a coat to keep us warm and dry; perhaps we're aiming to succeed in a job and so dress to look the part; or we might be buying a ring, hoping to bring joy to someone we love. The purpose of this newly revised and updated text is twofold: to examine our many reasons for buying and using fashion goods, and to recognize how fashion marketers use their understanding of consumer behavior to inform and persuade us to try their products.

Welcome, then, to the intriguing world of consumer behavior, the series of thoughts we have and actions we go through in deciding to buy and use goods and services. The focus of this book is consumer behavior as it relates specifically to fashion goods—that is, the variety of products including apparel, cosmetics, furniture, mobile phones, home accessories, cars, and other designed goods that are popular at a given time. Because fashion, by its nature, can change rapidly—and because of the dramatically changing landscape created by social media and mobile/digital communications—this revised edition presents an updated examination of both the ways in which consumers make fashion decisions and the ways in which fashion marketers track and anticipate consumer behavior trends in order to satisfy our needs for goods and services.

In working to meet customer needs, marketers look for those product qualities that will make people feel good about their purchases; these qualities are known as consumer benefits. We buy emotionally and justify logically. Consumer benefits can be tangible—for example, the beauty and value of a diamond ring—or intangible, such as the delight the recipient will feel when presented with the gift. When people buy fashion goods, they are buying benefits—what the product will do for them. "Will the dark suit make me look slimmer?" "Does that bronzer make me look healthier?" "By driving that convertible, will I stand a chance with that certain someone?" "Will my friends be impressed by my new smartphone?" Of course, everyone's ideas of product benefits are different, but marketers have found that large groups of people may be looking for the same kinds of benefits and that their marketplace behavior is similar. Marketers identify these groups and organize them according to those similarities. Businesses, particularly fashion businesses, know that they cannot serve every customer equally well, so they have to decide which customers they can serve most efficiently and profitably. To do this, marketers use a process called market segmentation: dividing the total population into distinct groups seeking similar customer benefits and showing similar purchasing behaviors. In this way, fashion marketers can best work to meet customer needs.

There are many ways to identify customers who share similar behaviors and lifestyles. Furthermore, consumers are often grouped by characteristics including gender, age, geographic location, income, even apparel size, in order to provide the right products for a targeted customer group. For example, the mid-price retailer Gap recognized that many of its female customers were either too large or too short to wear regular sizes, so the company began offering plus and petite sizes. Market segmentation, then, allows fashion marketers to most accurately anticipate, identify, and respond to consumer fashion needs with the hope of keeping their customers' loyalty and thus staying in business and improving their profits. Another example of how companies cater to specific market segments can be seen in the efforts of handbag and accessories marketer Coach, which, in addition to its leather handbags in the upper price ranges, established a lower price handbag line for younger customers.

As you can tell, marketers respond to consumer needs because customers—as they decide what they will buy and use—are the reason for the existence of a business. However, any given business cannot serve everyone; therefore, by using strategies such as market segmentation, a business finds those customers it can best serve profitably. For example, Target understands that its customers want current fashions—even designer names like Missoni or Peter Pilotto—but at a very moderate price. Target needs to generate a profit in order to continue its business. Identifying customers' needs and focusing on the needs that a company can best serve while making a profit is the marketing concept. In the highly competitive fashion field, the most successful businesses pay close attention to the marketing concept—their very existence depends on it!

Today's fashion marketplace is global, and fashion news is spread instantly around the world via the Internet and mobile communications. At the same time, social media has opened a two-way dialogue between consumers and marketers—not to mention providing consumers with a vast source of fashion information and influence at their fingertips. This communications network permits consumers to express their needs and marketers to understand those needs and fulfill them at faster speeds than ever before. In this updated text, we explore the many ways in which digital communications and social media have changed the entire game plan both for consumers making fashion decisions and marketers eager to influence those decisions.

Our approach begins with a look at the relationship between consumers and the field of fashion, showing the contributions that consumers make to fashion and design. Next we explore the minds of consumers to observe how humans perceive and learn. We then look at what motivates consumers and how attitudes and values influence their selection and purchase of fashion goods. Our focus then shifts to examine how marketers' methods of persuasion work to influence consumer actions. As consumers we see ourselves a number of ways, and our self-perceptions can also influence our choice of fashion goods.

The outside world has an effect as well; factors such as family, age, and ethnicity can have an impact on our fashion purchases, as can our friends, social class, income, and lifestyle. Fashion marketers collect extensive information on consumer motivations and decisions in an effort to ensure their persuasion will lead to our ultimate satisfaction as consumers. Before buying, consumers may go through numerous decision-making steps, seeking information from sources such as social networks, stores, catalogs, the Internet, TV, and friends, among others. For some consumers, this search can be local; for others, it can be worldwide. Organizations (both private and governmental) have been created to help consumers in reaching buying decisions, and to protect consumers from potentially harmful products or business practices. These topics and more are what we will be exploring as we delve into the "why of the buy." Consumer behavior and fashion marketing are fascinating processes—let's see how they interact!

THE
WHY
OF THE
BUY

**FAIRCHILD
BOOKS**

Part I
WE ARE ALL CONSUMERS

SHOPPING has become an American pastime. Consumers buy both for need and for entertainment, as Part I describes.

Through learning as much as possible about consumers, fashion businesses can work to influence customer purchasing today and in the future. Chapter 1 lays the groundwork for *The Why of the Buy*, discussing what consumers want and how marketers can best serve them. Chapter 2 examines what consumers value, and the connection between companies and customers, followed by a description of how businesses gather consumer information, develop strategies, and create what they hope will be lasting marketing relationships with their customers.

CHAPTER 1

Why Is Consumer Behavior Important to the Fields of Fashion and Design?

WHAT DO I NEED TO KNOW ABOUT THE IMPORTANCE OF CONSUMER BEHAVIOR IN THE FASHION AND DESIGN FIELDS?

✔ The crucial roles that marketing, in general, and consumer behavior, specifically, play in the success of a product/service.

✔ Why an understanding of how people make purchasing decisions is the key to effectively communicating with consumers.

✔ Why marketers must study consumer behavior in order to determine and deliver what customers need and want.

✔ How culture influences buyers and how, combined with the zeitgeist, it is a major determinant of what people buy.

✔ Why market segmentation is vital to identifying the right customer at the right time.

Every January, the National Retail Federation, the world's largest retail trade association, holds its Annual Convention and Expo in New York City. At a recent convention, the most important topics included:

- The Subconscious Mind, Habits, and Behaviors of Consumers
- Retail Goes Personal: Creating Stores Shoppers Want
- Analytics to Understand the Multi-Channel and Multi-Device Customer
- Product Innovation for the People and by the People
- Understanding New Technologies and their Influences on Consumer Behavior
- "Catch and Keep" the Digital Shopper: How to Deliver Retail Their Way[1]

Why were these topics of such interest to convention attendees? Because they were seeking the answer to the eternal marketing question—the one that's asked again and again by businesspeople every day: What do customers want, and how can we best serve them?

It's an important question—one that addresses the very essence of doing business successfully. The more we learn about what people purchase and their behaviors before, during, and after those purchases, the more fascinating the issue becomes. Read these examples and you'll see what we mean.

Did you know that there is a group of young African men from the Republic of the Congo, known as *Sapeurs,* or members of the *Société des Ambianceurs et des Personnes Élégantes* (Society of Tastemakers and Elegant People), who, although chronically unemployed and living in the worst poverty, devote themselves to purchasing and wearing expensive clothing, made in the design houses of Paris, London, and Milan? To possess these precious pieces, *Sapeurs* do whatever it takes to make enough money to buy an ensemble and wear it with pride, while displaying the most gentlemanly bearing and behavior amidst their dismal surroundings (Figure 1.1).[2]

Did you know that in the United States, there is one group of consumers that shops using a tablet or mobile phone 70 percent more than other groups do, that is more than two and a half times more likely to judge the quality of a product by its packaging, and that is more than twice as likely to follow trends and try new products first? If you guessed that it's top income earners, or maybe the under-30 crowd, you guessed wrong. It's the Hispanic community, which is rapidly becoming the most influential voice in pop culture, business, and politics, and exerting a trendsetting impact that can make or break the success of a product or service.[3]

Did you know that a recent study reported that children between the ages of 2 and 17 watch an annual average of 15,000 to 18,000 hours of television during which they see 25,000 to 40,000 commercials? (Other studies' precise numbers differ slightly, but all are comparable.) Compare these numbers with the 12,000 hours spent per year in school. Approximately $15 to $17 billion is spent yearly by companies advertising to children in the United States, the impact of which is getting stronger due to the lessening of influence by parents and others in the older generation.[4]

These stories all lead to one essential question: Why? Why do people buy what they buy? What are the motivators behind our buying practices? To begin to uncover the answers, we must start with an understanding of the term **consumer behavior,** which is the central issue of this book. We define consumer behavior as the actions and decision-making processes of buyers as they recognize their desire for a product or service and engage in the search, evaluation, purchase, use, and disposal of that particular commodity. Consumer behavior is the study of **consumption:** the using up of a resource by the person who has selected, adopted, used, discarded, and (hopefully) recycled it.

FIGURE 1.1 The Congolese Sapeurs value dressing like gentlemen; this man proudly models his designer suit in Kinshasa, a city badly damaged by years of conflict and struggling under the weight of refugee camps and poverty.

Fashion and Design Purchases Are Unique

When it comes to the selection of fashion-related goods, some very specific influences determine our buying behavior. Why? We use fashionable items primarily to make statements about ourselves, our tastes, our values, our identities, our aspirations—that is, the way we want others to see us. People seek different goods for different reasons. Some of us are drawn to items that bear the names of famous designers, some to pieces that are comfortable and affordable, some to items that reflect elements of good design.

What, exactly, is *design*? In his book *By Design,* author Ralph Caplan calls it "a process for making things right, for shaping what people need. We all live with designed objects that we love, hate, use, break, and don't know how to fix . . . we live in a designed world."[5] *Webster's New World Dictionary* defines it as "to plan and carry out, especially by artistic arrangement or in a skillful way; to make original plans for or outcome aimed at."[6] Our working definition of **design** is a hybrid: a creative process, driven by a need, that leads to an invention of some sort, be it practical or artistic, functional or simply attractive, devised to enhance life in some way.

To be sure, fashion has an important relationship to design of all kinds, because the concept of fashion pertains to more than just clothing. It includes automobiles, furniture, accessories, cuisine, appliances, lighting, bathroom fixtures, jewelry, music, graphics, photography, industrial products, paint colors, electronics, and so on. Simply stated, design covers a lot of ground.

The term **fashion** applies to anything that's of the moment and subject to change; it's anything that members of a population deem desirable and appropriate at a given time. During the past few years, many celebrities have turned their pampered pooches into chic fashion accessories (Figure 1.2). These doggy darlings have accompanied their famous owners to fashion shows and galas, traveling in designer canine carriers, decked out in cashmere, sequins, and feathers (yes, we're talking about the pups!). Who knows what type of pet garb will be *de rigueur* by the time you read this book? But one thing is for sure: Fashion trendsetters will likely be on the trail of something entirely different by then.

Fashion and design are both about tuning into the **zeitgeist,** the spirit of the times. To be fashionable or engage productively in the process of design, one must be extremely well read, well rounded, in tune with current aesthetics, politics, popular products, culture, art, architecture, business—everything occurring in the present, which together make up the zeitgeist. Developing awareness and sensitivity must be top priorities, because success in the worlds of fashion and design requires a person to be up-to-date and in sync with the moment, for the moment is the indicator of all that is important, valued, and wanted by customers (whether it be symbolic or functional, real or perceived).

FIGURE 1.2 For La Toya Jackson, a pampered pup makes a great fashion statement.

How Marketing Influences the Purchase of Designed Goods

Suppose you want to develop your own fashion-related business in the future—a sportswear manufacturing firm, a video production company, an online designer resale boutique, an interior design consulting service, an art gallery, a contemporary furniture showroom in a bustling mart center, and so forth. There are so many possibilities in the world of design, retailing, wholesaling, and consulting that the choices seem endless. How will you begin? How will you determine who your customers are? How will you connect with them, once you identify them? How will you decide what to offer them next season and the season after that? How will you get them to keep coming back to you and not go somewhere else the next time they go shopping?

Moen Transforms Faucets into Jewelry

When was the last time you found yourself in the powder room at someone's home and thought, "Gee, that faucet would make a great necklace"? Never? Well, don't blame home-hardware brand Moen. The company believes the designs of its bathroom fixtures are so striking, they could be translated into equally striking jewelry—and set out to prove it by commissioning actual statement-piece necklaces based on its statement-piece faucets.

It was actually The Martin Agency, Moen's advertising firm, that created the campaign, inviting jewelry designers from around the world to submit sketches of necklaces inspired by several of Moen's distinctive faucets. The selected designs were then crafted into actual necklaces, which became the centerpiece of Moen's global advertising campaign. The TV ads used special effects to show the jewelry falling from models' necks and magically reassembling into the actual bathroom faucets that inspired the jewelry.

"Our industry often thinks of faucets as the jewelry of the bathroom," said Tim McDonough, Moen's vice president of global brand marketing, adding, "The perfect faucet can add glamour and style, and highlight a homeowner's personal taste."

Ultimately, six necklaces were produced for the advertising, crafted using a variety of techniques. Some of the jewelry pieces were designed and fabricated by hand, while others were created with the help of computer-assisted design, laser cutters, and even a 3D printer. Moen also had a limited number of the necklaces made to give as gifts to some of the company's key retailers and customers at several home-industry trade shows.

"We've tended over the years to focus more on innovation and reliability, but we always realized that style drives purchase," said McDonough. Thanks to the faucets-as-jewelry campaign, Moen is now putting style at the forefront of its "Buy it for looks, buy it for life" tagline.

Sources: Ann-Christine Diaz, "Moen Turns Its Home Hardware into Fashion Jewelry," *Advertising Age*, September 17, 2013, http://adage.com/article/news/moen-turns-home-hardware-fashion-jewelry/244173/?utm_source=daily_email&utm_medium=newsletter&utm_campaign=adage&ttl=1379988078; and Moen, "Moen Incorporated Makes a 'Statement' with New Global Ad Campaign," News release, September 19, 2013.

LET'S TALK

If you opened a retail or service business of your own, how would you let consumers know about it? How would you get them to continue buying from you, rather than from a competitor?

Certainly you need to have some kind of plan for the *marketing* of your idea—that is, getting the word out to the public that you exist and what it is that makes you unique. **Marketing** is a process that includes the communication of all information that sellers want to share with consumers, from the time a product or service is an idea through its purchase, use, evaluation, and disposal by the customer. Marketing covers a broad range of activities, from design, research, and test marketing to pricing, production, promotion, and distribution. And it doesn't stop there. Marketers must continuously evaluate and innovate, since no product or service can remain the same forever and still be desirable. Furthermore, marketers

need to concentrate on maintaining relationships with customers while seeking to attract new ones. Coordinate these activities successfully and you can give your product or service a **competitive advantage:** the delivery of benefits that exceed those supplied by the competition, making your product or service the best choice for the customer and the most profitable for your organization. In other words, if you listen to customers' needs, satisfy them by delivering the benefits they're seeking, and communicate your message effectively, you can greatly enhance your chance of success.

So, what are the actual areas of expertise that make up marketing? Think of marketing as an umbrella term that plays a role in many integrated activities, all of which are based on and enhanced by the study of consumer behavior. Why? If you don't know what people think they need, you can't give them what they think they want. Finding out as much as you can about your customers will help you successfully use the full gamut of marketing components or areas a marketer must master, which are listed in Figure 1.3 and explained here:

FIGURE 1.3 Areas of marketing.

Advertising. Communicating an organization's intended message by way of paid-for space (on TV, on a billboard, on the Internet, in a magazine, etc.)

Branding. Creating an identity and recognition for a product/service/company through the development and use of both visual symbols (color, letters, words) and intangibles (meanings, impressions) to build a brand's image and buyers' loyalty

Communications. Creatively and effectively sharing ideas to generate interest in products, services, and ideas

Community involvement. Implementing the societal marketing concept (see Chapter 2)

Customer relationship building and management. Having continuous and regular interaction with customers in order to encourage loyalty and drive repeat business

Direct marketing. Selling directly to the public via television, Internet, telephone, mail, catalogs, text messaging, and so on

Global marketing. Marketing to customers in foreign markets by learning about other cultures, values, and needs

Media planning. Selecting and purchasing advertising space in the media that will best reach the desired audience while staying within the organization's budget

Pricing strategies. Establishing prices that are attractive to customers and that benefit stakeholders

Product development. Devising innovative ideas to create new and better products

Professional selling. Focusing on personal attention and using effective communication to uncover customers' needs and assist them with buying decisions

Psychology and sociology. Using the study of individual and group behavior to influence consumer purchases and inspire customer loyalty

Public relations. Enhancing the image of a person, product, company, or service in the eyes of the customer

Sales promotion. Devising and implementing activities designed to increase sales in the immediate future

Social media and word of mouth. Employing online social networking to disseminate information, engage with consumers, and encourage wider sharing of the marketer's message

Supply chain management/distribution. Coordinating the organizations associated with the manufacture, delivery, and sale of a product/service

Website creation and implementation. Developing and maintaining an online destination that addresses marketing goals including communication of information, brand reinforcement, e-commerce sales, and more

Coordinating Marketing Efforts

Consumer behavior is the aspect of marketing that propels it into action. The discovery and information processing inherent in consumers' actions before, during, and after they buy keeps marketers on their toes. Savvy marketers want to influence these processes and direct potential customers to their products and services through expert use and careful implementation of their particular marketing specialty. Obviously, communication is a key element if all departments are to be coordinated efficiently. It makes sense that the advertising department should know what the sales promotion team is planning, so those plans can be included in current ads. Likewise, the sales associates need to know what promotions are either planned or under way so they can effectively encourage purchases and work to ensure good customer relationships. In other words, all of the cross-functional team members need to be in touch, via what is called an **integrated marketing system (IMS),** the continuous, efficient sharing of information and ideas supplied by team members. The intended result of an IMS is the organized and effective communication of a consistent and unified message to the desired audience, which includes employees, stakeholders, and, of course, targeted customers.

Here's what can happen without an IMS. A large department store is hosting a trunk show featuring the new evening wear collection of a well-known designer. In preparation, the sales associates in the second-floor Designer Salon send printed invitations to their best customers but do not request RSVPs. To make sure the event will be well attended, the store manager decides at the last minute that it should be opened to the public, so posts it on the store's website and Facebook page the night before. In addition, the store's well-connected public relations agent manages to get two local TV news commentators, on two different channels, to mention it during their broadcasts on the morning of the event. However, no one communicates to the store's sales associates that the event has been opened to the public. Hence, when customers who'd seen the online post or heard about the event on TV arrive without a formal invitation in hand and ask for directions to the right department, they are told, "We're sorry, but this is a private showing for our premier customers." Many leave in a huff, file complaints with the management, and say they will not return to the store unless they receive formal apologies.

So, who benefits from an integrated marketing system? Just about everyone who's involved with the process of creating, producing, selling, and buying, since coordinated marketing informs and helps provide consistent information about a product or a service. Additionally, better marketing, which includes inviting and integrating feedback from customers and employees by conveying a cohesive and uniform message, results in products, services, and customer experiences that are higher in quality and, therefore, higher in customer satisfaction. And isn't that the goal of the whole process? Without some kind of an IMS in place, the customer and the organization both lose.

Recent Approaches to Marketing

The fundamental purpose of marketing is to create goodwill, interest, excitement, and desire among prospective buyers. Marketers know that most people want to be in the know; they want to feel that they belong and, at the same time, that they're unique—a conflicting but common human condition we're all familiar with. The creation of **buzz,** the tongue wagging and ongoing chatter that's set in motion by marketers—particularly public relations and advertising experts—but then proliferates through public sharing, is a strategy being used more and more often to get the word out about new products. The theory is this: Everyone wants to participate in spreading the news about something exciting and avant-garde; people are flattered when they're part of the process. This results in wider exposure and greater momentum for the product, not to mention the positive feelings enjoyed by consumers when they believe they have "inside" information.

Hype is another device used by marketers to build excitement for a message; it's a set of activities put in motion before the actual appearance of a new product or service that helps create a supportive marketing environment and a spontaneously infectious kind of person-to-person image spinning. Then, when the product actually becomes available, consumers are eager to purchase it. Did you ever notice how, before a new movie opens, the starring actors seem to be everywhere—on late-night TV, on morning talk shows, making caviar pies with celebrity chefs, endorsing products—in general being highly visible and chatty? Then, the next day at school or work, people ask, "Did you see Kerry Washington last night on _____? Her movie is coming out this Friday." This is marketing hype in action.

There are those who protest that buzz and hype are not really spontaneous at all but, rather, calculated, covert operations by marketing agents in disguise and are therefore unethical. Clearly, marketers do plant the seeds that enable the message to take off. But some critics see devices such as these as nothing more than a way to get customers to spread promotional propaganda without knowing they've been recruited. Perhaps that's why the use of such methods is sometimes referred to as **guerilla marketing,** a term coined by Jay Conrad Levinson to describe unconventional marketing tactics designed to get maximum results from minimal resources. (See Figure 1.4 and Case in Point 1.2.) Among these techniques, all of which employ some element of surprise, are **ambush marketing** (placing unique marketing materials in unexpected venues that result in consumer and media attention), **viral marketing** (passing a marketing message to others with the goal of having it spread widely, much like passing a virus from one person to another), and **stealth advertising** (devising ads in which marketers attempt to conceal the fact that an ad is actually an ad—the theory being that marketing is most effective when

consumers don't recognize it as such, making it even more persuasive). These techniques are part of what's called **word-of-mouth marketing,** or **WOM**—the passing along from person to person of a marketing message or opinions about a product—and are all based on the sharing habits of human beings.

Fashion brands like Forever 21 and Adidas are adept at using WOM strategies in clever and attention-getting ways, as are design houses like Gucci, Tiffany, and Donna Karan. From surprise public events to "pop-up shops" (temporary stores that open and close within a few days or weeks, such as a Halloween shop that opens in September and closes at the end of October; Figure 1.5), it's obvious that this strategy is very effective at getting the attention of consumers who enjoy new experiences, especially ones that surprise them—and then can't wait to tell their friends all about it.

FINDING YOUR AUDIENCE

Whatever the preferences of shoppers might be, the marketer needs to identify those preferences, along with the lifestyles and habits of the customers who share them. This homogeneous group of buyers displaying like needs, wants, values, and buying behaviors is called a **market segment.**

Consumer behavior experts provide marketers with the research they need to learn everything possible about the types of customers they want to attract. These market segments are studied and carefully considered; then, one or more is selected to become the basis of the organization's **target market,** an incorporation of the likely groups of potential customers who share similar lifestyles and preferences, on which a company intends to focus its marketing efforts. (See Chapters 2, 7, 8,

Putting the "Buzz" into Marketing

In the Internet/social media age, consumers are bombarded with competing information from brands eager to grab their attention and their purchasing dollars. So to break through the noise and clutter, all marketers dream of unlocking the power of buzz marketing—getting people to spontaneously talk about a product and tell their friends, who'll tell their friends, and so on, and so on.

But how can companies plant the seed that will grow into full-fledged organic buzz? Believe it or not, there is actually a science to generating buzz, and author Mark Hughes in his book *Buzzmarketing* explains the formula with several basic principles—the most fundamental being: If you want to generate buzz, you need to give people something to talk about. Sounds simple, right? But it's only simple once you understand the types of topics that reliably get people talking. In other words, there are certain conversation-starting topics that work better than others to generate buzz. Based on his research, Hughes has identified some of those topics and calls them "the six buttons of buzz":

1. *The Taboo.* People tend to talk about things they shouldn't talk about, like friends who can't resist discussing another friend's indiscretions. Tsk-tsk! Taboo can also mean controversial or edgy, so a brand will create better buzz with topics that give people something to argue about, debate, or dispute.
2. *The Unusual.* A marketer's goal is to create a product or positioning strategy that is unique. To stand out from the crowd, the brand cannot follow along and do the same thing as everyone else in its industry, but rather must offer something unusual or unconventional about its product to get people talking.
3. *The Remarkable.* When everyone else is creating something average, the buzz marketer's goal is to create something significantly *better* than average, something *outstanding*. When a product or service goes above and beyond their expectations, that's when people start talking about it.
4. *The Outrageous.* People definitely talk about shocking things, but "outrageousness" just for the sake of being outrageous doesn't generate positive buzz if there's no beneficial connection made with the brand. In other words, outrageous marketing content has to connect meaningfully to a brand and promote its benefits.
5. *The Hilarious.* People are very quick to share videos and articles that they think are hilarious because everybody likes to laugh and to talk about things they find funny. But when it comes to business, being funny isn't always easy—and like the outrageous button, this one only works when people remember that it came from or was about the sponsor brand (and in a good way).

(continued)

6. *The Secrets.* There are two things about secrets that get people talking—either when the secret is kept or when it's revealed. Something in our DNA seems to make us want to find out about things that are supposed to be hidden from us or from others. And once we are privy to a secret, like a sneak preview of a new product before it's introduced, we take pleasure in sharing that inside scoop with other people, because we are then among the fab few who are "in the know."

As you can see, to generate buzz most effectively, marketers need to push the buttons that are known to get people talking. By following these principles, not only will a business stand out by doing things that are unique and remarkable, but it will also get people talking about what it does—which creates awareness, drives traffic, and increases sales and profits.

Sources: Joseph Putnam, "How to Apply Buzz Marketing Principles for Effective Internet Marketing," *KISSmetrics,* http://blog.kissmetrics.com /online-buzz-marketing; "Six Maxims of Creating Buzz," *Buzz Marketing Web site,* http://buzzmarketing.com/2010/11/26/6-maxims-of-creating-buzz/.

and 9 for additional segmentation information.) For example, if you're using this textbook, you might be a member of a market segment often referred to as "Millennials," people born roughly between the early 1980s and early 2000s. Because they are a target market for many businesses, there have been scores of research studies about the shopping habits of Millennials. Without consumer research, which uncovers and keeps marketers up-to-date with the wants and needs of a diverse marketplace as well as specific market segments being targeted, all organizations might still be relying on the traditional method of **mass marketing,** the mass distribution and mass promotion of the same product to all potential customers. Today that method is no longer considered efficient in reaching a target audience; there is simply too much competition and a new wealth of options for reaching more focused groups of consumers. Furthermore, customers do their own careful research in order to get the greatest benefit from each item they purchase. They want to know that a product fulfills their own individual needs and wants, rather than being a "one size fits all" selection.

Consumers Can Be Inconsistent

Do you recognize the name Claude Montana? Once upon a time, he was a world-famous designer, hailed as a visionary and leader in cutting-edge concepts. Rudi Gernreich was also very popular at one time, but have you ever heard of him? Gernreich is considered by many to be one of the ten most influential designers of the twentieth century, having changed the face of modern fashion with his concept called "unisex" dressing

FIGURE 1.4 Guerilla marketing in progress: Not a scene commuters would expect to see at New York's Grand Central Station—a gathering of athletes, all dressed in Moncler Grenoble workout wear, exercising in style during Fashion Week.

(which was once considered crazy) and his invention of the soft, unstructured "no bra" bra. He was so well known that he remains among a handful of designers who appeared on the cover of *TIME,* once the most respected newsmagazine in the United States.

When it comes to fashion-related and designed goods, people tend to be fickle, forget quickly, and for the most part, want novelty and newness. Consumer behavior, therefore, can be inconsistent and capricious. Inevitably, something more desirable will come along and dethrone what was previously at the top of everyone's most-wanted list, because many purchasers of designed goods pay close attention to trends. A **trend** is a direction in which something is moving, be it a trend in climate change,

population growth, real estate, politics, technological devices, kitchen appliances, textiles, and so on. Some trends last for many years, while others slow and decline rather quickly. Many consumers want to be up-to-date regarding trends; this awareness signals that they are knowledgeable about what's considered to be "the latest."

Buyers Often Stick Together

Consumers tend to accept or reject various goods in large numbers; buyers actually cast a "vote" in the marketplace regarding what they like and don't like, want and don't want, purchase or refuse to purchase. This voting of sorts has been referred to as the theory of **collective selection,** a process by

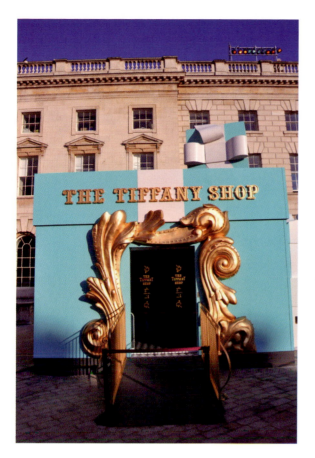

FIGURE 1.5 Two cleverly designed pop-up shops that generated lots of attention. (left) Quite a surprise . . . an "extra-large" version of the coveted Tiffany blue box that's actually a pop-up store. (above) Visitors to Grand Central Terminal at the Target and Sonia Kashuk Bath & Body Collection pop-up store in New York. Shoppers got to preview the designer's new bath and body products, which would not be available in Target stores until a week later. The promotional event was for one day only and featured hundreds of balloons as well as a woman in a bathtub atop the display.

which a mass of people formulate certain collective tastes reflected by the goods or services they choose, and their selections illustrate the beliefs and values of the group's social system. Only those goods most consistent with the sociocultural environment win.[7] Consumer researchers point to a collective buying behavior that first appeared a decade or so ago: the demand for luxury goods by shoppers at many income levels. While true luxury products and services are generally out of reach of all but the very wealthy, marketers recognized the collective desire for premium products—or at least those that *appear* to be premium—and they began offering upscale everything, from bottled water to in-home spas. Whether or not a product is truly deserving of the label or simply the subject of a desired marketing bump, today it seems that "luxury" is everywhere. Marketers regularly invent new terms to qualify luxury: true luxury, masstige, premium, ultra-premium, opuluxe, casual luxury, accessible luxury, hyper-luxury, and meta-luxury. But instead of clarifying the concept of luxury, this semantic creativity may only add to the confusion. If everything is "luxury," then the term no longer has any meaning.[8] What, therefore, constitutes a luxury product, luxury brand, or luxury company? In Point of View 1.2, a strategic planning director attempts to understand what luxury really means to consumers and how marketers can best convey a luxury image.

Guerilla Marketing: Battling for Consumers' Attention

OK, you're a consumer, right? What happens when you sense an advertisement coming? Is your finger already on the DVR remote to zap through the commercial, or on the keypad to browse elsewhere until the ad runs its course? In today's video-on-demand age, that's what happens more often than not—so you can see the dilemma for marketers, who must constantly try to outdo themselves in the creative department just to win a moment of consumers' attention.

Sure, making ads that are truly fun to watch is one solution. Did you ever get tired of watching the GEICO camel strolling through the office trying to get coworkers to admit it was "hump" day? That one did get people talking, but it's not always easy to second-guess what will click with consumers. Or how many times have you watched an episode of a favorite show and clearly noticed the characters tapping on a MacBook? Placing products in movies or TV shows can sometimes be effective. But sometimes it takes even more creativity, or should we say, downright guile. Sometimes, to *really* get consumers' attention, it takes . . . guerrilla marketing.

Some have described guerrilla marketing as advertising "with a wink," because the very concept is based on sneakiness. Consumers are often sucked into the message before they realize what's happening; and with a truly cunning and creative campaign, by the time they understand they've been tricked, they don't mind because they appreciate how ingenious the whole thing was.

Some guerilla marketing is fairly whimsical, like the seafood restaurant that tucked its flyers into oversized "clam shells" and scattered them across a beach for consumers to discover; or the casino that transformed the nearby airport's baggage carousel into a giant "roulette wheel." At other times it can border on the macabre, like the HBO campaign that dangled an "arm" out of the trunk of a New York City taxi, next to a bumper sticker for *The Sopranos.*

One of the masters of guerilla marketing is videogame maker Acclaim Entertainment, which operates under an "all publicity is good publicity" philosophy. Acclaim regularly uses guerilla tactics to drum up attention for new game releases—such as the time it offered £500 to British residents who would legally change their names to Turok to promote the launch of "Turok: Evolution." (Believe it or not, nearly 3,000 people tried to claim the prize money!) Not to stop there, the company also offered a $10,000 savings bond to the first U.S. parents to name their baby Turok within a specified time frame.

But surely the guerilla marketing campaign to end all guerilla marketing campaigns is the one set in motion by the makers of the 1999 film *The Blair Witch Project.* University of Central Florida Film School cohorts Daniel Myrick

(continued)

and Eduardo Sánchez initially planted the seed by engineering a website devoted to the "Blair Witch," a specter who had supposedly been snatching kids out of the Maryland woods for the last century. Then they created a tagline for the film that set the stage further: "In October of 1994, three student filmmakers disappeared in the woods near Burkittsville, Maryland, while shooting a documentary. A year later, their footage was found." Never mind that the legend was total fiction. Or that the presumably dead "students" were doing media interviews about the film's release. Many filmgoers refused to believe that the Blair Witch was not real—and even those who accepted the con were caught up in the buzz and the "have to see for myself" mentality . . . to the extent that the movie ended up grossing $250 million at the box office world-wide. That's a kind of success that would make any marketer eager to deceive!

Sources: Ryan Lum, "6 Great Guerilla Marketing Campaigns," *Creative Guerilla Marketing*, July 6, 2010, http://www.creativeguerrillamarketing .com/guerrilla-marketing/6-great-guerrilla-marketing-campaigns/; "20 Creative Guerilla Marketing Campaigns," *Designer Daily*, March 2, 2011, http://www.designer-daily.com/cool-and-creative-guerilla-marketing-campaigns-13471; David Becker, "'Turok' Maker Plays the Name Game," *CNET*, August 27, 2002, http://news.cnet.com/Turok-maker-plays-the-name-game/2100-1040_3-955594.html.

Let's Talk

How do you decide what to buy? Do you base your decisions on current trends, on an item's usefulness and practicality, on the brand name, or on the suggestions of friends?

CULTURE INFLUENCES BUYING HABITS

One of the more fascinating aspects of the study of buying behavior is so firmly tied to a particular concept that it's critical to the understanding of consumer behavior. We're referring to culture, the compass that guides us and affects every observation and decision we make. **Culture** is composed of all the shared beliefs, values, and traditions learned and practiced by a group of people, rich or poor, educated or uneducated, whether they live close to one another or far apart, all of whom are focused on a common quest. A quest is a search, a pursuit, like that of the famous fictional character Don Quixote, who spent his life pursuing the impossible dream. Americans, no matter who we are, share the ongoing pursuit of freedom and independence, and our absolute commitment to it unites us as one culture. One of the ways we express this value is through the products and services we consume, and to be sure, we are among the most savvy and complex risk takers in making purchasing decisions.

Why Don't Millennials Shop More Online?

As a population segment, Millennials—those born approximately between the early 1980s and the early 2000s—are the first to have grown up using the Internet. Yet according to market research firm NPD Group, Millennials not only have the lowest shopping conversion rate of all generations (meaning their shopping activity results in fewer actual purchases), but when they do make a purchase, they spend far more of their retail dollars in a physical store than online.

Based on its study, "Winning the Fight for Millennial Shoppers," NPD found that Millennials spent only 19 percent of their shopping dollars online, as compared to 81 percent that they spent in brick-and-mortar stores. And even though they actually make a purchase in only 57 percent of their shopping trips, they clearly enjoy shopping: In a typical week, more than half—53 percent—of Millennials go to a store to shop.

It may seem odd that this first generation of consumers who grew up using computers and digital devices doesn't make more purchases by means of those devices. But another report, this one by management consulting firm Accenture, helps shed light on the paradox. In its study, "Who Are the Millennial Shoppers? And What Do They Really Want?," Accenture found that Millennials, who number some 80 million in the United States and spend some $600 billion, are digitally savvy shoppers, using online and mobile channels to research products, read reviews, and compare prices. But they actually prefer shopping in person in stores. As one of those surveyed put it, "You want to touch it; you want to smell it; you want to pick it up."

As Marshal Cohen, NPD's chief industry analyst, noted, "Millennial shoppers are the most elusive generation and the most challenging to keep engaged. In order to get more Millennial consumers in store, retailers need to understand how Millennials' shopping habits differ from other generations. Previous generations were more easily impressed by marketing and advertising strategies. With this group you must have a strategy to grab their attention in- and out-of-store."

If there are questions about Millennials' low in-store conversion, that aspect of the generation is not really so surprising considering their still-young age and earning power. A recent Times and Trends Report from market researcher IRI, "Millennial Shoppers: Tapping Into the Next Growth Segment," reveals how deeply Millennials have been impacted by the ongoing effects of the recent economic crisis and recession, resulting in their being downright frugal in regard to their spending habits. As a result, these consumers are drawn to retailers like dollar stores, secondhand stores, and other off-price channels that focus on

(continued)

offering value; and they don't hesitate to use social media and smartphone apps to search out the best deals. That doesn't mean, however, that they'll settle for boring: Even when they're searching out good prices, for Millennials, a retailer's "fun factor" is essential.

Sources: Santi Briglia, "Why Aren't Millennials Big E-Spenders?", *RetailWire,* August 30, 2013, http://www.retailwire.com/discussion/16995/why-arent-millennials-big-e-spenders; NPD Group, "NPD Group Reports Most of Millennial Dollars are Spent in Stores vs. Online," News release, August 27, 2013; Christopher Donnelly and Renato Scaff, "Who Are the Millennial Shoppers? And What Do They Really Want?," *Accenture,* June 2013, http://www.accenture.com/us-en/outlook/Pages/outlook-journal-2013-who-are-millennial-shoppers-what-do-they-really-want-retail.aspx; IRI, "Millennial Shoppers: Tapping into the Next Growth Segment," June/July 2012.

In today's marketplace, information abounds, and all of it influences buying behavior. That's why the jobs of consumer researchers are both evolving and demanding. Clearly, one of the biggest challenges is staying a few steps ahead of purchasers. By studying psychology, sociology, history, economics, and the causes of change, and through constant, close observation, marketers can increase their knowledge and expertise, becoming both effective and efficient in determining what consumers are likely to want next.

WHAT WILL CUSTOMERS WANT TOMORROW?

Does this mean consumer behaviorists have to add fortune-telling to their résumés, in addition to all the other subjects they have to master? Not exactly, but they probably will be asked on occasion to draw conclusions from their findings and make some reliable predictions as to what's most likely to occur in the future. This is another tool that successful marketers use. It's called **forecasting,** a creative process used by industry professionals, which can be understood, practiced, and applied by those familiar with the applicable theories and tools.[9] (See Chapter 14 for information about trend forecasting services.)

Accurate forecasts are compiled using information from the past and present to calculate what's likely to happen in the future, and are crucial to the success of every business. Because we live in a time when change occurs with amazing speed, designers, product developers, analysts, and other marketing professionals must explore all possible futures in order to establish directions for their companies. Consumer researchers play a crucial role in this effort. They systematically gather the kind of data that helps forecasters make informed predictions on subjects such as population shifts, cultural changes, attitude fluctuations, economic deviations, and the emergence of new products and businesses—all of which may be significant to executives and planners who are plotting a company's future. Research and evaluation are essential elements in the study of consumer behavior; without them, there is no basis

What Does "Luxury" Really Mean?

"I think every girl deep inside dreams about having the money to be able to buy the Louis Vuitton bag or being at the red carpet herself and wearing a beautiful Chanel dress."

If you're like most people, you can probably identify as "luxury" the brands mentioned in that quote, from a participant in a 2010 qualitative research study conducted in the United Arab Emirates. But could you pinpoint exactly what it is that makes Louis Vuitton, Louis Vuitton? Or Chanel, Chanel? What are the specific ingredients or components that constitute a luxury brand? What is it precisely that makes a luxury brand desirable?

Those are the questions that Rohit Arora, strategic planning director at Bates Pan Gulf (BPG Group), headquartered in Dubai, United Arab Emirates, and one of the largest marketing solutions firms in the Middle East/North Africa region, set out to answer in the "8 P's of Luxury Brand Marketing."

According to Arora, many equate luxury with purely "physical/functional attributes like product quality, craftsmanship, design, technology," and he quotes a respondent from the research study as saying, "When you buy something with really high quality, you can genuinely feel the difference. It is in the touch, the feel of the material; it's in the smoothness, it's in its minute details . . ."

For others, Arora finds, luxury may be the "self-asserting emotional stimulation" of letting everyone around them know that they have achieved success and have a taste for the finer things in life. As another study respondent said, "I bought my BMW just to keep my key on the table during the meeting."

Or perhaps, notes Arora, it's that luxury brands are "just the stepladder to move to the right circle or an appropriate thing to have or wear in that circle." Yet another study respondent said, "There is a proverb which says if you wear nice shoes you enter nice place."

By analyzing the research, Arora developed a list of "8 Pillars of Luxury Brand Marketing," encompassing *performance*, the delivery of superior experience; *pedigree*, the brand's heritage and years of mastery; *paucity*, scarcity that increases desirability; *persona*, the brand's personality, mystique, and emotional values; *public figures*, to enhance credibility and impact; *placement*, a retail environment that heightens the consumer experience and brand aura; *public relations*, to influence opinion and maintain the brand's exclusive image; and *pricing*, at a level that maximizes perceived value.

"Luxury brands have always been a fascinating space and luxury brand marketing one of the most complicated ones," Arora writes. "The 8 P's may not be a 'universal methodology,' yet [they] present a strong analytical 'toolbox' to audit and leverage the brand potential."

Source: Rohit Arora, "8 P's of Luxury Brand Marketing," http://www.brandchannel.com/images/papers/533_8ps_of_luxury_branding.pdf.

on which to strategically plan. And in business, planning precedes success.

But are forecasters always right in their determinations of what customers are likely to want? One example of what was deemed accurate and useable forecasting was applied to the creation of a retail chain, Forth & Towne, a specialty store division of Gap, Inc. Researchers had been carefully tracking the buying behavior of the baby boomer population for years and anticipating the tremendous cultural shift that would take place when the group reached middle age.

A baby boomer is someone born during a period of increased birth rates, such as those born in the United States during the period of economic prosperity after World War II, 1946 to 1964 (see Chapter 7 for more about baby boomers). Forecasters have predicted for decades that the mind-sets and buying habits of boomers would force marketers to employ new and different tactics, and clearly they were right. Boomers, some 76 million of them, make up the single largest group in the United States today (more than a quarter of the total population) and spend some $3 trillion on goods and services each year. Over the next 25 years, their retail purchases are expected to continue to increase, in addition to what they'll be spending on new homes, travel, and leisure activities.

Despite those statistics, the fashion industry has largely ignored this group, especially women, opting to direct its marketing efforts almost exclusively at the young, whom designers prefer to dress. Part of our cultural belief system is that youth is synonymous with beauty, while aging makes people less attractive. But after assessing vast amounts of data supplied by researchers about the needs and preferences of boomer women, Gap marketers determined several years ago that it was the right time to focus on this huge market segment whose female members were hungry for chic and stylish clothing.

The opening of Forth & Towne made national headlines. All cultural indicators pointed to success, since in both planning and execution, Gap had utilized the most essential marketing activity: determining what customers want and giving it to them. (In addition to its numerous other definitions, marketing is also referred to as *problem solving*.)

However, the Forth & Towne stores performed poorly. Although the targeted group was (and is) a large one with a lot of money to spend, the eclectic tastes and diverse lifestyles of the segment were harder to pinpoint than anticipated. That, along with various corporate challenges facing Gap at the time, ultimately led to the closing of Forth & Towne, less than two years after its launch.

Yes, marketers do make mistakes, and mistakes come in many forms besides faulty forecasting. What's more, because of the instant and massive impact of social media, mistakes today can result in more than a loss of money. Read Case in Point 1.4 and consider the public's response to a Kenneth Cole tweet that was seen by many as a disaster for the designer. But did that stop him from doing it again?

On what consumer research did Kenneth Cole base his marketing strategy? Are there limits regarding how far an organization should go to differentiate itself? Perhaps "mistakes" aren't always what they seem, or perhaps some marketers are able make their errors look like they were just part of a clever strategy all along.

Tweeting Up a Firestorm

Designer Kenneth Cole is no stranger to controversy—not in terms of his fashions but in terms of his tweets. In fact, to many observers, the designer who established Awearness, The Kenneth Cole Foundation, to encourage and inspire meaningful social change with particular focus on HIV/AIDS, civil liberties, freedom of expression, and disaster relief, has himself taken freedom of expression too far.

What could Cole have possibly said or done to deserve the outpouring of anger, outrage, and vitriol that has swirled around him in recent years? For one example, how about seeming to joke about the horrific situation as civil strife and violence raged in Syria, with the United States and other nations embroiled in debate over a proper international course of action? Picking up on the phrase "boots on the ground," used by both President Barack Obama and Secretary of State John Kerry in terms of possible options for an American response, Cole tweeted:

Kenneth Cole@KennethCole: Boots on the ground or not, let's not forget about sandals, pumps and loafers. #Footwear

Cole's attempt to piggyback on the international crisis in order to promote his shoes might have drawn slightly less attention if it hadn't followed another less-than-tactful Twitter post a couple of years earlier. In 2011, a Cole tweet referenced the riots that were escalating in Egypt at the time—in this instance, as a way to promote his new spring collection:

Kenneth Cole@KennethCole: Millions are in uproar in #Cairo. Rumor is they heard our new spring collection is now available online at http://bit.ly/KCairo –KC

Yet other Twitter posts have raised eyebrows and ire, such as one that tapped into the debate over gun control following the Newtown school massacre and that featured a link to his quote: "Regardless of the right to bear arms, we in no way condone the right to bare feet." Clever play on words? Sure. In questionable taste for the circumstances? Absolutely. But Cole openly admits it is all part of his deliberate plan to stir up the pot and get people talking. (See Point of View 1.1 about the six buttons of buzz.) In fact, when asked about the Egypt tweet for an interview with *Details Magazine*, Cole was not shy about describing his Twitter strategy as an attempt to get exposure by tweeting something offensive.

"Billions of people read my inappropriate, self-promoting tweet, I got a lot of harsh responses, and we hired a crisis management firm," Cole told *Details*. "If you look at lists of the biggest Twitter gaffes ever, we're always one through five. But our stock went up that day, our e-commerce business was better, the business at every one of our stores improved, and I picked

(continued)

up 3,000 new followers on Twitter. So on what criteria is this a gaffe?

"Within hours, I tweeted an explanation, which had to be vetted by lawyers," he added. "I'm not even sure I used the words I'm sorry—because I wasn't sorry."

Kenneth Cole@KennethCole: Re Egypt tweet: we weren't intending to make light of a serious situation. We understand the sensitivity of this historic moment -KC

Cole also told *Details* that he deliberately pushes the envelope in social media and advertising, while keeping his fashion itself more subdued. "We're clearly bolder with our social messages than we are with our fashion messages, and that's by design," said Cole.

Even so, after the outcry over his tweet about Syria, Cole again felt the need to explain his rationale to followers, even if not apologize—this time posting a video on Instagram.

"I've always used my platform to provoke dialogue about important issues, including HIV/AIDS, war, and homelessness," he said on Instagram. "I'm well aware of the risks that come with this approach, and if this encourages further awareness and discussion of critical issues, then all the better."

Sources: Kim Bhasin, "Kenneth Cole: Offensive Tweets Are Simply Good Business Strategy," *Huffington Post*, September 6, 2013, http://www.huffingtonpost.com/2013/09/06/kenneth-cole-twitter_n_3881085.html?utm_hp_ref=tw; Prachi Gupta, "Kenneth Cole Defends Abhorrent Syria Tweet," *Salon*, September 6, 2013, http://www.salon.com/2013/09/06/kenneth_cole_defends_abhorrent_syria_tweet/; Alexander Abad-Santos, "If There's a War, Kenneth Cole Will Co-Opt It," *The Wire*, September 5, 2013, http://www.thewire.com/entertainment/2013/09/kenneth-cole-twitter-war-syria-eypt/69096/; Awearness, The Kenneth Cole Foundation, www.awearness.com.

STANDING OUT FROM THE REST

Let's examine the idea of marketing as problem solving. The customer has a dilemma and is looking for a solution. It's up to the marketer to offer one (or two, or more). For many years, it's been the job of marketers to help businesses position their products or services as the best remedies for customers' problems. **Positioning** is creating a certain perception or image about the product in the minds of consumers that differentiates it from the competition. In the world of kitchen design, appliances by Thermador and Viking have been positioned as such high-tech options that their ovens were referred to as "kitchen jewelry" by the *Dallas Morning News*. And because saving time is so important to so many people today, TurboChef, a prestige appliance manufacturer, offers a very pricey oven that cooks a 21-pound turkey in only 75 minutes.

But how are these three high-end appliance makers going to make sure consumers don't confuse their products? By using a marketing strategy known as **product differentiation,** the way companies attempt to make their products seem unique when compared to similar products by competitors.

"Newism" Accelerates Innovation

In the twenty-first century, more than ever before, consumers crave what's new. And that can translate to either wild success or outright disaster for brands.

From emerging to mature economies, the entire world seems to be creating new products, services, and experiences at a breathtaking pace. Clearly, the new has never been more readily available—and this constant stream of innovation is moving "new" from being simply a trite marketing tactic by old brands touting something as "new and improved" to a truly exciting proposition for consumers.

Of course, a major contributor to newism is the online world, as it speeds the dissemination of information and excitement ever faster. Consider social media platform Instagram, which garnered 10 million users in under a year, or Draw Something, which captured 35 million users in just 6 weeks. And then consider that many Draw Something adopters quickly abandoned the app— probably for something even newer.

Indeed, any new innovation that taps into some pent-up demand or unfilled niche has the potential to burst onto the scene and spread like wildfire. Look at Taco Bell, which introduced its new Doritos Locos Tacos and proceeded to sell 100 million of them in just 10 weeks—the chain's fastest- ever product launch. And the simple tactic of making it easier for consumers to obtain what's new, or helping them to be ahead of the pack in finding, knowing, or doing something new, can represent an enormous opportunity for a brand. A case in point is when Nike recently launched several limited- edition, collectible athletic shoes using a reservation system set up on Twitter. During the course of the day of release, stores selling the sneakers randomly tweeted out specific product hashtags, and the first followers who included the information in a direct message back to the store were able to reserve a pair of the shoes.

Clearly, there is far more to newism than just traditional product innovation. It is also much more than simply replacing products for the sake of replacing them, especially when the new models are created in an eco-unfriendly manner. As a matter of fact, companies have introduced a plethora of new eco-friendly products and services that do not necessarily represent true newism.

What's more, the prevalence of newism does not mean that *all* consumer attention is or always will be focused only on the new. Heritage brands, long recognized for their constant, trusted quality, continue to have unmatched value for consumers. And there will be always be strong value in brands or products that have well-told, compelling stories, or that offer a level of comfort or tradition. The

(continued)

POINT OF VIEW 1.3 (continued)

important thing to remember is that no trend applies to all consumers, all of the time—and that the new doesn't always kill the old.

In short, for both new and established brands, it comes down to being able to capture and hold consumers' attention. Granted, today's lightning communications and abundance of media may be making consumer attention spans shorter and shorter. But for brands that break through the clutter and reach their target customers, the rewards can be instant and enormous.

Source: "Newism," *trendwatching.com*, July–August 2012, www.trendwatching.com/trends/newism/.

Take blue jeans, for example. A lot has happened to this widely regarded symbol of the American worker. Jeans have certainly evolved from their origins as the uniform of prospectors and cattle ranchers in the 1800s. For more than four decades, blue jeans have taken over as *the uniform,* period. And what about the endless choice of styles, cuts, treatments, and embellishments? What is it that differentiates Levi's jeans from those by True Religion or Diesel, for which people pay anywhere from $19.95 to $595.00? Is it the actual quality of the denim, the finish, or the fit? Or is it something more elusive? Perhaps it has to do with people's *ideas* about jeans and what jeans *symbolize*, more than their value as a physical product.

Marketers know that the meanings consumers attach to items are every bit as powerful (sometimes more so) as the actual contents or quality of the product itself. Of course, this is not to diminish the importance of high quality and fine design, but that may not be enough in today's competitive marketplace. The title of the 1981 best seller by marketing gurus Al Ries and Jack Trout says it all—marketing is "The Battle for Your Mind."

So, if the customer thinks she will be more satisfied . . . attractive . . . special . . . desirable. . . wearing $250 jeans than in $50 jeans, and she has the means to make that purchase, then the marketers of those jeans have done their jobs.

WHAT'S IN A NAME?

When it comes to elusive qualities, nothing is more fascinating than consumers' attraction to certain brands. A **brand** is everything that is known and felt about a product or service or organization, from its recognizable name, logo, slogan, and packaging to the power it holds in peoples' minds. You might say that we actually become emotionally attached to certain brands, and you'd be right. Think about Coke and Pepsi. You probably know people who will argue vehemently that one is better than the other, that the two drinks taste different, and that even if they were blindfolded, they could tell which one is which. Researchers have found, however, that blind taste tests show quite the opposite—most people can't really tell the difference, and they're less influenced by the actual taste and more influenced by the advertising, promotion, and affiliations the products have with certain celebrities and/or activities they enjoy.

Much of the time, consumers respond to a **brand image,** the deliberate, consistent way the company communicates a product's qualities and essence. Imagine you're traveling and want something to eat, but no place looks appealing. You see a sign indicating that a familiar fast-food spot is a short distance ahead. Even though you've never eaten at this particular location, you expect a friendly place with tasty food because the name and logo evoke positive feelings, based on your past experience. The creation of a positive brand image will draw targeted buyers to that particular brand and keep them coming back. That's a big part of successful marketing—developing **brand loyalty,** behavior exhibited by customers who have strong connections to their favorite brands; this includes purchasing a certain brand again and again. Are you loyal to a specific hair product, a certain brand of cologne or toothpaste? Do you tend to buy these items time after time? If so, you're brand loyal. When brand image and brand loyalty have both been achieved, the result is **brand equity,** the power a brand derives from a group of strong assets that include value, esteem, worth—all of the intangibles that help create satisfaction, retention, and demand in the marketplace.

Customers can become very attached to certain brands and refuse to buy others for a variety of reasons that range from emotional (their parents used it, their ex-boyfriend used it, it reminds them of a special evening) to rational (they prefer the taste, the price, the convenience, the use of natural ingredients). Whatever their motivation, their brand loyalty can be attributed to the success of the integrated marketing system in creating a brand image that resonates with customers in a way that is more appealing than that of competitors.

IS NEW NECESSARILY BEST?

Numerous theories exist about people's relationships with their possessions. Some of these date back more than 100 years. Most of the time these theories, regardless of when they were developed, share one common "truth": the attraction of consumers to designed goods results from their curiosity about **innovation,** something new or different being seen or experienced for the first time. Consumers are drawn to an item by the belief that inherent in the object they desire is something that is new; however, it doesn't have to be new in actuality—it just has to be regarded as new by the person viewing it. Think of a young woman in a consignment shop discovering a gorgeous vintage gown, which is clearly not new but is unlike anything else she's ever worn before.

People are naturally curious about what's new, but newness doesn't guarantee success. Adopting something new requires people to be willing to change their behavior in some way. That's where innovations become challenges—how much are customers willing to change? Of course, the answer depends on the individual; some consumers might be ready for a radical departure from what they're currently doing, using, wanting, purchasing, while others might not want their habits disrupted. Some people might be influenced by peers or celebrities and jump on the bandwagon right away; others might be extremely slow to respond to newness or reject an innovation, calling it silly or even potentially harmful. There are certain goods that companies would simply like to get into the hands of customers, confident that if they try the item, they'll like it, and they'll purchase it, hopefully more than once. So, how do marketers encourage shoppers to try something new? Giving out samples is always a good idea, though in some cases, it's not feasible. So, what do marketers need to think about when it comes to what's new?

LET'S TALK

How do you feel when you hear about a product introduction like new running shoes, a new watch, a new mascara, or a new mobile device? Are you curious or skeptical about "newness"? What is it that makes something not only new, but truly innovative? What would get you to purchase something brand new?

The following chapters address these issues with some practical and workable ideas. This text can assist you, the student who is looking ahead to a productive career in the fashion or design fields, by enhancing your understanding of the principles of consumer behavior. The knowledge you gain should enable you to both choose the methods that fit your business needs and use them effectively.

Summary

Consumer behavior is the decision-making process that buyers go through prior to making actual purchases. An understanding of consumer behavior is necessary for successful marketing, a group of activities designed to persuade prospective buyers to choose one product, service, or company over others. Consumer behaviorists identify those who are most likely to need and want certain goods, be they designed objects, fashion-related products, or any consumable item. Designed goods have a special place in the minds of consumers; this is largely driven by a combination of two conflicting behaviors: wanting (then buying) what the rest of the crowd wants, and seeking (then purchasing) what's truly unique and innovative. To address this issue, marketers try to develop and impart to the purchaser a special set of characteristics and qualities that distinguishes a product, service, or company from those of competitors. There are various ways to accomplish this, some traditional and some less conventional. But regardless of the approach used, all marketers must listen to their customers and give them what they want.

KEY TERMS

Ambush marketing

Brand

Brand equity

Brand image

Brand loyalty

Buzz

Collective selection

Competitive advantage

Consumer behavior

Consumption

Culture

Design

Fashion

Forecasting

Guerilla marketing

Hype

Innovation

Integrated marketing system (IMS)

Market segment

Marketing

Mass marketing

Positioning

Product differentiation

Target market

Trend

Stealth advertising

Viral marketing

Word-of-mouth marketing (WOM)

Zeitgeist

QUESTIONS FOR REVIEW

1. What kinds of criteria do consumers use when deciding whether to buy fashion and designed goods that they probably don't use when evaluating other types of products?

2. Explain the importance of the zeitgeist as it relates to fashion and designed goods. What is the current zeitgeist and what influences has it had on recent creations by your favorite designer?

3. Choose three components of marketing from the list on page 11 and explain how each might be implemented in the fashion and design arenas.

4. Cite and explain an instance in your own employment experience when an IMS was or was not in place. What were the results?

5. Clearly explain the importance of branding, brand image, and brand equity when it comes to the customer's selection of fashion and design-related goods. Give specific examples of brands you are familiar with that demonstrate successful branding.

ACTIVITIES

1. People can be marketed as well as products. Identify a new designer in your field. List some of the marketing techniques that are being used to create interest in this person.

2. List three stores where you like to shop, and note the marketing efforts each store uses to get your business and develop loyalty.

3. Go online and find five answers to the question: "What is consumer behavior?" Are the responses all similar or did you find additional information not covered in this chapter? If so, make a note of your findings, and suggest them for class discussion.

4. Read through your favorite fashion magazine and find examples of public relations activities and sales promotions that are featured. Determine what percentage of the magazine is actual news, what percentage is advertising, and what percentage is framed as news but is probably promotionally driven.

5. Subscribe to either of these free online newsletters: NRF SmartBrief (https://www2 .smartbrief.com/signupSystem/subscribe.action ?pageSequence=1&briefName=nrf/) or Shop .org SmartBrief (https://www.smartbrief.com /signupSystem/subscribe.action?pageSequence =1&briefName=shop).

6. Visit the Word of Mouth Marketing Association (WOMMA) website: www.womma.com. Look at the mission statement of this organization and learn how members view the potential of word of mouth versus traditional marketing methods.

MINI-PROJECTS

1. Hold an in-class panel discussion and ask panelists what they look for when choosing designed goods that will be visible to others. What matters most to them? Uniqueness? Aesthetic appeal? The responses of peers? Why is this important to them? How would the discoveries made during this discussion help a marketer plan an effective branding strategy? Relate your findings to the class in a 5-minute presentation.

2. Visit a retail store that sells designed goods, such as jewelry, clothing, appliances, or furniture. Identify a specific item and the audience that is most likely being targeted, choosing from among the following age groups:

   18–25 years
   25–35 years
   35–49 years
   Over 50

Name a few innovative ways to modify the item so it would appeal to a completely different age group. Why do you feel these innovations will work? Relate your findings to the class in a 5-minute presentation.

REFERENCES

1. National Retail Federation, Conference Schedule, http://events.nrf.com/annual2013/public/Calendaraspx?SuperTrackId=9&TrackId=&AssociationId=&DateId=&FormatId=&DurationId=&SpeakerId=&SessionTypeId=&SubExpoId=&Keyword=&&SearchEvent=&sortMenu=105001.

2. Angela Evancie, "The Surprising Sartorial Culture of Congolese 'Sapeurs,'" *NPR,* http://www.npr.org/blogs/pictureshow/2013/05/07/181704510/the-surprising-sartorial-culture-of-congolese-sapeurs, May 7, 2013.

3. Glenn Llopis, "Advertisers Must Pay Attention to Hispanic Consumers as Rising Trendsetters in 2013," *Forbes,* January 9, 2013, http://www.forbes.com/sites/glennllopis/2013/01/09/advertisers-must-pay-attention-to-hispanic-consumers-as-rising-trendsetters-in-2013/.

4. Anup Shah, "Children as Consumers," *Global Issues,* November 21, 2010, http://www.globalissues.org/article/237/children-as-consumers.

5. Ralph Caplan, *By Design,* 2nd ed. (New York: Fairchild Publications, 2005).

6. *Webster's New World Dictionary of American English,* 3rd college ed. (New York: Simon and Shuster, 1988).

7. George B. Sproles and Leslie D. Burns, *Changing Appearances: Understanding Dress in Contemporary Society* (New York: Fairchild Publications, 1994).

8. Jean-Noel Kapferer and Vincent Bastien, *The Luxury Strategy: Break the Rules of Marketing to Build Luxury Brands,* 2nd ed. (London: Kogan Page, 2012).

9. Evelyn L Brannon, *Fashion Forecasting,* 2nd ed. (New York: Fairchild Publications, 2005).

ADDITIONAL RESOURCES

American Academy of Pediatrics. Television and the Family fact sheet. http://pediatrics.aappublications.org/content/118/6/2563.full.

Calvert, Sandra L. "Children as Consumers: Advertising and Marketing." *Children and Electronic Media* 18: 1 (Spring 2008). http://futureofchildren.org/publications/journals/article/index.xml?journalid=32&articleid=62&sectionid=304.

Conlin, Brian. "Marketing to Baby Boomers Online: Where and How to Reach Them." *Vocus,* March 1, 2013. http://www.vocus.com/blog/marketing-to-baby-boomers-online/.

Fromm, Jeff. "How to Get Millennials to Love and Share Your Product." *Ad Age,* August 14, 2013. http://adage.com/article/cmo-strategy/millennials-love-brand/243624/.

Harrell, Gilbert D. *Marketing: Connecting with Customers,* 2nd ed. Upper Saddle River, NJ: Prentice Hall, 2002.

Horn, Marilyn J., and Lois M. Gurel. *The Second Skin: An Interdisciplinary Study of Clothing,* 3rd ed. Boston: Houghton Mifflin Company, 1975.

Kapferer, Jean-Noel, and Vincent Bastien. *The Luxury Strategy: Break the Rules of Marketing to Build Luxury Brands.* 2nd ed. London and Philadelphia: Kogan Page, 2012.

Kellogg, Ann T., Amy T. Peterson, Stefani Bay, and Natalie Swindell. *In an Influential Fashion: An Encyclopedia of Nineteenth and Twentieth Century Fashion Designers and Retailers Who Transformed Dress.* Westport CT: Greenwood Press, 2002.

Popcorn, Faith. *The Popcorn Report.* New York: Doubleday, 1991.

Ries, Al, and Jack Trout. *Positioning: The Battle for Your Mind*. New York: McGraw-Hill. 2000.

"What Is Guerrilla Marketing?" *Creative Guerilla Marketing*. http://www.creativeguerrillamarketing.com/what-is-guerrilla-marketing/#sthash.2ZfFdkGq.dpuf

White, Sara. *The Complete Idiot's Guide to Marketing*. New York: Alpha Books, 2003.

Wilson, Eric. "Gap's New Chain Store Aims at the Fashionably Mature Woman." *New York Times*, August 24, 2005. http://www.nytimes.com/2005/08/24/business/24gap.html?pagewanted=all&_r=0.

Vitelli, Romeo, Ph.D. "Television, Commercials, and Your Child." *Psychology Today*, Media Spotlight blog, July 22, 2013. http://www.psychologytoday.com/blog/media-spotlight/201307/television-commercials-and-your-child.

Consumer Behavior, Marketing, and Fashion: A Working Relationship

Understanding the Marketplace

As you learned in the first chapter, marketing is much more than just promoting a business, a product, or a service. Marketing includes a range of activities that span from the time a product or service is simply an idea, through its evaluation, purchase, use, and disposal by the customer. Businesses, and the marketers they employ, must integrate activities such as sales promotion, social media strategy, and community involvement (see Figure 1.3 in Chapter 1 for a more comprehensive list) to increase their chances of success in the marketplace. However, they also need to understand marketplace conditions and be able to respond appropriately. Let's start by looking at the difference between a buyer's market and a seller's market.

BUYER'S MARKET VERSUS SELLER'S MARKET

In a **buyer's market,** a marketplace situation in which there are more sellers than buyers, an excess of supply over demand results in lower prices for consumers. This means that buyers can be more selective about their purchases because there are many choices available to them. In *A Wealth of Nations* (1776), economist Adam Smith suggested that competition among companies would help customers get the best products and prices; as a result, only the best would survive in the marketplace.[1] Because buyers have more clout in these situations, they can make more demands on companies during a buyer's market cycle, such as insisting on more service and higher quality. It's been said that shoppers want quality merchandise and lots of options. They want things they can't find at other stores, unusual pieces that have friends asking, "Where did you find that?" And it all has to be wrapped up with a certain expected level of service.[2]

On the other hand, a **seller's market** is a marketplace situation in which there are more buyers than sellers; increased demand and low supply result in higher prices. Simply stated, many people want a product, but a limited supply gives sellers an advantage so they can charge more.

LET'S TALK

Can you list some products or services that you personally use and categorize the marketplace for them as either a buyer's or seller's market?

Value versus Cost

According to Peter Drucker (often referred to as the father of modern business management), "The aim of business is to create a customer."[3] When customers believe that an item has an attractive rate of return in terms of time, money, or some other benefit, then the value begins to outweigh the item's price.

For example, in July 2013, Kanye West's capsule collection, a fashion collaboration with French label A.P.C., quickly sold out (and even crashed the A.P.C. website) because of high demand, and then some financial schemers benefitted tremendously by reposting their original purchases on eBay at double or triple the original price.[4] So, exclusivity helps to raise the desirability factor and, therefore, the value points, of a product. The same concept is evidenced by a recent Burberry announcement that it would raise prices to increase its appeal to the upper end of its customer base, while also attracting new, wealthier customers.[5] Think of the items you've seen—or maybe even bought—that have sold at inflated prices because they were in high demand and short supply.

What are some other reasons that consumers are willing to pay high prices or stand in long lines to buy something? When sellers add **value**—tangible or intangible attributes that improve the desirability of a product or service—to the buying experience, it increases the likelihood that customers will buy. A store's ambiance, helpful employees, or customer service that exceeds expectations all might add value to a buying experience. For example, Nordstrom provides customers with a superior level of service that's well regarded in the marketplace.

CALCULATING THE COST

Math has been used to identify, account for, and tabulate things throughout the centuries, but what part does it play in our discussion of the fashion business? Whether customers are buying products or services, it's important to keep a running total of potential benefits. Here's an equation that can help customers and marketers keep score. The equation **P/V = Perceived cost,** where **P** = Price and **V** = Value, demonstrates that as the denominator (**V**) gets larger, the overall **perceived cost,** the balance between the benefits received and the actual price paid, appears smaller. Conversely, if the **V** (Value) decreases, then the overall perceived cost increases. When customers perceive that something has value, it's valuable. (See Chapter 3 for a discussion of perception.)

Examples: P (Price) / V (Value) = Perceived cost

1. The *denominator* V (Value) increases, thereby reducing the Perceived cost. ↓
   A. $100 / 2 = $50 where P = $100, V = 2, then Perceived cost = $50
   B. $100 / 4 = $25 where P = $100, V = 4, then Perceived cost = $25
   C. $100 / 5 = $20 where P = $100, V = 5, then Perceived cost = $20

   Or

2. The *denominator* V (value) decreases, thereby increasing the Perceived cost. ↑
   A. $200 / 5 = $40 where P = $200, V = 5, then Perceived cost = $40
   B. $200 / 4 = $50 where P = $200, V = 4, then Perceived cost = $50
   C. $200 / 2 = $100 where P = $200, V = 2, then Perceived cost = $100

This exercise demonstrates a fundamental marketing idea: Identify what is valued by (important to) the customer, and then provide and communicate that characteristic. This will reduce the customer's perceived cost, and may help that consumer justify spending extra dollars because of added perceived value. Businesses of all types try to turn today's buyer into tomorrow's loyal customer by continuously searching for and implementing ways to add value to multiple parts of the shopping experience. If distinct value is not added to the transaction, that consumer may not buy a specific product, service, or brand initially, or in the future.

Buyer Requirements

Consumer researchers have discovered that more and more customers are demanding products and services that are unique and tailored to them individually. Writer Catherine Getches summed up this issue nicely in an article in the *Boston Globe:* "It's as if marketers want to make us feel like our shopping experience is as customized as our Starbucks concoction."[6]

CUSTOMIZATION

From T-shirts to M&Ms, consumers can personalize a wide array of products including phones, stamps, breakfast cereal, clothing, and many other items with their own choice of comments, photos, colors, wrapping, or packaging (Figure 2.1). In some cases, they can even submit their body measurements to a company and purchase an apparel item that is constructed to fit their exact shape and size. **Customization** is the integration of individual requirements into a product.

FIGURE 2.1 Customization allows fashion consumers to create products with details of their own choosing.

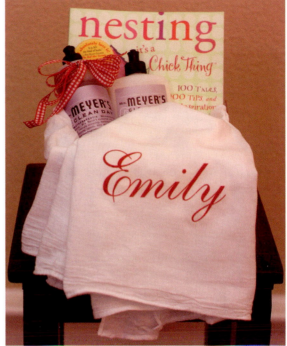

Obviously, there are various levels of customization. In 1996 Joseph Lampel, assistant professor, New York University, and Henry Mintzberg, professor, McGill University, noted a *continuum of customization strategies*. "In tailored customization, a product prototype is adapted to a customer's wishes, as a suit is tailored to a customer, but customization does not enter the design process. In pure customization, however, customization reaches all the way to the design, as custom jewelry is made to customer specifications."[7] Less than two decades later, product customization was more than just an option; it had become part of the marketplace fabric because customers no longer took a back seat. Consumers are the catalyst, and those manufacturers and marketers that better research what their target consumers want will be in a stronger position to improve customer experiences by providing appropriate product solutions and customizations. This customization and customer-driven manufacturing movement has clearly taken hold; according to Forrester Research, a global independent research organization, more than 35 percent of U.S. online consumers are interested in customizing product features or in purchasing build-to-order products that use their specifications.[8]

Today's digital world makes it even easier for consumers to get what they want. Social media encourage consumers to be in the driver's seat (see Chapter 11), and the Internet enables consumers to first search online for product options to explore, compare, and buy, or maybe visit a store to compare even more options or purchase on the spot. The Internet has also enabled small companies, no matter where they're located, to sell to a nationwide (or even worldwide) audience. Those smaller firms are, in general, better equipped than large manufacturers to undertake the customization of products for individual customers.

There is no question that the customization trend continues to grow, and there is an increasing number of customized or personalized products and services available in the marketplace. Perhaps you've bought or seen coffee mugs, postage stamps, or T-shirts with personalized photos, or heard about the dolls that are customized to look like the little girls who own them. Online marketers are even able to customize the very act of shopping, with recommendations for products and services targeted to individual consumers. (See Case in Point 2.1.)

LET'S TALK

What kind of personalized services or products do you request? Have you ever had your name or personal messages imprinted on any clothing, tattoo, jewelry, or other product?

In addition, the customization trend extends to homes that are being built using "green products" (natural materials) or other specialty materials requested by the homeowner, new vehicles that are purchased with specific upgrades or options ordered by customers, and mail and package deliveries that include options enabling the sender to track them via digital devices. With NIKEiD, consumers can customize their favorite shoe style with team colors, camouflage prints, glow-in-the-dark accents, and other embellishments. Ask your grandparents or parents what options they had at your age; you might be surprised by what they tell you.

The term *marketing customization* refers to the crafting of marketing campaigns and messages to address a particular market. If a marketing message is more focused, the response rate (the number of people who actually respond) is greater.

FINDING THE ANSWERS

In order to effectively connect with the marketplace, how does a company find out what established or new customers value? A company uses **primary data,** original information that is collected firsthand (via personal interviews, focus groups, surveys, or digital device tracking), as well as **secondary data,** information that has previously been collected from other studies or sources such as textbooks, magazines, the Internet, and other published materials, to learn about the buying habits of specific customer segments. This information provides a strong foundation for making solid business decisions. For example, has anyone ever stopped you in a shopping mall or gotten your attention with an online pop-up box, and then asked if you would mind answering a series of questions for a survey? If you complied, you participated in primary research. On the other hand, if you search the Internet or go to the local library to collect specific data already compiled, you are reviewing secondary research. (See Chapter 10, "How Marketers Obtain and Use Consumer Information," for more on market research.)

Simply stated, value and customization are critical success factors for many businesses. Delivering value to the customer and personalizing it better than the competition while earning a profit can help one company to thrive while another company that doesn't excel at these activities might merely

Personalizing Online Shopping

What does personalization mean to online businesses in our digital age? For one thing, it can mean the opportunity to create personalized shopping experiences for consumers across all channels. How is that possible? First, today's broad range of digital and mobile devices provides many opportunities for marketers to collect valuable consumer data. In turn, analysis of that data can open the door for apps, mobile platforms, and websites to deliver personalized, targeted business messages when, where, and how consumers want them, regardless of their shopping channel. Companies using such data-driven merchandising tools unlock shopping insights and can effectively influence consumer behavior, as well as brand loyalty and equity.

One company that facilitates personalized shopping experiences for online retailers is RichRelevance, founded in 2006 by David Selinger. Selinger was formerly head of Amazon's product personalization engine team—the team responsible for the giant e-tailer's pioneering method of nudging customers toward additional purchases with automated suggestions such as "you-bought-this, you-might-like-that" and "the people-who-bought-X-also-bought-Y." According to Selinger, the formula behind RichRelevance's capabilities is "ensemble learning," a proven machine learning engine that uses multiple algorithms to analyze consumers' online shopping behavior, noting not only what they buy, but also what they may shop for and don't buy. Individual shoppers' patterns are compared to those of a range of other shoppers, and through its sophisticated data-crunching, RichRelevance can produce targeted recommendations of products that are likely to appeal to specific buyers. Within just seven years of the company's formation, it was driving more than a billion product recommendations each and every day for six of the top ten U.S online retailers.

RichRelevance's ensemble learning allows for customization in reaching, attracting, and securing new customers because it adds personalized value to consumers' experience. They get timely, relevant, and quality content they can use in making key buying decisions. And it's not just about collecting historical purchase data. The large quantities of data harvested from a variety of social and non-social digital platforms can paint a detailed mural of the consumer that potentially raises the level of personalization for the online retailer logarithmically.

As much as the digital shopping experience has helped to change the landscape in the last decade, look for even more innovative ways for retailers to address consumers' needs and wants as further advances in online data personalization continue to mold the retail experience. And as more companies acquire this individual consumer information, collected and assembled via sophisticated digital algorithms, they will find new value for their customers.

Sources: RichRelevance, "Internet Retailer Ranks RichRelevance #1 for Personalization," News release, September 3, 2013; RichRelevance, "Inside the RichRelevance Core Platform: Dynamic Ensemble Learning," http://www.richrelevance.com/wp-content/uploads/2011/01/Speak-Geek2_EnsembleLearning_RichRelevance.pdf; and John Koetsier, "1 Billion Daily Product Recommendations Driving 'Multiple Billions' in Sales for RichRelevance Clients," *VentureBeat News*, March 7, 2013, http://venturebeat.com/2013/03/07/e-commerce-personalization-richrelevance-now-making-1-billion-product-recommendations-daily-driving-multiple-billions-in-sales/.

survive. How is the effectiveness of a company's efforts measured? Marketers need to measure the responses to their efforts (for example, online pop-ups or banner ads, magazine ads, or surveys). To do this, they use a method called **quantifying,** measuring and expressing a result as a number equivalent. By measuring responses in this manner, marketers can get a quick "snapshot" of the success of their efforts. Consider the following example of how you could quantify a response to a question:

> Q: On a scale of 1 to 5, where 1 represents fear of interacting online, 3 is average, and 5 is expert, how good are your social networking skills?
>
> A: I would consider myself a 4.

This quantified response quickly gives the researcher valuable information.

Staying on Track

"Plan your work and work your plan" is a saying that has been around for decades. It's a reminder to take the time to create a **strategic marketing plan,** a road map that identifies a specific target market, the preferences of that market's members, and specific ways to connect with and keep them. This gives the businessperson an advantage over competitors who have not taken the time to plan for success. A key element to include in this planning process is the ability to adapt in an evolving marketplace. Figure 2.2, for example, shows how cell phones have evolved to meet changing consumer needs and expectations.

Companies that cannot interpret changes and then adapt to them face the threat of serious losses.

Consider this example: During an annual conference of the Association of National Advertisers in Phoenix, Arizona, more than 900 executives discussed the rapid and often bewildering changes rippling across the marketing and media landscape and noted that none of the parties involved in any brand-building effort could be exactly sure what the market or media realities would look like six months down the road.[9]

FASHIONABLE SOLUTIONS

We've all read about the changes that evolution has brought since the times of dinosaurs and cavemen, and you have probably witnessed multiple fashion changes in the last 12 years, but what do these have in common? Change, especially fashion-related, does not take a vacation. The term "fashion" was defined in Chapter 1 as anything that's popular at the moment and subject to change; it's anything that members of a population deem desirable and appropriate at a given time, and includes clothes, vehicles, furniture, appliances, electronics, and so on. So, fashion solutions respond to rapid marketplace changes. "It seems that each year what we're seeing in the women's fashion luxury market has been a migration from one category to the next," said Marshal Cohen, chief retail analyst for The NPD Group, a leading market research firm. "A few years ago it was shoes, and then it was jeans. The reign of the handbag began in 2005. Shoppers' infatuation with handbags has lent that category significant clout, to the point where retailers and industry analysts say that bags have supplanted shoes, jeans, and even jewelry as consumers' choice signifier of affluence, social standing, and hipness."[10]

FIGURE 2.2 Consumers look for "what's new," so fashions continually change and evolve.

Figure 2.3 illustrates that fashion marketing is the combination of a tailored marketing plan and current fashion.

What encourages fashion-minded buyers to buy? Hiring celebrities to endorse brands or fashion designers to reimagine specific products is an effective tactic in consumer marketing. Celebrities include established influencers in movies, music, sports, arts, visual media, designers, socialites, models, or any well-known person in a related industry.

Hopefully the chosen celebrity brings a base of fans/followers and product usage integrity (an honest link between product and celebrity), in addition to very real opportunities to attract and engage consumers. Although the "digerati"—people who navigate very well in the digital community—are very influential across various social media platforms, a well-positioned celebrity endorsement can create strong global brand awareness. Having a passion for fashion does not mean that one's creative expression

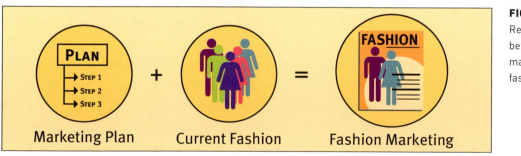

FIGURE 2.3
Relationship between marketing and fashion.

should be limited to only the primary and recognized medium for that person. Chapter 1 stated that "fashion has an important relationship to design of all kinds and pertains to more than just clothing." Case in point: the challenge presented to two fashion designers to make a special-edition car, the Infiniti Q50, reflect a new shine and turn heads even more than those turned by the structural design engineers. As you read Case in Point 2.2, consider how each designer's work reflected his creative vision.

Although the manner for winning over style- and fashion-minded urban professionals is more digitally influenced today, even the less traditional and more grassroots and lifestyle-oriented marketing efforts (using down-to-earth ways to spread the news about a product or service, streetwise methods) are effective. Companies are ever conscious, interested, and proactive about reaching fashion-minded buyers.

Approaching the Marketplace

Graham, a first-time business owner, needed advice on promoting his business. He called his friend Michi, who worked as a marketing specialist for a furniture manufacturer, and asked her for help. When they met the next day, Michi had Graham describe his target market and asked him how he'd segmented the marketplace. Confused by the question, Graham asked Michi to explain.

"You have to have a strategy," she said. A **strategy** is a plan of action for reaching a specific goal; in marketing, a strategy addresses how companies respond to consumers and competitors in the marketplace. "Think about that saying, 'Plan your work and work your plan,'" she told him. In *The Concept of Corporate Strategy*, Professor Kenneth Andrews of Harvard Business School (and also a former editor at *Harvard Business Review*) defines "business strategy" as the basis of competition for a given business.[11] Michael Porter, another business author, says strategy is about competitive positioning and separating your company from others by doing things differently than your competitors to modify the customer's perception.[12]

Michi said to Graham, "First, figure out who your customers are, where they are, what they like and don't like." But that's not always an easy thing to do. Then she told him about the **STP** formula, a way to help organize marketing activities for greater effectiveness.

Step 1:

S = *Segment potential buyers into similar groups (parts).*

You'll recall from Chapter 1 that marketers evaluate different market segments in order to identify their target market. **Market segmentation** is the method for dividing markets into smaller homogeneous clusters of possible customers who reflect similar characteristics, wants, and needs.

Why segment? To identify the best market prospects. For example, customers at Ann Taylor, Talbots, or Brooks Brothers are likely to be more conservative than the younger customers of Abercrombie & Fitch, Zara, Forever 21, or American Eagle Outfitters. Businesses segment their market by first identifying specific demographic or psychographic factors that describe the ideal customer, and then using a "funnel" approach to narrow each segment even further for greater efficiency in terms of

Fashion Designers Sway Consumers with More than Just Apparel

There is no question that successful fashion designers would not be successful without a following of loyal customers who watch for and seek out their newest creations from season to season. But will consumers gravitate to a favored designer even for products outside the designer's normal realm?

The answer, in many cases, is yes, since a keen eye and talent for design can clearly translate to a range of different product categories—and a designer's cachet can carry clout with consumers for a variety of purchases. Take two examples that couldn't be further apart: tissue boxes and automobiles.

You may not immediately think "design" when you think of Kleenex, but the facial tissue brand was actually the pioneer in transforming the sneeze-catchers' plain boxes into decorative home accessories. And to celebrate its 90th anniversary in 2014, Kleenex decided to elevate its passion for design even higher by partnering with style icon Isaac Mizrahi, who was enlisted to create four unique designs for the Kleenex Expressions line.

Mizrahi developed special-edition Kleenex box patterns based on fashion trends that he also incorporated into his spring apparel and home collections. To add to the allure, the company held a special "Catwalk or Kleenex" contest in which entrants had to view pairs of photos and guess which was a dress design and which was a Kleenex box design. Prizes for sweepstakes winners included a $5,000 award and a trip to a New York event where they could meet Mizrahi in person.

At the opposite end of the spectrum was car maker Infiniti, which wanted to create two truly special special-edition versions of its Infiniti Q50 luxury sport sedan—and asked two well-known fashion designers to each weave their distinct fashion sensibilities into the task: Thom Browne, the 2013 recipient of the CFDA (Council of Fashion Designers of America) Menswear Designer of the Year Award, and Zac Posen, designer to movie, music, and TV celebrities.

Browne's customized Q50 featured a gleaming silver exterior that carried through to interior accessories such as the shifter. "They asked us to reflect their customers," he quipped, explaining that a chrome appliqué film created the mirror-like effect. Browne also incorporated his trademark red, white, and blue ribbon across the upholstery as well as around the door frames, among other touches. Completing the ensemble were matching accessories, including a set of luggage adorned with the tricolor ribbon, plus a complementary sterling silver business card case.

Posen's approach could not have been more different, involving a highly

(continued)

sophisticated, 32-coat exterior paint job that went from matte to glossy and from silver to darker gray, from the front of the sedan to the rear. "I wanted to create a finish that emphasized the form of the car," he said. The car's interior was lined with plush red carpet in a nod to Posen's Hollywood connection, while the steering wheel and armrests were adorned with shagreen, another name for stingray skin, to complement the car's metamorphic colors and textures. A mobile phone case of matching red leather put the finishing touch on his design.

As part of a joint marketing program with online fashion retailer Gilt.com, Infiniti took both Q50s on a five-city tour, and also put them on display in "concept room" pop-up stores that the two designers created. After the tour, the cars were offered for sale on Gilt.com for $75,000 each, with a portion of the proceeds donated to St. Jude Children's Research Hospital. In addition, each of the designers planned to sell limited editions of the matching accessories on Gilt.com, including 100 of Browne's silver card case for $650 each, and 350 of Zac Posen's red leather smartphone clutches at $250 each.

Sources: Kimberly-Clark, "Kleenex Brand Celebrates 90 Years of Design; Announces Partnership with Xcel Brands, Inc. & Style Expert Isaac Mizrahi," News release, January 6, 2014; Jack Neff, "Kleenex Inks Deal with Isaac Mizrahi for Designer Tissues," *AdAge,* January 4, 2014, http://adage.com/article/news/kleenex-enlists-designer-isaac-mizraki/290913/; Phil Patton, "Fashion Designers Customize Two Infiniti Q50s," *New York Times,* September 26, 2013, http://wheels.blogs.nytimes.com/2013/09/19/fashion-designers-customize-two-infiniti-q50s/?_r=0; Matthew de Paula, "What the 2014 Infiniti Q50 Looks Like with a Makeover by a Fashion Designer," *Forbes,* December 11, 2013, www.forbes.com/sites/matthewdepaula/2013/12/11/now-your-infiniti-q50-can-wear-fashion-designers-thom-browne-and-zac-posen-too/.

reaching that particular segment while saving time and money (Figure 2.4).

How is segmenting done? Let's say we're selling shoes. Who might buy these shoes? Men? Women? On a separate sheet of paper, draw a pie graph (which is nothing more than a circle). The first step in segmenting potential buyers, as shown in Figure 2.5a, is to designate a portion (in this case, 25 percent) to men and a portion (in this case, 75 percent) to women buyers. This shows you how the total marketplace is divided. Of course, the data needed to create this pie graph must come from reliable research (discussed in Chapter 10).

Segmentation 2, shown in Figure 2.5b, subdivides only one of the groups (women from Segmentation 1) into smaller segments with similar characteristics. Segmenting group members by demographics divides them into subgroups according to some objective factors, such as age, marital status, income, education, and occupation. Segmentation 2 could include different age groups, such as 18 to 30 years, 31 to 41 years, and so forth, or financial brackets, such as $35,000 annual income, $65,000 annual income, and so on. If a businessperson segments the marketplace well, it makes the next step in the STP process much more effective.

How else can groups be subdivided? Some general marketplace segmentation categories are listed in Table 2.1. (See Chapter 9 for a complete discussion of demographics and psychographics.)

Step 2:

T = *Target (identify) a particular segment(s) to pursue.*

A target is a reference point to shoot at; it can also be defined as a goal to be achieved. Decide which subgroup or groups are important (this consists of people who are likely to buy your product or service). Effectively marketing to your target, a defined segment of the market that is the strategic focus of a business or a marketing plan, should save time and money. Why? Because with **target marketing,** you're promoting your product or service only to your specific segment(s), not the entire marketplace.

The following questions may help clarify whether selecting a desired target market is a good business decision:

- *Specify.* Can you actually designate and/or quantify specific segmentation parts, or are you using a series of guesses?
- *Enough.* Can you generate enough revenue (or interest) within the target market to satisfy all

Insert all or some of these items in the funnel:

Age: Tweens (8-12)
Ethnicity: Caucasian
Gender: Female
Technology Interests: Twitter, Video Games, PS4.

Here's the ideal target market: A Caucasian female tween interested in Twitter, video games, and PS4

FIGURE 2.4 Funnel approach.

stakeholders? (A **stakeholder** is any person or organization with an interest in the company.)
- *Growth.* How much will the target market grow or change during business cycles?
- *Cost.* How cost-effective is it to reach that specific market segment?

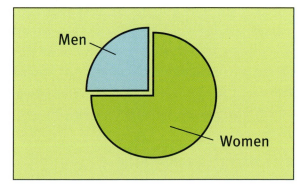

FIGURE 2.5A Segmentation #1 Total Market by Gender.

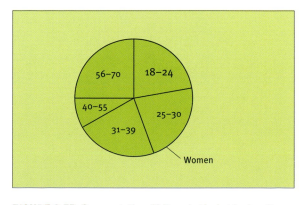

FIGURE 2.5B Segmentation #2 Female Market by Age Group.

TABLE 2.1 Marketplace Segmentation Categories

Type	Example
Demographic	Age, Sex, Marital Status, Income, Education, Occupation
Dominant Benefit	Convenience, Value, Social Rank, Political
Geographic	Domestic: state, city, region; International: country, zone
Hybrid	Combination of any groups
Psychographic	Lifestyle
Sociocultural	Culture, Religion, Ethnicity, Class, Family
Usage	Quantifying and Qualifying Criteria: rate/loyalty/activity/location

On the same sheet of paper you used for Step 1 (Segment), draw an arrow that points to one or more of the segments that identify your target customer(s). (See Figure 2.6.)

Completing the first two steps of STP—segmenting and targeting—helps to identify the specific market that is of interest. How can you make your product or service stand out from those of competitors? Chapter 1 defined positioning as creating a certain perception or image about the product or service in the minds of consumers; this is an idea we need to look at more closely.

Step 3:

P = *Position the product or service and company.*

To position means to align or put in place. In the book *Positioning: The Battle for Your Mind,* authors Al Ries and Jack Trout describe how to create a leading "position" in prospective customers' minds; that is, how to get the company's name and message into the "collective subconscious" of the target market and keep it there. It gives customers concrete reasons to select one competitor over another.[13]

THE MARKETING MIX

In order to position a product or service or company, you need to implement a combination of

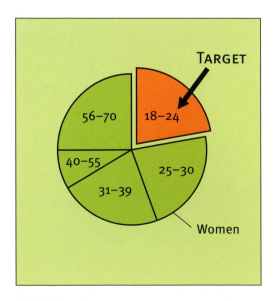

FIGURE 2.6 Target market is women ages 18–24.

marketing tools (described below and illustrated in Figure 2.7). By doing so, the consumer will presumably come to believe that you provide the service or deliver the product in a better way than your competitor. Figure out how to best serve your customers based upon some objective factors (for example, more physical distribution locations or self-serve computer checkout counters). Understanding what the customer really wants and why he or she wants it, then combining that understanding with your study of how your competitors serve that same market segment, will help you succeed.

The four key marketing tools used by all marketers today were delineated in 1960 by E. Jerome McCarthy, a professor and marketing consultant who identified the marketing mix as: *product, place* (also known as distribution), *promotion,* and *price*—commonly referred to as "The 4 P's."[14] Two ancillary tools may also be considered: *people (employees)* and *procedures (factors of efficiency and comfort for both internal and external customers, employees, and consumers).* Let's look at what each of these tools mean to marketers:

4 P's

Product. Is it the best it can be in terms of what customers want? Get feedback about it; improve it; use research to anticipate evolving physical (tangible) and mental (intangible) needs and wants.

Place. How can customers get the product or service at the right place and right time more easily, quickly, conveniently? Improve access and the distribution channels (the ways that customers get the products and services).

Promotion. What communications, promotions, media, and digital technology will interest and encourage customers to buy?

Price. What realistic supply and demand pricing strategies make sense, add value, and stimulate purchases?

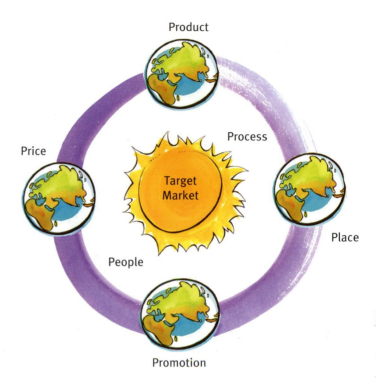

FIGURE 2.7 Marketing mix.

Ancillary Tools

People. How do you hire, train, motivate, develop, and retain employees to provide excellent service to customers?

Process/procedure. What will make the delivery of the product or service more efficient and cost-effective for both customers and employees?

Successful companies pay attention to details, and these details (marketing tools) add value to various levels of the **supply chain,** the organizations and related activities associated with the manufacture and delivery of a product or service. The supply chain represents the workflow from supplier to manufacturer to wholesaler to retailer to the end user, the consumer. (See examples in Table 2.2.) With a well-executed marketing mix, the final result of the STP process is the perception by the customer that the product or service has value and is worth

TABLE 2.2 Examples of Participants in a Supply Chain

Company Provides	Item	Some of the People Involved in the Supply Chain
Service	Restaurant	Raw materials supplier, farmer, truck driver, wholesaler, chef, server, hostess, and others until the customer actually eats
Product	Purse	Raw materials supplier, manufacturer, truck driver, wholesaler, boutique manager, salesperson, and others until the customer actually buys the purse

purchasing. Perception, the process of interpreting our surroundings through our senses, implies awareness and comprehension and can vary tremendously from segment to segment.

Customizing each of the variables of the marketing mix more effectively than the competition—so the benefits exceed customer expectations—should result in a competitive advantage for the company. Keeping current with research and adding value (for example, through new products or improved services) to the customer's experience should sustain a company's growth and revenue generation. As technology and the marketplace continue to evolve, so too will successful marketing tools. See Point of View 2.1 for one opinion on how the marketing mix can already be adapted further to today's marketplace.

LET'S TALK

Think of a fashion item you purchased recently. Which of the marketing mix tools do you think had the most influence on your purchase decision? Could the marketer have improved one or more aspects to make your experience better?

SATISFYING CUSTOMERS

The **marketing concept** is a design that focuses on knowing your customers or clients (buyers), satisfying their needs, and doing so more effectively than the competitors. This makes the buyer the center of all business initiatives. Simply put, marketers must find out what customers want and then give it to them at a profit, because the profit enables the company to stay in business. The more an organization understands and addresses the real wants and needs of its customers, the more likely it is to have satisfied buyers who not only become repeat purchasers but also influence their friends' decisions about where to shop and/or which brands to buy and even motivate others via social networking. A successful, effective marketing program also includes feedback mechanisms; companies should listen to both customers and suppliers, be alert to changes in the marketplace, and continuously track the business activities of competitors. (Refer to Chapter 11 for discussion of social media marketing tools.) The company is then on the path to creating a win-win situation, satisfying both its customers and its own strategic goals.

In the early 1960s, marketers started to use this knowledge to sell more products more efficiently. They began to test the waters through **market research,** the collecting of information to define the size, location, and/or makeup of the market for a product or service (see Chapter 10). This research helped marketers to identify consumer needs and wants.

In 1954 Peter Drucker noted that "what the customer thinks he/she is buying, what he/she considers 'value' is decisive—it determines what a business is, what it produces, and whether it will prosper."[15] However, many companies continued to practice the **selling concept,** which focused on trying to sell what the company had already made, not what the customer wanted. Today we know better, and most companies now base their efforts on the marketing concept.

Why do today's companies follow the marketing concept and not the selling concept? According to the American Marketing Association, the marketing concept is preferable for several reasons:[16]

- Surveys demonstrate that it costs as much as five times more to acquire a new customer than it does to service an existing one.
- The average company gets 65 percent of its business from its present and satisfied customers.
- Customers tell twice as many people directly about a bad experience as about a good one. Think of how that information, good and bad, can spread like wildfire in today's world of instant digital communications.

In a nutshell, organizations that address the needs and wants of customers stand a better chance of sustaining a competitive advantage in the marketplace.

Additionally, a new way of thinking has gained traction in the marketplace in recent decades, one that brings an even broader perspective to marketers' activities as previously described in this chapter. Consider the following:

> *"It is what we do when we don't have to that determines what we will be when we can no longer help it."* —*Anonymous*

> *"Hold yourself responsible for a higher standard than anybody else expects of you."* —*Henry Ward Beecher (mid-nineteenth-century clergyman and abolitionist)*

> *"Ethics are . . . the reverence for and the maintaining, promoting, and enhancing of life . . ."* —*Albert Schweitzer (1952 Nobel Prize recipient)*

The above quotes are intended to help illustrate that there are times when merely satisfying customers' needs better than the competition is just *not* enough. What if these solutions (as products and services are sometimes referred to) are harmful to people, the environment, or future generations? These days, businesses carefully balance the needs of individuals, the organization, *and* society, because ethics and responsibility are key components for the success of today's companies—not merely food for thought.

The **societal marketing concept** considers the interests of all of an organization's stakeholders—anyone from administrators to vendors, from stockholders to members of the cleaning crew, as well as clients and customers, who have an interest in an organization—as well as the greater good to society as a whole. The four key ideas that must be balanced for this concept to work are as follows:

1. Customer wants
2. Competitors' actions
3. Society's interests
4. Company profits

Modernizing the Marketing Mix?

Question: Is the marketing mix an out-of-date relic of another era when marketers told consumers what they should want and conversation about products traveled just one way, from the brand to the customer? Or is it an evolving framework that enables marketers to keep one eye on the basic tenets while adapting to a very new consumer landscape?

As you know, the original marketing mix was introduced more than 50 years ago and consisted of four Ps (product, price, promotion, and place), the tools that E. Jerome McCarthy identified as being crucial for marketers to succeed in the marketplace. Before long, other marketing gurus began adding their own elements to the mix—such as Ries and Trout with positioning, by which companies were tasked with finding market niches they could fill with their product.

As companies continued placing an ever higher premium on consumer-centered marketing and the study of consumer behavior took hold, however, some began to view the 4Ps as being too product-oriented or even obsolete. Yet marketers still wanted a framework on which to organize their strategy. As a result, new versions of the marketing mix began to be broached, looking at marketing from the customer's point of view. One model, dubbed the 4Cs, consists of: *customer needs and wants* (replacing product); *cost to the user* (replacing price); *communication* (replacing promotion); and *convenience* (replacing place).

Going further, in today's world of instant digital communications and social networking—where consumers suddenly have unparalleled access to information, unlimited choices of what to buy and where, not to mention control over the marketing conversation—some are suggesting even more tweaking of the model. An executive with the global advertising firm Saatchi & Saatchi, for example, redefined the 4Ps as *purpose, passion, participation,* and *profit.* And author, brand strategist, and marketing consultant Bernadette Jiwa suggests yet four different Ps as a new marketing mix for the 21st century:

Purpose—It's not a question of what you do, but why you do it. A company has to have a fundamental reason to exist that goes beyond simply bringing a product to market.

People—It's a matter of who you serve, not what you sell. A company needs to convey a compelling story about the benefits of its product or service and the real difference it will make in the lives of its customers.

Personal—The important thing is to become more relevant and significant to the people who are your customers. How they feel about a company's product is far less important than how the company makes them feel about themselves when they own or use the brand.

(continued)

Perception—You must be believed and believed in, not simply noticed. A company can tell its customers what to think over and over again, but that flies out the window if it doesn't match up with what those customers actually believe about the company.

The key is not just finding holes in the market or gaining share of mind among consumers, it's setting out to fill a void in customers' lives, Jiwa states. Half a century ago the secret of successful marketing was to simply be dominant; today, she notes, it is to *matter.* As a consumer, wouldn't you agree?

Sources: Andrew Bryson, "The New 4Ps of Marketing," *Saatchi & Saatchi Asia Pacific,* December 13, 2013, http://www.saatchiasiapacific. com/2013/12/the-new-4ps-of-marketing/; and Bernadette Jiwa, "The New Marketing Mix: 4 Different Ps," *The Story of Telling,* http:// thestoryoftelling.com/the-new-marketing-mix-4-different-ps/.

This concept both embraces and reflects the idea that companies should balance customer interests and wants, competitive intelligence, and long-term consumer and societal well-being. A few years ago, for example, Dove made the conscious decision to use women with average body builds rather than very thin models in its advertisements; the company suggested that this might help improve self-image issues among females and particularly impressionable young girls (in addition to increasing sales). Along those same lines, a growing number of brands, such as Old Navy, Canada's Reitmans, Monif C., and H&M, have increased their use of plus-size models in their marketing efforts. In fact, a recent H&M promotion for a new swimwear collection not only side-stepped fashion norms by featuring the beachwear on plus-size model Jennie Runk but did so without even mentioning plus size

or calling attention to it through an online media blast or other publicity.[17]

Other examples include some fast-food restaurants that incorporate menu choices containing less fat, and "smart" homebuilders that provide convenient safety and energy management options for disabled individuals. StarKist Seafood Company is committed to protecting dolphins and will not purchase any tuna caught by means that endanger these creatures. The American Marketing Association specifically addresses the social obligations companies have to all stakeholders in the responsibility and citizenship sections of its code of ethics.[18] (Ethics and responsibility are discussed in greater detail in Chapter 15.)

Taking this issue further is the concept of **cause-related marketing,** the public association of a for-profit company with a nonprofit organization in which a for-profit company pairs with a nonprofit's social cause. One of the front-runners in this effort was American Express. In 1983 it participated in the restoration of the Statue of Liberty, pledging a minimum of $3 million through its various fund-raising efforts. Companies that employ this concept increase corporate sales and customer loyalty while demonstrating social concern and involvement. Today companies and individuals want to do good things; philanthropy (helping others through charitable contributions) has become very fashionable as well as good business. Kmart, for instance, was named Corporate Partner of the Year more than once by St. Jude Children's Research Hospital, in part due to the retailer's annual St. Jude Thanks and Giving fund-raising campaign that has raised millions of dollars to support childhood cancer research and treatment.[19] Refer to the online Cause Marketing Forum at http://www.causemarketingforum .com for related information.

Developing fashionable solutions, from the company's perspective, means understanding what is currently valued and wanted by its customers. But what about the consumer's perspective? What is it that helps create that perspective—at a very basic level? How do consumers interpret and learn? The next chapter provides some answers.

Summary

Buying and selling come together in the exchange process when the buyer perceives value, tangible or intangible attributes that improve the desirability of a product or service. After the marketer identifies that perceived value in specific market segments, products or services that address those client needs and wants are sometimes customized to increase their appeal to the consumer.

A company that creates a strategic marketing plan (a road map that connects and positions product and service solutions to buyers) and adapts, as needed, to evolving fashion expectations, will thrive in today's marketplace. The emerging expectation is that organizations will provide products and services that add value in a socially responsible manner—not just generate revenue for the company.

KEY TERMS

Buyer's market

Cause-related marketing

Customization

Market research

Market segmentation

Marketing concept

Perceived cost

Primary data

Quantifying

Secondary data

Seller's market

Selling concept

Societal marketing concept

Stakeholder

Strategic marketing plan

Strategy

Supply chain

Target marketing

Value

QUESTIONS FOR REVIEW

1. Describe the differences between a buyer's market and a seller's market and give a specific example of each.
2. Explain the equation P (Price) ÷ V (Value) = PC (Perceived Cost), and provide a numerical example showing what happens to PC when the denominator increases. How do actual and perceived costs differ?
3. What is meant by "quantifying" and why is it an important business tool? Support your answer with two examples.
4. What is the STP process, why is it important to a marketer, and what steps are involved?
5. Discuss the differences between the selling, marketing, and societal marketing concepts.

ACTIVITIES

1. Price, value, and perceived cost (P/V = PC): You are a buyer, not the seller. Assume that you have the extra dollars to make a purchase. Select three items in the same product or service category that have low, medium, and high price points (for example, Jeans: $35/$75/$195).
   A. Explain this equation in terms of the product or service at the lowest and highest price levels.
   B. Identify specific value factors.
   C. List other value-added factors that might motivate you to spend more on the product or service.

2. Customization: Select a company that's both *product* and *service* oriented. Discuss the following:
   A. Ways the company customizes its offerings
   B. Your perception of this customization
   C. How you would improve it
3. Quantifying (measuring and expressing a result as a number equivalent): Think of a particular company that provides a service, and identify three areas in which quantifying results is important. Then:
   A. List and explain one specific method of measurement for each area.
   B. Recommend one improvement to maximize efficiency in each area.
4. Buyer's and seller's market: Select two designed products or services and explain how they moved from a buyer's market to a seller's market (for example, blue jeans).
5. Societal marketing concept: Find the mission statements of three not-for-profit organizations. Then pair each one with an existing for-profit company, explaining why you feel each is a good match (for example, Kenneth Cole and the Save the Children Foundation). Hint: Check http://www.causemarketingforum .com/site/c.bkLUKcOTLkK4E/b.6381267/k .B2B8/Cause_Marketing_Forum_Helping_ Businesses_Nonprofits_Succeed_Together.htm.

MINI-PROJECT

STP Process (Segment–Target–Position)

Assume the role of a business owner. Dream for a moment: What kind of business interests you? What product(s) do you sell or what service(s) do you provide? Then identify a new line or a service add-on you think would be good for your bottom line. Remember, you don't want to add a new product or service blindly. Illustrate and explain the STP process at work by segmenting your market and targeting and positioning your product or service.

REFERENCES

1. Adam Smith, *The Wealth of Nations*, www.bibliomania.com/2/1/65/112/frameset.html.

2. Susan Chandler. "What Do Shoppers Want," *Chicago Tribune*, September 25, 2005.

3. Peter Drucker, www.peter-drucker.com.

4. Alex Rees, "Kanye West's Capsule Collection for A.P.C. Almost All Sold Out Already," *BuzzFeed*, July 15, 2013, http://www.buzzfeed.com/alexrees/kanye-wests-capsule-collection-for-apc-almost-all-sold-out-a.

5. Lauren Sherman, "Fashion Inflation: Why Are Prices Rising So Fast?," *The Business of Fashion*, August 2, 2013, http://www.businessoffashion.com/2013/08/fashion-inflation-why-are-the-prices-of-designer-goods-rising-so-fast.html.

6. Catherine Getches, "Brand Boggled," *New York Times*, September 1, 2005.

7. Henry Mintzberg and Joseph Lampel, "Customizing Customization," *MIT Sloan Review* 38 Topic: Corporate Strategy Reprint 3812, no. 1 (Fall 1996): 21–30.

8. Barb Schmitz, "Demands for Increased Product Customization on the Rise," *PTC Creo*, March 25, 2013, http://creo.ptc.com/2013/03/25/demands-for-increased-product-customization-on-the-rise/.

9. James B. Arndorfer, "Grappling with Marketing's 'Tsunami,'" *AdAge.com* online edition, October 7, 2005, http://adage.com/news.cms?newsId=46320#.

10. Ruth La Ferla, "Over the Shoulder, Over the Top," *New York Times*, October 6, 2005, http://www.nytimes.com/2005/10/06/fashion/thursdaystyles/06handbags.html?pagewanted=print&_r=0.

11. Kenneth Andrews, *The Concept of Corporate Strategy*, 2nd ed. (Homewood, IL: Dow Jones-Irwin, 1980).

12. Michael Porter, *Competitive Strategy* (Cambridge, MA: Harvard Business School Press, 1986).

13. Al Ries and Jack Trout, *Positioning: The Battle for Your Mind* (New York: McGraw-Hill, 2001).

14. J. McCarthy, *Basic Marketing: A Managerial Approach*, 13th ed. (Homewood, IL: Irwin, 2001).

15. Peter Drucker, *The Practice of Management* (New York: HarperCollins Publishers, Inc., 1954).

16. Peter D. Bennett, ed., *Dictionary of Marketing Terms*, 2nd ed. (Chicago: American Marketing Association, 1995).

17. Asha Dahya, "How Dare They! H&M Uses Plus Size Model in Regular Campaign without Pointing It Out," *Girl Talk HQ*, May 2, 2013, girltalkhq.com/how-dare-they-hm-uses-plus-size-model-in-regular-campaign-without-pointing-it-out; and "H&M Uses Plus-Size Model for Swimwear Campaign Photos,"

HuffPost Style Canada, April 30, 2013, www
.huffingtonpost.ca/2013/04/30/hm-plus-size-
model-swimwear-photos_n_3186016.html.

18. "American Marketing Association Code of
Ethics," www.ama.org; www.marketingpower
.com/content435.php.

19. Sears Holdings, "Holiday Giving Starts Early As
Top National Partner Kmart Launches Its 2013
St. Jude Thanks and Giving Campaign," News
release, September 19, 2013.

ADDITIONAL RESOURCES

American Express. "American Express Launches
National Campaign to Help Reopen the Statue
of Liberty; Pledges a Minimum of $3 Million
with Cardmember Support." November 25, 2003.
http://home3.americanexpress.com/corp
/pc/2003/statue_liberty.asp.

Borden, N. "The Concept of the Marketing Mix."
Journal of Advertising Research 4 (June 1964): 2–7.

Davis, Wynn. *The Best of Success: A Treasury of Success
Ideas.* Lombard, IL: Great Quotations, Inc., 1988.

England, Lizabeth. "Marketing with a Conscience:
Sales and Ethics." Chapter 10 in *Business Ethics*
volume of *Language and Civil Society* journal.
Published online at http://exchanges.state.gov
/forum/journal/bus10background.htm.

Hughlett, Mike. "A Field's, Frango Frenzy." *Chicago
Tribune,* December 23, 2005.

Investor Words.com. www.investorwords.com.

Investor's Glossary. Contra the Heard Web site.
www.contratheheard.com/cth/glossary.

MarketingProfs Web site. www.marketingprofs
.com/5/kaden1.asp.

Martin, James. "Color Trends for Custom Homes."
Residential Design & Build, April 2007.

"Motorola Pininfarina i833 Announced."
MobileTracker Web site, August 18, 2004.
www.mobiletracker.net/archives/2004/08/18
/motorola_pininf.php.

Mplans.com Web site. www.mplans.com.

Nobelprize.org Web site. Biography of Albert
Schweitzer. http://nobelprize.org/nobel_prizes
/peace/laureates/1952/schweitzer-bio.html.

Schweitzer, Albert. *Civilization and Ethics.* New
York: Macmillan, 1949.

Scott, David L. *Wall Street Words: An A to Z Guide
to Investment Terms for Today's Investor.* Boston:
Houghton Mifflin Company.

SmartHomeUSA Web site. www.smarthomeusa.com.

Vielkind, Jimmy and Nancy Dillon. "Swoosh! Big
Women Taking Ads by Storm." *New York Daily
News,* August 16, 2005.

Voorn, R. *The Marketing Plan Made Simple.* 3rd ed.
Costa Mesa, CA: James Publishing, 1997.

Webster's New World Dictionary. 3rd ed. New York:
Simon & Schuster.

"What Is Strategy?" *Harvard Business Review,*
November–December, 1996.

Wikipedia. "Consumption" entry. http://en.wikipedia
.org/wiki/Consumption.

www.trexfiles.com/2007/02/why_fashion_has
_turned_to_cause_marketing.php.

"What Is Cause-Related Marketing?" From the
Foundation Center's Web site. http://foundation
center.org/getstarted/faqs/html/cause_
marketing.html.

Part II

INTERNAL FACTORS INFLUENCE FASHION CONSUMERS

NUMEROUS psychological and behavioral elements influence individual consumers in their actions and attitudes toward fashion—some of these elements are explored in Part II.

Chapter 3 describes how people perceive, learn, and remember. The various human needs and wants that motivate purchases, and the rational versus emotional drivers that influence purchase decisions, are examined in Chapter 4. The consumer's attitudes and values, and how those traits influence behavior, are the topic of Chapter 5. Part II concludes with the Chapter 6 discussion of how personality and self-concept relate to the consumption of fashion.

CHAPTER 3

How Fashion Consumers Perceive, Learn, and Remember

WHAT DO I NEED TO KNOW ABOUT HOW FASHION CONSUMERS PERCEIVE, LEARN, AND REMEMBER?

✔ What stimuli are and how they influence our five senses

✔ The meaning of perception and what the perception process includes

✔ How we learn and the difference between behavioral and cognitive learning for fashion consumers

✔ The three kinds of memory and how they work

Brad had not worn a wristwatch since he was about 10 years old—but the array of smart watches at the electronics store caught his eye immediately. Some featured traditional analog clock hands, while others had touch screens and scrolling displays to alert the wearer to incoming cell phone calls, text messages, and tweets. There were even styles with full-blown speakerphones or built-in music players. Brad was completely fascinated with all the smart watches' bells and whistles—the opposite of his sister Alyssa's reaction: She found the devices to be much too chunky and heavy to even think about wearing on her wrist.

Before people can react—form an opinion or reach a decision—they must be exposed to a physical sensation as Brad and Alyssa were when they looked at the store's smart watch display; **exposure** is what happens when we encounter a stimulus through our senses: seeing, hearing, smelling, touching, or tasting. Stimuli such as rock music on the radio, the aroma of coffee, or strong light bombard us constantly, and we cannot possibly register everything we encounter. Instead, we choose the exposure we want. For example, to discover fashion trends, women may flip through hundreds of ads in *Vogue* or *InStyle,* noting only those looks that appeal to them. Fashion marketers work to maximize the possibility of exposure for their products, creating eye-catching ads and commercials and placing their products prominently in stores. Note how the various merchandise displays in Figure 3.1 attract attention.

To better understand this concept, let's look further at Alyssa. She has been working as a cashier at a J. Crew store on weekends for several months to help pay for college (with a major in fashion). The job fits her schedule, and the store's merchandise has a certain trendy look her friends at school are wearing.

"This look appeals to my friends as well as some older people," she thinks as she rings up customers' purchases. Although some customers are indeed her age, Alyssa begins to note that a number of career-age women and men are also frequent shoppers. They talk about the polished look of the suits, dress shirts, ties, cashmere sweaters, and khakis—apparel that the executives in their companies seem to favor. Quality is also a factor; some goods are higher quality than others, and Alyssa finds herself impressed by some customers' ability to distinguish more sustainable but expensive merchandise from that intended for lower price lines. Finding the right ensemble for business can be a challenge, but Alyssa could see that savvy careerists felt it worth the effort to try to look as professional and "put together" as possible. She learned that in the J. Crew "look," these customers perceived a life of fashionable work and leisure; with their purchases, they were buying an image of fashion and success.

How Stimuli Influence Our Five Senses

As noted earlier, we receive stimuli through our five senses: vision, touch, smell, hearing, and taste. Let's consider each and the role each plays in the world of fashion and design.

VISION

In fashion, vision is the most obvious stimulus. Entering a room, we gain a sense of its design and purpose by looking at its furnishings and their arrangement. At a fashion show, we are exposed to an amazing assortment of garment colors and shapes, or as we walk in a city, we encounter a huge variety of building shapes and styles and apparel silhouettes and colors. In fashion, color is an especially vital element of vision. Color has an emotional appeal: red, yellow, and orange denote warmth, while green, blue, and purple are cool colors. Forecasting color trends is a basic part of creating fashion goods, including apparel, home furnishings, and even automobiles and airplanes. Years before a color is seen by the public, color companies and organizations such as Pantone and the Color Association of the United States track and indicate upcoming color palettes to textile and fashion designers, who then create their lines using these latest color combinations.[1] As the seasons change, designers plan apparel and home furnishings in the latest warm or cool colors.[2] The designs of Angela Missoni and the colorful stripes and prints of Missoni knits draw customers who enjoy those vibrant looks and want them for their wardrobes year-round. Businesses

FIGURE 3.1 Fashion businesses employ a creative variety of stimuli to maximize customers' exposure to a particular brand.

also identify themselves through colors.[3] Think of Tiffany packaging, a blue-green box enhanced by a white satin ribbon etched with the company name, elegant and refined, while an ad for Target, with its bull's-eye logo in red and white, is cheery and inviting. Consider the many bright colors you see on the Internet encouraging you to click on to the next site.

TOUCH

Essential also to the total fashion presence is the sense of touch. The plush feel of velvet, the smoothness of microfiber, the slight scratch and weight of denim each create a physical sensation on contact with the skin.

When discussing textiles, fashion professionals use the term "hand" to describe how a certain fabric feels. As you can imagine, designers can be quite particular about fabric. Ralph Lauren, for instance, launched his fashion empire by making men's ties wider and thicker (at one point he cut the upholstery off a sofa to obtain the "hand" of the fabric he was seeking).[4]

Obviously, customers can touch a fabric only when they are in the store with it, a disadvantage of shopping via catalog or Internet. In fact, some formerly Web-only retailers such as Gap's Piperlime opt to open stores in order to give customers the experience of touching and trying on merchandise, thus preventing the online need to order several sizes to see which is the best fit.

SMELL

In receiving stimuli, our sense of smell is strong and swift. Stimuli received through our eyes and ears need to be interpreted by the *thalamus,* a sensory way station in our brain. Odors, though, run directly for processing in the *olfactory cortex,* an outer part of the brain, right into the brain's *limbic system,* a series of nerves and networks controlling our basic emotions.[5] That is why the aroma of barbeque, watermelon, and chocolate brownies might instantly recall a summer picnic from years ago. Or the cool freshness of a pine forest or the fragrance of a bouquet of flowers may instantly evoke other distant memories. According to research, humans can distinguish 10,000 separate aromas.[6] A dog, however, has a sense of smell possibly 10,000 times more sensitive than ours! Smell has an evocative power, causing people to think of unpleasant (skunk) or pleasant (flowers) environments. Perfume and cologne, soaps, moisturizers, bath oils, aftershaves, cosmetics of all kinds, room fresheners, dresser drawer liners, and candles appeal to us because of their pleasant fragrance. Retailers including Nordstrom, Victoria's Secret, and Mrs. Fields use aromas to draw customers through their doors; the scents help to create a persuasive ambience inside the store as well.

The field of aromatherapy, with its promise of relaxation and renewal, is based on the attributes of certain odors. Consider scent strips in fashion magazines: these obvious indicators with an appeal to the sense of smell help marketers expose potential customers to their products. In addition, many people feel that one of the joys of owning the latest automobile is its "new car smell." The sense of smell is closely related to that of taste—just think how the aroma of warm apple pie can make your mouth water as you anticipate the sensation!

Can You Tell What Smells Good?

Only our noses reveal odors, and typically we seek out those aromas that are most agreeable. Fragrances—pervasive, stimulating, and at times intoxicating—have appealed to people everywhere over the centuries. Ancient peoples in the Middle East burned incense from fragrant trees to carry their prayers up to the gods. A thousand years before Christ, Egyptians soothed their bodies with perfumed oils as protection against that country's relentless blazing sun. Cedar, rose, jasmine, and sandalwood were among the available fragrance choices of the day.

Today, consumers, both men and women, have a wide and ever-changing assortment of aromas from which to choose. Some scents come from plants, trees, and flowers, while others emerge from laboratory-created chemicals. Well over a thousand new fragrances reach the market each year. No wonder most customers are stumped when trying to select a fragrance. According to one well-known *parfumier* (creator of new fragrances), although many customers may not know what they want, they do know what they don't like and can distinguish what they do like. This means that the fragrance industry works hard to meet customer demand by introducing an average of four new fragrances a day. These include new products bearing designer names such as Chanel and Jean Paul Gaultier and those of celebrities such as Justin Bieber and Lady Gaga.

Why is the fragrance industry so willing to offer such choices? One example: According to sales estimates for Vera Wang's recent fragrance "Bejeweled," available only at Kohl's Department Stores, sales could amount to $25 million in its first year alone. Clearly, the company believes that in this instance its customers *do* know what they like!

Sources: Eric Wilson, "Where Everything Smells Bad," *New York Times*, March 7, 2013, p. A24; and Julie Naughton, "A New Facet for Vera Wang's Empire," *Women's Wear Daily*, March 29, 2013, p. 6.

HEARING

On a day off, Alyssa decides to do some fashion research in a nearby city. When she enters a department store, she hears soft instrumental music drifting out from the sound system. Not exactly her style, but apparently it's soothing to many customers because they appear to be either oblivious to it or happily shopping. In the junior department she sees a bank of television sets blaring out the latest hit song and video. She moves on, heading for the store's fashion show, which features resort wear. There the lively beat of a combo announces the start of the show as the lights dim. The tropical music stirs excitement in the room; she can sense the audience anticipating the first models on the runway. Throughout the show, fun, playful music serves as the soundtrack as the models parade in swimwear, sunwear, and evening wear. After the show, she shops the department to try on one of the outfits. The salesperson's attention, knowledge of detail, and enthusiastic manner demonstrate to Alyssa how she can better help her own customers choose what's right for them. The sincerity and enthusiasm of the salesperson, along with the tone and sound of her voice, give Alyssa a feeling of confidence about the merchandise. Marketers reach customers many ways through sound.

TASTE

One day, Alyssa decides to have a Dove bar. She had seen an ad showing a silky curtain in chocolate brown emphasizing the smoothness of that candy compared with less expensive brands.[7] Not a designer chocolate, but quite fashionable in its appearance and taste just the same. Alyssa realizes that there are fashions in food just as there are fashions in apparel and home furnishings. Her friends were eating fewer hamburgers and more vegetables and fruit, and were experimenting with the flavors and cuisines of places as far away as Argentina, Ethiopia, and Thailand. Obviously, taste can introduce new experiences. Most humans recognize four flavors: sweet, sour, salty, and bitter; the Japanese claim a fifth flavor called "umami," with a taste similar to MSG.

The way we respond to these sensory stimuli makes up a part of the emotional aspect of our relationship to purchasing products and is known as **hedonic consumption.** For example, with the scent of roses a young woman recalls her grandmother's garden and the summer parties there. By purchasing rose-scented hand cream, she remembers the pleasant memories of those gatherings each time she uses it. Retailers look for many ways to appeal to consumers' desires for hedonic consumption. For instance, they might encourage shopping as a lifestyle experience by building personal relationships with consumers; make shopping more comfortable through plentiful and convenient parking spaces; and promote in-store restaurants such as the ones that shopping-weary consumers can find in stores including Neiman Marcus, Tommy Bahama, Ikea, and Target.

LET'S TALK

What fashion goods have you noticed recently whose appeal to consumers is based on hedonic consumption, the emotional relationship aspect of the purchase?

How We Perceive

Because as humans we can only process some of the stimuli that bombard us, we call the process of interpreting our surroundings through our senses **perception.** Drawing on the fields of psychology, sociology, as well as economics and social anthropology, perception concerns itself with both individuals and groups. Perception is subjective; that is, about our personal interpretations. What each of us perceives becomes our reality. How perception motivates us as members of specific consumer groups is a subject of marketers' ongoing research.

Interpreting our perception, supermarkets place the most popular items on shelves at eye-level and specialty stores display their newest wares in the front of the department. Customers often vary in their interpretations of fashions by young designers such as those in Figure 3.2.

In addition to exposure to sensory stimuli (discussed in the previous section), the perception process includes attention and interpretation. These topics are discussed later in the chapter.

ABSOLUTE THRESHOLD

Now that we have seen several examples of exposure through our five senses, we need to take this

FIGURE 3.2 The work of designers Dao-yi Chow and Maxwell Osborne reflects changing looks that draw the attention of fashion editors and customers from season to season.

information one step further. The lowest level at which our senses can recognize a stimulus is called the **absolute threshold.** The music in a store, in order not to detract people from shopping, is set at a scarcely discernible volume, an absolute threshold for many shoppers. When our senses can barely distinguish between two stimuli such as popular music and jazz, this represents the **just noticeable difference (j.n.d.).** The just noticeable difference is important to designers and marketers who want to make sure that customers can distinguish, for example, the difference between two sweaters priced $20 apart or two chairs priced $50 apart. Certain features of the more expensive item, perhaps the fiber content or the trimmings, must make it worth the higher price in the mind of the consumer. Or, if shirts are on sale, the reduced price must have a j.n.d. in price from the original price. In the mind of the customer, there is no j.n.d. in a sweater reduced from $80 to $78, but there is a significant difference in one reduced from $80 to $39. In this instance, the j.n.d. becomes another way consumers are encouraged to buy.

LET'S TALK

What recent examples can you think of that illustrate j.n.d.?

WEBER'S LAW

Nineteenth-century German experimental psychologist Ernst Weber gave us the basis for explaining j.n.d. when he developed the theory bearing his name. **Weber's Law** states that the more intense the first stimulus is, the stronger the next stimulus

Virtual Seeing, Hearing, and Tasting by Aiming Ultrasound at the Brain

The film series *The Matrix* showed some of the characters hooked up to a huge computer that was able to influence their vision, hearing, tasting, and other senses, but only in their imagination. While these "sensory experiences"—sounds, smells, tastes, and moving images—were fictitious in the movie, the entertainment giant Sony has taken out patents to create the actual technique. The project's goal is to use ultrasound to stimulate the brain to create virtual sensory experiences. The idea has long been a tool of science fiction writers, but how could the technology be used in real life?

There are several ways, according to Sony, a pioneer in the field of electronic entertainment with products including the Walkman and PlayStation. First, a film or videogame could be enhanced with a "personal sensory environment," taking entertainment to another level by letting participants believe they are really taking part in the situation—seeing, hearing, and smelling what was going on.

In the field of health, such sensory technology might well enable deaf and blind people to hear and see. In law enforcement, this technology could replace the rather unreliable lie detector by using "thermal facial imaging," which shows the flow of blood changing in the blood vessels when someone is not telling the truth. For example, bright circles show up around a person's eyes when faced with a question that he or she feels must be answered with a lie.

While these real-life applications remain in the future, Sony has integrated aspects of the concept into a retail store plan designed to give customers an interactive and entertaining shopping experience. At its flagship Sony Store in Century City, California, it created an immersive and stimulating sensory experience through a flexible digital signage system encompassing 50 separate zones within the store. Within each zone, the content on display can be unique to that zone and the products being merchandised, but all the signage is also time-synchronized so that every 12 minutes, a single "Sony Experience" message fills the entire store. What's more, sales associates can use a special mobile phone app to override the automated system, allowing them to customize the display content of a zone to their current customer's interests. When the customized display kicks in, the in-store audio broadcast is also adapted with corresponding messages, providing customers with a totally harmonized audio and visual experience.

Sources: "To Tell the Truth," *Trends Magazine Online*, August 22, 2005; and "Sony Flagship Integrates Digital Signage for Stimulating Consumer Sensory Experience," *Digital Signage Connection*, March 21, 2012, http://www.digitalsignageconnection.com/sony-flagship-integrates-digital-signage-stimulating-consumer-sensory-experience-806.

must be in order for people to see it as different.[8] For fashion marketers, Weber's Law has applications in design, color, pricing, and other areas. This season's fashion looks must stand out from last season's, or they will not excite fashion editors, professional buyers, and, eventually, customers. This season's color palette must appear different from last season's so that customers will be enticed to want the latest looks. In the area of price, Weber's Law is most important. Near the end of the summer, a set of wicker garden furniture marked down from $600 to $589 will hardly warrant a customer's glance, but a reduction to $449 could well attract interested buyers. In other words, there must be a lot more than a j.n.d. for Weber's Law to have an effect.

SUBLIMINAL PERCEPTION

An area exists below the absolute threshold where we perceive but are not capable of overtly recognizing stimuli. Suppose you were exposed to a fashion commercial on YouTube that flashed the words "plaids are in" at a speed you could not consciously see. The purpose of this message, repeated several times, would be to encourage viewers to buy plaid garments and home furnishings. The perception of stimuli by our senses below the level of conscious awareness (absolute threshold) is known as **subliminal perception.** The word "subliminal" comes from "limen," which is another term for "threshold." Subliminal perception was once a hotly debated topic. In 1957, a market researcher named James Vicary conducted an experiment at a movie theater in Fort Lee, New Jersey. He had the words "Drink Coca-Cola" and "Eat Popcorn" flashed subliminally on the movie screen (3/1,000 of a second, once every

5 seconds), and snack bar sales soared during the next several weeks. When the experiment couldn't be replicated with similar results and subsequent tests failed, interest waned in the use of subliminal advertising for marketing purposes. Nevertheless, many people see messages embedded in films, commercials, and print ads. The federal government believes that while subliminal advertising is an attempt to manipulate consumers and therefore is against public well-being, without proof that it actually works, legislation seems unnecessary.[9] Next, we will investigate how we continue to perceive and process stimuli.

How We Pay Attention

Just because we are exposed to a variety of sights, sounds, and smells doesn't mean we really notice all of them. Only when we apply our minds to a stimulus does it have our attention. **Attention,** then, is focusing our thoughts on a certain stimulus. Children and pets have a way of grabbing our attention (as you can tell from the soulful stare of the puppy in Figure 3.3).

Or, returning to Alyssa, she is thumbing through the latest issue of *Real Simple,* idly turning the pages until she sees a new home-decorating idea. The room design is the focus of her attention. Marketers work to accomplish this very goal: getting our attention is the first step in convincing us to buy. Notice one characteristic of attention, however: It does not last. Soon Alyssa turns the pages in search of even more appealing décor. Nor does the magazine have her full attention; she is listening to her iPod as she flips the pages.

FIGURE 3.3 The winsome look of a pet draws attention to an ad.

How do we choose which stimuli will merit our full attention? That depends on the kind of stimulus, what experience has told us to expect, and our current needs and desires. Let's first consider the stimulus itself, and then look at our personal characteristics.

STIMULUS CHARACTERISTICS

Certainly the type of item we focus attention on is essential and highly individual. An ad for a fishing rod may appeal to your grandfather, whereas an ad for a leather jacket is what really grabs your attention. Several factors are involved here; two of them are size and contrast. Large billboards along the highway draw our attention to nearby stores or restaurants, while small, exclusive jewelry store display windows might show a single diamond ring or clip. Using color is another way to draw attention. Consider the red star of Macy's, Nordstrom's silver packaging, Bloomingdale's little, medium, and large brown bags, or Nike's white "swoosh" on a red cap. The position of an ad in a magazine, or the placement of a logo on a package or product (such as the apple on an iPad), is also designed to attract attention.

PERSONAL CHARACTERISTICS

Since we cannot possibly process all of the stimuli we encounter, we pay attention to stimuli that touch on our needs and wants and (we hope) will meet our expectations. We practice **selective perception:** We choose to pay attention to the stimuli that connect to our needs. (To relate stimulus characteristics and personal characteristics, see Table 3.1.) When Alyssa wants to add a new skirt to her wardrobe, she skims the fashion magazines, surfs the Internet, and checks relevant mobile apps before searching through the skirt racks in several stores. She looks just at those skirts that interest her and disregards the rest. In reality, because we can deal with only a limited number of stimuli, we screen out others; we are practicing selective exposure and selective attention as well as selective perception. But we make

TABLE 3.1 Chart of Stimulus and Personal Characteristics

Stimulus Characteristics	Personal Characteristics
Type of item Size and contrast Color Position, placement	What we expect What we select to perceive What we select to reject

sure to be continually on the lookout over time for the things we need. For example, when Alyssa is at the beauty salon, she notices that a friend is wearing a skirt similar to the one she wants and learns that it is from a Boden catalog.

How We Process

How do we as consumers decide what to buy? Our first step is to organize the stimuli we have perceived into some meaningful form. The process of organization is explained by **gestalt psychology,** meaning that people reach a conclusion after seeing a total picture. The German word "Gestalt" means "pattern" or "configuration." Gestalt psychology is sometimes compared to a lightbulb turning on. Maybe you've seen a comic strip where the main character "gets the point," and to illustrate that, there is a lightbulb glowing over his or her head. That's the gestalt or "aha!" experience.[10] (Note the image in Figure 3.4.)

Three elements of perceptual organization are similarity, figure-and-ground, and closure. *Similarity* tells us that we like to group together similar ideas and objects. When we encounter a brand name such as Swatch, Honda, or JCPenney, we conjure up certain product likenesses. Retailers also use the concept of similarity to group similar merchandise so that customers can see related items together. Think, for example, of the display windows of Williams-Sonoma where you could see a group of red, yellow, or green kitchen appliances such as mixers, bread makers, waffle irons, and bowls displayed with coordinated print kitchen aprons and dish towels.

Another organizing concept, *figure-and-ground,* tells us that we organize stimuli so that part of the stimulus (the *figure*) is more prominent than the rest (the *ground*). Marketers use this principle in planning advertisements and merchandise displays so that the

FIGURE 3.4 The "aha" of the gestalt experience.

main objects, perhaps garments or jewelry, are distinct from the background. Interior designers place a solid-red sofa on a black-and-white floor so that the sofa stands out as the focal point. You can see one example of figure-and-ground in Figure 3.5.

Humans have a need for a complete picture. When what we see is incomplete, we tend to see it as complete anyway; this is known as the closure principle. A while ago, the Kellogg Company ran a billboard for its cereals, substituting a pair of bananas for the two letters "l" in the company name, and viewers automatically used closure to make the name complete. Marketers use the closure principle in ads to gain attention and to urge us to perceive and remember their messages. Interior designers group a collection of pictures on a living room wall, sometimes using the closure principle to create a complete look. As consumers, we develop an organized set of beliefs about a topic or product that is known as a *schema*. A client develops a schema when she or he learns that the grouping of pictures adds to the total effect of the interior.

How We Learn

When we're thinking about buying something new, we often want to find out as much as we can about that particular product or service. Alyssa noticed that customers frequently read the labels on the apparel and home furnishings in the store where she works. They were learning about fabric content and care. **Learning** is a process that changes behavior through experience. For example, two customers looking at a summer shorts outfit wanted to be certain of 100 percent cotton fabrication because only natural fibers would suit them.

People learn in several ways. Two major learning theories are behavioral learning and cognitive learning (Figure 3.6). Behavioral learning occurs when we respond to certain stimuli. Cognitive learning is a problem-solving process.

BEHAVIORAL LEARNING

The **behavioral learning** concept theorizes that learning takes place after exposure to external stimuli; two major types of behavioral learning are *classical conditioning* and *instrumental conditioning*. If you wonder sometimes why you see or hear advertising messages over and over again, behavioral learning theory could possibly be an element of that particular ad campaign. Classical conditioning and instrumental conditioning are both based on training that elicits a response to a stimulus. **Classical conditioning** pairs an artificial stimulus with

FIGURE 3.5 Here the handbag attracts attention because it stands out clearly from the background.

```
                    ┌─────────────────┐
                    │    Learning     │
                    │    Theories     │
                    └─────────────────┘
                      ↙             ↘
          ┌─────────────────┐   ┌─────────────────┐
          │   Behavioral    │   │   Cognitive     │
          │    Learning     │   │    Learning     │
          └─────────────────┘   └─────────────────┘
             ↙           ↘
    ┌─────────────────┐ ┌─────────────────┐
    │   Classical     │ │  Instrumental   │
    │  Conditioning   │ │  Conditioning   │
    └─────────────────┘ └─────────────────┘
```

FIGURE 3.6 Learning theories.

a natural one and eventually gains a response from the artificial stimulus alone. This theory was developed in Russia when physiologist Ivan Pavlov experimented with the way dogs anticipate food. Pavlov fed the dogs while ringing a bell. The dogs salivated naturally when given the food, but after much repetition, they began salivating when they just heard the bell. This is an example of a conditioned response.[11] The repeated experiment is the basis for the reason we may sometimes see the same furniture store commercial several times during a TV show, or notice the same ad in four different fashion magazines—or why a brand like Coach uses its signature "C" throughout its products' design. (See Figure 3.7.) This idea of conditioned response could be the reason why the private label on a regional drugstore's brand of shampoo almost mirrors that of the best-selling national brand and why so many food products in addition to soup bear the family brand name of Campbell's.

FIGURE 3.7 Repeating some identification of the manufacturer in a product's design or an appealing ad helps consumers identify the brand.

How Marketers Use the Learning Process in Selling Homes

With many affluent people owning not one but two or more homes and demanding custom touches such as professionally designed adjacent golf courses designed by pros, home builders are eager to see that the decision-making process is as appealing and convenient as possible. In addition, manufacturers of brand-name products such as General Electric, Kohler, and even John Deere are seeking out new markets by creating partnerships with home developers and making their goods an integral part of new building projects.

When a prospective new home buyer can choose General Electric kitchen appliances, Kohler bathroom fixtures, Andersen windows, or a John Deere tractor-mower to mow the lawn, or can play golf on an Arnold Palmer course, these brand names are already stored in memory. Because they are familiar, they can reduce the home buyer's stress in decision making, at least for these products. And often there is a carryover: If the customer has faith in the appliance brand names, that goodwill can spread to the builder.

For the marketer, the learning process is effective when customers have stored the brand names and product characteristics and recall them positively.

Source: Sharon Stangeness, "House Only Part of the Package," *Chicago Tribune*, June 18, 2005, Sec. 2, pp. 1 and 8.

When we have choices and begin to prefer a choice that produces a "reward" over one accompanied by "punishment," we encounter learning through **instrumental conditioning.** Suppose Alyssa's class project is to create a plan for remodeling her bedroom. She knows she should complete her assignment in order to succeed and earn a good grade. But her friends invite her out to the movies. If she opts for the night out, her project will be slapdash, and her grade will reflect it; however, if she spends time on her assignment, chances are that she will present it well in class. As consumers, we learn to behave in ways that bring rewards—and avoid punishment.

American psychologist B. F. Skinner refined the theory of instrumental conditioning through his work with rats that were rewarded with food by pushing one lever as opposed to another. Classical conditioning and instrumental conditioning obviously differ; in instrumental conditioning, a choice exists and the experiment's subject has the power to choose. If the right choice is made, there is a reward. If the wrong choice is made, there is nothing—or worse, a negative stimulus such as a shock. The right choice with repeated rewards reinforces the behavior, whereas no reward or receiving actual punishment for a choice discourages a subject from continuing with that choice.[12] As consumers, we continue to buy the same brands of apparel or appliances when we are satisfied with them; conversely, we avoid those products that we find may shrink in the wash or break too easily. Marketers use advertising, coupons, and rebates as rewards to attract and maintain loyal customers. When these promotions are no longer rewarding, we sometimes discontinue purchasing a given product.

COGNITIVE LEARNING

While behavioral learning occurs in reaction to a stimulus, **cognitive learning** is a problem-solving process where, as consumers, we actively seek out information in order to make an informed decision. Cognitive problem solving can be active (as when Alyssa tries several new paint colors on her bedroom walls until she finds the one she likes best), or it can occur through observation (as when she looks through a home-decorating magazine and selects the most appropriate window treatments for her room).

When do we rely on behavioral learning and when on cognitive learning? As consumers, we tend to be influenced through behavioral stimuli (for example, repeated ads for a brand of cereal or toothpaste) when the products we are considering are not high-involvement; that is, they don't represent expressions of our individuality and don't take a lot of energy to purchase. These low-involvement products are often staples such as dairy products or health and beauty aids. But we use cognitive learning strategies when considering goods that represent our personalities (such as a new outfit), or when making a substantial purchase (for example,

a home or apartment, a new automobile, or a vacation destination). We are more highly involved with these purchases—not just because they may be costly but because they make up part of our persona. Notice the Toshiba tablet product information presented in Figure 3.8.

LET'S TALK

What examples can you think of where fashion advertisers appeal to consumer learning behavior? Which type(s) of behavior?

How We Remember

Obviously, we need to be able to call on what we have learned when we need it. The process of storing and retrieving knowledge is called **memory.** There are three types of memory, each with a different purpose: sensory memory, short-term memory, and long-term memory.[13]

OUR THREE MEMORIES

We receive sensory stimuli automatically in our *sensory memory,* which holds them briefly. When Alyssa sees a family who is about to enter the store where she works (a visual stimulus), this image goes into her sensory memory for a few seconds and then disappears—unless she consciously records it, as she would if recognizing neighbors, for example.

If we do consciously record a stimulus, it enters our *short-term memory,* which allows us to remember something for a limited time. Alyssa would remember the neighbors entering the store. If a

FIGURE 3.8 Information on new products and improved technology helps consumers reach meaningful buying decisions.

customer were purchasing some T-shirts, sweaters, and pants, Alyssa would remember these items as she rings up the sale, but chances are that at the end of the day she wouldn't be able to recall every item in each sales transaction. Short-term memory is where most mental processing takes place in order to retain what we want to store.

To hold on to information readily, we encode it; in this sense, **encoding** means the way we select visual images or words in short-term memory to stand for what we want to store in our long-term memory. Visual images are often easier for us to store, and marketers devise brand symbols and corporate logos that are easy to remember. Marketers create symbols, or icons, such as the Ralph Lauren polo player, the Westinghouse W with a crown, and the Ford galloping Mustang horse that help us easily put those brands in long-term memory should those products be of interest to us.

The purpose of **long-term memory** is to store information we want to keep for permanent use and recall at will, almost like a computer's hard drive. Sometimes long-term memory retains items for years—even decades. For example, you can probably recall the name of your first really close friend, even though you may not have seen that person for 15 years or more. Marketers hope that by giving us symbols that are easy to encode, we will store them in long-term memory and retrieve them when considering purchases. We may store these symbols into knowledge structures made up of nodes, information that is linked to similar data in a kind of web. Humans can amass large amounts of encoded information on a topic, a process known as **chunking.** One example of chunking is when we add on to what we already know about appropriate fabrics for interior design as opposed to those for wearing apparel.

Often, we are bombarded with more information than we can process or store, a condition called **information overload.** When we learn that certain models of cell phones not only send, receive, record messages, and have photo and e-mail capability, and still others print movie tickets, turn on lights, and open garage doors, we have too much information and run the risk of making a poor buying decision as a result. Chunking helps consumers who have researched a given product or idea store much more information about it than those who have not.

STORING AND RETRIEVING INFORMATION

People can store information by its sensory interpretation, such as the brilliant yellow of a dandelion; semantically by its meaning in language, such as "surfers have great bods"; or autobiographically, as memories of events as they occurred to us, such as our high school graduation. Our semantic memories are interconnected through networks, sets of ideas, and schema (a set of beliefs and associations that trigger each other).

The process we go through to use information stored in memory is called **retrieval.** The strength of the associations in the memory network has an influence on the effectiveness of retrieval. If a student has a firm belief that the designs of Karl Lagerfeld influence both apparel and theatrical costuming trends, that person will be able to recall evidence to support this view. The speed at which information can be retrieved from the memory network is known as **activation.** Through spreading activation—that is, the linking of our memory nodes—we can recall a product through its brand name, a particular ad we saw, or some of its characteristics. For example, if we hear a radio commercial for a favorite restaurant, activation lets us recall the restaurant's location, the type of food it serves, and how the hosts treated us. The prominence of a product message also helps us retrieve information about it. A striking ad in *Vogue* or *Architectural Digest* can cause us to remember other information about the work of the designer featured.

But we are not able to retrieve everything stored in memory. Perhaps we can't recall a friend's telephone number or the birthday of an uncle. If we haven't used the information for a while, it could just disappear. When we learn new information, it may replace the old, which is then lost. At times, we unintentionally forget. Research indicates that older people and children have more difficulty remembering than people who are between those age groups; older people perhaps because they have had many experiences to remember and youngsters because they have had relatively few to build on.

In the next chapter, we will explore the topic of motivation, a key factor in buying decisions.

behavior. Major learning theories include classical and behavioral conditioning and cognitive learning. Classical conditioning demonstrates that a new stimulus used repeatedly with an original stimulus eventually produces the same reaction alone. Behavioral conditioning offers a choice, with the correct response bringing a reward. Marketers employ incentives based on conditioning learning theories when they offer product samples, coupons, and discounts that encourage consumers to purchase their products. Cognitive learning views learning as a problem-solving process: People go through a series of steps to determine the correct course of action. As consumers, we tend to use cognitive learning when considering high-involvement products, those that are more costly and closely related to our personalities, such as a new vehicle or apartment.

When storing information for future use, we rely on memory. We have different forms of memory based on the length of storage time. Sensory memory stores perceived stimuli for a few seconds, short-term memory enables us to remember for a few minutes, and long-term memory for months or years. We encode information and store it, retrieving it through networks, finding most easily what is familiar and important to us.

Summary

We are connected to the world through our perceptions. The way we perceive is through our five senses: vision, hearing, smell, taste, and touch. We are constantly exposed to these sensations and are only able to register some of them, so we focus on the stimuli that gain our attention and then select what we want to use. Through the continuing process of learning, we are capable of changing

KEY TERMS

Absolute threshold

Activation

Attention

Behavioral learning

Chunking

Classical conditioning

Cognitive learning

Encoding

Exposure

Gestalt psychology

Hedonic consumption

Information overload

Instrumental conditioning

Just noticeable difference (j.n.d.)

Learning

Long-term memory

Memory

Perception

Retrieval

Selective perception

Subliminal perception

Weber's Law

QUESTIONS FOR REVIEW

1. Using examples from your experience in design or fashion, describe each of the five kinds of sensory stimuli humans perceive.

2. Explain the importance of the concepts of absolute threshold, just noticeable difference, and Weber's Law both to consumers and to marketers.

3. As consumers, when do we tend to learn through classical or instrumental conditioning techniques and when through cognitive learning methods?

4. Identify the three levels of memory humans possess, and state which of these we use in recalling the brand names and characteristics of products we are considering purchasing. How do marketers hope to make this recall easier?

5. Why are perception, learning, and memory important to us both as consumers and marketers?

ACTIVITIES

1. Select three magazine ads, each of which appeals to a different sense. Identify which sense each ad appeals to and state what makes it appealing. Then explain how each ad attracts attention.

2. Visit the websites of two retailers, one with brick-and-mortar stores (such as www. Nordstrom.com) and one that is strictly point-and-click (such as www.Amazon.com). Describe the visual appeal of each site, indicating how each one promotes that retailer's image.

3. In small teams, visit a large supermarket to identify how customers use various learning theories. Look for examples of consumer behavior representing classical conditioning, instrumental conditioning, cognitive learning, and observational learning. Report your findings to the class.

4. Think of a brand of jeans or laptop computer that is marketed to your age group. Create a list of that product's characteristics that distinguish it from the competition. Select the features that would most appeal to your target market, and create the copy for a print ad or television commercial that would be based on cognitive learning theory. Share your results with the class.

5. Working in teams, recall as many product slogans and jingles as you can. Then create your own slogan or jingle. Ask other members of the class if they can remember the brand names that match your slogans. Recite your own slogan first, then the others. After classmates have identified the products on your list, ask them for the first slogan you gave them. Then ask them to determine whether these slogans are stored in sensory, short-term, or long-term memory.

MINI-PROJECT

As a group, develop the interior design for one room of a home. Create a household of three people and a clothing outfit for each. Explain how each group member (classmate) used perception and learning to select apparel for the residents and how together the group members applied cognitive learning theory in creating the design and selecting the furniture for the interior of the house. Present your project to the class.

REFERENCES

1. Elaine Stone, *The Dynamics of Fashion* (New York: Fairchild Publications, Inc., 2004), p. 315.
2. www.colorbox.com.
3. Color Association of the United States website, www.colorassociation.com.
4. Michael Gross, *Genuine Authentic: The Real Life of Ralph Lauren* (New York: HarperCollins, 2003), p. 98.
5. Natalie Angier, Basics, "The Nose, An Emotional Time Machine," *New York Times,* August 5, 2008, pp. D1 and D4.
6. Ken Druse, "She Smells Me Not," *New York Times,* June 9, 2005, Sec. D.
7. Stuart Elliott, "Advertising," *New York Times,* April 4, 2005, Sec. C.
8. *Encyclopedia Britannica,* "Weber's Law" entry, www.britannica.com/eb/article-9076393 /Webers-law#39123.hook; Lewis O. Harvey, Jr., *Psychology of Perception,* Psychology 4165- 100 (Fall 2004), http://psych.colorado .edu/~lharvey/P4165/P4165_2004_Fall/2004 _Fall_pdf/P4165_Lab1.pdf.
9. 39 Federal Register 3714, January 29, 1974. See also http://tribes.tribe.net/e388baea-51eb- 417f-9390-06fe37f92e41/thread/99d62700- d8c2-4905-b7dd-9426066cc759; http://www .psych.wright.edu/gordon/psy110/Psy110 Mod11a-outline.pdf.
10. Answers.com, "Gestalt psychology" entry, www .answers.com/topic/gestalt-psychology.
11. Ivan Pavlov biography, www.ivanpavlov.com.
12. B. F. Skinner biography, www.bfskinner.org /bio.asp.
13. April Holliday, "How Does Human Memory Work?," *USA Today,* March 12, 2007.

CHAPTER 4

Motivation and the Fashion Consumer

WHAT DO I NEED TO KNOW ABOUT MOTIVATION AND THE FASHION CONSUMER?

✔ What motivation actually means and how it affects human behavior

✔ The difference between needs and wants, and how marketers formulate strategies using their understanding of each concept

✔ How purchase decisions are influenced by rationally and emotionally driven behavior that's largely unconscious

✔ Why using emotion, conflict, and other stimuli can motivate consumers and even create demand

f you are among the growing number of consumers who are concerned about the environment and using eco-friendly products as a result, you probably look for clothing made with natural fibers, grown without the use of pesticides or man-made ingredients of any kind.

Other people may prefer the look and feel of real leather. Today, a variety of leather looks are achieved by applying various techniques, oils, and chemicals to the animal skins. From patent, metallic, and distressed to perforated, sueded, and pearlized finishes, leather clothing, accessories, and furniture are very popular.

Perhaps you have heard about the benefits of "functional foods," noninvasive, edible products that contain substances said to make users healthier

Shoppers as Modern Hunter-Gatherers

When American consumers enter a retail venue, it's almost as if some natural instinct kicks in and they have no choice but to hunt for deals and gather new purchases. But that's okay: Being hunter-gatherers is in our DNA, right?

Well, maybe not quite in our DNA . . . after all, a century or so ago, we weren't like that. But somewhere between then and now, America shifted from being a country that *creates* things to one that *consumes* things—and one that tends to spend money instead of saving money. It wasn't an overnight change, but a gradual change that sneaked up on us, making it less startling until you look back to where we used to be. It's enough to make wise old Benjamin Franklin roll over in his grave, since his saying, "Rather go to Bed Supperless than rise in Debt," seems to have been supplanted by such materialistic mottos as "Born to shop" and "I shop, therefore I am."

Helping the transition along were numerous changes and innovations that one could say "democratized" consumption. Sewing machines and off-the-rack clothes meant you didn't have to be wealthy to dress well. Department stores presented all kinds of goods that anyone could buy (or aspire to buy) at pre-established prices. Packaging became more than just a method of storage but an attractive wrapping meant to entice you to buy. And among the most dramatic changes: credit cards and installment plans, which let consumers have something before they can actually pay for it—in turn inspiring the new category of impulse purchases.

These innovations did not appear only in our country; but somehow our reaction to them was different from consumers elsewhere. As historian Daniel Boorstin wrote, by the late 20th century, Europeans still "went to market to buy what they wanted, while Americans went increasingly to see what they wanted."

So what's actually going on here? Believe it or not, scientists in the field of neuroeconomics—the study of how people spend money and manage risk—have discovered that when people come across unexpected rewards, they experience a rise in their levels of dopamine, a brain chemical associated with feelings of happiness and pleasure. So when you stumble upon a designer purse with a drastically reduced price tag at Nordstrom Rack or a rare Beatles vinyl album on eBay, your sense of delight is *really real*.

"Dopamine is one of the systems we use to learn how good or bad something is," says Paul Glimcher, a professor of neural science and psychology at New York University. "Shopping is

(continued)

fundamentally the same kind of foraging animals do every day. You move through a complex environment trying to find good stuff."

So the next time you're at the mall, think of it as a lab and yourself as a scientist, studying the research "subjects." Notice how when people walk into a store they tend to pause, looking around to see what's new and exciting. And watch as they discover that unexpected treasure and their face lights up with pleasure. Then ask yourself, is their smile because they got the last pair of boots in their size ... or is it just dopamine? Either way, it's a great feeling.

Source: Libby Copeland, "If Not Sublime, Then Silly: Holiday Shoppers Are the Hunter-Gatherers of the American Economy," *Washington Post*, December 19, 2005.

and more beautiful. For example, cold-water fish, such as salmon and sardines, are recommended for their omega-3 fatty acids, which promote healthy heart function and improve brain development, while the anthocyanin in fresh berries that gives them color offers numerous health promoting rewards. A friend of yours is thinking of going to an ashram where she'll be meditating each morning at 5:30 a.m. and eating two vegetarian meals a day, but you want to try a diet of functional foods that contain antioxidants, probiotics, or microalgae before committing to a trip to India where devotional chanting will be the only music you hear.

If you're about to purchase an engagement ring, you might be considering a diamond. Although diamonds are usually white, they also come in other colors. Premium colors, which are rare, and often more expensive, include canary yellow, pink, and blue, but shades such as champagne, cognac, and black might be less expensive. For some consumers, owning a diamond in an unusual color is an exciting prospect.

With so many choices, how do people decide what they really want? Why does one person choose bran flakes, another one oatmeal, and yet another scrambled eggs? What is at the core of each buying decision we make? How can marketers determine what customers want and present it to them in ways that please them?

These are the kinds of questions to which all marketers seek answers, and once they answer these questions, they should be able to predict *what* consumers are likely to want, and to understand *why* they want it. Are people interested in buying just to experience the act of consumption and ownership, because they consciously need something, or because of unrecognized, unconscious desires?

We need to understand human motivation in order to better explore what it is that creates in us the desire to buy in the first place. Is it a feeling that overwhelms people and can't be ignored? It might seem that way sometimes, and if that *is* what it is, where do these feelings come from?

Understanding Human Behavior

In order to successfully interpret consumer research data, we need to have some basic knowledge about the fundamentals of **psychology,** the study of individual behavior, and **sociology,** the study of group behavior. Once we agree that human behavior can be understood and that we can access and interpret these dynamics using the appropriate methods, we begin to recognize that there are certain patterns in consumer buying behavior, and these patterns can be influenced by applying relevant marketing strategies. In other words, marketers are able to create motives or **motivate** customers—they can impel, incite, or move a person into action, and, in this case, the action is buying. Both "motive" and "motivate" come from the Latin word "motivus," which means "to move or be caused to move." Thus, **motivation** is the result of forces acting either on or within a person to initiate or activate certain behavior. These forces can be physiological (for example, hunger activates the desire for food), psychological (for example, sadness evokes tears), or environmental (for example, storms move people to seek shelter). And the behavior that marketers want to activate or initiate is the purchase of a particular product.

How Motivation Works

Let's take a look at the following example to better understand motivation. Larry walks into a store that's well known for its state-of-the-art exercise equipment. What has brought him here? He could have been driven by several reasons. He wants to improve his stamina. He wants to increase his muscle mass. He's dieting and wants to tone as he loses weight. He let his health club membership lapse and has decided to work out at home. The store is currently offering some great discounts. His buddies mentioned that he looks like he's getting a little soft. Any or all of these reasons might serve as the motivating force behind his desire to purchase fitness equipment, and they all have one thing in common: They are causing Larry to experience some discomfort. That discomfort is referred to as a **stimulus,** an energizing force that causes a state of tension or arousal. (See Chapter 3 for a discussion of *stimulus characteristics*.) This tension has created in Larry a **need,** an internal state of discomfort that calls for a solution. Larry is trying to find a solution that will alleviate this feeling and provide some relief; he's trying to satisfy this need so that he can experience pleasure instead. By focusing on a **goal,** a particular outcome or end (which in this case is getting in shape), Larry is attempting to get rid of his discomfort. He hopes this will be achieved by the purchase of fitness equipment, resulting in **need satisfaction,** the experiencing of pleasure.

NEEDS VERSUS WANTS

"Listen, pal," his brother says when Larry tells him the plan, "you don't need to spend money on fancy equipment. Just do some running, and I'll lend you my weights. Then you can train without all that stuff around. It takes up a lot of room, and your apartment isn't that big." His brother is offering some good advice, but Larry is intent. He *wants* the equipment; he believes it will enable him to reach his goal more quickly. Both needs and wants are strong motivators, and both feelings emerge as the result of certain stimuli. But there is a difference between the two.

Studies have suggested that needs come from **instinct,** innate drives that we are born with, which are largely physiological, while **wants** are not necessities; although they can enhance the quality of our lives, they are not required for survival and, therefore, not driven by instinct, but rather by **desire,** a yearning or longing for something. Hence, what people *want* is largely the result of psychological and social forces in our environment.

Why can't consumers just explain to marketers why they buy what they buy and what the reasons are behind their purchases? The problem is that most people don't know what their motives are, and if they did, they probably wouldn't want anyone else to know. Motives can be **conscious,** in which case the individual is aware of what she wants and why, or **unconscious,** largely unknown to the individual because these motives are either repressed, dormant, or unrecognized.[1] To be sure, motives aren't always pretty (think of anger, fear, jealousy); that's why people often keep them secret—even from themselves.

NEED THEORIES

It's for these reasons that marketers turn to psychologists like Abraham Maslow, who, in 1943, was one of the first to formulate a practical theory about human needs (Figure 4.1). Many well-respected scientists, including David McClelland and Henry A. Murray, have developed other theories, some based on as few as three essential human needs (power, affiliation, and achievement are the basic needs identified by McClelland), and others that number more than 20 (see Table 4.1), but Maslow's theory has been used most frequently as the basis for understanding much of the modern consumer's behavior.

In Figure 4.1, you can see that humans' **basic** or **primary needs** are few: food, clothing, shelter,

FIGURE 4.1 Maslow's hierarchy of needs.

TABLE 4.1 Murray's Psychogenic Needs

Need	Definition
Abasement	To surrender and submit to others, accept blame and punishment. To enjoy pain and misfortune.
Achievement	To accomplish difficult tasks, overcoming obstacles and becoming expert.
Affiliation	To be close and loyal to another person, pleasing them and winning their friendship and attention.
Aggression	To forcefully overcome an opponent, controlling, taking revenge, or punishing them.
Autonomy	To break free from constraints, resisting coercion and dominating authority. To be irresponsible and independent.
Counteraction	To make up for failure by trying again, seeking pridefully to overcome obstacles.
Defendance	To defend oneself against attack or blame, hiding any failure of the self.
Deference	To admire a superior person, praising them and yielding to them and following their rules.
Dominance	To control one's environment, controlling other people through command or subtle persuasion.
Exhibition	To impress others through one's actions and words, even if these are shocking.
Harm avoidance	To escape or avoid pain, injury, and death.
Inavoidance	To avoid being humiliated or embarrassed.
Nurturance	To help the helpless, feeding them and keeping them from danger.
Order	To make things clean, neat, and tidy.
Play	To have fun, laugh, and relax, enjoying oneself.
Rejection	To separate oneself from a negatively viewed object or person, excluding or abandoning it.
Sentience	To seek out and enjoy sensual experiences.
Sex	To form a relationship that leads to sexual intercourse.
Succourance	To have one's needs satisfied by someone or something. Includes being loved, nursed, helped, forgiven, and consoled.
Understanding	To be curious, ask questions, and find answers.

Source: Adapted from http://changingminds.org/explanations/needs/murrays_needs.htm.

sleep, and so forth. Once these physiological needs are met, other needs can be addressed, such as the need to feel safe and secure, the need to feel connected to and valued by others, the need for praise and appreciation, and so on. Maslow has put these needs in a hierarchy, demonstrating that people put their efforts toward fulfilling their primary or "low" needs (also referred to as *biogenic* needs) before they attempt to fulfill "high" needs (also referred to as *psychogenic* needs). His theory contends that humans can't sufficiently progress, or even live normal lives, if basic physiological needs aren't met first. Only then can people attend to the other needs on his hierarchy, **acquired** or **secondary needs,** which are learned in accordance with the values of the specific culture a person is raised in. For example, people in the United States have developed acquired needs for money, education, freedom—things without which most Americans believe they could not survive. Could they?

LET'S TALK

Read Table 4.1, adapted from Explorations in Personality (1938) by Henry A. Murray. Which of these needs are primary and which are secondary? Are there any needs on Murray's list that can't be satisfied by the purchase of a product or service?

Motivation Is Complex

Motives can be driven by both **internal/nonsocial factors** and **external/social factors.** A couple may purchase a house because they really love it, the result of *internal* motivation (which comes from within), or because living on that particular street will afford them the status they desire, a result of *external* motivation (which derives from desires that are independent of the actual behavior).

We can also be motivated by either **positive** or **negative motivation.** A 19-year-old who's worked in the stock room of a department store since high school may decide she wants more out of life, so she joins the army in order to travel and get a free college education (*positive*). But another employee of the same age, who's worked in the shipping department since she quit school at 16, feels that she'll never make enough money to move out of her parents' place, so she joins the army, figuring that at least she'll have somewhere to go and will no longer have to worry about where she'll be living (*negative*).

Additionally, people are often motivated by the need to experience both **stability** and **variety,** or constancy and changeability. For example, we don't want to paint the bedroom a new color every single day (we need *stability*), nor do we want to repaint it the same color when we're ready for something different (we need *variety*).

To complicate matters, people are frequently motivated by multiple desires that are experienced simultaneously and thus create **conflict.** A conflict occurs when we view the outcome of our behavior as potentially positive and potentially negative. That is, we may want to both do something and not do it at the same time; or we find we must choose between two desirable outcomes; or we might even discover that we must choose between two undesirable outcomes. Essentially, there are three common types of motivational conflicts: **approach–avoidance,** **approach–approach,** and **avoidance–avoidance:**

Approach–avoidance. A simultaneous desire to engage in a certain behavior *and* to avoid it.

Approach–approach. A choice must be made between two desirable options.

Avoidance–avoidance. A choice must be made between two undesirable options.

In the first instance, *approach–avoidance,* a man may find himself experiencing a strong desire to buy an extravagant engagement ring for his fiancée (consistent with the needs for affection and prestige). However, he may also feel that if he purchases that ring, he'll be putting himself in debt, and he knows that that's no way to begin a marriage (inconsistent with the need for security).

In the second type of conflict, *approach–approach,* a newly graduated art student has just been given a generous check by her grandparents and is deciding how to spend the money. Should she purchase a painting she really likes by a famous artist whom all her friends will recognize and admire (consistent with the needs for recognition and self-esteem)? Or should she enroll in a six-month educational program that will allow her to study art abroad (consistent with the needs for enrichment and self-fulfillment)?

The third kind, *avoidance–avoidance,* is experienced by a single mom on a limited income who doesn't want to buy an expensive outfit for her class reunion, especially if she feels she won't wear it again (inconsistent with the need for financial security). But she certainly doesn't want to look frumpy or out-of-touch in front of her successful former classmates (inconsistent with needs for acceptance and recognition).

MARKETERS USE CONFLICT TO MOTIVATE CONSUMERS

By understanding the nature of conflict, marketing experts can create appealing ways to assist customers in the decision-making process, by either helping them resolve their conflicts or by tapping into those conflicts in ways that will encourage them to purchase. For example, marketers working in the professional selling field have developed programs that ease the minds of customers who may be conflicted about the amount of money they can comfortably spend, by allowing them to spread payments over extended periods. Or, if a customer has enough money for the required down payment but needs time to raise the rest, sellers offer plans that let buyers delay paying their balances for as much as a year, thus resolving any conflict that might stand in the way of completing the sale.

Marketers who specialize in product development also seek to create alternatives for customers who might be experiencing conflict. Many people are conflicted about buying fur because they've read or heard that extensive or unnecessary cruelty toward animals might be used in the process of creating fur garments and accessories. Thus, fake fur was developed, allowing those who want the warmth and look of fur to buy and wear those products without worrying about animal endangerment.

Marketers in the advertising field often make use of their knowledge regarding conflict when devising ad campaigns. A customer might be conflicted by the desire to look tan and the fact that sunbathing is unhealthy. An attractive ad for a product that promises that a person can actually look sun kissed while enjoying substantial protection from harmful rays will provide that customer with a resolution (Figure 4.2).

RATIONAL VERSUS EMOTIONAL MOTIVES

Consider what happened when Veronica had an argument with her significant other. She was feeling extremely sad and very lonely, so when her friend called and invited her to go shopping, she said yes, rather than sit home by herself. Soon after arriving at the mall, she found herself trying on a great-looking coat. Veronica knew she didn't *need* it—she'd bought one the previous month, in fact, which she really liked and had barely worn. But she *wanted* the coat she was trying on, even though she couldn't come up with a single logical reason to buy it—it was quite expensive, and it even resembled the new one at home in her closet! But she bought it anyway, and for an hour or two she felt a certain amount of satisfaction and excitement. However, later that evening, she began to question her purchase.

FIGURE 4.2 This advertisement for suntan lotion attempts to resolve the consumer's conflict: tanning to look healthy but not wanting to risk skin damage from the sun's harmful rays.

LET'S TALK

What might have motivated Veronica's impulsive purchase? Why did she feel such a strong desire to buy?

Early in this chapter, *motivation* was defined as the result of forces acting either *on* or *within* a person to initiate or activate certain behavior. Remember also that these forces can come from physical, psychological, or environmental stimuli. Thus, if Veronica had realized that she *actually* needed a coat to keep warm, she most likely would have followed

the **consumer decision-making process,** the steps buyers take when deciding whether or not to make purchases:

- Need recognition
- Information search
- Evaluation of alternatives
- Purchase
- Post-purchase evaluation

Veronica would have been acting on the basis of **rational needs** if her purchasing decision had been the result of a process using reasoning and logic—she *needed* protection from the cold, so actual physical and environmental realities motivated her to buy a coat. But sometimes we act because of certain **emotional needs;** these can inspire buying decisions that are made in a nonrational manner, without the benefit of an information search, a comparison of alternatives, and so on. In Veronica's case, the real motive of her coat purchase was a desire to ease the distress and unhappiness caused by a recent breakup and, therefore, she was acting based on emotional motivations.

When this happens, a person's post-purchase evaluation could include **post-purchase dissonance** (also known as "cognitive dissonance") or "buyer's remorse," which is when doubt about making a purchase decision follows the actual purchase and creates tension, or a state of dissonance. This can occur for any number of reasons. (In this particular case, doubt was brought on by allowing emotions to overrule rationality.)

So, although it might seem that consumer choices are quite random, each decision has some meaning behind it, even if the choice doesn't always appear to be rational. Purchasing decisions are motivated by any number of factors, including emotions, social situations, goals, and values. Obviously, all purchases resulting from motives that are emotional in origin do not necessarily end in dissatisfaction; in fact, many times the customer's decision leaves him or her feeling quite satisfied.

MARKETERS USE EMOTION TO MOTIVATE CONSUMERS

Using their understanding of basic psychology, marketers are able to motivate consumers by devising creative strategies that evoke emotional responses. We've all experienced various forms of emotional motivation, some as a result of our own envy, love, sorrow, fear, surprise, and so on, and some as a result of having our emotions stirred by marketers.

When presented with merchandising methods that evoke feelings of nostalgia, such as a display that resembles a flea market, a window that incorporates antique toys, or a sound system that plays "golden oldies" while customers shop, those who value the "good ol' days" are being motivated to purchase because of the positive emotions they are experiencing. This technique is particularly effective in encouraging the purchase of **unsought goods,** products or services that consumers do not actually seek or plan to buy, such as items that are purchased impulsively, without advance need recognition. The term *unsought goods* also pertains to things we don't want to buy until we absolutely have to, like cemetery plots or alarm systems.

Advertisers frequently use emotion to stimulate buying behavior. Think about the ads you see on a daily basis; many employ emotional appeals purposely designed to trigger positive emotional responses. Puppies, babies, beautiful scenery, grandparents playing with grandchildren, surprise visits from family members—the objective is that these kinds of images will become associated with the products that marketers are trying to sell. Marketers use beauty, humor, sex, camaraderie, and so on to encourage customers to buy, since chief among the benefits we seek from our purchases is simply to feel good. But they can also try to evoke negative emotions and then imply that their products will eliminate our bad feelings.

Similarly, unpleasant images can be just as effective. A car skidding in a storm or a burglar breaking into a home—these images can arouse fear, an

How Emotions Influence What We Buy

Studies have shown that the emotions felt by consumers when evaluating products are the primary determinants of what they ultimately buy. Huh? A lipstick evokes emotion? A running shoe conjures up feelings? Perhaps not the kind of emotion that brings tears to the eyes, but certainly, whether we recognize them or not, brands have personalities that are communicated through visual imagery, like packaging and advertising, and through the specific words used to describe the brand. Once a product "speaks" to a buyer, she or he is much more likely to buy it.

Marketers know that emotions drive sales; otherwise they wouldn't work so hard to position products in ways that evoke emotional responses that connect with customers. In a recent article, psychologist Peter Noble points out that when people are confronted with decisions of any kind, emotions from previous, related experiences attach themselves to whatever a buyer might be considering; that is, our decision making tends to result from an accumulation of views and feelings that we've developed over time. Hence, something about that lipstick or that running shoe induces us to feel a certain way toward a product, which will result in either the purchase or rejection of that item.

Psychological hocus-pocus? Well, consider this: Says Noble, "Emotions are the primary reason why consumers prefer brand name products. After all, many of the products we buy are available as generic and store brands with the same ingredients and at cheaper prices. Why do we decide to pay more for brand name products?"

Why indeed?

So back to our lipstick and running shoe. It's certainly true that we could find almost identical items, which cost less and perform the same way, but instead we choose to go with the item that "talks" to us, perhaps by stirring up a memory or bolstering our self-concepts.

Hence, what we buy is seldom a result of purely rational decision making; rather, it's how we *feel* about what we see, touch, smell, etc. that determines what we buy.

Source: Peter Noel Murray, Ph.D., "How Emotions Influence What We Buy," *Psychology Today,* Inside the Consumer Mind blog, February 26, 2013, http://www.psychologytoday.com/blog/inside-the-consumer-mind/201302/how-emotions-influence-what-we-buy.

emotion that can be powerful in motivating customers to purchase, for example, a new set of tires or a home security system.

The Power of Motivation

The science of evaluating and influencing consumer behavior is foremost in determining which marketing efforts will be used and when. Marketers spend a great deal of time and money discovering what compels consumers to make purchases.[2] There are two principal ways to evaluate the motivation behind consumer purchases: direction and intensity. **Direction** refers to what the customer wants from a product in terms of facts, features, or benefits. For example, if a customer is selecting a watch, she may like the fact that one watch is less expensive than another, but what she really wants is a timepiece that will last and keep accurate time, and she'll probably pay more if she thinks the more expensive brand will do those things more effectively. Marketers need to understand the principal motivation that leads to the purchase of each type of product in order to accurately target potential customers.

The other way to evaluate consumer behavior, **intensity,** refers to whether a customer's interest in a product is compelling enough that she will actually make the purchase. In other words, how badly does the customer want the particular item? Good marketing can create that kind of intensity. Positioning a particular handbag as not only chic but also as a special limited edition signed by the designer might create a sense of urgency that motivates the customer to buy that purse, and do so quickly.

Thus, understanding consumer motivation is the best way to increase buyer **incentive** (a reason to buy)—that is, to move the consumer from an actual state to a desired state. Most importantly, the customer's attention must somehow be focused on the specific goods the marketer wants to sell—and not on anyone else's products, and the drive has to be powerful enough for the customer to be willing to pay the price in terms of time, effort, and money to obtain the goods.[3]

MOTIVATION AND THE DESIRE TO ACQUIRE

"People like having stuff, and stuff is good for people," says Thomas O'Guinn, a professor of advertising at the University of Illinois and author of textbooks on marketing and consumption. "One thing modernity brought with it was all kinds of identities, the ability for [you] to choose who you want to be, how you want to decorate yourself, what kind of lifestyle you want. And what you consume cannot be separated from that."[4]

Marketers have had to adjust their strategies to accommodate ever-changing shopping habits. They also know that today's shoppers aren't as predictable as they once were. Perhaps that's why every day seems to bring something new to the marketplace, another enticement, a different method for arousing the desire to consume. One example of this is a retailing concept that's become popular recently: the temporary, or pop-up, store, designed to open and close within a short time (Figure 4.3).

Another example is the use of *experiential* marketing. *Experiential retailers* want to make their stores into destinations for customers, using the idea of retailing as theater. Imitation of Christ, the offbeat clothing line, frequently combined pop-up

FIGURE 4.3 A temporary JCPenney shop in New York's Times Square motivated shoppers by creating a destination that was there for a limited time and offered special merchandise, making it uniquely experiential.

and theatrics, opening a moveable store encased in a Plexiglas box that appeared in a different place in New York City every day for a week. The store had only a single item on sale each day, making it even more desirable and exclusive, and would close as soon as the product had sold out.[5] American Girl is another destination retail site, where parents and kids can spend the day at the store participating in a variety of activities designed to encourage customers to buy. Build-A-Bear Workshop, IKEA, and Apple all attempt to stimulate sales by creating experiences that engage consumers.

High-fashion designers are also offering new ways to attract consumers with lots of money to spend who may not only value the actual item they are purchasing but the customized encounters that go with them. (See Case in Point 4.1.) Other ways to motivate buying behavior include offering personalized products and customized goods. Timberland's Build Your Own Boot Program lets consumers choose the colors and monograms they want, while Fossil encourages consumers to design their own watches. A fragrance can now be created just for one person; jeans can also be customized to specifications. (See Chapter 2 for additional information about customization.) These are all ways to promote customer engagement.

Marketers can also connect with customers through convenience, an important issue for many

Selling a Luxury Experience

Anyone who follows fashion knows that the grand opening of an international luxury brand store can resemble the red carpet hoopla at the Academy Awards, with an invitation-only crowd of A-list celebrities, fashion VIPs, and top media. But today, even luxury brands, whose customers' spending tends to be relatively recession-proof, have to find creative ways to keep consumers buying—which is why Valentino, the Italian designer renowned for dresses and handbags that retail for thousands of dollars, decided to alter the strategy for the opening of its newest boutique in New York. For the gala affair, the company invited some of its non-celebrity customers to rub shoulders with the stars in attendance. But not for free. Those "regular" customers had to pay for the privilege, and did so happily.

What Valentino execs, along with other luxury fashion retailers, had learned is that customers want more than just sumptuous shoes or jaw-dropping jewelry. So these companies are now offering *experiences* along with their products, in the belief that customers will feel even more loyalty to the brand when they have attended one of its glitzy events or chatted with the designer face to face. "Everything has become more experiential," said Dante D'Angelo, brand and consumer development director at Valentino. "It's a new way of providing exclusivity, making customers feel important, unique."

The experiences these luxury companies are extending to customers vary. Some are giving consumers access to new products before their official launch, often at a limited number of stores for a strictly limited time. Lanvin, for example, invited its best customers to visit its Mount Street store in London by a certain date in order to purchase one of only a handful of black python handbags being sold for $4,000. Gucci has enticed its biggest customers with invitations to fashion shows, equestrian events, even tickets to the Cannes Film Festival—as well as offering key customers tours of its workshop in Florence, Italy, even if those customers don't happen to be major celebrities.

What all this makes clear is that affluent consumers, whose closets and drawers are already overflowing with opulent apparel and accessories, are looking for a way to treat themselves to something special that goes beyond simply acquiring more things. "In an era of over-consumption, people are realizing that there is more than just buying products," says Boston Consulting Group's Jean-Marc Bellaiche. "Buying experiences provides more pleasure and satisfaction."

Source: Andrew Roberts, "Building Luxury Brand Loyalty via Exclusive Experiences," *BusinessWeek,* January 31, 2013, http://www.businessweek.com/articles/2013-01-31/building-luxury-brand-loyalty-via-exclusive-experiences#r=lif-s.

of today's time-starved shoppers. Technology can play a key role in this regard. Some consumers are particularly interested in goods that can be easily purchased, such as through a mobile app. In Japan, for example, young women buy everything from subway passes to mascara with a swipe of their cell phones.[6] In the United States, texting has become one of the most effective ways for retailers to reach teens (see Case in Point 4.2).

MARKETERS CREATE CONSUMER NEEDS AND STIMULATE DEMAND

Studying the origins of motivation has enabled marketers to actually invent "needs" that people didn't know they had until marketers pointed them out. A recent TV commercial addressed the problem of "body soil," the invisible residue supposedly left in clothes after they've been washed, which can presumably irritate the skin, damage fabric, and so on. The solution? A specific bleaching product that claims to eliminate this problem. In this case, marketers actually *created a need;* people concerned with getting clothes as clean as possible were motivated to purchase by savvy marketers who aroused in them a need they hadn't previously recognized.

Some observers would say this is a good example of how marketers create or stimulate **demand,** the level of desire among consumers for a particular product and the price that people are willing to pay to obtain it. It is the job of marketers to create an atmosphere around a product or service that encourages consumers to take notice, experience a need/want, and ultimately purchase. However, some people question the ethics of creating artificial demand or **false need,** the desire for something to which we attribute more value than it is actually worth. In *An Essay on Liberation,* Herbert Marcuse argues that a capitalist system gives people what it wants them to want, and that it generates needs supportive of mass consumption rather than stimulating creative human development. Modern capitalist economies, he feels, are based upon a degree of production that can only be maintained through conspicuous consumption and a terrific degree of waste. These economies must therefore train their citizens to "need" the things the system produces, whether they're good for us or not. For example, adolescents often regard drinking alcohol as a cool thing to do, a sign of maturity, rather than a behavior that could lead to addiction, illness, and even death. However, the images they see in liquor ads are of glamorous models, often with glamorous friends in glamorous settings, and they seek to emulate that behavior. Because teenagers see only the positive side of drinking, they overestimate the true worth of liquor and often use a sizable portion of their allowance (and even phony identification) to buy it.[7]

Other researchers believe that U.S. consumers make purchases largely as a result of surplus—a condition in which a society has more than enough of everything; yet, we are programmed for deficit—the feeling that we never have enough. Using this premise, modern marketers may use several "little lies" to get us to keep buying, such as, *"Everyone has one of these . . . except you!* Yes, we spent $30 million on national advertising to reach the last holdout—you!" and, *"New and improved is better than old and reliable! Yes, it's better to buy a shiny new power screwdriver with enhanced accessories (that will eventually*

Charlotte Russe Finds Texts "Gr8" Way to Reach Teens

Ask any parent what's the best way to reach a teenage child who's out and about, and the answer will almost certainly be: texting. And it's not only teens, but twenty-somethings and even older consumers who are sending and responding to text messages with far greater frequency and speed than other types of communication, including phone calls and e-mails.

So it shouldn't be at all surprising that when Charlotte Russe wanted to invite customers to a special "Happy Hour" sale—a late-afternoon event at which customers could buy a pair of sunglasses for $1 when they spent $30 on other goods—the trendy retailer knew just how to go about it. It sent a text message that read: "Forward 2 ur girls!"

Charlotte Russe is hardly alone in using texts to communicate with its customers. Other youth-oriented fashion brands like Claire's Boutique and Vans are also finding that marketing messages sent via text to customers in their teens and twenties generate a higher and a much quicker response than do e-mails. What's more, some are adding pictures and videos to their texts to better grab the attention of their youthful target customers. One Charlotte Russe text, for example, incorporated a video of a handsome young man smiling romantically and saying, "I'll give you the moon . . . and a $5 shopping pass. Anything to win your heart."

Customers responded by sharing the video so widely the company grew its database by a full third in just one weekend!

There are a few drawbacks for marketers using text messages, however. For one thing, because texting is regulated by telecom companies, marketers can only send texts to consumers who have requested them, or "opted in." In addition, unlike lists of e-mail addresses, lists of mobile phone numbers cannot legally be sold, so marketers have to rely even more on consumers wanting to share their contact number. To encourage opting in, at the top of Charlotte Russe's Web page is the tempting offer: "BFF us and get 10 percent off," with a spot for consumers to enter their cell phone number or e-mail address. The retailer also has in-store signs encouraging shoppers to text its "short code," or text address (which spells out "style") as another way to opt in. To reach a more diverse customer base, Charlotte Russe has also begun texting in Spanish.

The effort is worthwhile, since research has shown that people are five times more likely to open a text than an e-mail—and response rates are swift: Consumers generally respond to texts within one to three minutes. As a result, retailers and brands often make their offers very timely and with strict expirations. One recent text Charlotte Russe "Happy Hour" alert, for instance,

(continued)

proclaimed, "All corsets $15! Yes, please!" to accompany a coupon deal that was available for just three hours that very afternoon.

The sense of immediacy and urgency works. Just ask Dahvi Cohen, a 13-year-old from Irvine, California, who was shopping at a local mall when she saw a store sign offering anyone who texted the retailer a 15 percent discount on jewelry. "I used the coupon that day," she says.

Source: Christina Binkley, "Teen Stores Try Texts as Gr8 Nu Way to Reach Out," *Wall Street Journal,* August 21, 2012, http://online.wsj.com /article/SB10000872396390444405804577561093050635960.html.

have to be replaced), rather than keeping that plain, old-fashioned one that, even after decades of use, your children will probably inherit from you!"[8]

LET'S TALK

Consider the two concepts of stimulating demand and creating false needs. Are they the same thing? In your opinion, is it acceptable for marketers to use these techniques to encourage customer purchases?

Motivation and Design

Many of the purchases we make are of designed goods or design-related products, and these serve several purposes in our lives. First, researchers have determined that humans seek to eliminate boredom; thus, we are motivated to own fashionable clothing and accessories, visit the newest clubs, attend museum and art exhibitions, see the latest movies, vacation at beautiful resorts, update our kitchens, obtain the latest technological innovations—all of which are not only symbols of newness but also the aesthetically pleasing results of good design; they invite us to experience them for personal stimulation, self-expression, and differentiation.[9]

Furthermore, the adoption of designed objects may satisfy the human need for social identity and increase feelings of personal security. Possessing or experiencing them also enables us to feel up-to-date, current, modern, and therefore better able to adjust to social change and better prepared to face the future.[10]

Humans are highly motivated to learn and possess. Designed goods—our homes, clothing, gardens, vehicles, art objects—become symbols, codes, ways to express ourselves nonverbally and elicit positive responses from people whose impressions we value, especially ourselves.

Although it is very important for consumer behaviorists to understand the principles of motivation, that knowledge generates additional questions whose answers could have deeper implications. For

Are You Defined by What You Do, or by What You Own?

While there are some people who live to shop and never seem to think they have enough "stuff," many others have long harbored the idea that experiences, such as trips abroad, ziplining, or dinners with friends, make us happier than buying and owning things, such as clothes, cars, and jewelry. Now, psychological research has shown that to indeed be the case—and one study in particular finds that the value of experiences over possessions goes even further than previously thought.

To find out *why* experiences are more important than possessions, researchers Travis J. Carter and Thomas Gilovich launched a study to test their theory that people use experiences more than they use possessions to define their sense of self. Their findings, reported in "I Am What I Do, Not What I Have: The Differential Centrality of Experiential and Material Purchases to the Self," proved their theory to be true. For example, when people in the study related their "life stories," they talked more about the experiences they had had than about their possessions. And when they did talk about things they'd bought or owned, they were more likely to view a purchase as a representation of who they were if they discussed it relative to their *experience* with the possession, as opposed to simply describing the item's physical attributes.

In addition, participants in the study believed that they would gain more understanding about who another person really is by knowing what experiences that person had had, not just what things he or she had bought. The researchers concluded that because people treasure the memory of interesting or significant experiences, they find those experiences more satisfying than mere possessions.

Thinking about these research results, there is a clear takeaway for anyone marketing fashion or other products: The emphasis should be on the experiences consumers can have with a product, rather than simply what it looks or feels like, or what it will be like to own it.

Source: Susan Weinschenk, "Experiences vs. Possessions: You Are What You've Done, Not What You Own," *The Brain Lady Blog*, February 28, 2012, http://www.blog.theteamw.com/2012/02/28/experiences-vs-possessions-youve-done-not-own-2/.

example, are we to believe that we as consumers are like pawns in a chess game, to be moved around—manipulated—by clever marketers? Or are we thinking beings with specific individual needs that we seek to satisfy by determining which purchases best suit our particular situations and personalities?

In order to be effective, marketers also need to understand the complexities of motivation. Through ongoing data collection concerning human needs and wants, researchers can convey important, relevant information to marketers, resulting in greater satisfaction for the purchasers of designed goods.

But motivation isn't the only determinant of buying behavior; marketers also must examine how attitudes and values influence customer decision making. In the next chapter we'll explore the formation and adoption of these two elements, and the important role they play in motivating the purchase of designed goods.

Summary

What is it that creates within us the desire to consume? By studying the basic principles of psychology and sociology, consumer behaviorists have discovered that motivation plays a major role in the buying process. Using techniques that stimulate primary and secondary human needs, which must be met in order to eliminate discomfort, marketers seek to direct customers to their products and ultimately activate buying behavior.

Needs, driven by instinct, and wants, driven by desire, are complex and are often unknown to consumers themselves. For example, one person may buy things simply to satisfy his own needs, while another feels the need to impress his friends. Or, a person may only purchase goods he feels are absolutely necessary, while another may spend freely on luxury items. Sometimes buyers experience conflict when making purchases, like the woman who wonders if she should buy the lined boots that will keep her feet warm and dry when it gets cold and snowy, or the high-heeled leather boots that are incredibly sexy. Purchasing the lined boots would be the result of rational decision making, while buying the other pair might be driven by emotion or her needs for recognition and differentiation.

By understanding need and motivation, marketers can create demand for products in more efficient and effective ways, even presenting solutions to problems that consumers might not have previously recognized.

People both need and want new products that satisfy a multitude of diverse desires, and the more the appeal addresses our motives, the more likely we are to buy.

KEY TERMS

Approach–avoidance

Approach–approach

Avoidance–avoidance

Conflict

Conscious motives

Consumer decision-making process

Demand

Desire

Direction

Emotional needs

External/social factors

False needs

Goal

Incentive

Instinct

Intensity

Internal /nonsocial factors

Motivate

Motivation

Need

Need satisfaction

Negative motivation

Positive motivation

Post-purchase dissonance

Primary (basic) needs

Psychology

Rational needs

Secondary (acquired) needs

Sociology

Stability

Stimulus

Unconscious motives

Unsought goods

Variety

Wants

QUESTIONS FOR REVIEW

1. Why is it important to understand the difference between needs and wants with regard to activating customer motivation? Should primary and secondary needs be equally considered when determining the most effective type of stimuli?

2. Some observers of our culture say that a marketer's job, at least in part, is to create false needs. Explain the concept of false needs and how it might motivate consumers to purchase things they don't really need.

3. Explain the difference between making a purchase decision based on rational needs versus based on emotional needs, and identify which leads more often to post-purchase dissonance, or buyer's remorse. Did you ever experience buyer's remorse? Can you remember what your motivations were when making that purchase? What did you do to change your dissonant state?

4. Why is it important to determine the direction and intensity of a customer's motivation to purchase? How can marketers create intensity, thereby increasing the likelihood that the customer will buy now (or perhaps postpone his purchase of a different product)?

5. Using your own experience, describe a buying situation in which you had to resolve some sort of motivational conflict.

6. Have you ever purchased something as a result of external motivation, rather than internal? Explain the situation and describe what motivated you.

ACTIVITIES

1. Using either books or the Internet, find three theories on human needs that are not discussed in this chapter. Take notes on your findings and share them with the class.

2. Choose three advertisements that appeal to customers via different stimuli. Using the terms and concepts from this chapter, write a description of the specific stimulus used in each ad.

3. *Materialism* can be defined as the degree to which one values material possessions. By creating demand for fashions and other designed goods that are merely decorative, explain how marketers are or are not helping to create a materialistic society.

4. Select a designed product and devise a marketing strategy created to address each of the three types of motivational conflict. Discuss how each method would alleviate your customer's conflict and motivate purchase.

MINI-PROJECTS

1. Visit a supermarket with two other classmates and shop separately for cereal, soup, and soda. Then meet to discuss the individual motivation behind your purchases. Why did each of you select the particular type of item (root beer, diet cola, ginger ale, etc.), and why did you each choose particular brands? Relate your findings to the class in a 5- to 7-minute presentation.

2. You have $1,500 to spend on a vacation. Choose three places you'd like to visit that are within your means, and rank them in order of desirable location, activities available, and so on. Identify your top choice, and explain your motivation for selecting that particular place to the class in a 4- to 6-minute presentation.

REFERENCES

1. Nessim Hanna and Richard Wozniak, *Consumer Behavior: An Applied Approach* (Upper Saddle River, NJ: Prentice Hall, 2001), p. 214.

2. "Consumer Behavior," Reference for Business Web site, www.referenceforbusiness.com/management/Comp-De/Consumer-Behavior.html.

3. Ibid.

4. Jennifer Steinhauer, "When the Joneses Wear Jeans," *New York Times,* May 25, 2005.

5. "Imitation of Christ," *Final Year* (blog), August 13, 2010, http://level6fashionstudies.blogspot.com/2010/08/imitation-of-christ.html.

6. Kate Betts, "Editor's Note," *TIME.* Style & Design issue. (Spring 2006).

7. Robert Woods, "A Critical Evaluation of Herbert Marcuse's *Essay on Liberation,*" http://prizedwriting.ucdavis.edu/past/1989-1990/woods.html

8. P. Lutus, "Consumer Angst," www.arachnoid.com/lutusp/consumerangst.html, Copyright © 2007.

9. George B. Sproles and Leslie D. Burns, *Changing Appearances: Understanding Dress in Contemporary Society* (New York: Fairchild Publications, 1994), pp. 181–182.

10. Ibid., pp. 191–192.

ADDITIONAL RESOURCES

American Marketing Association. "Dictionary." https://www.ama.org/resources/Pages/Dictionary.aspx.

Changing Minds Web site. "Murray Needs" entry. http://changingminds.org/explanations/needs/murrays_needs.html.

Encyclopedia Britannica. "Motivation" entry. www.britannica.com/eb/article-9108744.

Huitt, W. "Maslow's Hierarchy of Needs." *Educational Psychology Interactive.* Valdosta, GA: Valdosta State University, 2007. http://www.edpsycinteractive.org/topics/conation/maslow.html

Katz, Roy. "Identifying Customer Wants." *Inside Self-Storage,* October 1, 2002. www.insideselfstorage.com/articles/2a1results.html.

Maslow, Abraham H. *Motivation and Personality.* 2nd ed. New York: Harper & Row, 1970.

Perner, Lars. www.consumerpsychologist.com# Motivation.

Schiffman, Leon G., and Leslie L. Kanuk. *Consumer Behavior.* 7th ed. Upper Saddle River, NJ: Prentice Hall, 2000.

Shepherd, Nia E. "A Fragrance for You, and Only You." *TIME*, Style & Design issue, Spring 2006.

Solomon, Michael R. *Consumer Behavior: Buying, Having and Being.* 6th ed. New York: Prentice Hall, 2003.

Toyama, Michiko. "Boutique in Hand." *TIME*, Style & Design issue, Spring 2006.

Attitude and the Fashion Consumer

WHAT DO I NEED TO KNOW ABOUT ATTITUDE AND THE FASHION CONSUMER?

✔ The meaning of attitude and its three elements

✔ The hierarchy of effects and how marketers appeal to each of its levels

✔ Four factors that influence attitude formation and how each operates

✔ Two theories of the effect of attitudes on buying behavior

✔ Two methods marketers use to change fashion consumers' attitudes

or decades, American families shopped loyally at JCPenney stores across the country. In addition to a selection of well-known national brand merchandise, consumers sought out the casual denim styles of Penney's own private brand, Arizona Blue, and the smart career wear of the retailer's St. John's Bay and Worthington brands, all current looks at reasonable prices. Famous for providing fashionable yet moderately priced ready-to-wear and home goods, the company maintained a solid base of loyal patrons—so much so that a few years ago, chief executive Myron "Mike" Ullman felt it would be safe for him to retire after more than a decade at the company's helm.

Penney's board of directors, although sorry to see Ullman go, believed they had found a promising replacement. After all, their candidate had been responsible for opening Apple's first retail stores in that company's golden era. He had done an outstanding job, focusing on modern store exteriors, sleek interior design, artful product arrangements, and a knowledgeable sales force. The stores drew in customers from the first day. In addition, the candidate, Ron Johnson, had previous merchandising experience with Target before joining Apple. Just the man to spark up JCPenney, thought the board.

Johnson, in fact, did more than "spark up" the venerable chain. He set out to develop a whole new image, based on what he had learned at Apple. His decisions arose from previous experience and were based on intuition. Typically, retailers who want to learn their customers' preferences rely on information gathered from research such as customer focus groups. Johnson recalled what his boss Steve Jobs had told him: People don't know what they want until they see it. Then Johnson went to work fast. Where Penney customers had been used to discount coupons and frequent sales, he set up an everyday low price policy. Customers suddenly felt deprived of bargains. To give the stores a new look, he began to establish vendors' stores-within-stores, each carrying well-known brand names; at the same time, he deemphasized Penney's own private labels. He initiated contemporary looks in apparel, fashion-forward and more narrowly cut, and he designed a new store label featuring only the three initials JCP.

Customers became confused when they couldn't find their favorite brands and the clothes they tried on didn't fit. They balked at losing coupons and sale days. Their attitude toward the company changed significantly over the eighteen months Ron Johnson was CEO. Sales plummeted and so did the stock price of JCPenney. The board, seeing its mistake, let Johnson go and called back Mike Ullman. He began to undo some of his predecessor's changes: bringing back coupons and sale days; beefing up orders to traditional private label suppliers; having vendors cut goods more generously for older customers; and slowing down store-within-a-store projects. Most important, Penney communicated directly to consumers (including via Twitter and Facebook), letting them know the company was listening to them and wanted their advice. Sales figures in the seasons ahead will tell whether or not Penney customers fully regain their more positive attitudes toward the retailer. But early responses indicated that customers were slowly returning, pleased to have coupons and sale days again, and relieved that clothing sizes fit.[1]

What Is "Attitude"?

Over the years, JCPenney customers had built a positive attitude toward the company, but with the arrival of new merchandising and pricing policies, that attitude clearly changed. But what does the term "attitude" really mean? An **attitude** is our settled opinion—either positive or negative—about people, places, ideas, or objects. By "settled opinion," we mean that attitudes are formed after some thought, they are learned, and they occur within given circumstances. For example, Penney's customers had learned over time that the retailer's merchandise fit their needs and the frequent coupons and sales motivated them to shop, giving them a positive attitude about the store. When the assortment changed drastically and there were no longer the same sales events to draw them in, their attitudes about shopping there became negative.

Notice that we hold attitudes about people, ourselves included; objects, such as products, brands, manufacturers, places, and retailers, as we've just described; and ideas, such as those we see in print advertisements or on TV and the Internet. For example, in thumbing through a magazine, we may see ads about new digital cameras, certain kinds of tanning lotions, the latest foreign car, an exotic vacation spot, and our favorite discount store, all within a few pages, and as we look, we may form attitudes. In consumer research, those things that we form attitudes about are called **attitude objects.** For many customers, Penney's St. John's Bay and Worthington clothing are attitude objects they seek out when shopping.

LET'S TALK

What is your attitude toward a well-known fashion attitude object such as a pair of shoes by Jimmy Choo or the latest iPad?

Although we tend to maintain the same opinions over time, attitudes may change, and marketers continually strive to bring about attitude change, encouraging us to favor their offerings over others. For example, Target has carved out a niche in discount retailing by emphasizing its fashion connections and crafting agreements with designers such as Phillip Lim, Missoni, and Philippe Starck to create stylish goods at budget prices. Many consumers recognize and support this effort.[2]

What Goes into Our Attitudes?

Three elements contribute to the way we create attitudes: (1) *cognitive*—what we perceive and believe about an object, as Penney's customers traditionally believed the company coupons and private labels represented better values; (2) *affective*—how we feel about it, our positive or negative emotions, as

customers became upset when Penney eliminated coupons; and (3) *behavioral*—what we do about it, as many customers no longer shopped the store until they perceived changes, with the reappearance of coupons and better-fitting clothing. (See Figure 5.1, The Elements of Attitude.)

But we do not develop attitudes in a vacuum. Our emotions play a part. If we are happy, sad, angry, or distressed, our attitude tends not only to reflect our feelings but also how we think and act. Attitudes are also affected by other influences such as our individual personalities, past experiences, family and friends, media, and marketing efforts.

THE COGNITIVE ELEMENT

The **cognitive element** of our attitudes—that is, what we know—comes from what we have seen, read, or experienced concerning an attitude object; it forms the basis of our beliefs about that object. A fashion student learning about the features of

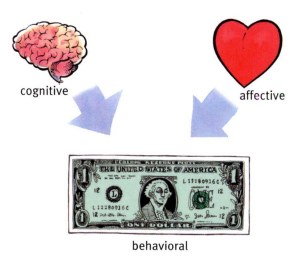

FIGURE 5.1 The ABC's of attitude: affective, behavioral, and cognitive elements are the primary influencers of attitude.

Spandex in apparel fabrics, for instance, believes that garments with some stretch in them look neater and more fashionable than those made solely of traditional fabrics.

Marketers appeal to our cognitive element by providing information about the product they are offering. For example, advertisements for wireless headsets fully describe the many features of Bluetooth technology, such as its clear sound, unobtrusiveness, and hands-free ease of use, all of which appeal to our cognitive, or reasoning, capabilities.[3] In learning, when reaching a complex or expensive (high-involvement) purchasing decision, such as deciding on our career education or a place to live,

we use problem-solving skills that rely heavily on our cognitive attitudes.[4]

Marketers appeal to our cognitive abilities by using credible sources, from a reputable home appliance manufacturer providing information about new product features to an appeal to use energy efficiently, as shown in Figure 5.2.[5]

THE AFFECTIVE ELEMENT

Remember seeing a fashion item on a website—a pair of shoes, jacket, or complete outfit—that was so appealing it just blew you away? That's an example of your attitude's affective element at work. The **affective element** of attitude is made up of our emotions toward an attitude object. Even those who don't care much about fashion may experience a thrill of excitement when they see the glamorous eveningwear of designers such as Vera Wang or Badgley Mischka. Countless movie fans crowd into the theater to see the latest film of Scarlett Johansson, Ben Affleck, or Jennifer Lawrence because they "just love" these performers and admire their work. Marketers appeal to the affective element by touching our emotions. For example, an interior designer tells a client how a certain demi-lune table enhances an entryway. Appealing subjects, such as photogenic models and celebrities, children and pets, and persuasive messages using humor or sex, reach out emotionally to a variety of consumers (Figure 5.3). Also, advertisers may also use emotional appeals to our affective side to counteract the fact that we might not be paying much attention to the purchase we're making, as when we buy staple goods like laundry soap or pet biscuits.[6]

Of course, how we feel internally when we encounter an affective appeal is also a contributing

FIGURE 5.2 Significant information about a product's benefits can appeal to the cognitive element of attitude.

factor. For example, if we are happy when browsing a retailer's website, we could have a positive reaction to an emotional appeal for an item, pull out our credit or debit card, and order it right then and there. But if we felt sad or distressed, our reaction could be negative to the very same image or message, and the persuasive effort would escape us.

There are also times when we may select a product off the shelf almost automatically, with a minimum of thought or effort. Knowing that, some advertisers try to make an impression through repetition, using basic methods such as behavioral learning techniques (described in Chapter 3). This is the reason that duplicate advertisements for certain cosmetics appear in four fashion magazines during the same month, why television ads for a particular store are sprinkled throughout a series of programs, or why the same product ad pops up in the sidebar of multiple websites you visit.

THE BEHAVIORAL ELEMENT

The third part of attitude, the **behavioral element,** is how we intend to act toward the attitude object. We can act negatively (for example, avoiding a certain fast-food drive-in because a friend became ill there), or we can do nothing. Or, many times we act positively and buy a particular product because all three attitude elements point in this direction. Thus, our intentions to act positively become our decision to buy. Marketers, of course, aim their efforts at dispensing information and techniques of persuasion toward this goal by making it as easy as possible to purchase goods and services. Advertisements appealing to our cognitive and affective elements, multichannel marketing (that is, selling

FIGURE 5.3 Emotional messages, such as those featuring celebrities or pets, can stimulate desire for a product.

through stores, catalogs, and/or websites), personable and knowledgeable salespeople, and pleasant shopping environments along with accessible credit all contribute to the behavior that both customers and marketers desire. Influencing consumer behavior is a major goal for many organizations, including both profit-making companies like Target and

FIGURE 5.4 By including a website, the advertiser encourages action after appealing to our emotions and thought processes.

nonprofits such as Americans for the Arts. (In Figure 5.4, notice how Clinique is seeking immediate response through persuasive techniques based on cognitive and emotional appeals.)

The Hierarchy of Effects

The term **hierarchy of effects** refers to the series of steps—beliefs, feelings, actions—that we go through in forming our attitudes. The order of these steps depends on how involved we are with the attitude object and is designated: (1) high-involvement

hierarchy, (2) low-involvement hierarchy, and (3) experiential hierarchy.

HIGH-INVOLVEMENT HIERARCHY

In the **high-involvement hierarchy,** customers use a problem-solving process to reach buying decisions about a product, usually when contemplating an important purchase, such as the latest portable electronic device. (Does this item have the major features you want? Will it fit safely and comfortably into a backpack? Is the price within your budget?) We actively study product features and benefits; and what we learn—our cognitions—become beliefs about a product. These beliefs then lead to our forming affective (positive or negative) feelings about the product. When, as consumers, we participate in the high-involvement hierarchy, we are serious about our planned purchase; we seek out information, evaluate the alternatives, and after a great deal of thought, decide. Marketers key into consumer problem-solving skills using advertising that is heavy on copy, containing complete explanations of product features and benefits, or communicating knowledge and values the consumer already understands. Figure 5.5 shows the similarities and differences among the three hierarchies of effect.

LOW-INVOLVEMENT HIERARCHY

With **low-involvement hierarchy** situations, the purchase is usually insignificant and we do not prefer one brand over another; here, we act before forming firm attitudes, and our attitudes emerge after we have used and evaluated a product. We may select a product out of habit or availability, such as paper

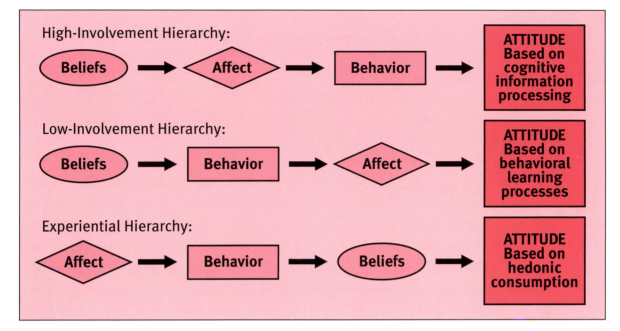

FIGURE 5.5 Three hierarchies of effects.

towels. We do not identify with those items, nor do we care much about them. Therefore, our selection of a certain brand is passive, based on existing beliefs and requiring minimum energy. Our positive or negative attitudes develop from our experience with the product after we purchase it. Here, while no single brand seems to be a favorite, emotional appeals in the form of television commercials, print and social media advertising, and particularly point-of-purchase materials influence our beliefs and, hence, our decisions to buy. For example, say that Kim is looking for a new shampoo. She glances at the department store brands but is not impressed. At the drug store, she notices a counter card and a display of a L'Oréal ultra-nourishing haircare system claiming it leaves each strand of hair soft and shimmering. Only after purchasing and using the product does she form positive or negative feelings about it.

EXPERIENTIAL HIERARCHY

Consumption for pleasure (hedonic consumption) is the basis of the **experiential hierarchy;** as consumers, we are interested in enjoying the product and its symbols and emotional meanings before learning about its features and benefits. Moreover, as opposed to the low-involvement hierarchy, we care about the product and may even identify with it. A young designer may be struck by the fine lines of an Armani suit and decide to save his earnings to purchase one. Upon wearing it, he grows to appreciate the quality of fabric, workmanship, and attention to detail that went into its creation. Before buying the suit, he had seen articles about Giorgio Armani and his apparel empire, and the Italian designer's signature look, which originally caught his attention. After buying and wearing his suit, he comes to know

Target Corporation: Influencing Consumer Attitude through Design

The main way that discount stores attract customers is through their low prices, right? Wrong. Or at least wrong in the case of Target, the second largest discount store in the United States, after Walmart. Instead of keying on the lowest prices to be found, Target's strategy is to position itself in consumers' minds as *the* place to find great design at reasonable cost. With its motto of "Expect More. Pay Less," Target's emphasis on great product design, in-trend fashion, and consumer convenience is meant to influence the way consumers feel, think, and act toward patronizing its stores.

In promoting design, Target frequently partners with well-known designers to offer exclusive merchandise through its stores, such as the home furnishings of Thomas O'Brien, known for his high-end store in New York and his luxury bedding line in Chicago stores. O'Brien's line for Target has included furniture, lamps, tableware, rugs, clocks, towels, and more—and his creations join an array of other designer products the store has featured in recent years, such as toasters and teapots by architect Michael Graves, household goods by Nate Berkus, Philippe Starck, and Todd Oldham, and the Simply Shabby Chic line by designer Rachel Ashwell. Other design collaborations that have contributed to Target's cachet in recent years include collections of home furnishings and sportswear by Isaac Mizrahi, clothing lines by Mossimo Giannulli, intimate apparel by Gilligan & O'Malley, plus the British cosmetics line Boots, among others.

Design permeates store operations, too. Large parking lots, clean and brightly lit interiors, and large shopping carts to wheel down wide aisles all add to the ambiance and ease of shopping. The average Target store offers over 70,000 items sourced from around the globe, and even more on its website, www.target.com. If a customer in the store cannot find an item, a call on a bright red telephone on a nearby fixture brings an employee prepared to answer shoppers' questions and find merchandise. At purchasing time, Target's own REDcard credit and debit cards plus store gift cards make buying easy—and as of early 2015, also more secure. Following a late 2013 security breach in which hackers stole credit data related to millions of Target customers, the retailer quickly took steps to minimize the damage, and fast-tracked a program to update to chip-enabled smart card technology in all its stores.

Target innovates in promoting its image. For example, during three sweltering days in New York one summer, Target sent out "Deliver the Shiver" trucks loaded with air-conditioning units; the air conditioners were sold in the neighborhoods and customers could wheel them home on Target carts. For a November

(continued)

sale, customers could arrange to have a wake-up call from Darth Vader or other celebrity voices. At Christmastime, a Target ship pulled alongside a New York dock for a while, enabling customers to shop on board. One summer, the advertising in an entire issue of the stylish *New Yorker* magazine was devoted to Target, featuring the signature red and white bulls-eye from the cover to the very last page, its message indicating that the retailer's merchandise appeals to a far wider spectrum of customers than just the budget-conscious. In its humanitarian efforts, the corporation donates a portion of store sales to local schools and works with a number of charitable organizations to promote social responsibility. These are some of the ways a discount store has been able to influence consumer attitudes by design.

Sources: "The Power of One: One Vision. One Brand," Target Corporation *Annual Report* 2004; Alex Kuczynski, "Consumer Philosophy by Tar-zhay," *New York Times*, Critical Shopper column, July 21, 2005, pp. E1 and E5; Eils Lotozo, "Target Rolls Out Thomas O'Brien Collection," *Chicago Tribune*, October 9, 2005, Sec. 15, p. 13; *New Yorker*, August 22, 2005; Target Corporation *Annual Report* 2006; 2013 Top 100 Retailers, *Stores*, July 2013.

for himself the elegant "hand" of Italian fabrics and recognizes the inspiration and sophisticated design elements inherent in the suit. Plus, he knows how very well dressed he feels wearing his Armani, and he believes that Armani apparel is in a class by itself. However, an emphasis on style and design does not occur just at the highest price level. For years, Target Corporation has highlighted design in its merchandising strategy, an appeal to the experiential hierarchy. (See Case in Point 5.1.)

While the experiential hierarchy may seem similar to the high-involvement hierarchy, there is a difference. Since the experiential hierarchy is based on consuming for pleasure, emotional appeals and symbols are prominent, whereas in the high-involvement hierarchy, specific product features and customer benefits predominate. Many marketers understand this difference when framing their messages to consumers. Automobile manufacturers that emphasize a vehicle's sporty look, lush leather interior, and high-end sound system are reaching out to the experiential hierarchy, while those that promote a car's fuel economy, low maintenance, and high safety ranking are appealing to the high-involvement hierarchy. Take a look at Figures 5.6 a, b, and c, and decide to which hierarchy level each ad appeals.

LET'S TALK

For each of the last three fashion purchases you made, which of the three elements of the hierarchy of attitude was the greatest influence? Explain.

VERSACE

FIGURE 5.6 Depending on a consumer's attitude level, advertisers use a variety of appeals; here, the reputations of the manufacturers appeal to the high- and low-involvement hierarchy knowledge and beliefs, while experiential levels are influenced by affective appeals.

How Do Attitudes Serve Us?

Attitudes help give us a sense of balance in life. Psychologist Daniel Katz developed a theory on the **functions of attitudes,** which tells us that attitudes serve us in the following four classifications:

- Utilitarian
- Value-expressive
- Ego-defensive
- Knowledge[7]

The *utilitarian function* of attitude helps us reach our goals by focusing on product benefits. For example, if we want to prevent slipping on winter ice, we will shop for boots with nonskid soles and avoid those with smooth leather soles. Marketers work to change our attitudes about utilitarian function by indicating the problem-solving capabilities of their products. In the case of the boots, for instance, L.L. Bean advertises its "chain grip rubber outsole."

In applying the *value-expressive function* of attitude, we are expressing our personality and self-image through the goods we buy. For instance, the saying "Dress for the job you want, not for the one you have" means that if you want a promotion, give the appearance that you already have it (that is, you are moving toward your ideal self-image). Marketers make great use of the value-expressive function of attitude by promising a more successful or happier life when you possess their products, whether paintings, cosmetics, or Zen meditation classes.

We also form attitudes to protect us from anxieties; this is the *ego-defensive function*. We are concerned about acceptance in business, so we pay attention to our grooming and use products that eliminate body odors. We know we should pay attention to our health; marketers promoting smoking-cessation methods are appealing to our ego-defensive functions by offering ways to combat the addiction.

Every day, we are inundated with more stimuli than we can ever absorb. The *knowledge function* of attitude helps us to order the information we encounter. Marketing information proclaiming new product features and new products themselves reaches us through all kinds of media, including billboards, magazines, the Internet, and television. An editorial feature in this month's *Vogue* shows the latest fashions from Milan and Paris, describing new fashion trends—information we store and use when considering our next apparel purchases. An ad in *Better Homes and Gardens* tells us about the features and advantages of indoor/outdoor carpeting for balconies and patios; if the information is relevant, we may store it for later use. Humans are naturally inquisitive and collect information on many topics.

Because we differ in our values—what is important to us—the way we use our attitude functions varies. Marketers are aware of these differences and reach out to us in a number of ways: through the utilitarian function of attitude, as when Colgate toothpaste promotes its cavity-fighting capabilities; or through the value-expressive function of attitude, making claims about Colgate's teeth-whitening capabilities. (See Figures 5.7 and 5.8.)

What Influences Our Attitude Formation?

Many influences contribute to how we form attitudes, including (1) our own personality, (2) the experience and information we encounter, (3) our family, and (4) our friends and peer groups.

A

B

FIGURE 5.7 (a) How does this ad appeal to the utilitarian function of attitude? (b) To which values does this NYDJ ad appeal?

PERSONALITY

Human **personality** consists of the individual psychological characteristics that routinely influence the way people react to their surroundings. Those characteristics that make us unique from other people, characteristics such as whether we are more extroverts or introverts, passive or active, leaders or followers, are part of our personality. (For additional information on personality, see Chapter 6.) For example, when considering adopting a new fashion look, someone who is more of a follower than a leader will wait until she sees others wearing that style before she will adopt it. Each person's own individual sets of characteristics influence the attitudes he or she forms, as well as that person's decisions and resulting behavior.

EXPERIENCE AND INFORMATION

Our personal experience with a product, plus what we have learned about it, influence the kinds of attitudes we form. For instance, if we have experienced success with a certain brand of suntan lotion, we do not hesitate to buy the same brand again. Or, we may have purchased a North Face jacket and found it sturdy, dependable, and fashionable enough over several years. Having formed a positive attitude about that brand, we look for the brand again when it's time to replace that jacket. Or, when deciding between purchasing a laptop computer and a tablet, after studying information about each model, we know we can make a buying decision that is most appropriate for us. To help us gain experience, we gather information. Often we don't even have to look for it, because the media bombard us

FIGURE 5.8 (a) In what ways does this L.E.I. jeans ad appeal to the ego-defensive function of attitude? (b) How does this Yaz ad target the knowledge function of attitude?

with marketing messages that may or may not be targeted to us and, if so, may or may not be useful, depending on our attitude and buying intentions.

Consumers develop attitudes not only toward products but also toward the advertisements for those products. For example, if we are interested in a new cell phone and see an ad for one, we might study the copy seriously to learn more about its capabilities and form beliefs (cognitions) about the product. Another time, an exciting TV commercial for a new film could send us straight to the theater. Both beliefs and affections defined through advertising can lead us to form positive attitudes toward the advertisement as well as the product.

FAMILY

Our families can play important roles in the formation of our attitudes, particularly when we are young because they are the dominant factor in our lives as children. Also, they influence us heavily during that time because we simply have not yet lived long enough to be exposed to other influences for a sustained period. Say, for example, the adults in a family believe that a certain brand of cereal like Special K is more nutritious than other brands. Their children would tend to feel the same way about that cereal, whether or not they enjoyed eating it. As we mature, we become more independent and develop

Sean John Changes Puff Daddy Attitude

Born in Harlem and growing up in nearby New Rochelle, New York, with next to nothing except a family fashion tradition and his own musical and entrepreneurial skills, by delivering newspapers at age 13, Sean John "Diddy" Combs was earning $300 a week. In college, he decided to pursue a music career, and the rap music he produced as Puff Daddy or P. Diddy became a hit among urban teens and hip hop fans. As a rapper he won multiple Grammy Awards, enabling him to begin his first business, Bad Boy World Entertainment.

Combs' love for apparel became evident when he began creating urban styles for teens including jailhouse stripes, low-crotch pants, and baggy logo-embossed T-shirts and hoodies, and founded his own apparel company, Sean John. Before long, however, realizing the baggy urban look had peaked, Combs set out to overhaul his fashion emphasis—and his customers' attitudes toward his brand. He shifted his focus to creating casual men's wear with an edgy yet mainstream look. In addition, he launched two signature men's fragrances and a women's fragrance through a partnership with Estée Lauder. And in 2010, he signed an agreement with Macy's to be the exclusive U.S. department store retailer for the Sean John men's sportswear collection.

Clearly, the total merchandise package creates an image distant from that of the urban rapper; and so far, Combs' offerings are right in tune with the changing attitudes of his customers: By 2013, Sean John accounted for more than $525 million in sales in the United States alone.

Sources: Seanjohn.com; Tracie Rozhon, "The Rap on Puffy's Empire," *New York Times*, July 24, 2005, Sec. 3, pp. 1 and 6.

our own attitudes that, in many instances, may be similar to those of our parents but in others may be quite different. Today, children tend to express their own attitudes at earlier ages than in the past. When it comes to choosing their own apparel or decorating their own rooms, many children are influencing their parents' buying decisions at a younger age. (For more information on the influence of family, see Chapter 7.)

FRIENDS AND PEERS

Friends and peers can also influence our attitude formation from childhood on. For example, teens hanging out together often have similar attitudes toward a number of things, including fashions in apparel, food, hobbies, and entertainment. Teens' influences on each other's buying behavior are heavy and contagious. In the world of work, other employees contribute to our forming attitudes toward the culture of the workplace, proper dress, and business etiquette. Acquaintances at college or clubs, as well as our very good friends, contribute to our attitude formation; a tennis partner may praise the performance of his new racquet; a good friend may suggest shopping at a certain website. This influence is even more pervasive thanks to the growth of social media and social networking. (The influence of friends and peers is discussed further in Chapter 8, and social media is explored in Chapter 11.)

Let's Talk

Consider a recent significant purchase made by your family—a car, home, or vacation. What roles did personality, experience and information, family members, and friends play in the purchasing decision?

How Do Marketers Use Attitudes?

Marketers study our attitudes in order to learn the effectiveness of their strategies and to plan for the future. To more fully understand and better connect with consumers, marketers divide the total market (all of the possible customers) for their goods or services into smaller, more homogeneous units in order to most effectively reach the most likely customers, a process known as market segmentation. They may do this in any number of ways, depending on what they want to find out. For instance, to learn about consumer attitudes toward products, researchers may segment markets according to consumer

benefits. (For a more detailed discussion of market segments, see Chapter 1.)

Through a graphics technique known as **perceptual mapping,** shown frequently in two dimensions, marketers can visualize consumers' attitudes toward their existing products and see where their goods stand in relation to their competitors. Map dimensions are created by selecting relevant attributes to be measured such as quality, timeliness, or customer service. For example, items appearing close together on a perceptual map are often seen by customers as "me too" products, while gaps indicate that no products exist and perhaps there is opportunity to satisfy an unmet consumer need. Marketers can then position their products to meet those needs. Thus, perceptual mapping also helps marketers focus on planning distinctive advertising and promotional activities.

Figure 5.9 presents a perceptual map of customer attitudes toward major department stores in the United States, arranged according to price and fashion leadership. Price appears along the horizontal axis and fashion leadership along the vertical axis. Note that American customers have a range of options in both price and style when shopping department stores. Not so with the neighbors to the north, in Canada. While some specialty stores there offer limited merchandise selections, two major department stores dominate the Canadian scene: Hudson's Bay Company (HBC) and Holt Renfrew. Hudson's Bay, whose customers are similar to Macy's but more conservative and moderate in spending, maintains a chain of some 90 department stores and 69 home furnishings stores throughout Canada. Holt Renfrew, with its nine retail stores

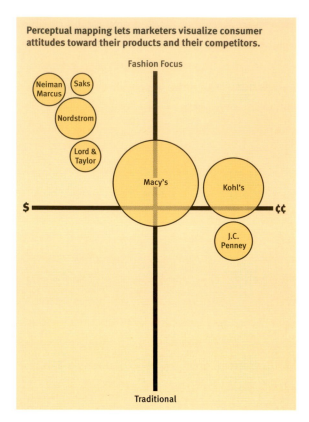

Perceptual mapping lets marketers visualize consumer attitudes toward their products and their competitors.

FIGURE 5.9 Perceptual map of selected department stores in the United States.

in Canada's major cities, is more fashion-centered and exclusive with higher prices. Within the past decade, however, Hudson's Bay and Lord & Taylor (Figure 5.10) were both acquired by the same parent company, which before long realized that HBC customers wanted a greater selection of designer brand merchandise and were ready to pay the price. The result was that Hudson's Bay then purchased Saks.[8] By envisioning the placement of these retailers on a Canadian perceptual map, it is easy to tell that with Lord & Taylor and especially Saks among its properties, Hudson's Bay is positioning itself to compete more effectively with established Canadian specialty stores, and in particular with Holt Renfrew.

What Is the Effect of Attitudes on Our Buying Behavior?

Marketers know that sales volume for their products depends not only on positive consumer attitudes about their offerings, but also on consumers' acting on these attitudes by purchasing their goods. Therefore, marketers are vitally interested in the ways our buying behaviors are influenced by the cognitive and affective elements of our attitudes, since our purchasing behavior reflects the effectiveness of marketers' promotional strategies. Advertising that leads consumers to develop positive attitudes about a product may well encourage them to buy that product, and successful experience with the product could well mean repeat purchases.

THE RELATIONSHIP BETWEEN BELIEFS AND ATTITUDES

While there are several theories explaining the relationship of beliefs and attitudes in the marketplace, most point out that consumers want to maintain harmony in their buying activities. Among the theories, two of the most relevant are balance theory and multi-attribute theory (the basis for the Theory of Reasoned Action).

Balance Theory

Balance theory states that people want to maintain harmony or balance in their attitudes—that is, their beliefs and feelings, whether positive or negative. An example of balance theory happened when Sears, renowned for its tools and appliance "hard goods," tried to enhance its apparel fashion image by

FIGURE 5.10 When Canadian retailer Hudson's Bay Company purchased Lord & Taylor and Saks, it opened up a wider selection of goods for both Americans and Canadians.

promoting "the softer side of Sears." One part of its strategy was to purchase the nautical sporting goods and apparel firm Lands' End. At the time, Lands' End had many loyal customers, while fewer people purchased apparel from Sears. When Sears started offering Lands' End apparel, the negative object (Sears) connected to a positive one (Lands' End), creating a negative imbalance, and customers saw them both as negative. Lands' End apparel, when made by Sears, took on a negative appeal and consumers began buying less of it. Sears' apparel sales also

fell below expectations, resulting in a total negative balance (Figure 5.11). The huge retailer put Lands' End up for sale, then had second thoughts and created Lands' End boutiques in Sears stores, hoping to achieve balance in apparel sales. Over time, these departments became successful for Sears and represented a bright spot for the retailer, even as the company continued to struggle as a whole. However, by late 2013, Sears decided to spin off Lands' End into a separate company and offered its stock for sale on the market, leaving open the possibility of creating

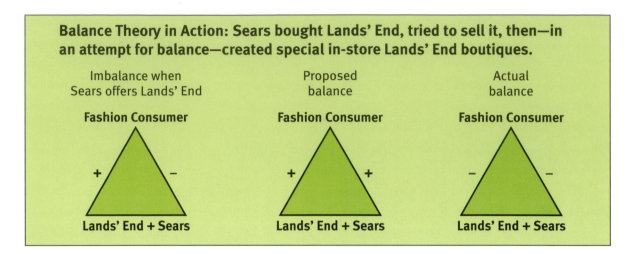

Balance Theory in Action: Sears bought Lands' End, tried to sell it, then—in an attempt for balance—created special in-store Lands' End boutiques.

Imbalance when Sears offers Lands' End

Fashion Consumer

\+ −

Lands' End + Sears

Proposed balance

Fashion Consumer

\+ +

Lands' End + Sears

Actual balance

Fashion Consumer

− −

Lands' End + Sears

FIGURE 5.11 Balance theory.

a more even balance between the two stores in customers' minds.[9] The outcome remains to be seen.

As mentioned, the main concept of balance theory is that people are more comfortable when their attitudes are in balance. Moreover, as consumers, we like to associate ourselves with positive attitude objects.[10] Serious fashion apparel consumers are drawn to the quality and style of names such as Prada, Burberry, and Chanel; many interior design practitioners have high regard for names such as Baker, Miele, and Kohler.

Balance theory also helps explain the use of celebrity product endorsements. The balance is created because consumers like to identify with positive attitude objects, here represented by a well-known person. Marketers hope to transfer our positive feelings toward the celebrity to the product the celebrity endorses, thus creating a favorable balance in our minds toward the product. Celebrities such as Beyoncé and Justin Bieber, among others, endorse new fragrances in hopes that we as consumers will buy them because we have transferred our positive

attitudes toward these celebrities to the products. Popular athletes such as Phil Mickelson and Tiger Woods endorse golf wear and accessories. Celebrity Jennifer Lopez has created a full look book for the Jennifer Lopez Collection of apparel for Kohl's, believing her star image will transfer positively to the merchandise. A celebrity's negative image also can influence consumers' attitudes, as when allegations of drug use by model Kate Moss hit the news. This caused the cancellation of a number of her commercial contracts, such as one with apparel retailer H&M. Later, Moss was cleared of all charges and successfully renewed her modeling career, as well as going on to introduce her own fashion collection and fragrance line.

Multi-Attribute Models

The idea that consumers purchase products based on the latter's characteristics or attributes became the basis for the development of Fishbein's **multi-attribute model,** which states that a combination of consumers' beliefs, derived from their knowledge about the attributes of a product, reveals the consumer's overall attitude toward the product.[11] For example, a young couple searching for furniture for their new apartment had developed beliefs about IKEA's attributes and how they filled their needs.

The multi-attribute chart in Table 5.1 compares three furniture retailers: IKEA, Crate & Barrel, and Pier 1. The furniture attributes sought by the couple are listed in the first column. In the second column are the couple's rankings, on a scale of 1 to 10, of the importance of each attribute in this situation, with low cost being the most important attribute. Then each retailer is accorded points based on the twosome's evaluation of that company's attributes. Adding up the attributes, we see that for the couple's purposes, their beliefs about IKEA's furniture are that it would best meet their goals. For these young people, price and transportability are the most important factors. Neither Crate & Barrel (with a score of 37) nor Pier 1 (with a score of 34) fulfills all of the attributes combined as well as IKEA (with a score of 50).

LET'S TALK

What are three or four of the attributes of your college that influenced your decision to attend? How would you prioritize them?

Theory of Reasoned Action (TORA)

While we as consumers may hold favorable attitudes about products, those attitudes may not lead to our purchasing them. For example, we might think highly of a BMW convertible or a French chaise lounge in a Provençal print, but something—perhaps money—keeps us from pulling out our wallets. Realizing that positive attitudes do not necessarily mean increased sales led to the creation of a more precise theory

TABLE 5.1 Multi-Attribute Theory

Attributes	Importance	IKEA	Crate & Barrel	Pier 1
Modern-looking	3	8	9	6
Sturdy	5	6	10	5
Flexible construction	4	9	3	6
Accommodating design	6	8	9	4
Easy-to-move	2	9	3	5
Inexpensive	1	10	3	8
Total		50	37	34

Source: Adapted from Michael Solomon's *Consumer Behavior*, 6th ed., Upper Saddle River, NJ: Pearson/Prentice Hall, 2004, Table 7.1, p. 252.

dealing with consumers' intent to purchase. The **Theory of Reasoned Action (TORA)** includes the affective, cognitive, and behavioral components of attitude in addition to other influences on our decision making (Figure 5.12). These influences, known as **subjective norms,** include our **normative beliefs;** that is, the opinions about the purchase held by other people who matter to us (such as friends and family), plus the extent to which we're motivated to go along with others' opinions.

For example, Pam, a college design student, hears about a school trip to Paris and wants very much to go. Analyzing Pam's attitude using TORA, we can determine the likelihood of her intention to take the trip. Her attitude toward the excursion is that it will be educational, somewhat costly, fun, but foreign and perhaps unsettling. Her beliefs about the educational value and the fun outweigh her concerns about both the cost and the fact that she has never been to a foreign country before. Evaluating the consequences of the trip, she will need to borrow money to pay for it, plus she will miss the income from her job while she is away. But her attitude toward the trip remains positive. She asks her

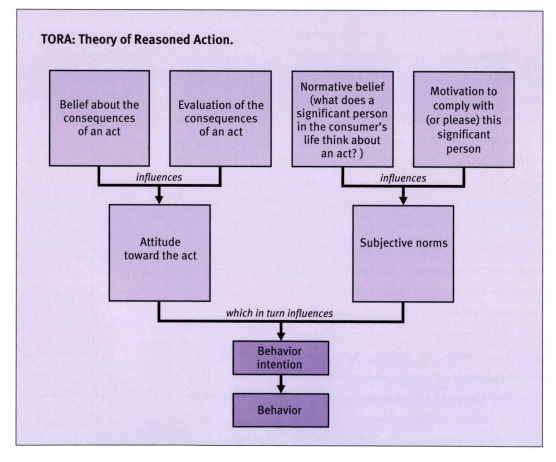

FIGURE 5.12 The Theory of Reasoned Action combines our attitude toward the act with subjective norms that influence our intent to buy.

parents for their opinion, and they are enthusiastic, even offering to underwrite some of her expenses. She then turns to her boyfriend; he is totally against her going away at all. While she is quite fond of him, she believes that if their relationship is to last, whether or not she takes the trip will not be the deciding factor. She is motivated to take the trip and intends to sign up for it. TORA is a more precise gauge of consumer behavior because it strives to measure consumers' attitudes toward *intending* to buy rather than their attitudes toward the object being considered for purchase.

One application of TORA can be seen in a survey by *Women's Wear Daily* on how people perceive fashion brands, namely that style and color outrank marketing efforts such as celebrity promotion. Consider the information in Point of View 5.1 on how consumer attitudes can be changed.

Theory of Cognitive Dissonance

After buying a product, we want to assure ourselves that we have made the right decision, an effort that helps us maintain balance. According to the **theory of cognitive dissonance**—sometimes called buyer's remorse—we are uncomfortable when we have conflicting attitudes or behaviors concerning an attitude object and work to resolve them. Remember Veronica in Chapter 4, who bought a coat she didn't really need after breaking up with her boyfriend? For consumers, cognitive dissonance tends to appear after making a large purchase. For example, perhaps you spent a lot of money on a new outfit. When you get it home and try it on, you ask yourself, "Should I have bought the gray one that had a more stylish jacket?" or "Was the striped one more flattering?" You think about your answers and

decide that you were right in the first place, or you take steps to return the outfit and find something more suitable, thus restoring balance. Marketers are quite aware of the power of cognitive dissonance, one of the reasons why salespeople at stores such as Nordstrom send customers notes of appreciation after a significant purchase, and why, for customers buying a new car, automobile dealers like Cadillac used to include a CD that lauded the features of the vehicle (to be played as the new owner drove away from the showroom).[12] Marketers work to reinforce doubts about the features of the brands we rejected by emphasizing the attributes of the one we actually purchased.

COMMON METHODS MARKETERS USE TO CHANGE FASHION CONSUMERS' ATTITUDES

Marketers use numerous ways to change our attitudes; one is repetition, which stems from Pavlov's system of classical conditioning (described in Chapter 3). We see over and over again the latest fashions promoted by manufacturers and marketers in a multitude of newspaper and magazine ads and articles, through the Internet, in catalogs, and on television.

Attitude Change through Repetition and Emotion

The act of repetition (repeated exposure through advertising and promotion) can make a product or service seem familiar to us, so, if it meets our needs and we develop a favorable attitude toward it, then we buy it—and the marketing goal has been achieved.

When the message itself is appealing to us, with attractive visuals (children, pets, or celebrities), when

Are Fashion Marketers Doing Enough to Sway Consumers' Attitudes?

Apparently not. At least not in great numbers. According to a study conducted by the marketing consulting firm Brand Keys, too few fashion brands sway consumer attitudes favorably enough in their direction. In the survey, 500 men and women, ages 18 to 59, ranked 50 fashion brands in terms of attributes they value, such as style, color, and comfort, along a continuum ranging from price-driven commodities at the low end to the high end, designated human brands.

Of the brands rated, only five (10 percent of the brands surveyed) made it to the highest or *human* level: Chanel, Donald Trump, Isaac Mizrahi, Ralph Lauren, and Victoria's Secret. Consumers' attitudes toward these brand attributes were most positive. Surprisingly, only two brands relied on celebrity mojo: Chanel, through its successful promotions enhanced by Nicole Kidman, and Donald Trump (marketing his fragrance and menswear), through his real estate and reality television image of over-the-top living that appeals to some wannabe affluents.

The second-highest level, labeled *21st century* brands, contains 34 brands (17 percent) positive in consumers' attitudes but not high enough to rank as human brands. These include Abercrombie & Fitch, Christian Dior, Louis Vuitton, Nike, and Skechers, among others. At the third level, designated *label* and containing 12 brands (24 percent), consumers' positive attitudes toward the brand attributes were weakening. Some of these brands include Anne Klein, Dockers, Gucci, and Tommy Hilfiger. The *commodity* group, primarily driven by price, contains 16 brands (32 percent), among them: Champion, Gap, Guess, JCPenney, Old Navy, and Wrangler.

The survey produced some astounding results for fashion marketers. First, of the 50 fashion brands included, only a small number of five reached the very highest level. Second, of the many brands with strong attributes in the next category (over a third of all brands surveyed), not enough of them were seen to have influenced consumer attitudes sufficiently enough to rate as human brands. Additional research pointed out that celebrity promotions of fashion goods influence the purchasing of 9 percent of clothing bought by men and women, whereas style, color, and comfort are far stronger influences on buying behavior (62 percent for the first two, 44 percent for the third, with the percentages totalling more than 100 percent because consumers have multiple reasons for purchasing). Clearly, fashion marketers have more to do in their efforts to influence consumer attitudes!

Source: Valerie Seckler, "There's No Banking on Star Power," *Women's Wear Daily,* November 16, 2005, p. 8.

the sound of a commercial features music we enjoy, when there is humor, or even better, sex—perhaps the most powerful of all attitude changers and a gargantuan selling tool in the world of fashion—marketers are hoping to change our beliefs and feelings toward a new fashion look, or for just about any product, service, or company (Figure 5.13).

Changing the Multi-Attribute Model

Changing beliefs, attitudes, and intentions to purchase by altering aspects of the multi-attribute model is another approach marketers use to increase sales. One popular method is to change beliefs about product attributes. What customers believe about a fashion look affects its popularity. For example, if fashion leaders are wearing knee-length gaucho trousers, then fashion followers who had been wearing ankle-length pants begin to believe that knee-length is the latest look, and to be in fashion they must adopt the new length. Another way that fashion marketers work to change consumers' beliefs is by adding a product attribute. With fashion goods, adding an attribute may be as simple as putting lace on the neckline and cuffs of this season's "hot" silk blouse, or altering the look of a room by placing colorful cushions on the sofa. Changing beliefs about a competitor is another way fashion marketers work to change attitudes. In the budget fashion market, Walmart—not generally perceived as a fashion leader—tried introducing Metro 7, a trendy line of women's wear, hoping to lure young urban consumers away from the pull of Mossimo and Isaac Mizrahi at Target. Unfortunately, the fashion change was too dramatic for Walmart's mainstream customers, and the company not only discontinued the line, but actually ended up paring

FIGURE 5.13 Fashion promotion of all kinds frequently contains sexual overtones.

down its apparel offerings to focus on staples like jeans, socks, and underwear.[13]

Another way that fashion marketers can sway customer attitudes about owning an attitude object (product) is by making buying easier. Carpeting, furniture, and appliance retailers, for instance, promise introductory discounts or low interest rates and "no payment until next year" to customers who are considering doing some interior decorating. Or, some promotions may be based on changing our normative beliefs, that is, others' opinions of certain fashion decisions. The group People for the Ethical Treatment of Animals (PETA), renowned for its disapproval of the commercial treatment of fur-bearing animals, actively campaigns against the use of fur in fashion apparel and home furnishings in hopes of convincing all consumers that the many possible substitutes available today make fur unnecessary.

How do our attitudes relate to our individual personalities? We'll find out more about that topic in Chapter 6, "Personality and the Fashion Consumer."

Summary

We all hold attitudes; these are our settled opinions (either positive or negative) about people, ideas, places, or objects. Our attitudes consist of three parts: cognitive, our beliefs; affective, our feelings; and behavioral, our actions. In forming attitudes, we go through the hierarchy of effects, a series of steps, the order depending on our level of involvement with the attitude object. In a high-involvement situation, we use a problem-solving process, first gaining knowledge, then developing positive feelings, and finally taking action. In a low-involvement situation, we act on our beliefs—in this case, buying the product—and then develop positive or negative feelings about it as we use it. In an experiential situation, based on consumption for pleasure, we are caught up by the emotional appeal of the product, and by using it, we develop beliefs about it.

Our attitudes give us balance by meeting our needs through their functions: utilitarian, being useful in problem solving; value-expressive, representing our personalities and self-image; ego-defensive, protecting us from anxiety; and knowledge, ordering our information-processing. Influences on our attitudes include our personalities; our experience and information; as well as our family, friends, and peers.

Through perceptual mapping, fashion marketers use their knowledge of consumer attitudes toward their products both to assess their current strategies and to reveal new marketing opportunities.

By studying the relationship between beliefs and attitudes, marketers have learned that customers like to maintain balance (balance theory) and do so by association with positive attitude objects such as celebrities. Consumers develop attitudes about products by citing product attributes and weighing their importance. To go beyond attitudes and learn consumers' intent to purchase, marketers use the Theory of Reasoned Action (TORA), which factors in attitudes plus the importance of others' influence in the purchasing decision.

Some of the most popular ways of influencing attitudes in fashion marketing include the use of repetition and attractive messages featuring celebrities, pleasant visuals, sound, sex, and humor. Changing our perceptions of a product's attributes and making the purchase of fashion goods easy are also marketing efforts designed to encourage us to buy.

KEY TERMS

Affective element

Attitude

Attitude object

Balance theory

Behavioral element

Cognitive element

Experiential hierarchy

Functions of attitudes

Hierarchy of effects

High-involvement hierarchy

Low-involvement hierarchy

Multi-attribute model

Normative beliefs

Perceptual mapping

Personality

Subjective norms

Theory of cognitive dissonance

Theory of reasoned action (TORA)

QUESTIONS FOR REVIEW

1. Explain the relationship of an "attitude" to an "attitude object," and describe each of the elements that compose an attitude.

2. Name the three classifications of the hierarchy of effects, and explain why appealing to each is useful to fashion marketers.

3. Cite the four classifications of the functions of attitude, and supply an example of how a fashion goods marketer could appeal to each.

4. Describe four influences on attitude formation, with examples of each.

5. Explain what is meant by "perceptual mapping" and how fashion marketers would use it.

6. Give examples of how fashion marketers could apply the following: balance theory, multi-attribute model, and TORA.

ACTIVITIES

1. Select one designer about whose work you have developed strong feelings—either positive or negative—and state whether your attitude stems mainly from cognitive or affective elements, or a combination. Cite the contribution of each element to your attitude formation, and state their combined effect on your purchase behavior.

2. Think of a fashion item you have purchased, and explain how your feelings, beliefs, and behavior developed, and in which order. Create a diagram of the hierarchy of effect that depicts your choice, and describe it to the class.

3. From recent fashion magazines, select a series of advertisements that appeal to the four functions of attitude. Try to find at least one ad that appeals to each function. Share your findings with the class. Ads appealing to which attitude function were easiest to find? Why?

4. Working with one or two partners, select a fashion goods manufacturer or retailer, and create a perceptual map positioning that business in relation to its competition. Based on your findings, what are your suggestions for advertising campaigns for this company? Are there gaps that the company might fill with new divisions or products?

5. List four or five attributes of your college. Then applying TORA, indicate how you arrived at the decision to attend this school as opposed to others you could have selected.

MINI-PROJECT

Working alone or with a team, think of three stores (or fashion goods designers or manufacturers) you have a positive or negative attitude about. Create a multi-attribute model for your chosen subjects consisting of the attributes you have selected, their importance, and the ranking of your beliefs about each one. Add up each attitude score, and report your findings to the class.

REFERENCES

1. David Moin, "Penney's B-T-S Strategy Seen as Key to Revival," *Women's Wear Daily,* April 29, 2013, pp. 1 and 12; Sidney Finkelstein, "Johnson and Penney's: Anatomy of a Bad Fit," *Women's Wear Daily,* Think Tank column, April 29, 2013, pp. 1 and 13.

2. Alex Kuczynski, "Consumer Philosophy by Tar-zhay," *New York Times,* Critical Shopper column, July 2, 2005, Sec. E.

3. Shawn Young and Li Yuan, "You Talkin' to Me?" *Wall Street Journal,* September 16, 2005, Sec. B.

4. Martin E. Goldberg et al., eds., *Social Marketing* (Mahwah, NJ: Lawrence Erlbaum Associates Publishers, 1997).

5. Robert J. Marzano, *Designing a New Taxonomy of Educational Objectives* (Thousand Oaks, CA: Corwin Press, 2001).

6. Brian Mullen, *The Psychology of Human Behavior* (Mahwah, NJ: Lawrence Erlbaum Associates, 1990).

7. Daniel Katz, "The Functional Approach to the Study of Attitudes," *Public Opinion Quarterly* 24 (Summer 1960): 163–204.

8. David Moin, "HBC'S $2.9B Bet on Saks," *Women's Wear Daily,* July 30, 2013, pp. 1, 4, and 6.

9. Maria Ajit Thomas and Aditi Shrivastava, "Struggling Sears to Spin Off Lands' End Clothing Business," Reuters, December 6, 2013, http://www.reuters.com/article/2013/12/06/us-sears-landsend-idUSBRE9B50K120131206

10. John C. Mowen, *Consumer Behavior* (New York: Prentice Hall, 1997).

11. Kenneth Miller, "A Situational Multi-Attribute Model," *Advances in Consumer Research* (Association for Consumer Research) 2 (1975): 455–464.

12. Robert A. Wicklund and Jack W. Brehm, *Perspectives on Cognitive Dissonance* (Hillsdale, NJ: Lawrence Erlbaum Associates, 1976).

13. Alyce Lomax, "Wal-Mart's Latest Fashion Fail Proves Again That It's No Target," *Daily Finance,* November 1, 2011, http://www.dailyfinance.com/2011/11/01/wal-marts-latest-fashion-fail-proves-again-that-its-no-target/.

CHAPTER 6

Personality and the Fashion Consumer

WHAT DO I NEED TO KNOW ABOUT PERSONALITY AND THE FASHION CONSUMER?

✔ What comprises personality and what influence it has on fashion consumers

✔ The effect of three personality theories on fashion consumer buying behavior

✔ The trait theories that are useful to fashion designers and marketers in better understanding fashion buyer behavior

✔ Why fashion marketers work to endow their products with personalities as a means of influencing consumer behavior

What do Raf Simons, Lady Gaga, Jay-Z, Tom Hanks, Yo-Yo Ma, and Sofia Coppola have in common? Beyond the fact that they all contribute to our culture, each is internationally known, frequently in the news, and much discussed. In other words, according to a standard definition, they are all "personalities."

But well-known people are not the only possessors of personality. We all are personalities, because the term *personality* also means the characteristics that each of us has that make us unique from other people.

What Is Personality?

While our perceptions and attitudes play an important part in how we choose fashion goods, our personalities also influence our actual purchasing behavior. As we defined in the previous chapter, personality is made up of those individual psychological characteristics that routinely influence the way people react to their surroundings, including how they make buying decisions. In addition, while personalities are lasting, they can change, through

127

maturing, or after an accident, illness, or other very significant event. One example of this could be a mean-spirited relative who "mellowed out" after either marrying or divorcing his or her spouse.

Effect of Personality on the Fashion Consumer

Although marketers often segment consumers by obvious means such as gender, income, or occupation, by using personality-based dimensions, they also probe to discern more about customers' deep-seated purchasing behavior. For example, fashion experts know that when shopping for apparel and home furnishings, assertive and outgoing customers tend to choose bright colors and patterns harmonizing with their personalities, while more timid people, in order to blend in, tend to stick to basic neutrals and pastels.

Major Personality Theories

In order to look more deeply into the core aspects of consumers' buying behavior, marketers examine some of the major theories of personality, including (1) psychoanalytic theory, (2) social cultural theory, (3) self-concept theory, and (4) trait theory.[1]

PSYCHOANALYTIC THEORY

During the early twentieth century, Austrian psychiatrist Sigmund Freud studied many aspects of human behavior, developing theories that revolutionized the study of personality and making major contributions to the advancement of psychoanalysis. According to Freud's **psychoanalytic theory,** many of

our behaviors and our dreams come from our unconscious, where thoughts we are largely unaware of are stored. The personality develops as a reaction to the ways one deals with childhood conflicts and is influenced by the three components of personality: the id, the ego, and the superego. The **id,** or libido, while unconscious, is the component that controls our biological drives of hunger, sex, and self-preservation; it is with us from birth and its impulses require immediate gratification. The purpose of the id is to seek pleasure and avoid pain. If unchecked, it is wild and acts freely, and can be a source of destruction—and of creativity.[2] The id plays a significant role in the lives of many people in the fields of design and fashion.

The second component, the **ego,** is the conscious part of our personality, our sense of ourselves; it reacts to reality in a socially acceptable way, serving as a mediator between the desires of the id and the restraint of the superego.[3] Operating under the ego's influence, a consumer purchasing an outfit for work would select something that both blends into that environment and accurately reflects how she feels about herself. The late designer Gianni Versace, interpreting the ego in his own way, at one time remarked, "I like to dress egos. If you haven't got an ego today, you can forget it."[4]

The third component, the **superego**—manifesting the traditional values of society customarily transmitted by parents—acts as a conscience, promoting acceptable standards of behavior and restraining the impulsive id by creating feelings of guilt to punish misconduct, real or imagined. A graduate student who would like very much to own an expensive watch, but also not wanting to see his debts mount, opts for a Timex instead. His superego puts a brake on his id's demand for immediate gratification, and the ego tells him the watch he chose is practical, durable, and completely acceptable for now. In this situation, the ego has acted to balance the desires of the id and the superego in a way that maintains the personality's equilibrium; this is known as the *reality principle* and takes place in the unconscious, so that the consumer often may not know the real basis for some buying behavior.

LET'S TALK

Can you think of an example of a recent fashion item that you, or someone you know, chose where id, ego, or superego could have played a part leading up to the purchase decision?

Through the work of Freud, marketers are able to envision the relationship between our biological urges (represented by the id) and our human consciousness (shown by the ego) to the customs and traditions of society (represented by the superego). These three influences are the basis for understanding the needs and motivations of consumers and their behavior. Note in Figure 6.1 how Levi Strauss uses psychoanalytic theory to create and advertise products that appeal to the id, ego, and superego.[5]

The field of **motivational research,** developed when researchers applied some of Freud's theories to marketing, studies the effect of the unconscious id and the superego on motives in purchasing behavior. *Depth interviews,* prodding for unconscious motives through a series of questions, and *focus groups,*

FIGURE 6.1 What messages is this ad conveying to the ego, superego, and id?

guided discussions on marketing behavior, both grew out of the psychoanalytic approach. (For a more detailed discussion of motivation, see Chapter 4.)

SOCIAL-CULTURAL THEORIES

Two students of Sigmund Freud, Carl Jung and Alfred Adler, carried the psychoanalytic view a step further. They believed that the social and cultural influences on personality were far stronger than the biological drives cited by Freud. They also felt that knowledge about personality would best reveal itself through studying people behaving normally in their environments, as opposed to Freud's methodology of working primarily with abnormal patients. Jung developed the concept that shared memories of the past were the basis for the present culture; he called these memories **archetypes.** Some of these archetypes relating cultural memories included wizards, enchanted beings, and the "earth mother." To convey

the shared meanings, advertisers sometimes incorporate archetypes into their campaigns. For example, the French government has used actress Catherine Deneuve and other stars to depict Marianne, France's national symbol of courage and freedom ("earth mother"). The characters from *The Chronicles of Narnia* or *Harry Potter* are archetypes that enthrall us today. In the *Pirates of the Caribbean* series, Johnny Depp's Captain Jack Sparrow represents the archetype of the swashbuckling adventurer coping with the eternal powers of the sea (Figure 6.2).

FIGURE 6.2 Recalling archetypes such as the characters in *Pirates of the Caribbean* relates shared memories to today's culture.

LET'S TALK

What archetypes can you think of that play a role in today's marketing of fashion goods and services?

Alfred Adler, an early twentieth-century Austrian physician and psychologist, worked with Sigmund Freud in Vienna for a while, but then broke away to develop the school of individual psychology. Adler's emphasis centered on the individual's relationship to his or her environment and on maturing by overcoming feelings of inferiority. Contemporary marketers incorporate Adler's theories by showing how consumers sometimes gain feelings of superiority through association with the products of luxury brands such as Rolls-Royce, Rolex, and Ritz-Carlton, and even with other goods and services that are more moderately priced (Figure 6.3).

Karen Horney was another twentieth-century social theorist. A physician by training, she worked at the Chicago Institute for Psychoanalysis, founded the Association for the Advancement of Psychoanalysis, and later taught at the New York School of

FIGURE 6.3 Which personality characteristics are the focus of this advertisement?

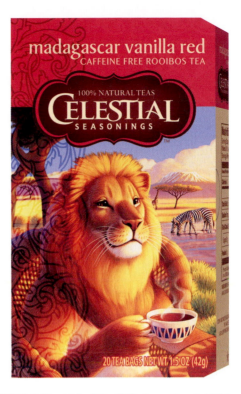

FIGURE 6.4 To which of the CAD elements might this advertisement apply?

Medicine. Her theories were based on the idea that personality develops as an individual learns to cope with anxieties originating in childhood relationships with parents. She developed three hypotheses that describe ways people deal with this anxiety: compliance, an effort to move toward people, to be accepted and loved by others; aggressiveness, to move against people, to compete and gain power; and detachment, to move away from people, to be independent and self-sufficient. She believed that the reality-based ego was more influential than aggressive or sexually driven motivations in guiding human behavior and sought to strengthen her patients' feelings of competency and self-worth.[6]

Joel Cohen built on Horney's theories by creating the CAD scale, a device that measured degrees of compliance, aggressiveness, and detachment. He discovered that compliant people used more mouthwash than others and postulated that this was part of their ongoing efforts to be accepted; aggressives, he learned, bought more aftershave—possibly as a means to dominating a group; and detached people drank more tea, perhaps as a way to enjoy themselves in a relaxed environment.[7] Research such as that using the CAD scale is important because it is rooted in personality theory, and its marketing applications focus on consumer behavior (Figure 6.4).

SELF-CONCEPT THEORY

A third theory addresses personality by looking at the self, our characteristics and attributes, that

Fashion Sizing: Paying Attention to Larger Personalities

Just because a woman may not have what is considered an "ideal" body shape, that does not mean that her self-concept isn't one of being fashion-forward. Yet for years, the plus size group of fashion consumers has been consistently underserved, if not ignored. According to Atlanta's Center for Disease Control, the average woman in the United States is 5 feet 4 inches tall and weighs 167 pounds. How many fashion models have you seen who display those measurements? How many clothing manufacturers make stylish looks for the customers who wear size 14 (which should fit the average woman described above) and larger?

Statistics quoted by The NPD Group, a leading marketing research organization, reveal that while around 65 percent of fashion consumers are plus size candidates, only 14 percent are buying from plus size retailers such as Lane Bryant. Plus size women fall in all age groups but many brand marketers have yet to realize their needs and their willingness to spend. A while back, an Abercrombie & Fitch executive, referring to large size customers, said, "A lot of people don't belong [in our clothes]." Lululemon's CEO recently resigned after making a similar comment about his firm's yoga apparel. Yet research by the apparel organization ModCloth shows that plus size customers spend 25 percent more on clothing than regular size customers and buy 17 percent more items.

Across the board, the fashion industry is catching on, moved in part by *Vogue* editor Anna Wintour's placing voluptuous model Kate Upton's photo on the magazine's cover, and chiding the apparel industry for ignoring larger-size customers. A number of designers and brand marketers are responding to calls for plus size fashions. Among them are Donna Karan, Calvin Klein, and Michael Kors. On his website, designer Tadashi Shoji has gowns to size 24, which clients can purchase online. Forever 21 Plus offers dresses and shorts, while tennis star Serena Williams includes plus sizes in the line she markets on QVC. The fashion industry is beginning to understand the buying power of the average-and-larger customer and to bring greater diversity to its fashion offerings.

Source: Christina Binkley, "On Plus Side: New Fashion Choices for Size 18," *Wall Street Journal*, On Style, June 13, 2013, p. D3.

is, our **self-concept.** As consumers, our buying behavior tends to support our self-concept: We tend to shop in the stores and select the products that fit in with our views of ourselves. For example, Kim prefers to shop for kitchen appliances at Sears because she believes that the durability and price of Kenmore (Sears' private label) products reinforce her view of herself as a practical and frugal person. Tony, on the other hand, thinks that his newly rebuilt Porsche accurately reflects his self-confidence and risk-taking abilities as a computer games designer.

In actuality, we all have **multiple selves**—that is, we take on many roles. To explore this point further, let's learn more about Kim. She has a degree in merchandising, works as an assistant manager in a small boutique, and is a fashion stylist for a music group on the side. She lives in a small house with two roommates and has a brother, a sister, and a significant other. In each of these relationships, or roles, she responds differently. Likewise, her needs for goods and services vary depending on her role. Just like anyone else, Kim has multiple aspects to her personality. Many marketers understand the concept of multiple selves, segmenting their markets and aiming their promotions accordingly. For example, in surfing the Internet to find a birthday present for her sister, Kim is attracted to colorful photos of decorative gloves and scarves; later, while looking for a blouse to wear to work, she is drawn to the description of a fitted style in a wrinkle-free fabric, noting the garment's easy-care features.

In addition to the concept of multiple selves, according to **self-concept theory,** we envision ourselves both privately and in our relationships to others. Privately, the **actual self** (self-image) is who we think we are, while the **ideal self** represents who we would like to be. When she was a college student shopping for her school wardrobe, Kim combed the thrift shops for rock-bottom prices on brand-name sweaters and jeans, reflecting her actual student self-image (and budget). For her job at the boutique and in her role as a stylist, however, she buys fashion-forward designer looks whenever she can, approaching her ideal private self-image. In our relationships to others, our **social self-image** represents how others see us, and our **ideal**

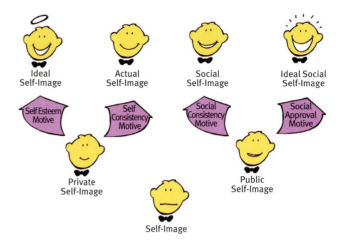

FIGURE 6.5 Our private and public self-images.

social self-image is how we would like others to see us (Figure 6.5). Part of Kim's social self-image is that she has a knack for entertaining with great music and food at her parties. In her ideal social self-image, Kim wants to be known for entertaining gatherings of designers, musicians, and other celebrities in her own elegantly furnished home.

Self-concept theory includes the ideas of consistency and of working to improve one's self-esteem, or opinion of oneself (described in greater detail in the following paragraph). It grows out of psychoanalytic theory in that the actual self is close to the ego, our internal mediator, while the ideal self is similar to the superego, both concerned with their version of the way things *should* be. Marketers of fashion goods of all kinds such as jewelry, clothing, automobiles, homes and interiors, as well as travel (also a consumer item) frequently appeal to our ideal self-images with advertisements that portray an ideal. One outstanding example of this is Ralph Lauren, with his tailored British looks for men and clubby upper-class British furniture, fabrics, and wall paint. The company's promotions as much as declare, "Buy these goods and live the life!"

LET'S TALK

When considering buying fashion goods, which manufacturers and stores do you feel most comfortable patronizing? Why?

Self-Esteem

The concept of the ideal self focuses on **self-esteem,** that is, our positive and negative opinions of ourselves and our estimate of our self-worth. The closer the resemblance between the actual and the ideal self, the higher one's self-esteem. Having an ideal and working toward it can obviously influence buying behavior—and self-esteem. Unfortunately, much advertising that appeals to the ideal self tends to accentuate the differences between the real and the ideal, frequently contributing to a viewer's diminished self-esteem. The advertisements themselves are unreal, creating their own ideal by using models whose bodies are often surgically enhanced and graphics technology such as airbrushing to alter reality. Consider any fashion model in an advertisement. What real people do you know with such proportions, such smooth complexions, and such perfectly arranged hairstyles? Striving for such unattainable ideals can be disappointing and stressful, and can result in compulsive and unfulfilling buying behavior, at the extreme.

The Extended Self

The relationship between ourselves and our possessions is known as the **extended self;** in other words, "We are what we own." In the film *Pulp Fiction,* one of the main characters, Butch (Bruce Willis), although running for his life, must drive back to his apartment and a potentially lethal situation to pick up the watch he inherited from his father and grandfather. That watch was part of Butch's extended self. Perhaps you have been given a gift that you enjoy and treasure highly; owning it adds to your self-esteem. Or, if you lost or gave up that item, you feel diminished in self-esteem. Consider Eleanor, who is in a public restroom. After removing an heirloom sapphire ring to wash her hands, she inadvertently leaves it on the edge of the sink. Realizing her forgetfulness just a few minutes later, she rushes back to retrieve the ring, but finds it is gone. Eleanor is devastated, ashamed of her carelessness; her self-esteem tumbles. Possessions as forms of our extended selves can have numerous meanings. According to research, they can actually enhance or extend our personalities in these ways: (1) *actually,* as in learning a new skill by using new scuba diving equipment; (2) *symbolically,* as winning a contest prize for creating a garment; (3) *conferring status,* as being the first among friends to own the latest Samsung smartphone; (4) *bestowing symbols of immortality,* as preserving a wedding gown for future family brides; and (5) by *containing magical powers,* as did Dorothy's red slippers in *The Wizard of Oz.*[8,9] The ornate Asian necklace in Figure 6.6 is a likely candidate representing someone's extended self.

LET'S TALK

Think of a fashion item you would like to own. In what ways might it enhance your self-esteem? Then consider one of your possessions that you believe represents your extended self. In which of the five ways described above do you see this item as part of your extended self?

Celebrating Diversity Lets Authentic Personalities Shine Through

Defying the fashion trend to pinch, pad, and puff, many consumers today, men as well as women, are opting for a more natural look. According to Faith Popcorn, head of Brain Reserve, a New York research organization, the interest in a more realistic look began when, as a society, we started celebrating the black and Hispanic cultures where having a visible derrière and even a mustache (for women) are totally acceptable and often "cool."

In marketing, the natural look may have started when Jamie Lee Curtis appeared in an ad wearing sports gear but no makeup and without photo retouching. The advertising industry was quick to act on consumers' desires to see advertisements with more realistic models. To promote its Intensive Firming Lotion and other products, the health and beauty aids brand Dove created billboards and ads featuring six women of various sizes, who were not professional models, dressed in their underwear. Their appearance caused a stir in the media and society in general and included a segment on the *Today* show and a *New York Times* editorial. This moderately priced beauty products manufacturer was reaching real women. Nike was quick to follow, showing people with outsized shoulders, thighs, and backsides in its ads for exercise outfits.

Dove's emphasis on promoting the natural look grew from more than a whim to counter consumer dissatisfaction. As part of the British conglomerate Unilever, and in order to learn consumers' views on beauty, Dove surveyed girls and women in the United Kingdom, Canada, and the United States. Some of the results were disturbing; for example, in Britain, more that half of those surveyed said their bodies "disgusted" them. Six out of ten girls believed they would be happier if they were thinner, but actually fewer than two out of ten were in fact overweight. Apparently, fashion's images of artificially curvaceous models and celebrities had wreaked not a little havoc on young self-concepts.

From its findings, Dove created a self-esteem fund to help girls and women build confidence. In Britain and Canada, the fund devotes itself to combating eating disorders, 90 percent of which are found in young girls. In the United States the fund works with the Girls Scouts to build self-image through the *uniquely ME!* program to build self-esteem. Activities include exercises in recognizing one's strengths, identifying core values, and handling stress, among others. The message conveyed: An attractive, natural appearance grows from a healthy outlook on life. And the company is not stopping there. Dove continues to conduct research on the topic and incorporate the healthy self-image message into its ongoing Dove Campaign for Real Beauty.

Sources: Stuart Elliott, "For Everyday Products, Ads Using Everyday Woman," *New York Times*, August 17, 2005, pp. C1 and C2; Rich Thomaselli, "News Steers Advertising toward Reality Anatomy," *AdAge.com*, August 15, 2005; Rob Walker, "Social Lubricant," *New York Times* Magazine, September 4, 2005, p. 23; Dove Support: the Dove self-esteem fund, www.campaignforrealbeauty.com; Dove, Social Mission, www.dove.us /social-mission/campaign-for-real-beauty.aspx.

FIGURE 6.6 An heirloom object, such as this enamel-over-copper vessel on a necklace by Stefani B, can become part of a consumer's extended self.

TRAIT THEORIES

Another way of studying personality is by looking at our traits or personal behavioral tendencies. We each have **traits**—distinct characteristics that differentiate us from others and contribute to our behavior. Many psychologists have identified and studied traits such as friendliness, innovativeness, and the desire for power. It was Carl Jung, however, who identified people according to whether they were **introverts,** choosing to turn inward, or **extroverts,** sociable and outgoing, concerned with external matters.[10] As consumers in the decision-making process, introverts do not ask others for product information but prefer to rely on themselves, whereas extroverts get product advice from various sources and tend to buy products that are accepted by others.

To better understand consumer behavior, many researchers have undertaken studies of personality traits. Because its results apply to almost all cultures, one of the most important theories is the five-trait model. These traits are (1) extroversion, (2) neuroticism, (3) openness to experience, (4) agreeableness, and (5) conscientiousness.

Researchers have also noted various personality traits that designers and marketers are interested in understanding better. These are discussed below.

Extroversion and Introversion

Extroverted people are active and outgoing as opposed to introverts, who are more centered inwardly. According to research, extrovert consumers tend to react more positively than negatively to certain upbeat TV commercials.[11] Therefore, marketers aim cheerful and optimistic messages, such as travel agencies depicting fun-filled vacation resorts, or design firms emphasizing the glamour and efficiency of a new kitchen. Viral or "buzz" marketing (word-of-mouth promotion, discussed in Chapter 1) is a popular way of enabling extroverts to become part of a promotion, as when teens talk, talk, and talk about the latest look in denim—and then all want to own it.

Negativism

A person's level of negativism is shown by the tendency to express negative rather than positive emotions, as opposed to having a more realistic or balanced outlook. Negativism can be a manifestation of a **neurosis,** a mental disorder with emotionally painful symptoms that can surface as anxiety, compulsion, and depression. A marketing appeal to neurotic tendencies would cue in on negative feelings of insecurity and inadequacy. A fashion magazine touting the season's newest looks has a not-so-hidden agenda of making readers feel dissatisfied with their present outfits. A more realistically oriented personality would identify the information that could be useful in wardrobe planning and put aside feelings of discontent about not being able to acquire an entire closet full of the latest fashions.

One extreme form of neurosis—compulsion—is seen in the fashion world when consumers purchase goods indiscriminately, which is known as **compulsive buying behavior.** Consider Imelda Marcos, wife of a former president of the Philippines; at one time she owned more than 2,000 pairs of shoes! Extreme compulsive shopping is an illness, a form of addiction, similar to other addictions to activities such as gambling and drug use.

Desire for Knowledge

Some consumers have a strong urge to learn everything they can about a product before purchasing it; others do not need to know all the details. The desire for knowledge is called the **need for cognition (NC).** Studies have shown that consumers with a high NC react positively to advertisements explaining product features and customer benefits in great detail, while consumers with low NC seem to prefer attractive illustrations featuring celebrities.[12]

While some people prefer to learn through reading, others are more open and respond better to images. Cognitive research has developed two classifications for consumers: *visualizers,* consumers who prefer to learn through viewing pictures in movies or on sites like Pinterest or Instagram, and *verbalizers,* those who prefer to learn by reading texts or ads or listening to lectures or podcasts.[13] Advertisers of fashion goods, aiming at visualizers, stress the assets of their products in appealing illustrations, while marketers of technical products such as electronics, aiming at verbalizers, provide extensive written information about these items. (See Figure 6.7.)

Innovation and Opinion Leadership

Some people are the first to buy new designs for themselves and their surroundings. The people who buy the earliest and are the first visual communicators of the season's styles are known as **fashion innovators.**[14] In the rarified atmosphere of haute couture, they are often among those 1,500 or so individual clients of the famous couturiers. They are also the ones who can recognize and afford the newest in design. Fashion innovators want to stand out from the crowd, to be the first to own a new product; they are often said to have a *need for differentiation or uniqueness.* To be an acknowledged fashion

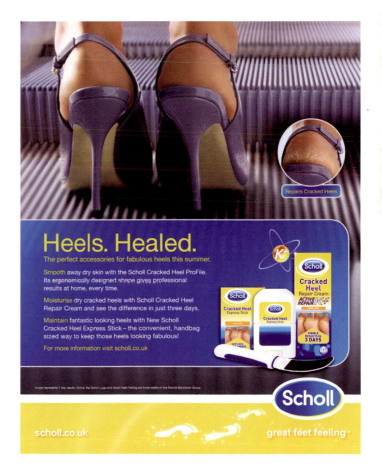

FIGURE 6.7 In this Scholl's ad aimed at verbalizers, the copy clinches the message.

FIGURE 6.8 The popularity of Mary-Kate and Ashley Olsen contributes to their influence on fashion trends.

innovator takes a lot of originality and a big check-book, although a few very creative fashion devotees are able to originate looks putting imagination to work with items they already own, or can devise.

People who recognize and endorse what innovators are wearing and doing are known as **fashion influentials** or the visible elite; they are usually members of an aggressive, fast-moving group of opinion leaders. They include royals, the wealthy, and celebrities worldwide. They are not necessarily fashion innovators but rather set the standards for apparel worn for a given event or the surroundings created for a certain lifestyle.[15] Current fashion opinion leaders include David Linley (grandson of Britain's Queen Elizabeth, furniture maker, and chairman of the auction house Christie's UK) and his wife Serena, whose house in Provence is the subject of articles in high-end shelter magazines such as *Architectural Digest;* socialites, such as Anne Hearst and Mercedes T. Bass; the wealthy, such as Donald Trump (whose hairstyle and face seem to be everywhere in the media); and others in the public eye, such as Queen Latifah, Ashley and Mary-Kate Olsen, Brad Pitt, Ben Affleck, Lupita Nyong'o, and Amy Adams (Figure 6.8). In accepting and approving new fashion looks, fashion innovators and influencers are frequently tolerant of and open to new ideas, as opposed to people who are rigid and dogmatic or closed-minded and do not readily accept innovation.[16] For this reason, fashion marketers direct their promotions to the affluent, socially mobile, and fashion-centered, those who tend to accept new looks readily and who consciously seek out the latest styles among friends and in the media.

Need for Stimulation

Some people have a greater need than others to explore their surroundings and seek stimulation; they may also be more open to new ways of thinking than other people are. For example, Mark might feel invigorated, alert, and ready to party after completing a brisk walk or run, while a lively discussion of the season's latest hues might energize Chris to devise new color combinations for his interior designs.

According to the theory of **optimal stimulation level (OSL),** people have different needs for stimulation, most preferring moderate stimulation over high stimulation. People with a high need for stimulation seek out strenuous physical activities such as mountain climbing, paragliding, or bungee jumping.[17] As consumers, those with a high need for stimulation react differently than do people with a low need. For example, according to research, consumers with high OSL traits tend to seek out information about products and are often innovators looking for uniqueness who are willing to make riskier decisions (such as buying a controversial work of contemporary art) than consumers with low OSL. When encountering advertising, those with high OSLs search for more information but become bored with repetitive ads.[18] To reach high OSL consumers, marketers try to provide a variety of promotional approaches with the advertising containing more product information than usual and not repeated in the same way. For example, GEICO is famous for running frequent, often clever ads that all tout the company's "15 minutes could save you 15 percent or more on car insurance," but that feature a variety of different themes and characters, ranging from the GEICO gecko to an office-strolling camel happy about its being "hump" day.

Need for Affiliation, Achievement, and Power

Some people are quite independent, preferring to be by themselves or with just one or two friends or family members. Others place strong emphasis on gaining friends, maintaining close relationships, and belonging to groups; these people have a strong **need for affiliation.** They often buy products to reinforce their affiliations. For example, affiliation to one's employment is obvious: The uniforms worn by members of the military, postal employees, train conductors, airline employees, and others overtly indicate a work affiliation. Scout pins and wedding rings are signs of other affiliations. College posters, pennants, sweatshirts, and dorm room furnishings instantly signify students' school affiliations. Marketers of these products stress achieving a sense of belonging through buying and using these goods. Many consumers striving to maintain a particular standing in society patronize certain restaurants, theaters, museums, resorts, and charities, all to validate their affiliation with a social class. To encourage these patrons, marketers promote the sense of uniqueness and quality in their offerings in order to appeal to consumer needs for affiliation.

Some people want to stand out from the crowd, to do better than others; this trait is the **need for achievement.** An example of this can be seen in the behavior of competitive people who want to excel; they would have a tendency to look for features in products that would add to their expertise. A marketing manager might find the latest tablet computer to be most efficient in handling work outside his or her office. An interior designer realizes her work would be more accurate and professional with the most recent room-planning software. A boutique owner consulting with an advertising agency learns that a multimedia promotional campaign with a strong social media presence plus mailers and magazine ads is likely to produce a higher sales volume for her next designer trunk show. Marketers appealing to the need for achievement stress the superiority of their products and services in fulfilling their customers' goals to succeed.

While some people have traits stressing a need to belong and others to achieve, still others want to be powerful. People who want to influence or control others are said to have a **need for power.** When people are taking charge, displaying their authority, and seeking attention, they may well be showing their need for power. Certainly, infamous tyrants Genghis Khan, Adolf Hitler, and Pol Pot displayed this trait in excess; thankfully, few people in history have possessed it to that degree! Tests measuring the need for power, however, do reveal that business executives, psychologists, and teachers (among other professionals) can score high on the power trait.[19] People with a strong power trait often want to focus attention on themselves. In the 1980s when businesswomen as a group were beginning to rise to executive levels, they made the broad-shouldered "power suit" the fashion trend, perhaps in part to show that their shoulders could bear the heavier job responsibility. Obviously, the "power look" is found not strictly among women. Male and female lawyers, stockbrokers, and bankers have a certain look to their apparel aimed at conveying power, control, and authority. In addition to apparel, consumers purchase many other items to boost their sense of power, including the latest electronics, expensive cars and homes, club memberships, and even trips to outer space. These goods and services draw admiration and indicate that the consumer has some degree of control over his or her surroundings. Marketers appealing to the power trait emphasize how consumers using their products become the center of attention and are in charge of the situation. Note how the Ford truck ad in Figure 6.9 conveys the image of power. (For additional information on human needs, see Chapter 4.)

FIGURE 6.9 This Ford truck advertisement appeals to the power trait.

While personality traits can strongly influence individual purchases at times, and while marketers can appeal to a given trait—for example, as the Ford truck ad shown appeals to some consumers with a desire for power—researchers have also found that traits alone are not always an accurate predictor of consumer behavior. By combining trait information with statistics such as age or income, marketers can obtain more reliable indicators of buyers' behavior, such as customers' willingness to try healthier food items.[20] What marketers can do to appeal to personality traits is to endow their products and brands with personalities that key into consumer needs.

Products and Their Personalities

As we saw in the earlier discussion of self-concept, people tend to shop in stores and choose goods and services that make them feel comfortable. Plus, as consumers, we want the goods we buy (such as apparel, home furnishings, and automobiles) to say something about us, to reflect our personas. We tend to look at products as symbols of certain qualities; the study of symbols and their meanings is called **semiotics.** Consider the attorney who wears a gray pinstripe suit, white shirt, and regimental tie. In semiotic terms, these product symbols say he is smart, conservative, and well organized. The real estate agent in her designer dress and matching coat, accessorized with Ferragamo pumps and Prada handbag, conveys an image of style, knowledge, and success. Semiotics is important to marketers because consumers often express their personality characteristics through the symbolic meanings of the brands they purchase.

Studies by Alan Hirsch, published in his book, *What Flavor Is Your Personality?,* show the relationship between consumers' personality characteristics and their ice cream preferences. Participants were given a battery of standard personality tests and then asked to select their favorite among six flavors of ice cream. Six personality types appeared. You would think that respondents choosing vanilla would be mild with bland personalities. Not so! According to the findings, they are risk takers, even overcommitted. The results are summarized in Table 6.1.[21]

BRAND PERSONALITY

Because our personalities are reflected in the products we choose, marketers seek to create personalities for their brands that match what we want. For example, at a recent Paris auto show, Daimler-Chrysler promoted its new Mercedes-Benz as being innovative, created with passion, and possessing high quality.[22] Advertisers give certain brands human characteristics that relate to personality characteristics, like those of friends whom consumers would like to associate with; this is called **brand personification.** Consider the following list

Fashion and Semiotics: The Hidden Meanings of a Style

When we look at a startling fashion, or any new product for that matter, we try to make sense of it. The design might incorporate features or details that seem to have a significance that goes beyond a simple fashion statement, and—consciously or unconsciously—we attempt to decipher the designer's intent, to decode the symbols, within the context of our own experience and our own culture.

The interpretation of symbols and their meanings is the work of semioticians. In marketing, semiotics are particularly important in revealing what a product connotes to consumers, so that advertisers can attach appropriate symbols that will resonate with target customers and enhance their view of the product. The use of symbols is especially pervasive in fashion. As costume and fashion historian Pauline Weston Thomas wrote, "Fashion is a language of signs, symbols, and iconography that non-verbally communicate meanings about individuals and groups."

Consider the fall showing of designers Viktor Horsing and Rolf Snoeren in Paris a few years ago. Their collection featured polished trench coats and silvery frocks—yet on the runway, each of the models was outfitted with a grid mask, giving the effect, as noted in *Women's Wear Daily*, of a cross between a fencer and Hannibal Lector. What on earth did the masks symbolize? That depends on an individual's viewpoint and origin. One interpretation could be misogyny, a hatred of women; another could be a kind of cultural malaise, reflecting anxiety about political conditions of the day. A third could be a form of homage to Muslim culture, in which women's faces are hidden. Or, for some people, it might have been simply that the mask was an "in" trend of fashion that season.

Another example of symbolism in fashion relates to the punk movement. The impact of punk on high fashion was so profound that New York's Metropolitan Museum of Art mounted a Costume Institution exhibit in 2013 titled "PUNK: Chaos to Couture," illustrating how haute couture and ready-to-wear have borrowed heavily on punk's visual symbols.

Among the highlights of the exhibit were galleries spotlighting different aspects of punk's central do-it-yourself concept, including: "D.I.Y. Hardware," focusing on couture's incorporation of punk's iconic studs, spikes, chains, zippers, safety pins, and the like; "D.I.Y. Bricolage," highlighting ways in which fashion adopted punk's use of recycled materials from trash and consumer culture; and "D.I.Y. Destroy," examining the effect of punk's "rip-it-to-shreds" spirit on fashion design, via torn and shredded garments.

Clearly, 40 years after the movement's birth, the symbols of punk are still resonating—but would everyone have the same interpretation of their meaning? Noted a review of the Met exhibit in the *New

(continued)

York Daily News, "While the real-life punks loitering in Tompkins Square Park might scowl and toss expletives at the idea of their subculture on display, no one can deny that the visuals of fringe culture have become powerful symbol—which is exactly why it's catnip for designers."

Sources: "Ladies and Gentlemen," *Women's Wear Daily.* February 28, 2006, pp. 6 and 7; Stephanie Rosenbloom, "The Obscure and Uncertain Semiotics of Fashion," *New York Times,*" March 5, 2006, Section 4, p. 16; Pauline Weston Thomas, "Theories of Fashion Costume and Fashion History," *Fashion-Era.com,* http://www.fashion-era.com/sociology_semiotics.htm; Metropolitan Museum of Art, "Punk Fashion Is Focus of Costume Institute Exhibition at The Metropolitan Museum of Art," News release, May 9, 2013; Sheila McClear, "Punk's Influence on Fashion Is on Display at Metropolitan Museum of Art's 'Punk: Chaos to Couture,'" *New York Daily News,* May 5, 2013, http://www.nydailynews.com/life-style/fashion/punk-fashions-display-met-punk-chaos-couture-article-1.1334338.

TABLE 6.1 Selected Ice Cream Flavors and Personality Characteristics

Ice Cream Flavor	Personality Characteristics
Vanilla	Colorful, gregarious risk takers, possibly overcommitted, impulsive, set high goals, enjoy close relationships
Double Chocolate Chunk	Charming, lively, want attention, extroverts, romantic, trustworthy, followers rather than leaders
Strawberries and Cream	Shy, but emotionally strong, have high standards, can seem cranky and irritable, pessimistic
Banana Cream Pie	Easy-going, well-adjusted, good listeners, good marital partner
Chocolate Chip	Competitors, go-getters, can't stand losing, charming, generous
Butter Pecan	Set high standards, ethical, fair, tend to be rigid, aggressive in athletics

Source: Alan Hirsch, *What Flavor Is Your Personality?* Naperville, IL: Sourcebooks, 2001, pp. 69–71.

of characteristics and sample brands that have been promoted to reflect those characteristics:

- *Sincere, down-to-earth, family-oriented.* These terms could be used to describe GE, Hallmark, or Coca-Cola, products that are respected like a well-regarded friend.
- *Young, modern, outgoing.* In the soft drink category, this describes Pepsi, a friend to hang out with during free time.
- *Competent, influential, accomplished.* Hewlett-Packard and the *Wall Street Journal* are representative of these characteristics, like a business leader or teacher you respect for his or her achievements.
- *Sophisticated, wealthy, condescending.* These terms might describe brands such as Chanel or Baccarat, as opposed to Tommy Hilfiger or Mikasa. It has been suggested that a consumer's relationship with the first two brands might resemble one with a rich relative.[23]

In his book *Why Customers Do What They Do*, Marshal Cohen, chief industry analyst for the research organization The NPD Group, declares, "Branding is what makes the consumer associate himself or herself with the product. Branding gives the product personality and image, and, even more important, gives the consumer something to share with others."[24] Figure 6.10 depicts some of the personality characteristics that marketers work to incorporate into their brands.

HOW MARKETERS CREATE BRAND PERSONALITY

Marketers create personalities for companies as well as for products. Consider Macy's, for example; many people think of this retailer in terms of wide assortments, up-to-date fashions, and fair prices. The goal of a successful effort to create an effective brand personality is to build brand equity; that is, to gain

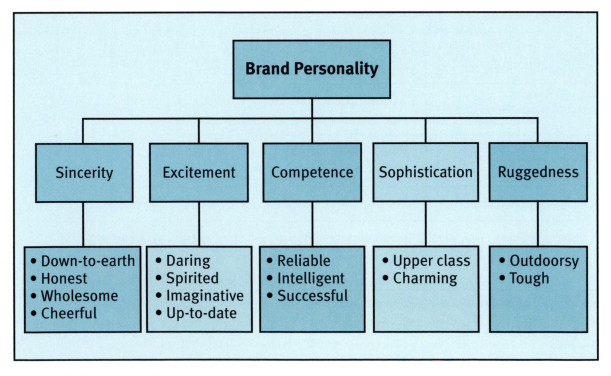

FIGURE 6.10 Brand personality.

a loyal customer for the long term. In developing a brand personality for a product or a company, one way is to build a personality that closely resembles that of the consumer. Following are the steps for developing a brand personality:

1. Define the target market.
2. Determine what those customers want, need, and like.
3. Create a consumer personality profile.
4. Build a product personality to coincide.[25]

Companies such as Levi-Strauss research their target markets thoroughly and find that building brand personalities is very useful. The company discovered the following characteristics for its master brand personality: original, masculine, sexy, youthful, and rebellious. For its signature button-fly 501 jeans, Levi's created the following brand personality that the company could market worldwide: romantic, sexually attractive, rebellious, strong, resourceful, and independent.[26]

COLOR AND BRAND PERSONALITY

According to research done by NPD Group, the main external influence on customer purchases is style (which includes color), followed by price, comfort, and fit; this is true not only for apparel but also for household appliances and electronics.[27] In describing how Apple changed the look of the office, home, and classroom by introducing computers in colorful housings (which strongly contrasted to the drab off-white and gray electronics then in use), graphic designer and consultant Beatrice Santiccioli said, "Giving things color is a way of inventing personalities."

Think of the image that color conveys for fashion organizations: The cosmetics firm Elizabeth Arden

and the online gift purveyor Red Envelope are nearly as recognizable as Coca-Cola for their use of that color; Alexander Julian, creator of apparel and home furnishings, is known for his signature "Colours" line; Clinique and Tiffany have their own shades of green and blue; Chanel and Nike make great use of black and white; Dior's gray is known worldwide. Even Kermit the Frog, who used to sing, "It's not easy being green," changed his tune when he saw a Ford Fusion Hybrid! Some colors have certain personality characteristics, as indicated in Table 6.2.

LET'S TALK

What additional fashion businesses or individuals can you think of that are associated with certain colors? What personality characteristics do these colors convey?

To encourage consumers to want the newest in fashions, and to move along the product life cycle, the apparel and home furnishings industries introduce new color combinations each season. Coordinating this effort, color-forecasting organizations provide advance trend information to manufacturers, retailers, and the media, enabling them to synchronize production and promotion. These organizations include companies such as the Color Marketing Group, and associations such as the Color Association of the United States (CAUS) and the International Color Authority (ICA).

In addition to the internal influences on consumer behavior, such as learning, motivation, attitude, and personality, that we have seen in Part II of this text, in Part III we will look at external factors

TABLE 6.2 Personality-Like Associations of Selected Colors

Color	Personality Link	Marketing Insights
Blue	Commands respect, authority	• America's favored color • IBM holds the title to blue • Associated with club soda • Men seek products packaged in blue • Houses painted blue are avoided • Low-calorie, skim milk • Coffee in a blue can perceived as "mild"
Yellow	Caution, novelty, temporary, warmth	• Eyes register it fastest • Coffee in a yellow can tasted "weak" • Stops traffic • Sells a house
Green	Secure, natural, relaxed or easygoing, living things	• Good work environment • Associated with vegetables and chewing gum • Canada Dry ginger ale sales increased when it changed sugar-free package from red to green and white
Red	Human, exciting, hot, passionate, strong	• Makes food "smell" better • Coffee in a red can perceived as "rich" • Women have a preference for bluish red • Men have a preference for yellowish red • Coca-Cola "owns" red
Orange	Powerful, affordable, informal	• Draws attention quickly
Brown	Informal and relaxed, masculine, nature	• Coffee in a dark-brown can was "too strong" • Men seek products packaged in brown
White	Goodness, purity, chastity, cleanliness, delicacy, refinement, formality	• Suggests reduced calories • Pure and wholesome food • Clean, bath products, feminine
Black	Sophistication, power, authority, mystery	• Powerful clothing • High-tech electronics
Silver, Gold, Platinum	Regal, wealthy, stately	• Suggests premium price

Source: Schiffman and Kanuk, Table 5–9, p. 141. *Original source:* Bernice Kanner, "Color Schemes," *New York* magazine, April 3, 1989, pp. 22–23.

such as family and society that constitute other revealing components of the why of the buy.

Summary

Our personalities are made up of those individual psychological characteristics that routinely influence the way we react to our surroundings. Four significant areas of personality theory are (1) Freud's psychoanalytic theory, (2) social-cultural theories, (3) self-concept theories, and (4) trait theories.

According to psychoanalytic theory, the unconscious, pleasure-seeking id often conflicts with the superego, or conscience; the realistic ego mediates these conflicts to create harmony. Since this activity occurs at the unconscious level and we may not be aware of the reasoning behind some purchase decisions, marketers use motivational research and focus groups in part to understand unconscious buying motives. Shared memories of the past, archetypes, can also influence our purchasing habits, as can the sense of superiority that some products strive to convey.

Social-cultural theories tell us that the conscious mind plays a big role in our decision making, and that our decision making may be compliant, aggressive, or detached. Each of these responses calls for a unique marketing approach, appealing to that specific characteristic.

Self-concept and self-image theories identify the many roles that humans play—that is, our multiple selves, such as student, employee, son, or daughter. Also, privately, our actual selves represent the way we are, and our ideal selves, the way we would like to be. Our social self-image is the way we appear to others; our ideal social self-image is the way we would like to appear to the world. Our self-esteem is made up of our positive and negative opinions of ourselves and our concept of self-worth. The term "extended selves" is used to describe the relationship between ourselves and our possessions.

Trait theories seek to examine and describe the distinct characteristics that distinguish us from others. Research in personality traits useful to fashion marketers includes: (1) extroversion and introversion, (2) negativism, (3) desire for knowledge, (4) innovation and opinion leadership, (5) need for stimulation, and (6) need for affection, achievement, and power. For example, when offering new color combinations or fabric innovations, fashion marketers can key into consumer traits such as the desire for knowledge and the desire to innovate.

Products, and often the symbols representing them, also have personalities. Semiotics is the study of symbols and their meanings. Consumers express their personalities through the brand symbols they purchase. Advertisers often give brands human characteristics, called brand personification, in hopes that consumers will respond by purchasing those brands that relate to their personalities.

In creating product or brand personalities, marketers go through steps that include defining the target market and building a product personality to match. Color adds personality to products, and certain colors contain specific personality traits (for example, red represents excitement in some Western cultures). Each season the fashion industry offers a new color palette providing fresh product choices to consumers, keying in to consumer and brand personalities.

KEY TERMS

Actual self

Archetypes

Brand personification

Compulsive buying behavior

Ego

Extended self

Extroverts

Fashion influentials

Fashion innovators

Id

Ideal self

Ideal social self-image

Introverts

Motivational research

Multiple selves

Need for achievement

Need for affiliation

Need for cognition (NC)

Need for power

Neurosis

Optimal stimulation level (OSL)

Psychoanalytic theory

Self-concept

Self-concept theory

Self-esteem

Semiotics

Social self-image

Superego

Traits

QUESTIONS FOR REVIEW

1. Name and describe the three components of personality according to psychoanalytic theory.

2. What were Karen Horney's and Joel Cohen's respective contributions to the social-cultural theory of personality?

3. Explain the various "selves" in the self-concept theory. What is the relationship between self-concept and buying behavior?

4. Cite the six personality traits presented in the text, and for each identify a marketing strategy that fashion businesses might use to target that trait.

5. Why are many fashion goods marketers concerned with creating brand personalities for their products?

ACTIVITIES

1. Select two apparel, home furnishings, or other fashion goods advertisements with origins in psychoanalytic theory, and two ads that stem from social-cultural theories. What is the main point of each ad?

2. With a classmate or by yourself, visit a fashion retail store where you are comfortable shopping and that appeals to your self-concept. Note the store layout and displays, the merchandise, and the salespeople. Determine how each of these elements enhances your self-concept. Then visit a store where you are not necessarily comfortable and that does not harmonize with your self-concept. Describe the displays,

merchandise, and sales force, and contrast your findings from the second store with those of the first. Which store element has the greatest influence, positive or negative, on your self-concept? Why?

3. Develop a profile of a college student based on the selected traits described in this chapter. How might fashion businesses use this information?

4. Describe your color preferences for apparel and home furnishings. Based on what you have read, how do these relate to your personality? Select five advertisements for apparel and/or home furnishings that appeal to you because of color, and state how the promotion matches your color preferences and personality. For more information on your color preferences, take an Internet color quiz such as the one given at www.colorquiz.com.

5. Describe two fashion brands that portray definite personalities. Explain the target market for each of these brands according to their brand personalities. State the relationship between the personality of the product and that of the targeted customer.

MINI-PROJECT

Create a customer profile and corresponding brand personality with at least four components for each of two fashion brands within the same product classification, for example, jeans, men's suits, or dining or living room sets.

REFERENCES

1. Henry Asseal, *Consumer Behavior: A Strategic Approach* (Boston: Houghton Mifflin Company, 2004), p. 295.
2. Sigmund Freud—Life and Work: www.freudfile.org/.
3. Eric Arnold et al., *Consumers,* Chapter 11 (New York: McGraw-Hill Higher Education, 2002).
4. Gianni Versace obituary, *The Guardian,* July 16, 1997.
5. Asseal.
6. Karen Horney, *Neurosis and Human Growth* (New York: Norton, 1950).
7. Joel B. Cohen, "An Interpersonal Orientation to the Study of Consumer Behavior," *Journal of Marketing Research* 4 (August 1967): 270–278; P. K. Tyagi, "Validation of the CAD Instrument: A Replication," in *Advances in Consumer Research* (Association for Consumer Research, Ann Arbor, Michigan) 10 (1983): 112–114.
8. Russell Belk, "Possessions and the Extended Self," *Journal of Consumer Research* 15 (September 1988): 139–168.
9. Amy J. Morgan, "The Evolving Self in Consumer Research," *Advances in Consumer Research* (Association for Consumer Research, Provo, Utah) 20 (1992): 429–432.
10. Carl G. Jung, *Man and His Symbols* (Garden City, NJ: Doubleday, 1964).
11. Todd A. Mooradian, "Personality and Ad-Evoked Feelings: The Case for Extraversion and Neuroticism," *Journal of the Academy of Marketing Science* 24 (Spring 1996): 99–109.
12. Susan Powell Mantel and Frank R. Kardes, "The Role of Direction of Comparison, Attribute-Based Processing, and Attitude-Based

Processing in Consumer Preference," *Journal of Consumer Research* 25 (March 1999): 335–352.

13. Leon J. Schiffman and Leslie L. Kanuk, *Consumer Behavior,* 8th ed. (Upper Saddle River, NJ: Pearson Prentice Hall, 2004), p. 131.

14. Evelyn J. Brannon, *Fashion Forecasting,* 2nd ed. (New York: Fairchild Publications, Inc., 2005), p. 92.

15. Elaine Stone, *The Dynamics of Fashion,* 2nd ed. (New York: Fairchild Publications, Inc., 2004), pp. 59–61.

16. P. S. Rajou, "Optimum Stimulation Levels in Relationship to Personality, Demographics and Exploratory Behavior," *Journal of Consumer Research* 7 (December 1980): 273.

17. Marvin Zuckerman, *Sensation Seeking: Beyond the Optimal Level of Arousal* (Hillsdale, NJ: Lawrence Erlbaum, 1979).

18. Jan-Benedict, E. M. Steenkamp, and Hans Baumgartner, "The Role of Optimum Stimulation Level in Exploratory Consumer Behavior," *Journal of Consumer Research* 19 (December 1992): 434–448.

19. D. G. Winter and A. J. Stewart, "The Power Motive," in H. London and J. Exner (eds.), *Dimensions of Personality* (New York: Wiley, 1978).

20. Gordon R. Foxall and Ronald E. Goldsmith, "Personality and Consumer Research: Another Look," *Journal of Marketing Research Society* 30, no. 2 (April 1988): 111–125.

21. Alan R. Hirsch, *What Flavor Is Your Personality?* (Naperville, IL: Sourcebooks, Inc., 2001).

22. www.idsa.org/idea 2005/b.1082.htm.

23. David A. Aaker, *Building Strong Brands* (Riverside, NJ: Free Press, 1995).

24. Marshal Cohen, *Why Customers Do What They Do* (New York: McGraw-Hill Companies, 2006).

25. www.indiaco.com/resource-center/building-brands-personality.html.

26. Ibid.

27. Cohen, p. 33.

Part III
EXTERNAL FACTORS INFLUENCE FASHION CONSUMERS

OBVIOUSLY, consumers do not make buying decisions in a vacuum. In addition to internal motivations, outside influences have a profound effect on fashion consumers—the focus of Part III.

Chapter 7 discusses the roles that family status, age, and life cycle stages play in consumers' purchasing behavior. The variety of social influences, both online and offline, on consumers' fashion choices is examined in Chapter 8; and Chapter 9 describes how marketers create profiles of consumers, using demographics, psychographics, and value-driven behaviors to target an ideal customer audience for their products.

Age, Family, and Life Cycle Influences

WHAT DO I NEED TO KNOW ABOUT AGE, FAMILY, AND LIFE CYCLE INFLUENCES?

✔ Why and how a consumer's age influences his or her purchasing behavior and product choices

✔ How the U.S. family has evolved and how the changes have altered the way marketers connect with consumers

✔ The stages of both the traditional and 21st-century family life cycles

✔ How the roles of various household decision makers influence the consumption process

The makeup of the American population is changing. Americans vary greatly in their attitudes, opinions, and lifestyles, and appear to be splintering into more and more diverse groups with more and more distinct behaviors and purchasing practices. What does this mean for marketers? Will a time come when marketers will have to anticipate and accommodate the desires of an even greater variety of consumers, with needs, attitudes, values, and expectations so vast that eventually there will be product and service options too numerous to count, and target markets so disparate that consumer researchers will continuously be identifying new groups and looking for new and better ways to satisfy them? What a nightmare! Well, Future Marketers, wake up—that time is already here.

The Changing Face of the American Consumer

It seems that every few months we hear about a new group of buyers with unique preferences and habits, along with new theories regarding the attitudes and motivations that lie behind those consumers' purchasing decisions. These groups are often identified by age—and by extension, by their current stage of life and family situation. You're surely familiar with many of these segments—designated by names like Millennials, GenXers, Boomers, and Tweens. What makes these segments important to the study of consumer behavior is that each has its own methods for learning about, choosing, and purchasing goods.

AGE INFLUENCES PURCHASING BEHAVIOR

No matter how else marketers "slice and dice" the population into homogeneous segments, there is one variable that appears to govern both customer preferences and the strategies marketers employ to reach those customers. That variable is age. Age is one of the biggest determinants of what people want; with changes in age come changes in the products and services a person seeks. Think about it. At age 3, most of us are mainly interested in toys. By age 10, we may have graduated to video games. At

16, many of us are focused on having a car; at 23, our own apartment; and at 30, perhaps a family and a house with all that goes with it. Clearly, each age brings different priorities and desires (Figure 7.1).

And segmenting goes even further. Not that long ago, the "birth to 12" age group was viewed as one unit, all of the children assumed to be quite satisfied with a variety of colorful toys, games, bicycles, dolls, and the like. However, current research indicates that marketers should no longer approach this age group as a whole, but should treat it as four distinct segments: newborns to 3-year-olds, 3- to 5-year-olds, 5- to 8-year-olds, and 8- to 12-year-olds. Why? Because members of each of these age groups demonstrate very different preferences from one another.

Today's children also differ from their parents in that they are much more technologically savvy; they've grown up in a world with ready access to gaming gadgetry and digital devices. While television remains the primary medium for advertising to kids, marketers are also looking at new media that children increasingly use. Of course, products and marketing campaigns still should be fun; after all, no matter how techno-savvy they are, 3- to 12-year-olds are still children. And, because they're still children, marketers need to demonstrate strong social consciousness and avoid crossing ethical boundaries.

Let's turn to teenagers. Generally speaking, today's 13- to 17-year-olds have developed a view of consumption that differs from their parents. They are also at an age of finding their own "voice," so may seem to purposely seek out their parents' disapproval regarding things they choose to wear or buy. A recent Back to School Survey, for example,

FIGURE 7.1 Buyers come in all sizes and ages. Studying family life cycle patterns has made it obvious that as we move from phase to phase, our purchasing habits evolve.

found that traditional back-to-school shopping at physical stores is stressful for about two-thirds of parents and teens alike. Among the stressors for the students in the survey, who ranged in age from 12 to 17, were arguing with parents about buying items not directly related to school, and disagreeing about how much to spend, fashion/style choices, desirable brands, and which stores to shop. Teens and their parents were also in disagreement when it came to choosing what to buy for starting the new school year, with popular items among students—but not parents—including tech gadgets such as laptops, smartphones, and tablets/e-readers.[1]

Teenagers today are accustomed to being the target of sales pitches, and tend to be more aware and sometimes skeptical of sales techniques as a

Children in Marketers' Crosshairs

Kids love to play games on their parents' mobile phones and tablets. But what happens when they suddenly run up huge credit card bills by making "in-app" purchases of products or services within those games—a capability that any Internet-enabled mobile device, such as an iPhone or iPad, is designed to facilitate? And they do so without their parents' knowledge or consent? In one case, the result was that Apple had to settle a lawsuit to the tune of $100 million, acknowledging the inadequate protections against excessive spending in mobile games, many of which are targeted to children yet allow microtransactions that show up later on the Apple user's credit card.

The controversy surrounding marketing to children is hardly a new phenomenon. Forty years ago, concerned parents and others were pushing for more stringent standards, which led, as one example, to the creation of the Children's Advertising Review Unit of the Council for Better Business Bureaus, established to promote responsible advertising to children under 12. But that hasn't stopped marketers from doing all they can to reach impressionable young minds. In fact, in a push from marketers and wave of eagerness to deregulate many industries during Ronald Reagan's presidency, rules regarding advertising to children were completely gutted. A recent documentary, *Consuming Kids,* looks at the impact of that deregulation and the resulting boom in marketing to children, citing concerns of health-care professionals, children's advocates, and industry insiders as it examines the issue.

The film pulls no punches in demonstrating that turning kids into loyal, lifelong consumers—consumers who will influence the spending of the whole family—is a central mission of the multibillion-dollar marketing industry. Highlighted are ways in which marketers employ tactics from psychology, anthropology, and neuroscience in their efforts to influence American children and mold them into a strong, profitable customer base for their brand.

Yes, marketing to children has turned into a true science. Research has told marketers that when children see the same commercial over and over again, they are more likely to remember what product was being advertised. What's more, marketers have learned how to create ads that can actually make children ask their parent or other adult repeatedly for a product—a tactic that frequently wears on parents' nerves to the point that they relent and buy the product just to stop the pestering. Among the other questionable techniques marketers employ to influence these youngest of consumers are stealth advertising, viral marketing, branded characters, computer-generated special effects, celebrity endorsements, and giveaways.

(continued)

POINT OF VIEW 7.1 (continued)

Along with research to benefit marketers, other studies have been conducted to better analyze the effect of advertising on young brains and psyches. One such research area involves how children's ability to understand commercial messages—and equally important, to understand their purpose and intent—differs at different ages. For instance, studies have found that children younger than age eight believe that commercials' purpose is to help them make decisions about purchases, and they are oblivious to the fact that the ads actually aim to persuade them to buy a certain product or brand.

As children develop, however, sometime between ages 7 and 11 they begin to realize that the purpose of advertising is to sell them products. But even then, they remain impressionable. It isn't until adolescence, around age 12 and older, that children's thought processes mature to the point where they can reason abstractly—at which point they understand much more clearly what advertisers' motives are and start to develop a healthy cynicism about what they see and hear in advertising.

Sources: Yannick LeJacq, "Apple Offers Compensation to Parents for Children's Excessive In-App Purchases," *International Business Times,* February 26, 2013, www.ibtimes.com/apple-offers-compensation-parents-childrens-excessive-app-purchases-1104974; Dr. Mercola, "'Consuming Kids' Reveals Shocking Tactics Used to Manipulate Your Children's Preferences and Habits," *Mercola.com,* June 8, 2013, http://articles.mercola.com/sites/articles/archive/2013/06/08/children-marketing.aspx; Sandra L. Calvert, "Children as Consumers: Advertising and Marketing," *Journal: Children and Electronic Media* 18 (1), Spring 2008, http://futureofchildren.org/publications/journals/article/index.xml?journalid=32&articleid=62&sectionid=304; D. Kunkel, APA Task Force on Advertising and Children: "Psychological Issues in the Increasing Commercialization of Childhood," Washington, DC: American Psychological Association, 2004.

result. And because today's multitasking teens are besieged by competing advertising and other promotional messaging—whether it's a commercial on TV, a text or tweet on their tablet or smartphone, or ads popping up on the myriad websites they visit—marketers work hard to position products in ways that really stand out; otherwise, they'll just become part of the clutter that teens have learned to ignore. Knowing what's important to teenagers (customization, green products, social networking) and zeroing in on their interests and habits is the most effective way for marketers to get teens' attention.

The Millennial market segment, also referred to as Generation Y, is made up of consumers who are currently roughly 18 to 34—the first age group that grew up with computers and cell phones. They are old enough to remember the 9/11 tragedy and to have

Teens to Parents: Get Off My Social Network

Has Facebook been getting less cool? Ask a teenager and the answer might be a thunderous "yes!" Consider this: The average age of U.S. Facebook users recently jumped from 38 to 41 in just a 2-year period, while the total number of active users fell by more than 7 percent in 6 months. And Tumblr surpassed Facebook—61 percent to 55 percent—as the social website/app teens are using most, according to research by Right Mix Marketing.

So what's going on? For one thing, by 2012 almost three quarters of moms were using Facebook, with nearly half of parents joining the network as a way to keep tabs on their children, Right Mix Marketing found. In fact, nearly three quarters admit to checking their child's page several times a week. The result: an exodus of teenagers from the site, with the primary reason being because their parents are increasingly active on the network. Getting more specific, one in three teens say they're embarrassed by the comments their parents post, and 30 percent would like to "unfriend" their parents, feeling they no longer get the privacy they seek on the site, the research shows.

Those findings could spell bad news for apparel companies that, after years of hesitation, had at last begun using Facebook as a marketing tool—and using the social network specifically to communicate with younger customers who tend to spend more per purchase than older consumers. But perhaps those brands will simply follow their target audience to one of the other social media venues teens frequent, including Tumblr, Twitter, Instagram, and Snapchat.

Sources: Tom Treanor, "Are Teenagers Abandoning Facebook? #Infographic," *Right Mix Marketing,* April 17, 2013, http://www.rightmixmarketing .com/facebook-tips-tools/teenagers-facebook-infographic/; Matthieu Guinebault, "Are Teenagers Deserting Facebook?," *FashionMag,* April 24, 2013, http://us.fashionmag.com/news/Are-teenagers-deserting-Facebook-,325958.html#.UmmR7RCFf8k.

experienced first-hand the challenges brought about by the recent economic crisis and recession, high unemployment rate, and stagnant wages, all of which have left them with understandable feelings of insecurity. Members of this market segment tend to look for value in the products they buy, and seek items that are environmentally safe, connected to a cause, and community friendly. For example, they may choose to shop at the local farmers' market to express their social responsibility; and their compassion regarding social issues extends to their brand preferences as well. Research shows that Millennials will seek out and buy brands that support a cause that aligns with their values, such as Nike, Target, and Gap.[2]

Of course, like any other sizable segment, this group has diverse members, but for marketers' purposes, Millennials share a common attraction to well-designed, well-performing products that imply luxury but are of good value. A recent survey of adults with a household income of at least $75,000 found that those aged 18 to 33 were more optimistic about their financial situation and planned to spend more than their older counterparts. The study also showed that Millennials care about getting superior service and exclusive products. That doesn't mean, however, that they're extravagant: The majority of them spent less than $250 on their most recent luxury purchase.[3]

Generation X, the generation born roughly between the early 1960s and early 1980s, is characterized by both spending a lot and spending carefully. Currently spanning ages from about 35 to 54, most Gen Xers have the money to make purchases, so price is not necessarily the deciding factor in their decisions, even though many are still raising children. Members of this market segment are also quite comfortable using technology, and their purchasing habits reflect that. Other priorities for people in this age group include fitness, health, and adventure. Marketing efforts directed at this group should appeal to their desired state of well-being and their focus on "getting out there and doing things," such as taking exotic trips and participating in extreme sports.

The Baby Boom generation, those born after World War II from about 1946 to 1964, is one of the most powerful consumer segments, due in part to its sheer size. This group numbers some 76 million, or about a quarter of the total U.S. population.

Although the oldest of the boomers are already at retirement age, many are energetic and prosperous, and want to hold off old age as long as they can. Thus, they are giving marketers opportunities in the areas of finance, hospitality, and wellness. Products and services that promise to keep them youthful are in high demand. Many people in this group have enjoyed the benefits of higher education, real estate investments, and so on, but they are still concerned about the future, particularly following the recent recession, which took its toll on the savings and income of all but the very wealthiest Americans. After all, living longer could increase their need for extended care. Today's marketers are hurrying to accommodate a rapidly growing population of seniors who inevitably will become less mobile as they reach their eighties. Product enhancements for the home, such as easily accessible bathtubs, special lighting, safer kitchen equipment, and senior-friendly technology are all intended to meet the needs of older consumers.

Data on population trends, age-related preferences, and other valuable information available through the government and market research enables companies to develop new products and services in a timely manner, advertise in media most likely to be accessed and trusted by their target markets, devise persuasive and effective promotions (including making prices appear more appealing), and ultimately move goods and services into the hands of consumers more efficiently. Marketers also have to learn the special language cues that can evoke responses from members of different age groups. At each stage of life, there are certain words that hold greater meaning than they did in the past

Table 7.1 "Buy Words"—Marketing Approaches That Appeal to Different Age Groups

Phase	Phrase
Teens	This is what you *need* in order to *belong.*
Twenties	This is what your *friends expect of you.*
Thirties	This is for a *good, solid person like you.*
Forties	This is what the *pros and experts* buy.
Fifties	This is something to *judge for yourself.*
Sixties+	This is very *effective* and *economical.*

Source: www.wcupa.edu/_Academics/sch_cas.psy/CareerPaths /Consumer/.

or might in the future; using those words effectively can be an important marketing tool. This idea of "a phrase for a phase" is illustrated in Table 7.1.

FAMILY INFLUENCES ON CONSUMER BEHAVIOR

There is a multitude of powerful forces that help determine purchasing behavior, most of which derive from observing the actions of various **reference groups,** any person or group serving as a point of comparison or frame of reference for an individual when that individual is forming his own beliefs and behaviors. (See Chapter 8 for an in-depth discussion of reference groups.) The first and primary reference group a child uses to gauge his or her behavior is the family. No matter what your age, you can probably remember a time when you were a child, shopping with your parents or grandparents, and how you were expected to behave. Perhaps you had to dress up a little to go to a fancy store. Maybe you were told in advance that you would not be getting a toy during that visit—and that there would be no whining or else you'd be taken straight home. Or you might have been asked what you thought about a certain item and then treated to ice cream for being "good." Consumer researchers have discovered that the behaviors and values parents teach their children and continuously reinforce as they grow are the ones that will guide them through their teens and into adulthood. Although children have numerous experiences each day outside the home, the family remains the strongest influence.

Today's Family

Traditionally, a **family** is defined as a group of individuals who live together and are related either by blood, adoption, or marriage. Some of these groups are **nuclear families:** the parents and children living together; some are **extended families:** grandparents, aunts, uncles, and other relatives may also live with the nuclear family. Curiously, although many people in the United States view the nuclear family as "typical," it is by no means the norm. In fact, that traditional view of the American family does not represent the majority of the groups of people who live together today. Rather, today's "family" is more often thought of as a **household,** a term that refers to any single person or group of persons who live together in a residential setting, regardless of whether or not they're related. Many researchers agree that the American family began to change soon after World War II, when more married women began working outside the home. The changes continued with the introduction of birth control, enabling women (and men) to better plan the size of their family; with fewer children to care for, women began to feel they had more opportunities to pursue a career. Additional changes in family structure, made possible by the evolution of societal norms, include increased acceptance of both cohabitation without marriage and nonmarital births. For example, unmarried heterosexual couples living together increased by 40.2 percent between 2000 and 2010.[4] And children born to unmarried women accounted for 3.8 percent of recorded births in 1940, while in 2013, 48 percent of first births took place outside of wedlock.[5]

Many different kinds of households exist today beyond the traditional nuclear family of married father and mother with children. There are **nontraditional families,** including single-parent families, step-families, blended families, and families with two same-sex parents, as well as households consisting of single people living alone, unmarried heterosexual and gay couples, married couples without children or whose children are not living at home, two or more single people who are roommates, and elderly parents who live with their grown children. Needless to say, the family of today takes many forms (Figure 7.2).

Marketers obviously need to keep track of the ongoing evolution of the modern household. As the composition of the family changes, the needs and wants of each household change—hence, the rise of furniture stores that cater to singles, resorts that

FIGURE 7.2 Today's definition of "family" reflects the changes that have taken place in American society over the past decades; that's why consumer researchers often use the more apt term "household."

The Changing Face of American Families

The traditional nuclear family, consisting of a married straight couple with children, may not be called "traditional" for much longer. Based on statistics from the 2010 census, that category of family dropped from 51.7 percent of households in 2000 to 48.4 percent in 2010—marking the first time since census data on families began to be collected in 1940 that less than half of U.S. households are made up of husband-wife couples with their own children.

Indeed, data from the 2010 census indicates a dramatic rise in nontraditional households in America. The biggest gains since the previous census were among households of unmarried couples, although the category represents just 6.6 percent of total. Those unmarried couple households involving opposite-sex partners grew by 40.2 percent, while those with unmarried same-sex couples increased by 80.4 percent. What can't be known from that last statistic, however, is whether there's really been such a huge increase in same-sex couples living together since 2000, or if changing societal attitudes simply made them more comfortable to say so.

Family households remain the biggest segment, at 66.4 percent, but the largest increases were among male householders with no spouse present, a group that grew by 35.6 percent for those without children and 27.3 percent with children. Despite those increases, the number of family households headed by females numbered almost three times as many as family households headed by males. And among nonfamily households, the census showed more than 17 million females living alone, while men living alone numbered 13.9 million.

The wealth of data available from the census also reveals characteristics of households of different racial and ethnic groups. For example, more Hispanics or Latinos (roughly 78 percent) and Asians (nearly three quarters) indicated they lived in family households than did whites (about 65 percent).

Sources: U.S. Census, "Households and Families: 2010," Census Brief, http://www.census.gov/prod/cen2010/briefs/c2010br-14.pdf; Doris Nhan, "Census: More in U.S. Report Nontraditional Households," *National Journal,* May 1, 2012, www.nationaljournal.com/thenextamerica /demographics/census-more-in-u-s-report-nontraditional-households-20120430.

target families, communities exclusively for retirees, and do-it-yourself classes for women who take care of their own cars and build their own sundecks.

Regardless of composition, the spending patterns of household members primarily depend on their age, income, relationships to one another, and the presence or absence of children. These factors are all part of the consumer decision-making process, which involves multiple influences and steps that we'll discuss in depth in Chapter 12. For now, however, we will focus our attention on the family, since it is the primary influencer and the unit that teaches each member the skills eventually needed to make buying decisions.

THE PRIMARY FUNCTIONS OF A FAMILY

The family, no matter its size and composition, has two main functions:

1. To create security (emotional and financial)
2. To educate and socialize the children

Both functions include preparing children for the future. Encouragement of positive qualities, self-respect, confidence, and the satisfaction of basic needs (as discussed in Chapter 4) all contribute to feelings of security, a sense of safety. Families educate and help prepare children for adulthood through **socialization,** the process of transmitting the skills, attitudes, cultural values, and general knowledge necessary for a person to effectively integrate into society. **Consumer socialization** refers to how children acquire knowledge about products and services, along with various consumption-related skills needed to function as consumers in the marketplace (such as how to politely talk to salespeople, search for bargains, find the best prices). Younger children acquire much of their consumer knowledge from their parents, but adolescents also learn from their peers. Also, children of every age learn consumer knowledge and skills from the media and from advertising. The socialization process continues throughout adulthood, and many lessons learned from our parents stay with us our whole life, with consumer behaviors from childhood still

influencing many of us in later years. Some adults, for example, continue buying the same brands their parents purchased, whether it's breakfast cereal or an automobile. It's not surprising then that developing early brand awareness and loyalty is an important marketing strategy for many companies. This is probably why so many successful fashion designers have introduced children's clothing lines; attracting and keeping loyal customers can never begin too early. The task for marketers is clearly ongoing.

> ## LET'S TALK
>
> *Are there specific skills we all have to learn in order to become productive members of society? What knowledge must we possess in order to successfully interact with others in settings such as classrooms, sporting events, stores, and so on?*

THE FAMILY LIFE CYCLE, DEFINED AND REDEFINED

The **traditional family life cycle** comprises the time-honored stages through which people predictably progress as they age (see Table 7.2); it has been used by marketers for decades as a guideline for the development of new products and the creative strategies used to sell those products. However, since more and more people belong to nontraditional families, for this textbook, we have reworked and expanded these stages to create a representation of the **21st-century family life cycle** (see Table 7.3) in hopes of making the stages more relevant for today's marketing professionals.

Table 7.2 The Traditional Family Life Cycle

Stage	Description
I Bachelorhood	Single, no longer living with parents
II Honeymooner	Newly married
III Full Nester	Parenthood, raising children of varying ages (infants to teenagers)
IV Empty Nester	Post-parenthood, children have left home (parents are still working or newly retired)
V Dissolution	One spouse dies, the widow(er) survives and lives alone

Different Stages, Different Needs and Products

Regardless of whether marketers are targeting members of a traditional or a nontraditional family, two ideas are clear:

1. The various stages of the life cycle create different needs, resulting in different allotments of available money, and different buying behaviors and patterns, all of which lead to the purchase of many different kinds of products and services.

2. For each life cycle stage, marketers must not only develop new products but also new marketing strategies, since what attracts a person in the midst of one stage might not interest him or her during another.

Needs and wants are fluid during each life cycle stage; what might be viewed as superfluous during one stage could be seen as a necessity during another, and vice versa. Consider the following list of products and services. Which do you think a person in the initial stage of parenthood would consider a top priority? Which product or service would be a top priority for someone in the empty-nest stage, or a person in the single household stage?

- Smart car
- Latest tablet computer
- Bed linens
- Personal trainer
- Patio furniture
- Designer handbag
- Life insurance policy
- Stain remover stick
- Lawn care service
- Online subscription to *The New York Times*

And with so many types of different household scenarios now common in the United States, how can marketers determine which household members are actually making the final purchasing decisions?

LET'S TALK

Do you live with another person, or more than one? How do you make purchasing decisions? Who ultimately decides what to buy when it comes to shared items?

Table 7.3 The 21st-Century Family Life Cycle

Stage	Description
I Child/Teen	Living with parent(s), dependent
II Single/Independent	Usually young, dating, living in residence separate from parents for first time, beginning career or job, answers only to self
III New Couple/ Partnership	Living together, adjusting to life together, two incomes usually allow for a comfortable lifestyle
IV Mid-Adulthood	**A. Parenthood**—Three scenarios: • **P-1**—Raising young children, under age 6 • **P-2**—Raising children, ages 6–12 • **P-3**—Raising teenagers *At any point, the following variations can be introduced:* • **V-1**—*Separation*: Creates single-parent household • **V-2**—*Re-coupling*: Single parent remarries, introducing step-parent to household • **V-3**—*Blending*: Step-siblings introduced to household
	B. Partners without children—Partners do not become parents
	C. Single household—Individual remains independent, does not partner
V Empty Nest	Two phases: • Phase 1—*Send-off*: Children have left home, adult(s) still working, looking forward to new experiences • Phase 2—*Retirement*: Adult(s) no longer working, slower pace is adopted
VI Dissolution	One partner dies; remaining partner lives alone or with adult children and possibly grandchildren (infants to teenagers)

Note: This discussion of households and life cycles refers primarily to those in the United States. In other countries, the family relationships and the obligations of the members can be very different (see Chapter 14 for more information).

Source: © Stefani Bay, 2006.

HOUSEHOLD ROLES IN THE FAMILY DECISION-MAKING AND PURCHASING PROCESS

In your family, who decides what to buy? Is it your mother or your father? Your younger sibling? Is it the person who's the most aware of what's new and exciting? Or is it the one who speaks with the loudest voice?

Suppose your family was thinking about buying another car. Who would have the last word on make, model, style, color, special features: the person who was paying for the car, or the one who would be driving it? Or would it be decided by family vote? Suppose your mother knew very little about smart TVs that connect wirelessly to the Internet, but you really wanted her to buy one. How would you approach her? Would you try to explain the benefits of owning one, or maybe have your more persuasive sibling talk to her instead? If she agreed to the purchase, would she stipulate that because the TV is expensive its purchase would involve important trade-offs in purchasing other products for the family? And, if that was the case, would you decide to drop the idea and remind yourself that you can still use the one your dad has when you're at his house on the weekends?

Each household does things differently, of course, but as a unit, all members must participate in some way, so together they can function as a whole. Developing positive interdependence is the key. In other words, members learn to operate as a team. In most households each member has a certain role to play in the decision-making process, whether conscious or unconscious. A **role** can be defined as the behavior expected of a person in a given setting. Roles are often performed automatically, but sometimes they change.

A person in a dominant role in a household might typically decide issues such as a child's bedtime and how chores are delegated (for example, who will wash the dishes, walk the dog, mow the lawn, and so on). One role of a teenager who is very tech-savvy might be to help the rest of the family with computer glitches.

Additionally, each household member usually plays a certain role regarding buying decisions, although these roles may shift slightly, depending on the product sought. Six primary roles exist in regard to consumption in a given household; each role is described in Table 7.4. A single member

Table 7.4 The Six Primary Consumption Roles of Household Decision Makers

Household Role	Accompanying Behaviors
Information gatherer/ influencer	Provides information/guidance to other members about products/services, newness, and availability
Gatekeeper	Screens/controls household members' access to product information; can veto purchases
Decision maker	Ultimately decides, with or without input of other members, which items will be considered purchased and how they will be used and disposed of
Purchaser	Secures/buys product(s)
User	Consumes (uses) product(s)
Disposer	Discards product(s) when no longer useful

might assume several roles, depending on the size of the household, the particular shopping context (supermarket, hardware store, boutique), or even the prevailing cultural attitudes, whether or not they are really true (for example, men know more about cars and are better at negotiating price on an automobile purchase).

Consumer researchers have found that the household decision-making process can sometimes cause tension and conflict resulting from numerous issues, including disagreements about how limited funds should be spent. In large families, two or more members might share a role, and in smaller households, one person might act in more than one capacity. Additionally, the person who uses the product isn't necessarily the one who actually buys the product. When conflicts arise, the role of the ultimate decision maker can be difficult because that person has the responsibility and power to determine what, where, when, which product, whether to buy, and how much to spend.

LET'S TALK

What ads or commercials have you seen where the marketers are aiming their message at a specific role player in the decision-making process?

Household Decision Making Today

When it comes to purchasing practices in the modern household, consumer researchers have detected several new patterns. Most important are the changes in decision-making styles and **consumption roles,**

the expected/prescribed behaviors of consumers within a household. Look again at Table 7.4. In the past, fathers traditionally served multiple roles. They were **information gatherers** (also called influencers), providers of information and guidance to other family members about products, services, newness, and availability; **gatekeepers,** those who screen and control access to product information and can veto purchases; and **decision makers,** who ultimately determine, with or without input of other members, which items will be considered, purchased, and how they will be used and discarded. Mothers might have participated with fathers as **purchasers,** those who actually buy the product, and, depending on the product, all family members were users, or those actually consuming the products or services. An additional role one could add to the list is that of **disposers,** who get rid of a product or discontinue use of a service[6] (a father hauls an old sofa to the curb for garbage collection; a mother stops a magazine subscription).

Today, however, household members often collaborate when it comes to purchases and prefer a certain amount of interaction during the decision-making process. Tweens and teenagers are increasingly becoming information gatherers, influencers, and purchasers, as well as users. And men are taking on more of the roles traditionally held by women. (See Case in Point 7.3.)

There are several reasons for this shift in consumer behavior. Primary is the change in the makeup of the U.S. household. As previously mentioned, what was once considered a traditional family is no longer the norm. Often both parents/partners work, and children are more likely—and more able—to discover new products and/or product advancements simply because they have more unsupervised free time and greater access to a wide

The Rise of the "Mansumer"

Once upon a time, fathers would arrive home from work expecting to sit down to a home-cooked meal before settling into their favorite chair to read the newspaper or watch television. Those days are all but gone. Men—and particularly Gen X men—are now taking a far more active role in the household, including making purchasing decisions, than their fathers or any previous generation ever did.

Global media agency BPN has called the shift "the rise of the mansumer," and it clearly can be traced to the dramatic changes in families in recent years. According to 2010 census figures, one out of five fathers of preschool-age kids whose wives work indicated that they are the children's primary caregiver. There are also millions of other fathers who may stay home part of the time to help take care of their children—or if not to that extent, who may cook meals, clean the bathrooms, and perform other tasks that traditionally were handled by moms.

It's a brand-new breed of men that BPN in a Retail Trends Report dubbed "Chief Buying Officer" for their household, with statistics to back that title up. According to the report, 40 percent of men are now the primary grocery shopper in the household; 44 percent say they equally share in housecleaning; and a whopping 86 percent agree that being a man means "doing what is necessary to keep the household running."

Because of this, marketers are stepping up to adapt to the way men approach shopping—which is different from the shopping behavior of women. While it's known that women tend to respond to beauty and luxury, men look more for durability and practicality. In addition, when men go shopping, they are intent on meeting a need or solving a problem; they get satisfaction and a sense of accomplishment from "hunting" for the goods they need, as opposed to women who enjoy the satisfaction of simply bringing goods into the house. Men's hunting instinct also shows up in their use of social media and the Web to research products, gather information, and read reviews, so that they can immediately go to the store, knowing exactly what they want. A final key difference? Unlike women, once they're at the store, men are rarely inclined to purchase other things while they're there.

Sources: BPN, "This Holiday Shopping Season, It's All About The 'Mansumer,'" News release, December 12, 2012; Craig Guillot, "Man Up," *Stores,* May 2013, http://www.stores.org/STORES%20Magazine%20March%202013/man.

range of media. Studies indicate that today's parents spend less time making purchase decisions for the whole family, which puts children in a unique position to influence product purchases more than ever before. This can have a positive impact, however, because children are often a driving force when it comes to buying environmentally friendly products.

Second is the evolution and daily barrage of media impacting all members of a household. In today's digital age, not only is more information available, but it's available virtually anywhere and at any time. Some older household members might have a hard time keeping up with all the latest technology and gadgets, so they depend more on younger members for information that's not accessible by traditional means. For example, your grandmother might not be interested in reading her e-mail on her cell phone, as the screen is just too small, but she asks you to help her set up a Skype account so she can keep in touch with your cousins who live across the country.

A third factor that has contributed to changing consumer behavior and household decision making is the growing influence of young people, who have definite ideas about how to express gender, political ideals, affiliations, creativity, and independence through their belongings—especially their clothing and accessories. Certainly young people have long differentiated themselves from the rest of society by wearing certain types of products (think raccoon coats of the 1920s and psychedelic T-shirts of the 1960s), but today those under the age of 18 generally have much more input into purchases and can substantially affect how household members spend their free time (for example, where they will go for vacation, which movies or TV shows they will watch,

at what restaurants they will have dinner). They also can influence where household members buy products, such as clothing and electronics, and can also help decide which actual products will be purchased. Furthermore, many preteens and teenagers today have more ready access to money than in the past and are willing to spend it to convey their uniqueness and personal style.

A final factor is that Americans are starved for time. For many, shopping is a nuisance that interferes with their leisure. Some research has indicated that about 60 percent of Americans think of shopping as a "have-to" rather than a "want-to." As a result, busy members of a household may yield decision making to other members who have more time, or may bypass the information gathering and gatekeeping functions altogether to simply make the purchase that is quickest and easiest. Their choice of where and how to buy can also be strongly influenced by their available time, which is just one reason behind the burgeoning trend of mobile shopping and making instant purchases through apps. (See Chapter 13 for more on how fashion consumers buy.) On the other hand, another recent survey has determined that many customers still view shopping as a treat—one that can lift their spirits when they need it, as explained in Point of View 7.2.

Families, households, and the roles and preferences of their members are definitely evolving, as are the needs of shoppers as they negotiate the changing marketplace and the vast array of new products and places to purchase them. So, now that we understand how age, family, and phases of the life cycle impact consumers' needs and desires, we'll go on to explore social influences on consumer behavior in Chapter 8.

Consumers Beat the Blues with Retail Therapy

While many time-starved consumers may not enjoy the activity of shopping—and may even foist it off on other members of the household whenever they get a chance—that is not the case for everyone. A recent survey of 1,000 adults actually found that shopping can be therapeutic.

According to the study, more than half (51.8 percent) of all Americans go shopping to improve their mood—and that number rises to almost two thirds (63.9 percent) for women. Among men, the number is lower, but still represents about four in 10 (39.8 percent). What is it that triggers those consumers to indulge in retail therapy? About one in five (18.9 percent) shop to feel better after a bad day at work; 14.6 percent go shopping after getting bad news; and 12.2 percent shop after having a fight with a significant other.

The next question is: What do those blue shoppers shop for to lift their spirits? For women, the top item is clothes (bought by nearly three out of five), followed by food, shoes, accessories, and books/magazines. For men, food ranks tops (a choice made by 28.1 percent), followed closely by electronics and music/movies, with clothes and games/toys rounding out the list.

An intriguing finding of the survey is that shoppers can benefit from retail therapy without going to a physical store. For two out of three consumers, online shopping is actually preferable when they need to shake the blues—indicating that the act of shopping is more important than the immediate gratification of having the possession in hand. Among the reasons given were not having to leave the house, greater convenience, not having to drive, and wider range of stores to browse.

But what makes consumers feel the very best when practicing retail therapy? For more than four out of five: getting a deal.

Source: Ebates.com, "Ebates Survey: More than Half (51.8%) of Americans Engage in Retail Therapy—63.9% of Women and 39.8% of Men Shop to Improve their Mood," News release, April 2, 2013.

Summary

While marketers have always known the impact of factors such as family, age, and life cycle stage on consumers, significant changes are taking place in the factors themselves and are causing marketers to reconsider how best to reach out to—and connect with—consumers in various circumstances.

For example, the behavior that was once expected of older people may no longer be the norm. Age-appropriate behavior among seniors has evolved significantly as a result of prolonged life expectancy and better quality of life. Many work long past the traditional retirement age of 65 and lead very busy lives, rather than slowing down, as was once expected.

Similarly, the traditional definition and makeup of the family has changed. A description of today's "typical" American family is not as clear-cut as it was in the past (when terms such as "nuclear" or "extended" were adequate descriptors). Situations in which both parents work, step-families live together, and same-sex parents raise children are becoming more common. Thus, there are many different kinds of households providing security for and guidance to today's children. The roles of father as breadwinner and mother as housewife are simply no longer "typical."

Finally, an onslaught of new media, products, and services (many of which are technology-driven) has made some older family members reliant on the younger ones for advice about which products are preferable and how to use them. One result of this situation is that children are now much more active in determining how families spend their money.

Marketers will depend more and more on consumer researchers to track changes resulting from societal shifts in family, age, and life cycle stage in order to serve buyers more effectively.

KEY TERMS

21st-century family life cycle

Consumer socialization

Consumption roles

Decision maker

Disposer

Extended family

Family

Gatekeeper

Household

Information gatherer/influencer

Nontraditional family

Nuclear family

Purchaser

Reference group

Role

Socialization

Traditional family life cycle

User

QUESTIONS FOR REVIEW

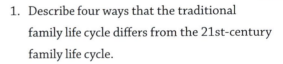

1. Describe four ways that the traditional family life cycle differs from the 21st-century family life cycle.

2. Explain the importance of the consumer socialization process as it relates to the development of a person's shopping habits and preferences.

3. What are the six roles of household members with regard to the decision-making process? Describe the behaviors that generally accompany each role.

4. Name three ways that access to information has changed how today's families make decisions.

5. How and why have teenagers' roles become more important in today's family decision-making process?

6. List three kinds of products or services that are geared specifically to modern seniors, and explain the appeal of each.

ACTIVITIES

1. Visit two or more of the following websites that appeal to young children: "Ice Block" (fruitloops.com), "Crunchling Adventure" (capncrunch.com), candystand.com, or pebblesplay.com, and lead a class discussion about the approaches these companies' sites use to engage children, along with the ethical implications.

2. Using the six primary consumption roles, create and present a chart that illustrates the dynamics of the decision-making process in your household. Be prepared to explain any changes that have occurred and give specific examples.

3. Prepare a 3- to 5-minute report on the consumer group Campaign for a Commercial-Free Childhood. Include both the mission and the techniques used to prevent companies from marketing directly to children. Discuss some of the group's activities and successes.

4. Select a product or service that would appeal to the 55- to 65-year-old age group. Based on the attitudes of today's mature consumers, devise a marketing strategy that would be likely to get their attention, and explain its appeal.

MINI-PROJECTS

1. Read any two chapters in the book *Party Shoes to School/Baseball Caps to Bed* by Marilise Flusser (Simon & Schuster, 1992). Choose two specific scenarios that effectively illustrate the consumer socialization process in your family and some of the clothing-related issues you and your parents dealt with when you were younger. In a two-page essay, discuss how these incidents helped shape your preferences regarding your current clothing choices.

2. Using Table 7.4, create a 3- to 5-minute skit with a few classmates that illustrates the various roles played by household members in the decision-making process, and how they might function as a unit in the purchase of a fashion- or design-related product or service. Present your skit in class.

REFERENCES

1. Ebates, "Traditional Back to School Shopping Stresses Both Parents & Kids," News release, July 18, 2013.

2. Jeff Fromm, "How to Get Millennials to Love and Share Your Product," *Advertising Age*, August 14, 2013, http://adage.com/article/cmo-strategy/millennials-love-brand/243624/.

3. Lucia Moses, "Wealthy Millennials Approach Shopping Differently Than Their Parents," *AdWeek*, September 3, 2013, www.adweek.com/news/advertising-branding/wealthy-millennials-approach-shopping-differently-their-parents-152140.

4. Doris Nhan, "Census: More in U.S. Report Nontraditional Households," *National Journal,* May 1, 2012, www.nationaljournal.com /thenextamerica/demographics/census-more-in-u-s-report-nontraditional-households-2012-20120430.

5. Michelle Castillo, "Almost Half of First Babies in U.S. Born to Unwed Mothers," *CBS News,* March 15, 2013, http://www.cbsnews .com/8301-204_162-57574599/almost-half-of-first-babies-in-u.s-born-to-unwed-mothers/.

6. Peter J. Olson, *Reference Groups and Family,* 2013, http://answers.mheducation.com /business/marketing/consumer-behavior /reference-groups-and-family#reference-group-influence.

ADDITIONAL RESOURCES

American Academy of Pediatrics. "Television and the Family Fact Sheet." 2011. www.aap.org /family/tv1.htm.

American Marketing Association. "Family life cycle." *Dictionary of Marketing Terms.* August 6, 2006. http://www.marketingpower.com/mg-dictionary-view3937.php.

Anderson, George. "What Can Merchants Do to Become Better Retail Therapists?" *Retail Wire,* April 2, 2013. http://www.retailwire.com /discussion/16684/what-can-merchants-do-to-become-better-retail-therapists.

Assael, Henry. *Consumer Behavior: A Strategic Approach* (Boston: Houghton Mifflin Company, 2004).

"Back-to-School Guide: Hack College," *MSN,* September 13, 2013. http://tech.ca.msn.com /back-to-school-guide/photogallery.aspx?cp-documentid=29925760&page=4.

Bagdikian, Ben H. *The Media Monopoly,* 6th ed. (Boston: Beacon Press, 2000).

Boone, Louis E., and David L Kurtz. *Contemporary Business,* 11th ed. (Mason, OH: Thomson/South-Western, 2005).

Briglia, Santos. "Why Aren't Millennials Big E-Spenders?" *Retail Wire,* July 20, 2013. http://www.retailwire.com/discussion/16995 /why-arent-millennials-big-e-spenders.

Carter, B., and M. McGoldrick, eds. *The Expanded Family Life Cycle,* 3rd ed. (Boston: Allyn and Bacon, 2005).

Consumer Behavior. San Diego State University. August 10, 2006. http://www-rohan.sdsu .edu/~renglish/370/notes/chapt05/.

Cook, Dan. "Kids and the Marketplace: Then and Now." *LiP Magazine,* August 20, 2001.

Dolliver, Mark. "Marketing to Today's 65-plus Consumers." *Adweek,* July 27, 2009. http://www .adweek.com/aw/content_display/news/client /mailto:mdolliver@adweek.com.

Kossek, Ellen. "Work-Family Balance," http:// ellenkossek.lir.msu.edu/documents/wfb2.pdf.

Kunkel, D. APA Task Force on Advertising and Children: "Psychological Issues in the Increasing Commercialization of Childhood." (Washington, DC: American Psychological Association, 2004).

Marketing Charts staff. "Family and Friends Still Most Trusted for Shopping Decisions." January 22, 2013. http://www.marketingcharts.com /wp/television/family-and-friends-still-most-trusted-for-shopping-decisions-26423/.

Perner, Lars. "Consumer Behavior: The Psychology of Marketing." University of Southern

California, July 28, 2006. http://www.consumer psychologist.com.

Sutton, Kelly. "How to Reach Those Crazy College Kids." June 18, 2010. http://www.imedia connection.com/content/27009.asp.

Vitelli, Romeo, Ph.D. "Television, Commercials, and Your Child." *Psychology Today*, Media Spotlight blog, July 22, 2013. http://www.psychology today.com/blog/media-spotlight/201307 /television-commercials-and-your-child.

CHAPTER 8

Social Influences on Fashion Consumers

WHAT DO I NEED TO KNOW ABOUT SOCIAL INFLUENCES ON FASHION CONSUMERS?

✔ What is meant by the term "social influence"

✔ The three theories of fashion diffusion and how they differ

✔ The different types of social influencers and how each affects consumer behavior

✔ The impact of groups on consumer decision making

✔ The influence of social media on fashion consumers

Question: What do friends, strangers, our family, a new movie, a post on Instagram, celebrities, a store display window, and any kind of media all have in common?

Answer: They provide us with information, they influence us, and they often exert a kind of social pressure on us—to which we may well respond by modifying our behavior, both as individuals and as consumers.

Forces That Influence Behavior

Each day we go online, take part in activities, buy products or services, or share our points of view with other people. Think of a typical day—haven't many of your activities been influenced by someone or something? Maybe you planned to study at the library after class but some classmates invited you to go with them to a movie so you did that instead. Or a friend pointed out a rip in your backpack so you decided to buy a new one, looking for the style you'd seen pictured on one of the fashion blogs you follow. Previous chapters have addressed the impact of various individual and family forces on how we choose the products and services that we buy; our discussion will now focus on social forces that change, reinforce, and drive our decisions.

What Is Social Influence?

In her book, *Fashion Forecasting*, Ellen Brannon writes about the balancing a person must do when trying to live in the moment, which often involves efforts to conform (perhaps by imitating others) and, at the same time, the desire to demonstrate uniqueness.[1] We all engage in these divergent, apparently contradictory behaviors—the simultaneous effort to both fit in and stand out. A multitude of social forces can tip the scales to one side or the other, and marketers do their best to identify, categorize, and make use of those forces for the benefit of both their organization and the consumers they seek to attract (Figure 8.1).

In a marketing context, **social influence** refers to the information or pressure that an individual,

FIGURE 8.1 Understanding the social influences affecting consumers clarifies the task of marketers, helping them to see a bigger picture. Each frame gets clearer as marketers address customer preferences.

group, or type of media presents to or exerts on consumers. Variables and related pressures (friends, social networks, marketers, politicians, TV, radio, and so forth) come into play between the moment of stimulation and the resulting action. (See Chapter 3 for information about stimuli and how we respond.) For example, a marketer that is interested in accelerating the buying process people use when purchasing a new car would want to identify appropriate buying triggers for target customers, determine who (individuals or groups) surrounding the target customer wields the most influence, what types of influence they exert, and how those influences affect the ultimate purchase. In their book *Consumer Behavior and Marketing Strategy,* marketing professors J. Paul Peter and Jerry C. Olson discuss

how both direct (for example, firsthand communication) and indirect (for example, observation) social interactions influence consumers' behaviors.[2]

More than 50 years ago, psychology professor Solomon Asch researched three responses to social influence; his discoveries are still valid today. He classified the responses in the following way: **conformity,** which occurs when a person is behaving like others in order to be accepted or feel like "one of the group"; **compliance,** when someone chooses to do something because he's been asked to do it; and **obedience,** when a person strictly obeys an order from an authoritative person or group.[3] Figure 8.2 shows how these responses might impact a buyer's decision making. These behaviors are illustrated in the following scenario. Assume you're alone in your

FIGURE 8.2 "Dad thinks it's too expensive, Jon likes it in red but Dylan likes it in black, Jennifer thinks the trunk is too small. . . . Who do I listen to??"

aunt's apartment, and you have the volume on her TV's surround sound system blasting to heighten the effects in the videogame you're playing.

- A neighbor asks you to turn the volume down and, unhappily, you *comply*.
- A police officer rings the doorbell; he tells you to turn down the volume, and you *obey*.
- After a while, you realize that the right thing to do is to turn the volume down; you know it's what your aunt would expect, so you *conform*.

Of course, numerous other influences exist (many of which are discussed in this book), but marketers are most interested in the ones that mold buying behaviors, particularly when it comes to the purchase of designed goods.

Influences on Fashion and Design

As previously mentioned, influence affects us in myriad ways, such as in what consumers buy and wear, what designers create, and what media marketers use; there are many sources of influence. Some of these sources we may not consciously consider, but they nonetheless have lasting effects on our choices and behavior. Three examples of such forces include social class, culture, and subculture. These forces in particular often determine the roles that are assigned or ascribed to us—that is, the roles we didn't choose, such as firstborn, only child, aunt—as well as the ones we strive for and achieve, such as designer, buyer, manager.

Social class refers to groups of individuals belonging to different levels of society; social classes are hierarchical and, for the most part, depend on

levels of prosperity and opportunity. Culture, as we defined in Chapter 1, includes the shared customs, values, and beliefs of a group of people who usually live close to each other, although proximity is not a requirement. Younger members of a culture are taught by older members to behave in expected and accepted ways, which were learned from the members of the previous generation. Some have described culture as society's personality and the lens through which we screen products and services.[4] **Subcultures** are smaller groups or "mini-cultures" that function within larger cultures; examples of subcultures include flappers, hippies, punks, skinheads, Goths, bikers, and cowboys. Figure 8.3 visually illustrates subgroups within larger groups.

Influences outside our immediate sphere are all part of the unending array of external influences we encounter on a daily basis. These include salespeople, advertisers, our favorite entertainers, athletes, politicians, teachers, role models, mentors, as well as TV shows and movies, websites, social

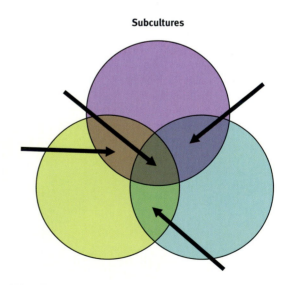

Subcultures

FIGURE 8.3 This visualization identifies several subgroups within larger groups.

media platforms, blogs, and so on. Review some of the websites that appear when you search for "fashion/design/culture/political . . . blog" on the Internet. You'll see comments posted from both large and small organizations as well as from individuals that provide insight, education, updates, and points of view that might influence our fashion and design behaviors. There is no question that Web-based communication is now a fact of life for most people, and its impact on consumer behavior is only growing. In a recent study of digital influences, more than half of consumers said that retail websites are influential in shaping their opinions and purchase decisions, while nearly a third said they are influenced in their purchase decisions by blogs and Facebook.[5] What's the downside to online behaviors? In some cases, there seems to be more incorrect or dubious information being posted or shared than there is valid and accurate information. Equally important, there is simply more of it than anyone could possibly absorb. Forbes suggested that the online consumption habits of today's consumers have led to digital and content "pollution"; every second there are 30 hours of new videos uploaded to YouTube, 100,000 new tweets, and over 204 million new e-mails sent.[6] These and other existing sources, plus new outlets or sources not yet invented, can certainly influence our consumption activities and decisions.

Social Influences and Fashion Diffusion

Obviously, members of "society" influence the fashion behaviors of others. How and where did this social influence begin? In the late 1800s, Thorstein Veblen, the Norwegian-American sociologist and economist, described a group of people whom he termed "the leisure class," wealthy members of society who spent their time and money acquiring extravagant clothing, homes, and art objects. Since they didn't have to work, their main pastime was buying for themselves; Veblen referred to these people as participating in a lifestyle that revolved around "conspicuous consumption." They purchased in order to entertain themselves and to show off. Since they were at the top of the social ladder, they were celebrities, of a sort, and those who rubbed shoulders with them wanted to imitate their style and attempted to do so (within their more limited means).[7] Thus, the first theory of **fashion diffusion,** the spread of a fashion throughout different societal groups, became known as the **downward flow theory** (trickle-down theory), whereby people look to those they consider to be above them (the upper classes) for fashion guidance, and the styles they've adopted continue to trickle down the social ladder. Of course, by the time members of the lower classes are wearing their version of that fashion or style, members of the upper class have moved on to something new.

LET'S TALK

In 1929, "Puttin' on the Ritz" was a slang expression for dressing fashionably and the title of Irving Berlin's song about "different types who wear a day coat, pants with stripes and cut away coat, perfect fits." What song lyrics have recently given you new insights into fashion? How have these same songs touched your friends?

Tracking Social Influence in a Digital World

There is no question that the Internet provides consumers with a wealth of information about products and brands. But in the vastness of cyberspace, what websites and social media are actually most influential in shaping consumers' opinions and purchase decisions? That's what Technorati Media set out to determine in its 2013 Digital Influence Report.

For the research, Technorati surveyed 1,200 consumers, 6,000 digital influencers, and 150 top brand marketers. Among the findings: When it comes to the influence of an online community, bigger is not better. More than half (54 percent) of consumers agreed that the smaller the community, the greater the influence.

The survey also found that many consumers turn to blogs when looking to make a purchase. Blogs were found to be the most influential digital resource (31 percent) among social media when consumers are making a decision about what to buy, topped only by retail sites (56 percent) and brand sites (34 percent). Of the online services that consumers found to be the most trustworthy, news sites ranked first, at 51 percent, with Facebook next (32 percent). Also most trusted by about three in 10 consumers were retail sites, YouTube, and blogs.

Clearly marketers recognize the importance of the Internet in reaching consumers with their brand message, and to maximize the impact on consumer behavior, two thirds (65 percent) of companies participate in influencer-based marketing—that is, getting their message to those who have established themselves as an authority in a specific area, such as fashion, and have a following of consumers who can be swayed by their views. In selecting which influencers to work with, marketers may look at criteria such as the person's number of Twitter followers, number of Facebook friends, number of Facebook likes, number of unique visitors to a blog, and number of blog page views.

And what of the digital influencers themselves? How do they wield their influence—and what influences them? Overwhelmingly, the majority of these influencers (86 percent) create influence by publishing one or more blogs, posting primarily text, but also employing photos and microblogging (like Twitter). And the greatest influence to them when it comes to choosing their own content to publish: other blogs.

Source: Technorati Media, 2013 Digital Influence Report.

Variations of this theory have emerged over the years, including the **upward flow theory** (trickle-up), the concept that a great new fashion idea can also start among the lower echelons of society and work its way up. One example of this is hip-hop fashion or urban wear, which originated in the 1980s among African American youth living in major cities; the style was eventually embraced all the way up the social ladder, and even showed up at one time in hip hop-inspired collections from Isaac Mizrahi and Chanel. Phat Farm is a clothing company that combines fashion elements of both urban and preppy culture; this business was launched in 1992 by Russell Simmons, co-founder of the hip hop record label, Def Jam. The clothing was adapted and became so influential in the look of the urban subculture of rap and hip-hop that it further solidified Simmons' identification as the founder of the hip-hop movement.[8] The trickle-up concept can also be used to explain how benefits and productive ideas result from simple customer engagement. For example, many companies that implement an effective CRM (customer relationship management) system frequently realize trickle-up benefits from listening to and being in tune with customer needs and desires. More users and increased data analysis lead to productive business decisions, satisfied clients, and repeat and new business opportunities.[9] This shows that consumer researchers can actually use a fashion theory to enhance their business practices.

The **horizontal flow theory** (trickle across) is the third theory of fashion diffusion and contends that influences among members of peer groups with similar demographic or psychographic profiles are what determine the adoption of fashions. (Psychographics is the study of consumer personality and lifestyle, a topic we'll discuss in Chapter 9.) For example, your college roommate got an iPod in a hot new color or an 8-inch high-def tablet computer, so you find yourself wanting one. Or perhaps a fashion leader in a particular group of suburban moms knowingly or unknowingly influences others in that same group to do something, wear something, dine somewhere, or purchase a specific product or service.

These three fashion-diffusion theories have themselves each been in fashion at various times. Juliet B. Schor, a professor of sociology at Boston College, noted that in the 21st century, "horizontal desire" (trickle-across theory), or the coveting of a neighbor's goods, seems to have been replaced by "vertical desire" (trickle-down theory), or coveting the goods of the rich and powerful, who are seen on television and in the movies.[10] Her research showed that "increased exposure to TV (the modern babysitter) increases individuals' annual spending because of lifestyle interests for the upper middle class and wealthy."[11] As you view Figure 8.4 consider how your fashion preferences are influenced.

LET'S TALK

Which fashion-diffusion theory do you think is most applicable in America right now? Which influences are the most powerful?

FIGURES 8.4A–D (a, b) Once seen as a runway extravagance and impractical for daily wear, sequins are a common accent for women's sportswear. (c, d) The "rocker chic" look, featuring skinny jeans and cropped leather jackets, has made the step up from the streets to the runway platform in fashionable form.

Types of Social Influence

To further increase our understanding of how social influences impact us, we can divide them into two main categories. As mentioned earlier, sometimes people do things simply because that's "the way things are done" at that moment in history. If we follow this pattern of not questioning our behavior, we know we will generally be rewarded with acceptance and approval. So, we identify and follow certain societal guidelines or rules of behavior that serve the common good (doing the right thing/ serving humanity). This is referred to as **normative social influence,** a type of pressure that requires a person to conform to the expectations of others. We might conform to avoid rejection or to gain acceptance. Society sets standards of behavior, evaluates subsequent performance, and uses rewards or punishments in response to the performance.[12,13]

Examples of normative social influence are easy to see. People frequently wear clothes they believe will grant them greater acceptance. For example, a young entrepreneur might believe that his well-tailored suit helps him to be seen as both a mature adult and serious, successful businessperson at a chamber of commerce event. Friends socializing in a club may order the same type of drinks. Or a shopper might select a specific gift because of an expectation that the recipient has expressed, either directly or indirectly. In a sense, our society has "programmed" us (via our parents and relatives, friends, employers, and members of institutions such as churches and schools) to believe that when we meet the expectations of others, good things happen (Figure 8.5). Maslow's Hierarchy of Needs, one of the models discussed in Chapter 4, can help us relate conformity to the belonging and esteem needs we seek to meet through

FIGURE 8.5 Normative social influence exerts pressure on an individual to conform to others' expectations.

the approval and friendship of others. Conformity can be a very powerful change agent (something or someone that motivates change), as we often modify our attitudes, actions, beliefs, and values so they are more in line with those of our key social groups and respected elders or authority figures.[14] On the other hand, sometimes we prefer not to conform for a variety of reasons, such as wanting to differentiate ourselves from these same groups. Avant-garde (leaders in new or unconventional movements) designers exemplify a nonconforming group.[15]

At other times, people seek specific guidance and direction in order to make the right choice. **Informational social influences** affect us when we copy the behavior of others because they directly or indirectly offer information to assist in our decision making. "Social proofing" is another term that describes this type of influence; we often think that others really know how to handle certain situations better than we do. For example, a college student might read *Vanity Fair* because her instructor does, and she believes her instructor to be very much "in the know." Perhaps a college graduate accepts a job in a specific city because, although he doesn't want to move, a respected family friend in the same field succeeded there. Or a newly married couple decide to accessorize their kitchen with black appliances instead of stainless steel because their developer told them black was the "in" color. Another example of informational social influence can be seen in Figure 8.6.

FIGURE 8.6 Informational social influence: Says one girl, "I wore my new Ralph Lauren pants, a sweater, and my pearls to last month's college Open House." Replies another, "Really! I wouldn't have thought of going like that, but okay, I guess I'll wear the same thing."

In Figure 8.6, one student did no research before making her decision; she was satisfied to follow what her friend had done. Of course, fashion marketers would prefer that she not depend solely on the word of a friend (except for those working for Ralph Lauren, of course!), but rather on the messages about their brands that they themselves disseminate via TV, radio, magazines, websites, social media, and so on. In this situation, marketers for Ralph Lauren competitors, such as Calvin Klein and Donna Karan, would want potential customers to look at their offerings before deciding to buy. Marketers encourage consumers to spend time learning about product or service alternatives instead of buying just because of informational social influencers' opinions. Naturally, marketers want to be the ones to provide the influences that people respond to, and they aim to use those influences effectively to encourage the "right" buying behavior.

What kinds of information do people consider most important when deciding to buy?

1. The ease of use of the product or service; how much work is required to use the components of the goods as compared to the competitor's offerings.

2. The types of risks involved in the purchase.

3. The levels of expertise of both themselves (the consumers), as well as the seller and the influencer.

4. The degree of comfort, security, and convenience that comes with the goods.

How does this information, and the idea of relying on the opinions of others, relate to the Internet?

Past research has indicated that potential Internet shoppers wait to learn how others like a specific website before making it part of their routine.[16] This suggests that many people do not want to be the first ones to do a specific activity; they don't want to experiment and prefer instead to seek the feedback of others before trying new things. Designers and marketers adapt these same ideas and "help" potential customers see others using similar products first.

LET'S TALK

What are some of your own shopping and buying habits—do you "rely on a friend"? Do you want other people to "test the waters" first with a particular product before you buy a similar item? Do you feel more secure about a product when you know that others are already buying and using it?

In the offline world, researchers have also determined that a physical presence of some kind can also lead people to make decisions more quickly than if no one were around. A study published in the *Journal of Consumer Research*, "The Influence of a Mere Social Presence in a Retail Context" (see Case in Point 8.2), noted that "the mere presence of another person or group of people is sufficient to elicit emotional and behavioral responses on the part of the consumer." So, a retail manager who maintains an amount of "social presence" (for example, sales associates, consultants, etc., who move around the store) could influence customers to make buying decisions more quickly.

HOW MANY INFLUENCERS ARE TOO MANY?

Are people more likely to be influenced in a given situation when there are fewer people or more people involved? The **social impact theory** suggests that the probability of influence increases depending on the number of people involved and the importance and proximity of the influencers. However, when the number of influencers increases, the influence of any one person is reduced. So, if one person goes shopping with ten other people, that shopper is more likely to disregard the opinions of the ten influencers. But if only three people were shopping together, each person's opinion would weigh more heavily (would have stronger influence). Perhaps your decision making has been influenced by a few people gathered together; put yourself in the shopping scenario shown in Figure 8.7.

FIGURE 8.7 The degree of social influence depends on how many people are involved, as well as their importance and proximity.

Influencing Consumer Behavior by Just Being There

It's easy to understand that when friends or family go shopping with you, they can easily influence what you buy and how much you spend. You might even invite them along specifically because you want their advice and opinion. Likewise, a helpful sales associate can be influential in what you select, especially when he or she listens to your needs and guides you to products that match up.

But what about the group of girls on the other side of the juniors department, or the couple ready to pay for their iPad at the nearby checkout, or the guy next to you at the supermarket who's also trying to decide which flavor of yogurt to get? You don't know them, and you're not interacting with them. Could they have an influence on what you buy or don't buy?

According to one research study, those other shoppers—representing a "mere social presence"—can indeed impact your purchase decisions. And the extent of that impact depends on a number of factors, including how many people make up the mere social presence and how physically close they are to you.

For instance, the study found that when consumers were alone in an aisle or area of a store, they tended to spend the least and to buy the cheapest, generic brand available. But when researchers added a social presence to the situation, having either one person or three people stand next to them, the consumers consistently spent more by purchasing a more expensive brand—never once choosing the generic brand when the social presence included three people.

Interestingly, having one other shopper in the proximity actually made consumers feel positive emotions; adding more shoppers to the mix, on the other hand, raised consumers' annoyance or frustration levels. But when the mere social presence was located at a distance, say the far end of the aisle, the influence was lessened no matter how many people there were. So what do these research findings mean? Retail marketers that are able to create the right level of social presence within the store may help influence consumers to feel good about their shopping choices and spend more money.

Source: Jennifer J. Argo, Darren W. Dahl, and Rajesh V. Manchanda, "The Influence of a Mere Social Presence in a Retail Context," *Journal of Consumer Research*, 32 (2005): 207–212.

THE IMPACT OF GROUPS

Sometimes situations involve multiple influencers that are grouped together and exert collective pressure on the person(s) making a decision.

Consider the following example. One day Inez, 18, came home from school and said to her parents, "Everyone is going on the trip to Disney World. It only costs $1,350. All the other parents are letting their kids go, so can I go?" Her parents discussed it for a few minutes and said, "Well, if everyone is going, and it's sanctioned by the school, you can go." In this case, the impact of the group's behavior on the parents (in this case, the decision makers) was powerful. A **group** is two or more people who share similar values and beliefs and communicate interdependently, sharing and relying upon another's opinion. Her parents agreed to let Inez go on a trip because they regarded her school group positively. In this example, the school group is a reference group, a specific type of group composed of individuals we respect, admire, and value; we use these groups as a guide when developing our own beliefs and behaviors.

Reference group members don't necessarily tell a person what to do; rather, the person is influenced by the group members' actions and the opinions they have. An example of this kind of influence is role modeling, but at the group level. When problem solving, the person might ask, "How would my uncles handle this situation?"

Just how strong is the influence of groups in our lives? Groups with which you have the most contact, such as family or close friends, serve as **direct** or **primary influencers;** their opinions are very powerful. **Indirect** or **secondary influencers** do not have as much power; they may include mere acquaintances or members of political/sports/entertainment groups you admire, but they are not included in your circle of closeness. Either group may exert pressure on you when it comes to prioritizing values, attitudes, and behaviors and in buying or not buying specific items or brands. For example, if a close friend (rather than someone you just know casually) suggests that you'd like a specific vacation destination, restaurant, or netbook, that comment could have an influence on you.

How the Reference Group Influences

Different types of reference groups serve different influential purposes. The American Marketing Association notes the three following purposes: informational, utilitarian, and value-expressive.

Informational influences come in the form of facts, figures, data, and so on to those seeking opinions from professionals who are familiar with a specific subject or brand. This can save consumers time and reduce the perceived risk involved with many purchases. Marketers can dispense information in the form of educational and/or awareness campaigns, positioning their products as the ones experts prefer. For example, an ad for a tooth-whitening product could feature the American Dental Association's endorsement of that particular whitening system.

Utilitarian influences are in effect when an individual yields to another person's or group's influence to gain recognition and reward or avoid punishment.[17] For example, if your boyfriend tells you he prefers the smell of gardenias over lilies, you may very well give up one fragrance and purchase another. You might do this to please your boyfriend; that is, to maintain favor with him. If a product helps you achieve a desired goal, your resulting attitude toward it will be positive.[18]

Value-expressive influences are those that address core values (for example, working hard is good for you; the customer is always right; be good to the environment), or the values a person believes one should possess to enhance his or her image in the eyes of others. One example of this is

Millennials Find Their Own Fashion Influence

All generations of consumers are vulnerable to a variety of social influences when shopping for fashion. But when it comes to the Millennial generation, there's a difference—and it lies in both their innate ease in using technology and their proclivity for social networking. Those factors mean that instead of conforming to the classic hierarchy of brands controlling the message of what consumers should consider desirable, Millennials are instead deciding for themselves and creating their own personalized shopping experiences.

Take 26-year-old Brittany Jasper. Working at a used bookstore, her financial resources are somewhat limited, and she can't really afford to buy the brands she likes at full price. So to meet her craving for new looks for her wardrobe, she devotes hours to browsing consignment stores, yard sales, and flea markets in a quest for items that suit her style and work with her budget—perhaps picking up a gently worn pair of Banana Republic chinos, or unbranded leggings and a vintage tunic if the look is right.

But that's not the end of the story. When Jasper gets home with her latest finds, she uploads photos of them to an online social media marketplace designed for sharing, buying, and selling among friends. Anything she decides she doesn't want to keep, she offers for sale on the site, and also shares it with her followers on Facebook and Twitter. For items she's happy with, she posts a photo and when someone "likes" the outfit, Jasper and her entire network get a notification, generating a expansive web of social approval and influence. As Jasper noted, "I really like that it's so social and tied into the people you like and what you like and what you express interest in. It kind of molds itself around you."

It's a dramatically different buying behavior from other, earlier generations of shoppers. Particularly at the younger end of the Millennial age cohort, these consumers are avid sharers, sending friends pictures of themselves in different outfits while still in a store dressing room in order to get instant feedback. And rather than head to a Zara or Forever 21 store for fashion inspiration, Millennials are taking their style cues from a host of different social networks, both online and off, and are using those same sources to find the version of a desired look that fits their budget.

As Samantha Bergeron, founder of market research agency Uncover, put it, the "emotional connection between brand and consumer is weakening. [Millennials] don't need to rely on [brands] so heavily for inspiration and resources. They have 2,500 bloggers and a variety of social networks telling them what to do."

Source: Emanuella Grinbert, "Cash-strapped Millennials Curate Style via Social Media," *CNN.com*, October 16, 2012, www.cnn.com/2012/10/12/living/millennials-shopping/index.html.

buying clothing that bears the "Made in the USA" tag, reflecting the value of national loyalty. Again, the marketer's goal is to identify these potential influences and respond in a manner that benefits all parties.

Reference groups impact our decision making in both obvious and subtle ways. Once marketers understand the shared beliefs of specific reference groups, they can use the group's influence to help promote their product or service, either directly or indirectly.

MEMBERSHIP INFLUENCES

We can also be influenced through membership relationships. Consumers consciously align themselves with potential influencers through individual and organizational memberships (Figure 8.8). The groups we do not actually belong to, but wish we did, are called **aspirational groups.** For example, we might want to belong to an admired downhill ski group or dream of joining an award-winning hip-hop dance troupe.

Associative groups are those we already belong to. For example, we might be members of the neighborhood volleyball team or a professional association. On the other hand, **disassociative groups** are those that do not interest us; in fact, we might disapprove of them.[19] For example, we might decide to avoid someone who belongs to a hunting group since we don't like the idea of killing animals for sport.

As was the case with the concept of informational social influence ("relying on a friend") discussed earlier in the chapter, research indicates that when consumers either don't know about a product or service or are just not sure about it, they may look

FIGURE 8.8 What do these groups have in common? They each influence their respective group members.

to others—in this instance, specific membership groups—as credible sources.[20] Consumer researchers use this type of information to help create strategies targeting appropriate market segments, using individuals who are perceived as reference group members and positive influencers for that segment. For example, if a woman's appearance-related aspirational group includes Angelina Jolie as an ideal, then companies that sell lip enhancers might hire the actress as their spokesperson or hire a model who resembles her to appear in ads or at special events.

CONTROL

In addition to all the influences we've discussed in this chapter, there's yet another group of influencers: the ones we don't know. What is their impact on consumer purchasing behavior?

You'll recall the role of the gatekeeper in household purchase decision making from Chapter 7. Figure 8.9 shows examples of another type of gatekeeper—knowledgeable or prominent individuals who can influence people to act or not act in specific ways. In the fields of fashion, design, and art, we are constantly bombarded by information from critics, seasoned professionals, high-profile influencers, and others who impact our decisions with their words or actions. We don't know them, yet they influence our choices. Additionally, as a result of advances in technology and the Information Age, a new group of influences exists in cyberspace: "e-gatekeepers," direct and indirect electronic data providers who try to influence users to do or not do something.

But are e-gatekeepers really powerful; do they actually have genuine influence in the real (nonvirtual) world? In his article "The New Gatekeepers,"

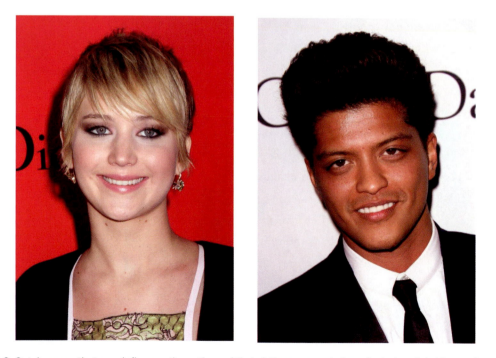

FIGURE 8.9 Gatekeepers that may influence the actions of their followers or admirers include celebrities such as Jennifer Lawrence and Bruno Mars.

writer Tristan Louis discussed the blogosphere and asked what might happen if a false rumor were perpetuated by an online gatekeeper. Would "top-ranked online bloggers" begin impacting the "non-blog world"? According to the writer, some gatekeepers use a combination of traditional and new technologies to guide their followers. For example, using a phone or fax to spread a rumor would be considered traditional in contrast to spreading a rumor via text, Twitter, blog, YouTube, or other digital medium.[21] This illustrates another concern about the potential power of gatekeepers in society and the role of technology. Recent examples of false rumors spread through cyberspace included that Kanye West had an affair with a gay Givenchy designer; Miley Cyrus announced onstage at the BET Hip Hop Awards that she was pregnant by Juicy J; and Troop Clothing was owned by the Ku Klux Klan. A decade earlier, both Liz Claiborne and Tommy Hilfiger were the targets of rumors accusing them of being racist and disseminated by anonymous Internet sources that seemed intent on harming their businesses.

Let's Talk

What information about celebrities have you found on the Internet that turned out to be simply rumors? What mainstream media ran the same story?

Whom do you go to for advice or guidance on subjects you don't really understand? You'd probably seek out an "expert" on that particular topic. An **opinion leader** is someone who is highly regarded by his or her peers and serves as a credible source or a liaison who transmits and translates information from mass media to those seeking advice. These advisors do not necessarily have to be famous (although they can be); they just need to have specific expertise in the area of concern to you. Opinion leaders might include the following:

- A friend who is a certified mechanic with eight years' experience working on Ferrari engines
- The hair colorist or stylist who works with well-known celebrities
- A highly trained and well-respected plastic surgeon
- Stella McCartney
- Imran Amed

Let's Talk

What opinion leaders have influenced your selections of music, movies, dress, friends, social events, or career paths?

Consumer Socialization Process

Also mentioned in Chapter 7, consumer socialization is a process by which children acquire the skills, knowledge, attitudes, and experiences necessary to function as consumers. Obviously, children learn from their parents, siblings, other relatives, friends, classmates, teachers, the media—and marketers. Marketers educate and motivate children to want goods by using TV programs, movies, and product placements in multimedia targeted to that specific market segment. Fast-food companies such as

McDonald's or Burger King create marketing campaigns that entice young people to buy toys and other nonfood items at these restaurants. Another example is Webkinz, the "website partner" that children are encouraged by marketers to use after purchasing a stuffed pet toy. The site teaches children how to care for stuffed toys and provides KinzCash that children use to pay for the redecorating of a virtual computer pet room, furniture, clothing, and food.[22] Marketers can use creativity as a way to teach children how to function as consumers.

When we shop, watch a TV show or webcast, listen to our iPod, flip through our favorite magazines, or read poster ads on public transportation vehicles, we are seeing marketers' efforts to educate and motivate us to try, buy, or switch products and services—to have some influence on both our thoughts and actions. Marketers also seek to develop a better understanding of the social forces affecting consumers, and then use that information about influencers to generate more product interest and sales. But marketers also need other statistics and "hard data" about consumers to accurately identify market segments and determine which potential customers to target; this type of research is discussed in Chapter 9, "Demographics, Psychographics, and the Fashion Consumer."

Summary

Marketers study the effect of influence on consumers in order to both predict and guide consumer behavior, as well as to understand the degree of impact that the influences have on buying behavior. Reference and other groups' (for example, positive and negative memberships) influences guide people to consider, reject, or accept products and services, among other things. These combined variables and the efforts of traditional and nontraditional marketing gatekeepers and new technologies make our buying decisions even more complicated. Purchasing choices are most certainly impacted by the influence of other people and/or forces. Because of this, marketers know that the ongoing process of consumer socialization is ever-changing, and they must adapt if marketing messages are to reach and impact consumers effectively before, during, and after a purchase. Marketers are therefore better able to create more successful campaigns when they understand the processes by which consumers allow people, places, events, culture, and so on, to affect their buying habits.

KEY TERMS

Aspirational groups

Associative groups

Compliance

Conformity

Direct (primary) influencers

Dissociative groups

Downward flow theory (trickle-down theory)

Fashion diffusion

Group

Horizontal flow theory (trickle-across theory)

Indirect (secondary) influencers

Informational influencers

Informational social influences

Normative social influence

Obedience

Opinion leader

QUESTIONS FOR REVIEW

1. Define and discuss normative and informational social influence. Provide examples of each from your own life.

2. Explain what the term "social class" means. How are the concepts of culture and subculture related? Illustrate their influences on consumers in relation to choosing designed goods.

3. How do the three "trickle" theories differ and why are they important to consumer researchers and marketers?

4. What is meant by the term "consumer socialization"?

ACTIVITIES

1. Select an element of home décor such as kitchen appliances or cabinetry, a piece of furniture, bathroom fixtures, or paint colors. Apply one of the diffusion theories (trickle up/trickle down/trickle across) by researching the origin and history of your selection and demonstrating how designed goods of all kinds spread through a population.

2. Select two items or services that cost more than $100 that you bought while shopping with a group of three or more people. Explain whether the people were direct or indirect influencers and how their comments (pressure) persuaded you to buy (or, if appropriate, *not* buy) the product or service.

3. Select two items you've considered purchasing that exemplify how either informational influencers, utilitarian influencers, or value-expressive influencers affected your buying decision.

4. Review your typical week at work, at school, and in social situations. List two potential gatekeepers from each of these categories. Explain why you consider them gatekeepers and tell how and why you responded to their input.

MINI-PROJECTS

1. Identify two opinion leaders, one found on the Web and one from another source. Compare and contrast the influence of each, taking into account traditional media, the reach of the Internet, and blogosphere opportunities.

2. Cite two memberships for each category (aspirational, associative, and disassociative) that you would personally consider joining or not joining, and explain the motivation behind your choices.

REFERENCES

1. Evelyn L. Brannon, *Fashion Forecasting* (New York: Fairchild Publications, 2005).

2. J. Paul Peter and Jerry C. Olson, *Consumer Behavior and Marketing Strategy* (New York: McGraw-Hill Irwin, 2008).

3. Solomon E. Asch, "Effects of Group Pressure upon the Modification and Distortion of Judgement." In *Groups, Leadership, and Men,* edited by H. Guetzkow (Pittsburgh: Carnegie Press, 1951).

4. Michael R. Solomon and Nancy Rabolt, *Consumer Behavior in Fashion* (Upper Saddle River, NJ: Prentice Hall, 2004).

5. John Swartz, "Technorati Media's 2013 Digital Influence Report," *Technorati,* February 5, 2013, http://technorati.com/business/article/technorati-medias-2013-digital-influence-report/.

6. Todd Wilms, "The Alarming Rise Of 'Digital And Content Pollution,'" *Forbes,* March 26, 2013, www.forbes.com/sites/sap/2013/03/26/the-alarming-rise-of-digital-and-content-pollution/.

7. Michael R. Solomon, *Consumer Behavior: Buying, Selling, and Being,* 7th ed. (Upper Saddle River, NJ: Pearson Prentice Hall, 2006), pp. 385–388 and 474–475.

8. Phat Farm website, www.phatfarm.com/about.

9. "Top 3 Design Considerations in CRM for Trickle Up Benefits: How Design Influences User Adoption," *crmBright,* May 24, 2013, http://crmbright.com/2013/05/24/top-3-design-considerations.

10. Jennifer Steinhauer, "When the Joneses Wear Jeans," *New York Times,* May 29, 2005, www.NYTimes.com.

11. Juliet Schor, "The Overspent American," Interview on Time.com, May 20, 1998, www.time.com/time/community/transcripts/chattr052098.html.

12. M. Deutsch and H. B. Gerard, "A Study of Normative and Information Social Influences upon Individual Judgement," *Journal of Abnormal and Social Psychology* 51 (1955): 629–636.

13. H. C. Kelman, "Compliance, Identification, and Internalization: Three Processes of Attitude Change," *Journal of Conflict Resolution* 2 (1958): 51–60.

14. ChangingMinds website, www.ChangingMinds.org.

15. *Webster's New World Dictionary,* 3rd ed. (New York: Simon & Schuster, 1988).

16. Matthew K. O. Lee, Christy M. K. Cheung, Choon Ling Sia, and Kai H. Lim, "How Positive Informational Social Influence Affects Consumers' Decision of Internet Shopping," HICSS, Proceedings of the 39th Annual Hawaii International Conference on System Sciences, Koloa, Kauai, Hawai'i (HICSS'06) Track 6, p. 115A, 2006.

17. Tudor and Carley, "Informational social influence" definition, 1998, http://ciadvertising.org/sa/spring_03/382J/jamie/term.html.

18. Nessim Hanna and Richard Wozniak, *Consumer Behavior: An Applied Approach* (Upper Saddle River, NJ: Prentice Hall, 2001) p. 177.

19. Katherine White and Darren W. Dahl, "To Be or *Not* Be? The Influence of Dissociative Reference Groups on Consumer Preferences," *Journal of Consumer Psychology* 16, no. 4 (October 1, 2006): 404–414.

20. Solomon.
21. Tristan Louis, "The New Gatekeepers," *TNL.net,* February 9, 2006. http://www.tnl.net/blog/2006/02/09/the-new-gatekeepers/.
22. Webkinz website, www.webkinz.com.

ADDITIONAL RESOURCES

Asch, S. E. "Forming Impressions of Personality." *Journal of Abnormal and Social Psychology* 41 (1946): 258–290.

———. "Opinions and Social Pressure." In A. P. Hare, E. F. Borgatta, and R. F. Bales, eds., *Small Groups: Studies in Social Interaction.* New York: Alfred A. Knopf, 1966, pp. 318–324.

———. "Studies of Independence and Conformity: A Minority of One against a Unanimous Majority." *Psychological Monographs* 70 (Whole no. 416), 1956.

ChangingMinds.org. "Informational Social Influence." http://changingminds.org/explanations/theories/informational_social_influence.htm.

Cialdini, R. *Influence: Science and Practice.* 3rd ed. New York: HarperCollins, 1993.

Latané, B. "The Psychology of Social Impact." *American Psychologist* 36 (1981): 343–356.

Latané, B., and S. Wolf. "The Social Impact of Majorities and Minorities." *Psychological Review* 88 (1981): 438–453.

Tanford, S., and S. Penrod, "Social Influence Model: A Formal Integration of Research on Majority and Minority Influence Processes." *Psychological Bulletin* 95 (1984): 189–225.

CHAPTER 9

Demographics, Psychographics, and the Fashion Consumer

WHAT DO I NEED TO KNOW ABOUT DEMOGRAPHICS, PSYCHOGRAPHICS, AND THE FASHION CONSUMER?

✔ The meaning and significance of demographics in relationship to fashion consumer behavior

✔ The effects of consumerism and materialism on fashion consumption

✔ Psychographics and its relationship to consumer lifestyles

✔ Examples of the ways researchers study and classify consumer lifestyles

f you're the kind of person who enjoys randomly surfing the Web to see what interesting things you can find, or happen to have a friend who loves to share fascinating tidbits discovered online, you may have seen a page or site with content similar to this:

If there were only 100 people on earth, and the existing human ratios remained the same, there would be:

50 males and 50 females; 26 would be children and 74 would be adults. Out of the 100, 60 would be Asians, 15 Africans, 14 from the Americas, and 11 Europeans. Twelve would speak Chinese, and 5 each would speak English and Spanish; 83 would be able to read and write but only 7 would have a college degree.

Urban dwellers would number 51 and rural dwellers 49. Just 77 people would have some type of roof over their head, and 23 would not; 13 would not have *clean, safe water to drink. One would be dying of starvation and 15 would be undernourished, while 21 would be overweight. Almost half, 48, would be living on less than $2 per day.*[1]

It's an intriguing way to analyze the world's population in microcosm, and an analogy that has evolved from one published in 1990 by Donella Meadows. Meadows was a pioneering American environmental scientist, teacher, and writer who tried to offer a framework for better understanding the vast diversity of the people who share our planet. The year her "State of the Village Report" was written, the world population had more than doubled in just 40 years—to more than 5 billion people. That number is not easy for most of us to wrap our heads around, particularly when we take into account the myriad countries and cultures it encompasses. And consider this: Since 1990, more than 2 billion additional people now call the planet home.

What does all this have to do with consumer behavior and fashion? Everything—because, as we began to explore in Chapter 7, when consumers consider what to buy, their decisions are influenced by a host of external factors including where and how they live, their gender and age, how much money they earn and can spend, what culture they relate to, their level of education, and other measurable statistics and personal characteristics that marketers use to analyze, interpret, and predict consumer behavior. But before we start examining those areas, we must first identify what makes up a consumer market.

Markets consist of people, specifically those people with an interest and ability to buy goods and services. Of the more than 7 billion people on the planet, just a small but growing number have much spending power, particularly the discretionary spending power used for non-essentials, which is the major concern of fashion marketers. Consider oil-rich Qatar, with a relatively small population of just over 2 million people but an estimated per capita (per person) income of nearly $104,000. Now look at impoverished Zimbabwe, with a population of over 13.7 million but a per capita income of only about $600. Which presents a more attractive consumer market for a fashion company?

According to information presented in Table 9.1, the countries with the highest population are China and India, each with over a billion inhabitants. Each also has a rapidly developing middle class (due to massive industrialization) whose spending power is increasing. No wonder Walmart is leading other retailers in expanding its presence in China, and site planners are designing in double digits shopping malls ten times larger than the Mall of America!

Although many people in highly industrialized nations such as the United States, Japan, Germany, and France enjoy a higher standard of living in comparison with citizens in developing countries, the former simply do not have the burgeoning societies or steadily rising income levels of China and India, and others such as Indonesia and Brazil.

What Are Demographics?

What does all this mean to marketers such as Home Depot, Gap, and Nike? Clearly, only a small fraction of the world's population are potential customers for goods offered by these international

Table 9.1 The World's 50 Most Populated Countries

Rank	Country	Population	Rank	Country	Population
1.	China	1,343,239,923	26.	South Africa	48,810,427
2.	India	1,205,073,612	27.	Spain	47,042,984
3.	United States	313,847,465	28.	Tanzania	46,912,768
4.	Indonesia	248,645,008	29.	Colombia	45,239,079
5.	Brazil	199,321,413	30.	Ukraine	44,854,065
6.	Pakistan	190,291,129	31.	Kenya	43,013,341
7.	Nigeria	170,123,740	32.	Argentina	42,192,494
8.	Bangladesh	161,083,804	33.	Poland	38,415,284
9.	Russia	142,517,670	34.	Algeria	37,367,226
10.	Japan	127,368,088	35.	Canada	34,300,083
11.	Mexico	114,975,046	36.	Sudan	34,206,710
12.	Philippines	103,775,002	37.	Uganda	33,640,833
13.	Vietnam	91,519,289	38.	Morocco	32,309,239
14.	Ethiopia	91,195,675	39.	Iraq	31,129,225
15.	Egypt	83,688,164	40.	Afghanistan	30,419,928
16.	Germany	81,305,856	41.	Nepal	29,890,686
17.	Turkey	79,749,461	42.	Peru	29,549,517
18.	Iran	78,868,711	43.	Malaysia	29,179,952
19.	Congo, Dem. Rep.	73,599,190	44.	Uzbekistan	28,394,180
20.	Thailand	67,091,089	45.	Venezuela	28,047,938
21.	France	65,630,692	46.	Saudi Arabia	26,534,504
22.	United Kingdom	63,047,162	47.	Yemen	24,771,809
23.	Italy	61,261,254	48.	Ghana	24,652,402
24.	Burma	54,584,650	49.	Korea, North	24,589,122
25.	Korea, South	48,860,500	50.	Mozambique	23,515,934

Source: CIA World Factbook.

retailers; marketers, therefore, have to determine whom they can best serve in order to earn a profit. To locate their best customers, then, businesses segment markets (discussed in greater detail in Chapter 1). Among the oldest and most efficient methods of market segmentation is according to **demographics,** the measurable statistics concerning a population, particularly its size, composition, and distribution. In this chapter, we will also discuss income, gender, education, and occupation. Other demographic measurements of interest to marketers are ethnicity, religion, age and family life cycle stage (discussed in Chapter 7), and social class (discussed in Chapter 8).

Marketers use demographic information to learn more about their markets—for example, where their customers live, what they do, how they spend their time, and the kinds of goods and services they need. They also use the information to identify trends, such as when products like the Apple iPad become popular and spawn the growth of other tablet computers, causing a greater demand in the personal electronics industry. And demographic information is used by marketers to increase sales—to learn, for example, when Michael Kors' successful stores in the United States would be ready for replication in Asia.

Examples of Typical Demographics

One of the most important demographic dimensions is population. As we saw earlier in this chapter, while the United States—plus the world's other industrialized countries such as France, Germany, and Japan—may not have the largest populations, the citizens do possess substantial disposable income (a topic discussed later in this chapter). First, let us consider the more than 316 million consumers in the United States. What information goes into demographic measurements of those consumers? Some of the statistics from the 2010 U.S. Census—a nationwide survey of U.S. households that is conducted every 10 years—indicate that:

- 50.8 percent of the population is female.
- 72.4 percent is white, although other races including African American and Asian are growing at a faster rate.
- The Hispanic population represents about 16.3 percent of the total, but its growth is outpacing that of the non-Hispanic population.
- The largest age group of Americans is 18 to 44 years old, but the fastest growing age group is 45 to 64 years old.
- Some 17.2 million women and 13.9 million men live alone.
- More people live in the South than in the Northeast, Midwest, or West, but both the South and West grew by double digits over the previous census.
- New York and Los Angeles remain the two most populous metro areas in the country.
- About two thirds of all Americans own their own home.

As you can tell, a significant amount of demographic information is available about the U.S. population: gender, age, location, home ownership, household composition, ethnicity/race, and more. This type of information helps marketers better connect with consumers.

POPULATION GROWTH AND DISTRIBUTION

Let's look in more detail at where Americans are living today. Census information tells us that many tend to prefer the two coasts and warmer states of California, Texas, Nevada, and Georgia, or scenic ones such as Colorado. Cities such as New York, Los Angeles, and Chicago also thrive; in fact, four out of five Americans live in metropolitan areas—that is, in or near a city with a population of at least 50,000. Table 9.2 shows the 10 largest U.S. cities by population. Home ownership is widespread, and the majority of households also possess at least

Table 9.2 Ten Largest Cities in the United States (2012 Population Estimate)

1. New York, NY	8,336,697
2. Los Angeles, CA	3,857,799
3. Chicago, IL	2,714,856
4. Houston, TX	2,160, 821
5. Philadelphia, PA	1,547,607
6. Phoenix, AZ	1,488,750
7. San Antonio, TX	1,382,951
8. San Diego, CA	1,338,348
9. Dallas, TX	1,241,162
10. San Jose, CA	982,765

Source: www.infoplease.com/ipa/A0763098.html.

one automobile. According to the census, over the decades the population center has moved steadily westward and more recently also southward, from Chestertown, Maryland, in 1790, to Plato, Missouri, in 2010.[2] In the Southwest, two rapidly expanding metropolitan regions in terms of population are Las Vegas, Nevada, and Phoenix, Arizona. Also, many people choose to leave the states where they were born; it is estimated that one out of every five people in the United States moves each year.

Moving to a new location frequently means spending on home improvements as well as new furnishings and appliances (Figure 9.1). Typical home buyers can spend as much as $4,900 more on their new home in the first year than homeowners who didn't move would spend.[3] When they move, some affluent people want more space in the form of larger homes, leading some places such as Marin County, California, to require those planning to build homes larger than 4,000 square feet to obtain approval from authorities, and communities such as Delray Beach, Florida, in an effort to safeguard its historic district, to ban construction of homes larger than 2,000 square feet.[4] The demand for home-building supplies and equipment provides opportunities for businesses ready to sell those types of products, such as Lowe's, Home Depot, and Menards, as well as for home furnishings retailers and design services such as Bed Bath & Beyond and Williams-Sonoma. National chain supermarkets and pharmacies such as Supervalu, Safeway, and CVS quickly occupy the newest shopping centers in American communities, as do clothing retailers like Gap, Kohl's, and Forever 21. Apparel designers are quick to understand consumer needs for home-related products, also. Calvin Klein attaches

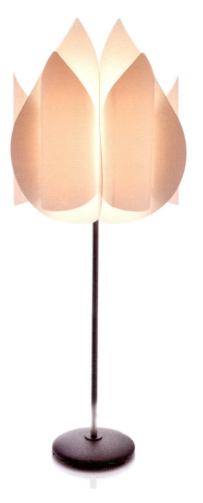

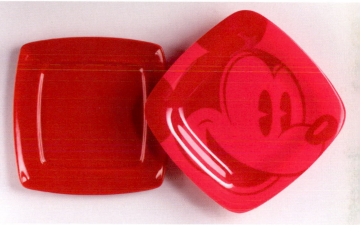

FIGURE 9.1 Frequent moves call for new household goods.

its brand name to furniture, and Vera Wang to mattresses, for example.

LET'S TALK

If you had your wish, where would you choose to live? Why? What kinds of retailers would you need to create the surroundings you prefer?

POPULATION SIZE FACTORS: BIRTHRATE, LIFE EXPECTANCY, AND IMMIGRATION

The size of a country's population depends on the following factors: birthrate, life expectancy, and immigration. **Birthrate** means the number of babies born each year; there must be a sufficient number to replace the population if a nation is to maintain its economy, and more if it is to expand.

Life expectancy means how long people will live, and, more important, how long they can be productive in the economy and in society. **Immigration** refers to the number of people who come into a country; it must be greater than the number leaving in order for the rate to remain constant.

Birthrate

Approximately 4 million babies are born in the United States each year, or 63 births per 1,000 women between the ages of 15 and 44 in recent years, with a slight increase in births among women over 30, according to the most recent census figures. The birthrate seems to be stabilizing after a decline over several years, due in a large part to the recession beginning in 2007. According to research by the Pew Research Center, nearly a quarter of 18- to 34-year-olds said they postponed starting families due to the state of the economy at the time.[5]

Marketers take note of the current birthrate for several reasons. First, all women giving birth have certain needs for consumable goods for themselves and their families, needs for maternity wear, infants' wear, and nursery furnishings (among others). Through their use of demographic statistics, marketers such as Sears, Target, Toys "R" Us, The Baby's Room, and others are able to offer products for this market segment (Figure 9.2). But the needs of women who decide to defer having families until they are older sometimes differ from those of younger mothers-to-be. In all likelihood, older women have been in the work force for a decade or more, and have been increasingly significant consumers of fashion apparel, home furnishings, entertainment, automobiles, and travel. Second, as women mature, their fashion tastes have also had

FIGURE 9.2 Young families have many needs for goods and services.

a chance to develop so that when they are ready to raise a family, their choices of maternity wear, infants' layettes, baby clothes, and nursery furnishings are different and probably more sophisticated than they would have been earlier. Third, their need for services could increase, particularly for those mothers planning to return to work. To maximize family time, they might hire people to provide housecleaning, landscaping, pet grooming, grocery delivery, and meal preparation services instead of doing these things themselves. Tables 9.3A and B indicate projected changes in U.S. population

Table 9.3A Projected Population of the United States, by Age and Sex: 2000 to 2050

Total Population by Age and Sex	2000	2010	2020	2030	2040	2050
POPULATION TOTAL (in thousands)						
TOTAL	282,125	308,936	335,805	363,584	391,946	419,854
0–4	19,218	21,426	22,932	24,272	26,299	28,080
5–19	61,331	61,810	65,955	70,832	75,326	81,067
20–44	104,075	104,444	108,632	114,747	121,659	130,897
45–64	62,440	81,012	83,653	82,280	88,611	93,104
65–84	30,794	34,120	47,363	61,850	64,640	65,844
85+	4,267	6,123	7,269	9,603	15,409	20,861
MALE						
TOTAL	138,411	151,815	165,093	178,563	192,405	206,477
0–4	9,831	10,947	11,716	12,399	13,437	14,348
5–19	31,454	31,622	33,704	36,199	38,496	41,435
20–44	52,294	52,732	54,966	58,000	61,450	66,152
45–64	30,381	39,502	40,966	40,622	43,961	46,214
65–84	13,212	15,069	21,337	28,003	29,488	30,579
85+	1,240	1,942	2,403	3,340	5,573	7,749
FEMALE						
TOTAL	143,713	157,121	170,711	185,022	199,540	213,377
0–4	9,387	10,479	11,216	11,873	12,863	13,732
5–19	29,877	30,187	32,251	34,633	36,831	39,632
20–44	51,781	51,711	53,666	56,747	60,209	64,745
45–64	32,059	41,510	42,687	41,658	44,650	46,891
65–84	17,582	19,051	26,026	33,848	35,152	35,265
85+	3,028	4,182	4,866	6,263	9,836	13,112

Table 9.3B

Percentage of Population by Age and Sex	2000	2010	2020	2030	2040	2050
PERCENTAGE OF TOTAL POPULATION						
TOTAL	100.0	100.0	100.0	100.0	100.0	100.0
0–4	6.8	6.9	6.8	6.7	6.7	6.7
5–19	21.7	20.0	19.6	19.5	19.2	19.3
20–44	36.9	33.8	32.3	31.6	31.0	31.2
45–64	22.1	26.2	24.9	22.6	22.6	22.2
65–84	10.9	11.0	14.1	17.0	16.5	15.7
85+	1.5	2.0	2.2	2.6	3.9	5.0
MALE						
TOTAL	100.0	100.0	100.0	100.0	100.0	100.0
0–4	7.1	7.2	7.1	6.9	7.0	6.9
5–19	22.7	20.8	20.4	20.3	20.0	20.1
20–44	37.8	34.7	33.3	32.5	31.9	32.0
45–64	21.9	26.0	24.8	22.7	22.8	22.4
65–84	9.5	9.9	12.9	15.7	15.3	14.8
85+	0.9	1.3	1.5	1.9	2.9	3.8
FEMALE						
TOTAL	100.0	100.0	100.0	100.0	100.0	100.0
0–4	6.5	6.7	6.6	6.4	6.4	6.4
5–19	20.8	19.2	18.9	18.7	18.5	18.6
20–44	36.0	32.9	31.4	30.7	30.2	30.3
45–64	22.3	26.4	25.0	22.5	22.4	22.0
65–84	12.2	12.1	15.2	18.3	17.6	16.5
85+	2.1	2.7	2.9	3.4	4.9	6.1

Source: U.S. Census Bureau, 2004, "U.S. Interim Projections by Age, Sex, Race, and Hispanic Origin," http://www.census.gov/ipc/www /usinterimproj,Internet Release Date: March 18, 2004.

between the years 2000 and 2050. No wonder fashion marketers are paying close attention to the needs of older age groups for apparel (think Chico's); cosmetics, health and beauty aids (think Lancôme "invisible night repair"); and travel and entertainment (think Elderhostel trips and home theaters).

Life Expectancy

People in the United States are living longer than ever; due to progress in fighting diseases, life expectancy for American men is around 76 years, and for women 81. The two leading causes of death, heart disease and cancer, are both in decline. The fact that people are living longer, healthier lives presents all kinds of marketing opportunities to meet the consumer needs of seniors, who may seek comfortable apparel; lower-chassis automobiles; home furnishings such as telephones with larger buttons, and draperies that are easy to operate; as well as relaxed recreation, travel, learning, and entertainment outlets (Figures 9.3 and 9.4).

FIGURE 9.3 Fashion marketers are paying attention to the older consumer's apparel needs.

FIGURE 9.4 Today many people live longer, with more opportunities to enjoy life.

Immigration

The United States has traditionally been a haven for people from other countries, and much of the nation's growth is due to immigrant talent and tenacity. After all, unless we can trace our ancestry to an indigenous American background, we all stem from immigrant stock. Due to the increases in birthrate and immigration over the years, the U.S. population more than doubled from 152 million in 1950 to 316 million in 2013, adding to concerns about overcrowding and the resulting stresses on the infrastructure (highways, bridges, and communications systems), social services (including schools and health care systems), and the environment. Some type of immigration reform, particularly regarding a possible path to citizenship for the millions of immigrants in the country illegally, continues to be discussed at the federal government level, but as of this writing, no new laws had yet made it through Congress.

Because the U.S. immigrant population is huge, marketers are eager to fulfill the diverse consumer needs of its various groups. In addition to the basic human needs of food, shelter, clothing, and health care, many immigrants have families here and the children require education, recreation, and supplies. At the same time, many want to maintain the traditions and customs of their origins; thus, marketers also have an opportunity to meet immigrants' needs for ethnic foods, apparel, household goods, and entertainment tailored to their tastes. In Los Angeles, for example, the most popular radio station broadcasts in Spanish. Because of California's large Hispanic population, *supermercados* (supermarkets) featuring Mexican foods and spices dot the landscape, and Mexican holidays such as Cinco

FIGURE 9.5 In this promotion featuring actress Eva Longoria, Target is focusing on the Hispanic customer.

de Mayo provide occasions for festivals and celebrations. For other daily living requirements, fashion marketers create apparel and home furnishings in bright colors to cater to the tastes of the Hispanic market (Figure 9.5).

INCOME

Perhaps the greatest single demographic indicator of consumer spending is **income,** the money or other assets that people receive typically in a year from their work, property, and other investments. There are two types of income that marketers pay attention to: **disposable income,** the amount of money after paying taxes that people have for necessities such as food, shelter, utilities, and transportation, of interest to supermarket chains and marketers in general, and **discretionary income,** the amount consumers have after meeting all expenditures for necessities, of particular interest to fashion and luxury goods marketers. Consumers tend to spend more when their discretionary income is up and they feel positive about general economic conditions—that their jobs are secure, that there are no imminent or foreseeable threats to their well-being, and that life in general is moving along fairly well. The level of **consumer confidence,** how consumers feel about the state of the economy, is another indicator that businesses monitor closely. If consumer confidence is high, people are willing to take greater economic risks (such as buying a more expensive home than originally planned), but if consumer confidence is low, as during the recent recession, people hold back, postponing major purchases in particular. Organizations such as The Conference Board periodically conduct surveys to determine the level of consumer confidence; fashion businesses can use this economic information to gauge planning for inventories and promotions.

Income Distribution

Obviously, the distribution of income throughout the population of a country is never evenly spread among all citizens; but in recent years it has become more polarized in the United States than it has been in nearly a century. According to a current analysis by an international group of university economists, financial inequality is at a high not seen since 1928 before the Great Depression. The study revealed that in 2012, almost half of all household income went to just the top 10 percent of the population.

Moreover, income among the wealthiest 1 percent grew 31.4 percent during the years 2009 to 2012, while incomes of the remaining 99 percent of the nation's earners grew only 0.4 percent.[6] Although economists agree that some income difference has the advantage of encouraging people to compete to get ahead (assuming opportunities to advance are there), others believe that too much income disparity stunts economic growth, since those without sufficient income cannot spend on goods and services that stimulate the economy for everyone.

These trends are important to marketers, since income is clearly one of the key factors by which they identify their customer base. While some companies such as Neiman Marcus, Gucci, Henredon Furniture, and Tauck Tours target their promotions to the high-income top 20 percent of consumers, others such as Lowe's, Old Navy, Walmart, and Kmart pay significant attention to the millions more people in the lower income brackets; this is an example of market segmentation based on the demographic of income (Figure 9.7). In 2012, the **per capita personal income,** total income divided by total population, in the United States was $42,693. As can be imagined, income distribution was not equal among states (Figure 9.6). Residents of Connecticut produced the highest per-capita income of $58,908, while residents of Mississippi had the nation's lowest per-capita income of $33,073.[7] The distribution of income (as well as population) has an effect on fashion marketers, because they are concerned with supplying their various retail stores throughout the country with the kinds of goods consumers need just before they recognize that need. Retailers from Macy's and Dick's to Sephora and Pottery Barn identify the economic conditions in each geographic

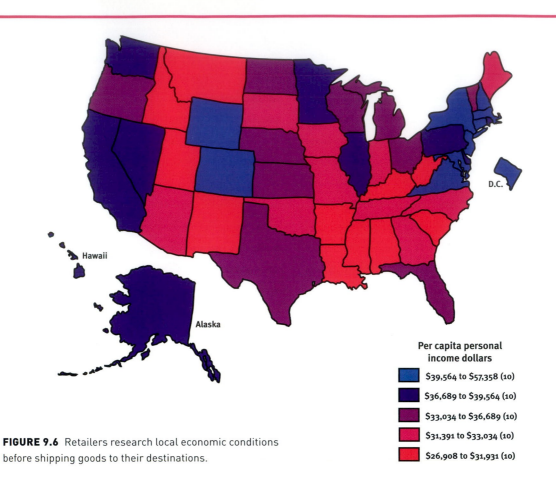

Per capita personal income dollars

FIGURE 9.6 Retailers research local economic conditions before shipping goods to their destinations.

FIGURE 9.7
Upper-income customers have considerable discretionary income to spend on fashion goods.

region they serve in order to successfully plan for the new season's merchandise distribution.

Spending Patterns

Obviously, the amount of money people spend varies according to income level, and age is also a significant factor (as discussed in Chapter 7). Consider children as consumers. According to census numbers, there are nearly 74 million children and young people in the United States who are under the age of 18; and their **purchasing power**—the amount of goods and services the dollar will buy—amounts to some $1.2 trillion per year, including expenditures their parents make for them, according to a report by global advertising agency Publicis. Children spend not only on clothing, food, and entertainment for themselves but also influence the purchasing of many items for the family. For example, according to the research, 60 percent of tweens have a say in the family's choice of an automobile.[8] Unfortunately, nearly 6 million young children in America, or one quarter of all of those under age 6, are living in poverty[9]—a matter the nation has yet to address in a meaningful way but surely must, as children represent the future of the country, including its potential prosperity.

The U.S. teenage population numbers upward of 25 million, and those teens spend more on apparel than their younger siblings. Yet because teen tastes change so swiftly and unpredictably, they create a "moving target" for retailers such as Forever 21, American Eagle Outfitters, H&M, Urban Outfitters, Pacific Sunwear, and Abercrombie & Fitch.

For Millennials, sometimes called Generation Y, the recent recession was a major factor shaping their young adulthood, so they tend to look for value when they shop. At the same time, being the first generation to grow up with the Internet, they are highly technologically savvy and use a variety of digital means to seek out products and services that meet both their budget and their desire for fun in shopping.

Generation Xers (born between 1965 and 1980) have spending patterns that reflect their interests, which are often centered on family and home—to be expected, as this generation is likely to still have children at home. Many are in their peak earning years, and they seek out large-screen TVs, brand-name sporting goods, high-end kitchen appliances, designer accessories, and roomy SUVs. Of course, not all Gen Xers are affluent. What's more, in addition to raising families of their own, some are also caring for aging parents, adding to the everyday expenditures they must make.

It is the baby boomers (born between 1946 and 1964 and accounting for nearly one-fourth of the U.S. population, or about 76 million people) who are the nation's biggest consumers, with an annual spending power of $3.4 trillion.[10] Eager to remain active even as they get older, much of boomers' spending goes to recreational and lifestyle pursuits like traveling, dining out, exercise activities, gyms, spas, and salons. They also spend money on technology, entertainment, household furnishings, landscaping, personal care, and gifts, and in one recent year, they spent $87 billion on new cars.[11] For boomer customers, fashion is part of their identity. Fashion marketers are realizing this in a number of ways: Luxury stores such as Neiman Marcus, Nordstrom, and Saks Fifth Avenue are paying greater attention to consumers age 50-plus, and specialty stores such as Talbots and Chico's cater to this consumer segment as well. The active boomer lifestyle also opens up opportunities for retailers such as Sports Authority, Travel Smith, L.L. Bean, and Magellan. What's more, boomers demand customization, not just in their music and clothing selections but also in their home theater systems, closets, and kitchen cabinets. New home builders encourage their customers (many of them boomers) to visit builder design centers and select customized tile, colors, and moveable non-load-bearing walls.[12]

But, as with younger consumer groups, not every member of this demographic is affluent, and the recent recession put a dent in both income and wealth for many Americans of all ages. Among working families in the United States, the median income (or exact middle, with half above and half below) is $51,107, representing a drop since the mid-2000s. The number varies based on ethnicity and race, as well. Median income for Asian Americans is higher, at $68,000; non-Hispanic whites $57,000; Hispanics $39,000; and African-Americans $33,000. By contrast, the top 5 percent of income earners have a median income of $191,000.[13] Clearly many consumers, and particularly the Hispanic and African-American communities, continue to struggle due to the lack of job opportunities and stagnant wages. Some lack sufficient education to be hired for many of the technical—and higher-paying—jobs needing workers. In such instances, covering necessities with disposable income is rarely feasible, and the concept of discretionary income does not exist.

Economic conditions impact the oldest segments of the population as well. Due to the sharp increase in the U.S. birth rate after World War II and increased longevity, one of the most rapidly expanding groups of consumers is people age 65 and older.

This group currently comprises 13 percent of the nation's population, encompassing some 43 million people, but is projected to double to 92 million by 2060. Households headed by seniors have a median income of $48,538,[14] and they spend their money on a variety of consumer goods including travel, housing, entertainment, and often gifts for their grandchildren. Even though the Internet was not a factor for much of their lives, nearly two thirds of seniors go online regularly,[15] including to shop for goods such as apparel, accessories, books, gifts, and flowers. As seniors live longer and healthier lives, their interests remain vital, and their purchasing power active. The problem is that between 2000 and 2012, seniors lost over a third of their buying power, a particularly difficult situation for middle- and low-income seniors for whom Social Security is their main source of income. Although Social Security benefits have risen nearly 40 percent, expenses— and particularly health-care costs—have soared, making it increasingly difficult for older Americans to live comfortably and securely.

LET'S TALK

Think of a shopping center or downtown area you know, and name three or four popular stores there. Which income and age groups do these stores cater to?

GENDER

It used to be that both marketers and consumers were quite certain about who bought what products, and advertisers knew whether to aim their promotions at men, women, or both. For example, men bought the family's car, while women bought the clothing—and marketers designed and directed their promotions accordingly. Automobile advertising stressed power and engine performance to men; department stores touted fashion and value to women. Today, however, marketers realize that women make up a significant market segment for a much wider variety of products including automobiles, homes, electronics—even extreme vacations like skydiving. In automobile advertising, along with the attributes of power, engine performance, and speed, traditionally of interest to men, manufacturers also highlight safety, aesthetic and comfort features, and fuel economy, considered strong draws for women.

Likewise, manufacturers of skin care and beauty aids, traditionally marketed to women, are targeting an increasingly important group of male customers. In addition to using shaving cream and deodorants, many men are also applying moisturizers, masks, aftershave lotions, and fragrances, with spending on grooming products expected to top $33 billion throughout the world in 2015.[16] Young men particularly find that these products not only make them feel better but can also enhance their appearance.

Moving toward Gender Equality

Over the past 50 years, an increasing number of women have joined the work force and pursued careers, many of them striving to "break the glass ceiling" and reach the top positions historically held only by men. In the majority of today's U.S. households, even those with children, both spouses work, and it often takes two incomes for a family to live comfortably. The rise of women in the work force has added to the growth of family income, and according to some experts, 100 percent of the growth of discretionary income. But the earnings of women working full-time, on average, still have a way to go before catching up to those of men. The so-called "gender gap" in earnings means that for every $1 a man earns, a woman doing a comparable job earns only 77 cents. However, with some federal government support, women are making some progress as they continue to push for income equality; and in more than 25 percent of all dual-income families, the woman now earns more than the man.[17]

Emerging Trends in Consuming

According to Michael Silverstein of the Boston Consulting Group and author of *Treasure Hunt: Inside the Mind of the New Consumer*, women's earning potential is rising. Women outnumber men in colleges and graduate schools. Their knowledge obviously includes shopping savvy, which they combine with control over the discretionary dollar. In the family, women tend to make the decisions about remodeling the kitchen, going on vacation, and dining out. When shopping, women are looking for pleasure, emotional "highs," and find them at both ends of the price spectrum, in small luxuries at one end (think Godiva chocolates) and fantastic values at the other (think Thomas O'Brien linens at Target).[18] Fashion stores such as Bloomingdale's, Tiffany, or designer boutiques display tempting luxuries, while Sam's Club, Nordstrom Rack, Price Chopper, and other discounters hone in on offering great bargains. Some marketers are responding to the small luxury preference by combining the desire for luxury with that for value. For example, the budget-priced

Reading the Trends to Predict Future Consumer Spending

There's no question that a downturn in the economy can have ramifications that go well beyond the immediate impact to many consumers' wallets. Indeed, in periods of economic stress, some people may feel forced to put off important events, such as marriage or buying a home, until circumstances stabilize. So it's not surprising that as the country eased its way back to stronger economic footing following the recent "Great Recession," trend-watchers began to see signs that consumers were ready to resume traditional activities for their life stages. *Stores* magazine compiled some of those insights from researchers and demographers, identifying key demographic shifts that could affect consumer behavior in coming years—including who is making purchases and where they're spending their money.

More Babies. According to Demographics Intelligence president W. Bradford Wilcox, the "baby bust" is over for now. "In the wake of the recession, about a million babies were postponed or foregone entirely between 2007 and 2011, [but] there are plenty of women out there who have waited to have a child. . . . The time is right now."

Older Mothers. Babies can be delayed, but not forever, thanks to women's biological clocks. Wilcox predicts that the biggest increase in births will be for women who are better educated, older, and more affluent. That translates to a 6 percent growth rate in births for college-educated women and for women over 30.

Gen Y as Homeowners. So-called "Boomerang Babies," members of Generation Y who faced a bleak job market so returned home after college to live with their boomer parents, are ready to fly the coop once and for all—which has led to a trend of parents taking advantage of a buyer's market in real estate and buying homes for their children. All those new households are expected to generate a huge surge in purchases of furnishings and other household goods, according to Ken Gronbach, demographer and author of *The Age Curve*.

Global Population Shifts. For decades, cheap labor has meant lower prices on products sourced in Asia, but a slowdown in population growth, particularly in China, means that a lot of manufacturing may move back to the United States. That not only means that prices on certain goods will go up, but also, with birthrates falling in various countries around the world, marketers will need to take a fresh look at their target customer bases and global strategies.

Strengthening of the Americas. So where should the smart marketer expand? Gronbach says that retailers should look to the Americas. He even forecasts that, at some point in the future, the

(continued)

countries of North and South America will join together to create a unified currency, much as the European Union did with the euro.

High-Spending Seniors. Returning the focus to today, which consumers are actually doing the most shopping? Older Americans, that's who. According to American Express Business Insights research, seniors surpassed all other age groups in spending on online luxury flash sale websites in 2011, spending 28 percent more on those sites than the year before. Boomers, by contrast, increased their spending by only 9 percent.

Gen Y Goes Luxury. Even as their boomer grandparents may be watching their wallets, it turns out that Generation Y is not afraid to spend on goods they really want—including luxury. In fact, this age group increased its full-price spending at online luxury retailers by 31 percent in 2011, according to American Express. Says Ed Jay, senior vice president at American Express Business Insights, "Retailers should consider this a good time to build lasting relationships with these Gen Y consumers who clearly have a taste for luxury brands. It's clear that as the Millennial group experiences luxury and designer merchandise through luxury flash sale sites, they are forming brand loyalties along the way. If this trend continues, as this group and their bank accounts mature, their spend on full-price luxury will continue to increase."

Source: Sandy Smith, "What Trends Portend," *Stores,* April 2012, www.stores.org/STORES%20Magazine%20April%202012/what-trends-portend.

Swedish fashion retailer H&M is known for collaborating with designers such as Karl Lagerfeld, Stella McCartney, and Viktor Horsting and Rolf Snoeren (Viktor and Rolf); the company offers name apparel especially created for its approximately 3,000 stores worldwide, thus providing luxury brands created to sell at bargain prices.

Marketing to Alternative Lifestyles

Although they make up a small percentage of all consumers, lesbian, gay, bisexual, and transgender (LGBT) people make up a vital part of the consumer market. Roughly estimated at about 4 percent of the total population, LGBTs do not fit into a single market segment, but their spending patterns are significant. With incomes estimated at $56,000 and above, many LGBTs are in professional and creative occupations, well educated, with an interest in the arts, travel, social reform, apparel, and home furnishings. As a growing number of states rewrite laws allowing same-sex couples to marry, and others at least permitting civil unions, the proportion of LGBTs living as families, often with children, will continue to increase, creating a new group of consumers for products such as children's apparel and toys, and additional household goods.

Today, advertisers use a variety of media, including the Internet and films, to reach LGBT customers. Sports events such as the Gay Games attract participants and fans from across the nation and abroad, providing numerous advertising, promotional, and sponsorship opportunities. Film festivals for gays and lesbians are also an important venue. The Pernod Ricard USA organization, owner of the Stolichnaya vodka brand, involved itself in film festivals by creating a 53-minute film for gay and lesbian audiences. Titled *Be Real,* the film carries Stoli's theme that the product is genuine Russian vodka and also emphasizes the company's commitment to the viewers.[19]

Cable television is another way that marketers successfully reach the LGBT audience. Logo TV, owned by MTV Networks and its parent Viacom, can be seen in more than 52 million households, and its website, logotv.com, has an even wider online reach. Many major companies advertise on Logo, among them Continental Airlines, Dell, Sears Holdings, and Subaru, with commercials geared to the audience. In addition, as greater tolerance and acceptance of the LGBT community spreads, marketers' messaging has become a little more mainstream. Some retailers and other marketers are making the conscious decision to feature same-sex couples in their advertising or on their catalogs or websites. JCPenney chose openly gay Ellen DeGeneres to be its advertising spokeswoman, and stuck with the popular comedian and talk show host even after a protest was launched by a small number of

conservative consumers. Highly rated TV shows like *Modern Family,* which features a gay married couple with a daughter, are also helping shift public opinion and therefore marketing tactics.

EDUCATION AND OCCUPATION

Another way by which marketers glean demographic information about customers is by segmenting markets according to education and/or occupation. Often researchers combine these elements with others such as income or age (Figure 9.8). For example, a marketer wants to reach middle-aged weekend motorcycle enthusiasts with careers in law, advertising, or dentistry. Research done by Harley-Davidson has shown that many affluent professionals seek adventure on the road and release from job stress, and for them, Harley has produced appealing motorcycles with power and style. In addition, the look is enhanced by accessories such as saddlebags and apparel, including leather jackets and pants, to complete the fashion picture. Finally the company creates a social life—Harley Owners' Group—built around Harley road trips and gatherings.

Typically, a college graduate tends to bring in a higher income than someone who completes only high school. And for many women today, education has become the key to more interesting, rewarding, and higher-paying careers. Marketers know that the more educated consumers become, the more goods and services they will want for themselves, and the more demanding they will be in their purchasing behavior—a result of their level of exposure to new ideas through travel, education, and life experience.

For example, an interior designer, once she gains experience, might design for wealthy clients, begin

FIGURE 9.8 Income, gender, and occupation are often essential demographics for marketers.

to buy period furniture and antiques for herself as well, and travel to exotic places to find just the right room accessories, and learn to distinguish an original piece of period furniture from a reproduction. As a result, she will become a more discriminating consumer; as a professional, she will be able to offer the benefit of her added expertise to her clients.

Marketers also use the demographic of occupation to reach target consumers. For example, people marketing New York theater productions and Las Vegas spectacles might target fashion professionals because the latter attend live performances for inspiration as well as entertainment; they have a professional/occupational interest. Mailers, flyers, and ads distributed at hotels and convention centers herald the shows most touted to market-week fashion buyers. Another example is the sport of golf. Among business executives, playing golf is considered a sign of job-related success. Many business deals have been made on the golf course over the decades. To reach this market, manufacturers of golfing equipment and accessories advertise in magazines that executives read (such as *Fortune* and *Bloomberg BusinessWeek*). Another example of marketers targeting a segment of consumers by occupation is the uniform industry. Many people wear uniforms on the job, including members of the military, emergency services personnel, airline and bank employees, health-care workers, and chefs (Figure 9.9).

Putting together all that we've covered so far, we can conclude that the demographic information of particular interest to fashion marketers includes population growth and location, income (especially as related to age and life cycle stage), gender, and occupation (Figure 9.10). Marketers need to know the size of potential markets and their location. Designers, noticing the population shift to the "sunshine states" (for example, Arizona) can respond by creating casual apparel for outdoor wear and furniture to be used in gardens and by swimming pools. The accumulation of wealth among a small percentage of people lets high-end fashion marketers (from tiny boutiques to Barneys) serve this demographic by offering distinctive apparel and accessories from prestigious designers. The great majority of consumers with more modest incomes create a market for retailers from Macy's to Costco to satisfy consumer wants. Apparel and home furnishings are

FIGURE 9.9 Uniforms serve to identify the members of an organization.

FIGURE 9.10 Nike is one of the brands that gears its messages toward particular markets.

designed with gender in mind, also, and often with occupation as well. Brooks Brothers offers conservative looks for men and women in business and similar professional fields, while Bed Bath & Beyond provides linens and home accessories created to appeal to women, men, or both.

LET'S TALK

As a college student, what three or four kinds of goods or services do fashion marketers aim specifically at you?

Values Driving Consumption

Our **values,** ideas that are important in life which become our principles for behavior, have an effect on what we do—including what and how we consume. We hold certain values, both as a culture and as individuals, and those values are often framed by demographics. For example, Americans in general believe in values such as freedom and democracy; the right to choose what we want to do in life, including the work we want to do; the connections to family we want to create; the lifestyle we prefer; and the right as individuals to pursue our own goals.

Other cultures (particularly in Asia) certainly share some of those but focus more heavily on different values, among them the supremacy of the family; respect for age; and decision making that benefits the group rather than an individual.

Humans have always consumed goods and services, but for centuries individuals were the sole producers of what they themselves consumed. In early civilizations, people would forage for food, shelter, and the makings of clothing, and would gather only what they needed to survive. Their connection with goods was intimate—they made what they ate, slept on, and wore. In fact, collecting more than they needed could cause hardship, as they regularly packed up and moved all they had from place to place. Life was simple, and resources were used efficiently.

Everyone needs to consume to survive, but the *way* we consume today is vastly different from the past. Over time, through population migration and wars, some people and nations gained control over resources. With control came waste, and great differences arose between those who were in charge of the means of production (such as farmland, mines, and later, factories) and those who were not. Even in the nineteenth and early twentieth centuries in the United States and Europe, consumption among most people was limited to necessities, and spending on luxuries was thought of as wasteful. Only the very wealthy were able to obtain the luxuries they desired (estates, jewels, works of art), a practice that had gone on for centuries in that class. According to writer Anup Shah in the article "Behind Consumption and Consumerism, Creating the Consumer," today almost everyone has access to luxuries, and many of these indeed have become "necessities," like hot and cold running water.[20]

THE RISE OF CONSUMERISM

Somewhere along the way in Western society, the rise of individualism and the popularity of an individual's pursuit of his or her own needs became more important than concern for the needs of society in general. Moreover, being able to pursue individual goals meant having the capability to consume whatever one could obtain.[21] The concept that emerged from this point of view has become a central issue in most modern societies. Known as **consumerism,** it has three meanings: (1) the movement protecting consumers by requiring honest packaging and product guarantees, (2) the theory that the greater consumption of goods is economically beneficial, and (3) attachment to materialistic values and possessions. The consumerism movement (protecting consumers) is discussed in Chapter 16; the theory presented in the second point reflects the idea that consumerism is actually beneficial to society (for example, by creating more jobs and a higher standard of living). The following discussion addresses the third definition of consumerism: the attachment to materialistic values and possessions.

What is the price of this lifestyle? The way modern humankind practices consumption produces the inequalities that accompany it across the globe, inequalities that are damaging to the world's resources (one example is the contribution of air pollution to climate change), according to the United Nations. Consumption affects people and the environment all over the planet. Consider the following figures: The wealthiest 20 percent of the world's population accounts for as much as 76.6 percent of total private consumption, while the world's poorest 20 percent of people account for just

Using Demographics to Give Consumers What They Want, When They Want It

Suppose, sometime in the future, you become interested in visiting some new spot on the globe, say a mountain ski resort, but you aren't quite sure exactly where the best one for you is located. Rather than spending hours and hours scouring the Internet to narrow down your choices, you could instead supply certain information about yourself—such as your address, income, occupation, and special interests—to a marketing technology company, or data broker. The data broker could then use the demographic details you provided to send you ads geared specifically to your interest, in this case, only mountain resorts specializing in great skiing and offering all-inclusive, moderately priced vacation packages.

How does this work? While still in the planning stages, the concept being developed by Acxiom Corporation, one of the largest data brokers, is to ask potential subscribers to send in certain data about themselves and their interests. From that data, the company would create an accurate consumer profile, but one the consumer may change at will. Then, when a specific subscriber request comes in, such as for a ski resort, the data broker would make sure that instead of receiving all kinds of skiing literature, the consumer receives only information that meets his or her criteria.

Acxiom (and other data brokers) already collect information about consumers to provide client companies with likely prospects for their products or services, and to determine for business clients (such as banks and credit card companies) whether a potential customer is who he or she claims to be. In order to provide this specific consumer information, data brokers amass quantities of data concerning individual customers. They generally secure these data from various sources including public records such as marriage licenses, birth certificates, property ownership, and professional licenses; magazine subscriptions and various consumer surveys; and recent customer purchases including product warranties. Acxiom then organizes its data according to six categories: personal characteristics, home and vehicle data, economic and shopping data, and household interests.

For an organization to be collecting and holding such vast amounts of consumers' personal data raises concerns from both consumers and the government over privacy and transparency issues. Acxiom's response is to provide a website (www.aboutthedata.com) where consumers can verify the accuracy of data collected about them and make changes where needed. Obviously, questions still persist concerning consumer privacy and other matters, but Acxiom's hope is that those concerns will be outweighed by the time savings and convenience consumers will enjoy when receiving only the most useful information in their product searches.

Source: Natasha Singer, "A Data Broker Offers a Peek Behind the Curtain," *New York Times*, September 1, 2013, pp. BU1, BU6; and Singer, "Acxiom Lets Consumers See Data It Collects," *New York Times*, September 5, 2013, p. B6.

1.5 percent. What's more, the richest 20 percent consume nearly 60 percent of the world's energy and own 87 percent of the world's vehicles, while the poorest 20 percent consume less than 4 percent of the world's energy and own less than 1 percent of its vehicles. To give it another perspective, the United States and Europe together spend more than $12 billion a year on perfumes. Worldwide spending on basic education for all totals only $6 billion.[22] Clearly, a dire need exists to erase poverty, hunger, and disease; to provide education and job opportunities; and to conserve and keep the environment free from degradation. These are issues of social responsibility, a topic that we'll examine further in Chapter 15.

MATERIALISM TODAY

The importance that we attach to the things we own is called **materialism.** People in the world's richest nations tend to be materialistic; they have accumulated the means to purchase many goods and services, which are readily available. And the people most devoted to materialism reside in the United States. We are fortunate in having access to so many products, and many of us in having the wherewithal to own them. But contrary to popular belief, owning and consuming products does *not* make many people truly happy. A recent consumer survey of American attitudes on materialism and consumption, commissioned by Merck Family Fund, revealed four major points regarding Americans' feelings about consuming:

- Many Americans believe our priorities are out of kilter, that materialism, greed, and selfishness are overtaking our public and private lives, and crowding out our dedication to family and sense of responsibility to society.

- Americans are concerned about their future. "The American Dream" is now defined by what people own and "keeping up with the Joneses," rather than by an opportunity to create a better society. In general, children are very materialistic—too centered on consuming things.

- People feel ambivalent creating changes. They want to be financially independent and comfortable, but they also have nonmaterial goals for the future (for example, raising healthy, well-rounded families). They know they buy more than they need, yet they cherish the idea of freedom to live as they choose.

- People connect materialistic concerns with the environment, realizing that the desire to consume more and more is not ecologically sustainable and, to maintain balance, priorities require serious changes—such as consuming far less oil and gas.[23]

LET'S TALK

Of the four concerns cited above, which, in your opinion, is the most important or urgent? Why?

WHAT'S TO BE DONE?

According to anthropologist, professor, and writer Dr. Leslie Jermyn, consumers have lost touch with the human element in the goods they purchase. If you knew Aunt Jessie had knitted that sweater just for you, you'd tend to keep it as long as you possibly could. A similar item made by a stranger overseas, however, could easily be replaced by next season's latest look. Dr. Jermyn has developed some ideas for "successful consuming":

- *Value what we have.* Appreciate the time and other resources that went into creating the wardrobes, furniture, and electronics that we already own. When it's time to dispose of an item, we can find out how someone else might use it. Give it to a charity.

- *Repair and reuse.* If a garment needs mending, instead of discarding it, we can fix it. If it's not the latest look, alter it. If slipcovers and spreads look out-of-date, dye them. They'll last longer and you can use that money for other purposes.

- *Shop alternatively.* When we need something, let's think of the many places we could obtain it: discount stores, thrift shops, vintage clothing and antique stores, fashion rental services. A Kansas City vintage clothing store on the second floor of a warehouse consists of several rooms, each of which is dedicated to a decade—the 1990s, 1980s, and so on to before World War II. Called Reruns, the store is visited by the general public as well as by costumers from Hollywood studios when they are doing period films, such as *Forrest Gump* and *Road to Perdition.* All of the apparel is sold at discount, and people come for miles to shop there. While other cities might not have stores exactly like this, towns of all sizes have thrift shops offering bargain assortments of vintage fashion goods.

- *Think before you buy.* Owning a certain product does not guarantee happiness. Owning a designer outfit does not make you a fashion plate. Using a certain soap or cosmetic will not change your basic appearance, so examine carefully what you need. By buying less often, you'll find you get more use out of what you do purchase, and you'll enjoy it longer.[24]

What Are Psychographics?

We have examined how marketers can analyze customers and segment consumer markets according to demographics—measurable statistics including population growth and distribution, gender, income, and education—but numbers alone don't give the full picture. To further explain (and try to predict) consumer behavior, many marketers make an effort to learn what goes on inside the consumer's mind, which can't be measured in numbers. The field of **psychographics,** the study of consumer personality and lifestyle, provides another dimension for marketers to understand and influence consumer behavior. Our **lifestyles** include our values and the way we express them in what we consume. A young woman who reads *Glamour* may have the same demographic characteristics as one who reads the *New Yorker,* but their psychographics and resulting buying behavior might be very different.

Marketers use psychographics in a number of ways, including defining a target market, positioning a product, and creating a marketing strategy. In defining a target market, a fabric store might try to reach college-age design students; in positioning a product, Callaway golf equipment might focus on the equipment needs of middle-aged country club golfers; in creating a far-reaching marketing

Social Media Offer Goldmine of Psychographic Data

Once upon a time, actually not too many years ago, marketers had little choice but to spend big bucks saturating the mass media in order to tell customers about their product. The problem is, even as they were spending lots of money on advertising, they knew full well that their message was falling on more than a few deaf ears, since many of the consumers hearing it were those who couldn't care less about the product or brand. Even when marketers chose a specific newspaper market or certain TV show, it was still hit or miss as to whether each message was getting through to exactly the right consumers.

But all that changed with the birth (and growth) of social media, which gives marketers an unprecedented capability to pinpoint customers based on personal information they are voluntarily sharing with the world. As social media strategist Cara Pring explains it, with social media, "all of a sudden [marketers] not only knew our name, age, gender, and location, but they knew just about everything else about our personality, lives, and interests, too."

If psychographics can be defined as a means of identifying consumers by their personality, values, attitudes, interests, and lifestyles, it's clear that social media is a goldmine for psychographic information. "It's not about how old you are or where you live, but the stuff that really defines who you are—like the fact that you enjoy Italian food, or *Mad Men*, or staying up late, or that you're an entrepreneur or stay-at-home mom with a 6-month-old," says Pring. "Do you think someone selling *Mad Men* merchandise would make a better return on investment targeting males 18–45 living in the United States, or by targeting everyone who likes *Mad Men*?"

The answer to that question is abundantly clear—and social networking sites like Facebook have made the capability a reality. That doesn't mean, however, that tapping social media for psychographic data is always easy. For instance, just because consumers tweet about a product doesn't mean they were the actual consumer; shoppers may have been impressed by something they bought as a gift, so targeting them for additional purchases could be spinning a marketer's wheels. At the same time, the goal behind social media is to encourage sharing, so limiting a psychographic profile to people a marketer thinks are most interested in actually consuming a product or service may leave out a wealth of other people who would eagerly pass the information along to friends they think would be interested.

That said, there's no question that psychographic targeting using social media has completely changed the game plan. And it can be very successful, but only if a marketer truly knows who its target market is.

Source: Cara Pring, "6 Considerations Before Engaging in Psychographic Targeting," *Ignite Social Media*, November 8, 2012, www.ignitesocialmedia.com/social-media-strategy/psychographic-targeting/.

strategy, an apparel specialty chain might offer mobile shopping in addition to its stores, website, and mail order catalogs.

THE ORIGIN OF LIFESTYLES

We frame our lives around what we consider important—that is, our values. Based on our values, our lifestyles consist of our activities, interests, and opinions (AIOs) and the goods and services we buy to confirm and support them. Psychographic analysis—done periodically through surveys and other market research (see Chapter 10)—reveals what people consider important and how they are consuming accordingly. For example, lifestyle research can indicate emerging trends in shopping

preferences, such as going to the mall, shopping online, browsing on a tablet or other mobile device, or ordering products from TV shopping channels. Table 9.4 shows popular AIO elements.

A psychographic system that many marketers employ to find out why customers make certain buying decisions, known as **VALS,** is based on psychological traits, motivation, and resources. Developed by the research organization SRI (now a separate organization operating under the name Strategic Business Insights), VALS originally stood for "values and lifestyles," but the system has been refined and is now based on consumer traits rather than values; however, the company continues to use the VALS name.

By conducting many consumer surveys, researchers using the VALS system arranged adult

Table 9.4 Examples of AIO (Activities/Interests/Opinions) Elements

Activities	Interests	Opinions	Demographics
Work	Family	Themselves	Age
Hobbies	Home	Social Issues	Education
Social events	Job	Politics	Income
Vacation	Community	Business	Occupation
Entertainment	Recreation	Economics	Family size
Club membership	Fashion	Education	Dwelling
Community	Food	Products	Geography
Shopping	Media	Future	City size
Sports	Achievements	Culture	Stage in life cycle

Source: AIO Elements, Wells & Tiger, *Journal of Advertising Research* 8, no. 71 pp. 27–35.

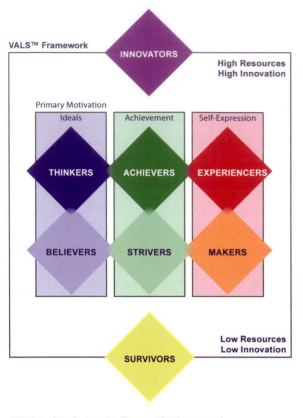

VALS™ Framework

INNOVATORS

High Resources
High Innovation

Primary Motivation

| Ideals | Achievement | Self-Expression |

THINKERS   ACHIEVERS   EXPERIENCERS

BELIEVERS   STRIVERS   MAKERS

Low Resources
Low Innovation

SURVIVORS

FIGURE 9.11 VALS framework.

U.S. consumers into one of eight segments, as shown in Figure 9.11. VALS created a framework based on consumers' motivation (the horizontal dimension) and resources (the vertical dimension). According to VALS, people's buying behavior is based on what gives them the greatest satisfaction, shape, or substance to their lives; that is, their motivation. VALS researchers found that one of three forces tends to motivate individual consumers: ideals or principles, achievement, and self-expression. Consumers motivated mainly by ideals and principles are guided by knowledge; therefore, when purchasing goods and services, these consumers are best reached by marketers providing thorough information on which to base decision making.[25]

For example, an advertiser of smart phones aiming marketing messages to "thinkers" and "believers" will stress ease of use, moderate cost, and functionality. Marketers know that consumers driven mainly by achievement ("achievers" and "strivers") seek goods and services that proclaim their accomplishments: luxury automobiles, designer apparel, and exclusive vacations. Prestige promotions for Gucci leathers or Tiffany jewelry get their attention—and dollars. For consumers motivated by variety and self-expression, such as a fashion merchandising student who plans to buy a dress for salsa dancing, ads highlighting glamour could draw attention. For other consumers seeking variety, a publisher of shelter magazines might offer detailed information on do-it-yourself decorating projects.

Geodemographic Measurements: An Example (PRIZM)

Research organizations also use another sophisticated method of market segmentation for industries such as communications, transportation, and fashion. Companies such as Nielsen Media Research, Gallup, JD Power, and The NPD Group use a **geodemographic system,** a consumer-measuring technique that combines geography with demographics. This system, first created in the early 1970s by Claritas and later acquired by the Nielsen Company, is known as Nielsen **PRIZM.** Continually being refined, this geodemographic system currently does the following:

- Segments markets down to the neighborhood and household levels by ZIP codes.
- Combines demographic information such as income and family size with lifestyles.
- Identifies areas of similar consumer behavior throughout the United States.

On the theory that "birds of a feather flock together" (that is, people with similar incomes and other characteristics tend to live near each other), PRIZM researchers have created 66 distinct market segments based on socioeconomic status, taking into account such characteristics as income, occupation, education, and home value. Each of these segments is further classified according to 14 different Social Groups (based on urbanization and socioeconomic rank) and 11 different Lifestage Groups (based on age, socioeconomic rank, and the presence of children in a household).

For example, one of the PRIZM Social Groups is labeled "Urban Uptown." In general, Urban Uptown consumers are affluent middle-class city dwellers, ethnically diverse, college educated, with a high representation of Asians and Hispanics. They patronize exclusive stores, travel, and use electronics extensively. One market segment of Urban Uptown is called "Young Digerati." These are tech-savvy, ethnically diverse couples and singles who live in trendy apartments or condos in fashionable neighborhoods filled with fitness clubs, clothing boutiques, casual restaurants, juice bars, and microbreweries. Young Digerati may also fall into the Lifestage Group of "Young Achievers," who've recently settled

into metro neighborhoods and tend to exhibit a progressive sensibility and enjoy a lively nightlife.[26] Figure 9.12 provides a sample of PRIZM segmentation.

It is easy to see how pinpointing consumers so precisely can be of great use to fashion marketers; among other efforts, they can use the information to design ads and promotions that will appeal to the specific targeted segment. One example of a fashion retailer's use of PRIZM occurred not long ago.

66 PRIZM marketing segments

PRIZM NE Social Groups

PRIZM divides the U.S. consumer into 14 different groups and 66 different segments. Below is a sampling of the information provided for each group and segment:

- Group U1 – Urban Uptown
- Group U2 – Midtown Mix
- Group U3 – Urban Cores
- Group S1 – Elite Suburbs
- Group S2 – The Affluentials
- Group S3 – Middleburbs
- Group S4 – Inner Suburbs
- Group C1 – 2nd City Society
- Group C2 – City Centers
- Group C3 – Micro-City Blues
- Group T1 – Landed Gentry
- Group T2 – Country Comfort
- Group T3 – Middle America
- Group T4 – Rustic Living

Group U1 – Urban Uptown

The five segments in Urban Uptown are home to the nation's wealthiest urban consumers. Members of this social group tend to be affluent to middle class, college educated and ethnically diverse, with above-average concentrations of Asian and Hispanic Americans. Although this group is diverse in terms of housing styles and family sizes, residents share an upscale urban perspective that's reflected in their marketplace choices. Urban Uptown consumers tend to frequent the arts, shop at exclusive retailers, drive luxury imports, travel abroad and spend heavily on computer and wireless technology.

FIGURE 9.12 PRIZM marketing segments.

A Midwestern department store chain, seeking to improve sales in the designer apparel sections of its stores, used PRIZM to locate its most likely target markets. The study revealed that the majority of designer department customers lived near six of the chain's 40 stores. The company quickly beefed up the prestige sections in those stores, closed some of the departments in other stores, and saw both sales and profits rise almost immediately. This demonstrates another way that marketers are able to use consumer information for the benefit of both the business and its customers.

In Part IV, we will see how fashion marketers reach out to consumers, and how consumers arrive at buying decisions.

Summary

Marketers seek to more thoroughly understand and influence consumer behavior through studying consumer demographics and psychographics. Demographics are measurable human statistics; among the most significant for marketers are population growth and distribution (including birthrate, life expectancy, and immigration), income distribution and spending patterns, age, and gender. The population of the United States today is approximately 316 million; however, we and the other industrialized nations consume a far larger proportion of the world's resources than do the rest of the world's population (more than 7 billion total). Fashion marketers adjust their product offerings according to the information they gather about population and income distribution.

As the role of women outside the home has evolved, more products such as automobiles, homes, and electronics are being bought by women. In addition, the recognition of lesbian, gay, bisexual, and transgender (LGBT) market segments has increased demand for products and services marketed to these groups. Also, marketers value information about occupation and education, and have found that people with more education are aware of a wider variety of goods and services, including fashions in apparel and interiors. For marketers of products like golf equipment and uniforms, targeting consumers by occupation can be a beneficial strategy.

Our consumption patterns are driven by what we consider to be important. In many societies, particularly the United States, we value the right of individuals to achieve the goals they set and, along the way, to buy and consume what they want. As a nation, Americans are materialistic—we attach great value to the objects we possess.

To further understand our lifestyles (the way we live), fashion marketers make use of psychographic systems such as VALS to determine whether we are motivated by ideals, achievements, or actions, and how our resources (including energy and commitment as well as income) influence our buying behavior. And through geodemographic segmentation such as Nielsen PRIZM, marketers can identify consumers throughout the United States by their ZIP codes and lifestyle characteristics.

KEY TERMS

QUESTIONS FOR REVIEW

1. What are three or four of the most useful demographic market segment categories and why is the information obtainable through demographic segmentation valuable to fashion marketers?

2. What is a major trend in income distribution in the United States and why is that information important to fashion marketers?

3. Give three examples of the ways marketers have become more sensitive to segmenting by gender.

4. As fashion consumers, what are three or four ways we can benefit from materialism, or successful consuming, according to Dr. Leslie Jermyn?

5. Why are segmentation systems incorporating psychographics, such as VALS, and those utilizing lifestyles and demographics, such as PRIZM, useful to fashion marketers?

ACTIVITIES

1. Organize a merchandise assortment for two small women's apparel stores, one geared to upper-middle-income boomers in a suburb of Los Angeles, the other to lower-middle-income seniors near Tampa, Florida. Include in your merchandise assortment items such as casual wear (pants and tops), rainwear and jackets, accessories, swimwear, and shoes. For each category of merchandise, describe the fashion look and fabrications you are seeking at each store.

2. Go to the website www.consumerworld.com. Under Resources, browse the Consumer News web page and create a consumer profile of its target market in terms of the audience income range, gender, and education.

3. Survey three people your age, friends and classmates, concerning their views on each of the four points of the Merck Survey about materialism. Then ask three people from older age groups, such as boomers or seniors, about their views on these four items. In what ways do your respondents agree or disagree with the

Merck Survey results? Do the two age groups you surveyed agree or disagree with each other on some issues? Which ones? What might be the reasons for the differences?

4. Select five or six fashion advertisements that you believe would appeal to a movie star, celebrity athlete, or someone you know, and state how each advertisement is geared to an aspect of that individual's demographics or psychographics. Write a paragraph for each ad, explaining the demographic or psychographic element and why you selected it.

5. To further explore the VALS system of market segmentation, collect a series of a dozen ads for fashion apparel and accessories and home furnishings. Three of these ads should be directed toward consumers guided by ideals, three toward those driven by achievement, and three to those guided by self-expression. The last three are ads of your choosing for any of the categories. Arrange your ads according to the VALS categories and, for each group, write a description explaining your reasoning in selecting the ads. Also, for each group, add a statement about the kinds of resources that would assist in motivating the consumer to buy.

MINI-PROJECT

Using the PRIZM system as a guide, go to www.MyBestSegments.com to find your own ZIP code. Using that ZIP code or another, create a print advertisement for a product or service that could be successfully aimed at one or more segments of that target market. Explain the reasons behind your choices.

REFERENCES

1. "100 People: A World Portrait," www.100people.org/statistics_detailed_statistics.php.

2. www.census.gov/2010census/datacenter-of-population.

3. Natalia Siniavskaia, "Spending Patterns of Home Buyers," National Association of Home Builders, December 4, 2008, http://www.nahb.org/generic.aspx?genericContentID=106491.

4. Earl Swift, "Is It Time to Buy or Sell?" *Parade Magazine,* May 21, 2006, p. 7.

5. Annalyn Kurtz, "Baby Bust: U.S. Births at Record Low," *CNN Money,* September 6, 2013, http://money.cnn.com/2013/09/06/news/economy/birth-rate-low/.

6. Scott Neuman, "Study Says America's Income Gap Widest Since Great Depression," *NPR,* September 10, 2013, http://www.npr.org/blogs/thetwo-way/2013/09/10/221124533/study-says-americas-income-gap-widest-since-great-depression.

7. University of New Mexico, "Per Capita Personal Income by State," bber.unm.edu/econ/us-pci.htm.

8. "Kids Spending and Influencing Power: $1.2 Trillion Says Leading Ad Firm," Center for Digital Democracy, November 1, 2012, http://www.democraticmedia.org/kids-spending-and-influencing-power-12-trillion-says-leading-ad-firm.

9. Hannah Matthews, "An Absurd Number of Children in the United States Are Living in Poverty," *Care2,* September 13, 2013, http://www.care2.com/causes/an-absurd-number-of-children-in-the-united-states-are-living-in-poverty.html.

10. "The New Target Demographic: Baby Boomers," *CBS News Sunday Morning,* March 6, 2011, www.cbsnews.com/8301-3445_162-20039772.html.

11. "Baby Boomers Are Shopping and Spending," *Examiner.com,* July 11, 2013, http://www.examiner.com/article/baby-boomers-are-shopping-and-spending.

12. Douglas Brown, "Baby Boomers Demand a Custom-Tailored Lifestyle," *Chicago Tribune,* September 30, 2004, Sec. 5, p. 11.

13. "Median Income and Poverty Rate Hold Steady," *New York Times,* September 27, 2013, www.nytimes.com/us/median-income-and-poverty-rate-hold-steady.

14. Department of Health and Human Services, Administration on Aging, "A Profile of Older Americans: 2012," http://www.aoa.gov/AoARoot/Aging_Statistics/Profile/2012/9.aspx.

15. Chris Horton, "Don't Forget the Seniors: They're Online, and Spending Money," *Social Media Today,* June 12, 2012, http://socialmediatoday.com/chris-horton/548628/don-t-forget-seniors-they-re-online-and-spending-money.

16. Global Industry Analysts, "Global Men's Grooming Products Market to Exceed $33.2 Billion by 2015, According to New Report by Global Industry Analysts, Inc.," News release, March 22, 2010.

17. Susan Chandler, "Women Direct More Dollars," *Chicago Tribune.* May 7, 2006, Sec. 5, p. 3.

18. Michael Silverstein, *Treasure Hunt: Inside the Mind of the New Consumer* (New York: Portfolio, 2006).

19. Stuart Elliott, "Hey, Gay Spender, Marketers Spending Time with You," *New York Times,* June 28, 2006, pp. C8, C31, C32.

20. Anup Shah, "Behind Consumption and Consumerism, Creating the Consumer," *Global Issues,* May 14, 2003, www.globalissues.org/TradeRelated/ConsumptionRise.asp.

21. Ibid.

22. Anup Shah, "Consumption and Consumerism," *Global Issues,* updated March 6, 2011, http://www.globalissues.org/issue/235/consumption-and-consumerism.

23. "American Attitudes about Materialism, Consumption, and the Environment," *Sustainable Consumption and Production Linkages Virtual Policy Dialog,* www.iisd.ca/consumer/mer_5.html.

24. Leslie Jermyn, "Great Temptations: The Trap of Materialism and How to Escape," www.globalaware.org/Articles_eng/great expectations.htm.

25. Strategic Business Insights website, http://www.strategicbusinessinsights.com/vals/.

26. Nielsen PRIZM website, http://www.claritas.com/MyBestSegments/Default.jsp?ID=70&pageName=Learn%2BMore&menuOption=learnmore.

ADDITIONAL RESOURCES

Barber, Benjamin. *Consumed.* New York: W.W. Norton & Company, 2007.

Churchland, Patricia S. *Touching a Nerve: The Self as Brain.* New York: W.W. Norton & Company, 2013.

Frank, Robert. *Richistan: A Journey through the American Wealth Boom and the Lives of the New Rich.* New York: Crown Publishers, 2007.

Thomas, Susan Gregory. *Buy, Buy Baby.* Boston: Houghton Mifflin Company. 2007.

Part IV

HOW FASHION MARKETERS COMMUNICATE AND CONSUMERS DECIDE

NEWS about fashion innovations spreads instantaneously in today's digital world, influencing both consumer behavior toward fashion and the way fashion marketers communicate their messages to the consuming public—subjects that are explored in Part IV.

Researchers help to identify and interpret consumer views about products and brands; Chapter 10 discusses some of the research methods by which fashion businesses obtain consumer data and explains how they use that information to formulate effective marketing strategies and disseminate their marketing message. The explosive growth of social media is examined in Chapter 11, which describes the impact on consumer behavior, as well as outlining how social media platforms have altered the way marketers reach and communicate with their target customers.

When making buying decisions, consumers take a series of both conscious and unconscious steps during the decision-making process; these are delineated in Chapter 12. Chapter 13 examines the topic of how fashion consumers buy, looking at the changing retail landscape and issues such as the growth and appeal of online and omnichannel retailing, and the importance of the shopping environment to influence a purchase decision. Chapter 14 tackles the subject of fashion on a global scale, exploring how the consumption of fashion goods is both universal and driven by local, cultural, and ethnic preferences.

CHAPTER 10

How Marketers Obtain and Use Consumer Information

WHAT DO I NEED TO KNOW ABOUT HOW MARKETERS OBTAIN AND USE CONSUMER INFORMATION?

✔ The importance of market research to understanding consumer behavior and meeting customer needs

✔ The difference between primary and secondary research and how each is conducted

✔ The methods that are used to conduct quantitative research and how they differ from those for qualitative research

✔ How marketers use research to determine the best ways to communicate with target customers

✔ Why digital communications and social media have changed the way marketers reach consumers with their messages

t's probably safe to assume that anyone reading this is familiar with Crocs, the company whose quirky rubber clogs propelled it to footwear fame when it launched in the early 2000s. Within a decade, the Colorado-based startup company had transformed into a billion-dollar global business—and in 2011, it hired its first chief marketing officer, Andrew Davison, who set about reshaping and expanding the brand by connecting with target shoppers, introducing a greater range of more stylish products, and focusing on emerging markets.

That effort began, said Davison, with a laser-like focus on the consumer: "Finding out who the consumer is, what is driving engagement, and asking what are the current behaviors and the intended behaviors we want to cultivate," he stated, adding that the company needed to understand how the consumer measures into its business goals, product strategy, and engagement strategies. And while Crocs had a great deal of anecdotal information about its customers, it wanted to delve deeper, to "map the entire purchase funnel and understand what drives behaviors."

Fortunately, the company's senior management understood the importance of investing in research and the value of a research-driven marketing strategy. Crocs undertook global studies that provided new insights about its target audience and identified market opportunity for the company, as well as revealing consumers' perceptions and feelings about the brand and how they engage with it. By conducting solid research, Davison said, the company "discovered what kind of permission we have as a brand, in terms of products, activities, silhouettes, and channels to grow our business."[1]

Conducting Market and Marketing Research

Having studied the preceding chapters, you understand how complex consumer behavior is—and why marketers work hard to decipher those complexities so that they can best meet the needs and wants of their target customers. But how do they do that? In large part, they do it by collecting information from and about consumers through research.

The field of market research was pioneered by Arthur C. Nielsen, Sr., who founded the ACNielsen company in 1923. (You may know that name from the often-cited Nielsen Television Ratings, which for decades has monitored how many households are tuned in to a given TV show, giving marketers a means for measuring the value of advertising on that show.) Nielsen developed many innovative research methods and techniques that are now standard industry practice, including the first objective and reliable methodology for measuring retail sales and competitive market share, and the impact of marketing and sales programs on revenues and profits.[2] Market research became even more important starting in the early 1960s when companies changed from using the selling concept to using the marketing concept (discussed in Chapter 2). Rather than trying to persuade consumers to buy products they'd already made, companies began making products they had confirmed, through research, that consumers wanted.

Today, research has reached new levels of sophistication and—although they are often used interchangeably—a distinction is made between the terms "market research" and "marketing research."

While market research (defined in Chapter 2) involves gathering information about a specific market or industry's size and trends, including number of competitors, product pricing, government regulations, and so on, **marketing research** goes further by analyzing a given marketing opportunity or problem and finding solutions, often through understanding the behaviors and preferences of the market's consumers. (See Figure 10.1.)

These two areas of research go hand in hand and are used either alone or together depending on the issues a marketer is facing. For example, if a manufacturer of fashionable luggage was thinking about adding a line of coordinating handbags to its offerings, it might conduct market research to learn more about the overall handbag market, including total annual sales, what competitors there were, what price ranges were most popular, and so on.

If results showed that the market conditions were favorable for the company, it might then use marketing research to determine specific design directions for its own handbags—perhaps by surveying its target consumers to pinpoint their preference for certain features (interior and exterior pockets, zippers versus snap closures), or what styling, detailing, and level of quality they would expect based on their perception of the brand. In general, market research is conducted periodically, such as when major changes occur in the market, or when a business is considering entering a new market or product category. Marketing research, on the other hand, should be an ongoing function within the sales and marketing department of a business as a way to stay in tune with its customer base.[3]

In this chapter, we'll look at different types of research and how each is conducted, and also

FIGURE 10.1
Fashion companies, such as Crocs, rely on research to better understand the attitudes and behavior of their target customers.

explore how research helps marketers refine their message and better communicate it to their target consumers.

THE RESEARCH PROCESS

Market and marketing research can take many forms and can range from formal, statistically sound surveys to informal, personal observations. Political pollsters, for example, create objectively worded questions and use scientific methods to reach a representative cross-section of voters when they track how candidates are faring before an election. By contrast, the owner of a high-end women's clothing boutique is conducting her own informal, yet equally valuable, research every time she scrutinizes the merchandise in her competitor's shop, or when she randomly observes customers in her own store or talks to them to learn what they like and don't like, and why (Figure 10.2). In all cases, however, research comes from one of two sources: secondary or primary.

Types of Research

Before undertaking any research, marketers must define the **objectives** of the study; they must identify specific information they want to learn. Once their objectives are established, they can determine

FIGURE 10.2 Retailers can conduct informal research just by watching customers browse and select merchandise.

what the best source of data will be. In some cases, the information might be available for them to cull and analyze from an existing source. Locating that existing data is called **secondary research.** If the information they want to gather is more specialized to their own business or otherwise unavailable from secondary sources, marketers conduct **primary research,** their own original study designed to address their specific objectives.

Secondary Research. The advantage of secondary research is that it can save marketers the time and expense of conducting their own original research or paying an outside firm to conduct it for them. Plus, depending on a marketer's needs, secondary data may be enough to answer the questions or solve the problem. Say a printed T-shirt company was considering extending its line by adding some graphic designs in Spanish but needed to be sure the market of potential customers was big enough. Through secondary research the company could learn that not only was the Hispanic population expected to grow 167 percent from 2010 to 2050, but that the group's buying power was projected to rise from $1 trillion to $1.5 trillion between 2010 and 2015.[4] Or say a boutique owner in Albuquerque was thinking about opening a second store in Santa Fe to sell his handcrafted leather belts and accessories, but wanted to be sure that potential customers there could afford the one-of-a-kind pieces. He could base his decision in part on existing statistics showing that the median household income in Santa Fe was actually several thousand dollars higher than in Albuquerque,[5] making the customer base there slightly more affluent even than his original customers.

There are numerous sources available for secondary research, and in some cases, their data is free. The federal government and many of its agencies, for example, offer a wealth of free information. The Census Bureau provides details on the number, geographic distribution, and social and economic characteristics of Americans, among other data; figures on employment, consumer expenditures, prices and living conditions, and other subjects are available from the Bureau of Labor Statistics, to name just two. Links to statistics from more than 100 government agencies are organized by subject and compiled online at www.fedstats.gov.

Other sources of secondary data are newspapers and magazines, including trade magazines. In the fashion industry, trade publications such as *Women's Wear Daily* (*WWD*) and *Home Textiles Today* not only report on the results of research conducted by other organizations, but often do their own market research. Marketers themselves can also be a source of secondary data through information found on their websites, in annual reports or other corporate material, as well as when they publicize findings of research they have done. In fact, a company's marketing department can often delve into its own sales department's statistics on orders, returns, pricing analysis, and other information for a "built-in" source of secondary research.

Trade associations, market research firms, and advertising agencies, among others, can also provide secondary data. Full results of their studies are often available only to clients or members; others can sometimes purchase the research reports for a fee. But even when full details of a study are not revealed, key findings may be made public in a press release or other published report. For example, highlights from a study by the market research company Packaged Facts titled "The U.S. Men's Market: Examining the Attitudes, Buying Habits, and Lifestyles of the Elusive Adult Male Consumer" were published in news articles by some media, although the full report would cost several thousand dollars to obtain. See Table 10.1 for examples of the wide variety of sources for secondary research.

Primary Research. When secondary research is not current or does not supply all the information a marketer needs, primary research can either provide all the necessary data, or, more often, supplement basic information from secondary sources. Depending on what information the company wants, it might do its research with existing customers, potential consumers, employees, vendors, or others, or possibly a combination of audiences.

Some companies may undertake the primary research themselves, but for most major studies, they will more likely hire a consultant or market research firm. In either case, the marketer's objectives will determine what research method should be used and how the study should be designed, whether by personal contact, written communication, or observation—techniques we'll discuss next.

Research Methodologies

In any marketing research, there are two types of methodologies: quantitative research and qualitative research. **Quantitative research** is objective, focusing on collecting numbers and facts that can be analyzed statistically. Has someone with a clipboard ever stopped you at the mall to ask you about the reason for your visit that day or maybe about your shopping habits in general? This type of survey

Table 10.1 A Few of the Many Sources of Secondary Data

Federal Government
• Bureau of Economic Analysis • Bureau of Labor Statistics • Census Bureau • Small Business Administration
Market Research Firms
• Nielsen • Claritas • Forrester Research • The NPD Group • Harris Interactive • The Futures Company
Publications
• *Ad Age* • *Women's Wear Daily* • *Stores* magazine • *Journal of Consumer Research* • *New York Times*
Trade Associations/Industry Organizations
• National Retail Federation • Cotton Incorporated • American Apparel and Footwear Association • Fashion Group International • Home Fashion Products Association

is commonly used to collect quantitative data that will enable the researcher to create statistics on how often shoppers of different ages go to the mall, how many stores they visit per shopping trip, how often they make a purchase, and so on. **Qualitative research,** on the other hand, is subjective, focusing on people's opinions and attitudes toward a product or service. If you've ever been asked to provide a review about a purchase or describe in your own words what you liked and didn't like about something, you were participating in qualitative research, meant to help the company better understand how you and other customers *felt* about the product or shopping experience.

Quantitative Research. Quantitative research is conducted in two main ways: through surveys and by observation.

Surveys are a flexible tool for quantitative research because they can be provided to respondents in written form by mail, e-mail, on a mobile device, or through a website; they can also be administered by an interviewer in person (for example, at a store or mall, or over the phone).

Surveys are conducted with questionnaires; the questions reflect the research objectives and include demographic questions to help identify respondents by population segment. Questions are generally closed-ended, meaning they can be answered with a simple response such as a number or a "yes" or "no," or by selecting from a multiple-choice list. This allows researchers to compile exact statistics and develop percentages for specific questions or categories. For example, a recent study conducted by The NPD Group on back-to-school spending provided quantitative data about where consumers planned to shop, how much they planned to spend at different types of stores, and what they planned to buy. Compared to the prior year, the report found that consumers intended to spend 8 percent less on back-to-school goods at mass merchants and 4 percent less at national chains, but spend 4 percent more online and at department stores; and they intended to increase their spending in almost all categories, particularly apparel (up 11 percent), footwear (up 9 percent), and apparel accessories and school bags (up 4 percent each).[6]

In addition to simple-response questions, surveys may include questions that allow consumers to express their feelings about a product or service but that also permit researchers to quantify those feelings. This is most frequently done with an **attitude scale,** a question format that lets respondents indicate their level of favorable or unfavorable opinion. The most popular attitude scale is the **Likert scale,** which presents a statement and asks consumers to select a degree of agreement or disagreement with the statement, with numbers usually representing the different levels. For example, a survey might include the statement, "I would be willing to spend twice as much money on a jacket if it had a designer label," and the respondent would choose a response ranging from 1 for "strongly disagree" to 5 for "strongly agree." Researchers are then able to assign numeric values to the results, such as "32 percent of consumers somewhat agree that they would spend twice as much money on a designer jacket, while 40 percent strongly disagree." See Figure 10.3 for other examples of Likert attitude scales.

LET'S TALK

Have you been asked recently to complete a survey using an attitude scale? Why do you think marketers seem to be using this type of survey more frequently?

Typical Uses of the Likert Scale

Measure of Agreement

For each of the following statements, please check the response that best describes the extent to which you agree or disagree with each statement:

I enjoy shopping online.

☐ Strongly Agree ☐ Somewhat Agree ☐ Neither Agree nor Disagree ☐ Somewhat Disagree ☐ Strongly Disagree

I worry about identity theft when shopping online.

☐ Strongly Agree ☐ Somewhat Agree ☐ Neither Agree nor Disagree ☐ Somewhat Disagree ☐ Strongly Disagree

Measure of Satisfaction

How satisfied are you with the selection of jackets at retailer X? Please check one:

☐ Very Satisfied ☐ Somewhat Satisfied ☐ Neither Satisfied nor Dissatisfied ☐ Somewhat Dissatisfied ☐ Very Dissatisfied

Measure of Importance

For each of the following features relating to bed sheets, please check the response that best expresses how important or unimportant that feature is to you:

All-natural fabric

☐ Extremely Important ☐ Somewhat Important ☐ Neither Important nor Unimportant ☐ Somewhat Unimportant ☐ Extremely Unimportant

Thread count

☐ Extremely Important ☐ Somewhat Important ☐ Neither Important nor Unimportant ☐ Somewhat Unimportant ☐ Extremely Unimportant

Price

☐ Extremely Important ☐ Somewhat Important ☐ Neither Important nor Unimportant ☐ Somewhat Unimportant ☐ Extremely Unimportant

FIGURE 10.3 Typical uses of the Likert scale.

Research that relies on observation has the advantage of not needing the active participation of the research subjects, and can even be conducted without their knowledge. A boutique owner, for example, can learn which styles and colors her customers are gravitating toward by simply observing their browsing and noting which items they choose to try on. Fashion reporters observe celebrities and other people attending fashion shows, benefits, and similar events to discover the most popular cut of men's suits or whether skirt lengths are trending up or down. If more formalized results are necessary, researchers might conduct a **count,** where an observer or team of observers keeps a written tally of variables within the category being studied, such as noting 17 men at a business seminar wearing khakis and sport coats but no tie, six wearing suits and ties, and 24 wearing khakis and dress shirts but no jacket or tie.

The Internet, and particularly social media, constitutes a treasure trove of observational research opportunities, enabling marketers to "observe" vast numbers of consumers and gauge their attitudes and preferences in real time. To assist in sifting through the huge amount of data found online, marketers can choose among a growing number of monitoring tools that help them track instances of consumers liking, posting, sharing, and tweeting about them and their products. (See Chapter 11 for more discussion on social media.)

Observational research can also be done mechanically or electronically. A department store might use an automatic counting device to find out how many customers enter a department featuring a category of merchandise that is new to the store; some marketers use location-based services and apps, such as Foursquare, to track when customers are in the vicinity (and perhaps text them a special offer). Frequent-shopper cards or store credit cards, when scanned at the cash register, record information every time a customer makes a purchase, providing a wealth of data about the customer's product preferences, buying frequency, and more. Similar information can be obtained when consumers shop online, whether they are using a store card or any other means of payment; in fact, marketers are able to gather some information about consumers who simply visit their site, "observing" which products they click on, whether or not they buy. In many cases, to facilitate the process, online merchants place invisible "cookies," or tiny text files that are saved to a computer user's

hard drive when he or she visits a website. For the most part, cookies are harmless, and simply enable an e-tailer or other site to identify a returning customer and retrieve stored information about past purchases or present new information that is personalized to that customer's preferences. Sometimes, however, websites install tracking cookies that "follow" consumers as they browse other sites and report that information back to the original site, or that enable ads for products consumers recently viewed to pop up on unrelated sites. Many consumers and consumer advocates consider tracking cookies to be an invasion of privacy, and some Internet surfers routinely run anti-spyware programs to delete them or use their browser's controls to block tracking cookies before they are installed. (See Chapter 15 for further discussion of cookies and ethics.)

Qualitative Research. Qualitative research, with its purpose of gleaning respondents' feelings and inner beliefs, has its roots in psychology, and requires a skilled researcher to conduct a study. In contrast to a quantitative study's closed-ended questions, qualitative research involves open-ended questions designed to encourage respondents to express their thoughts and opinions in detail. The two most common forms of qualitative research are focus groups and depth interviews.

A **focus group** is a gathering in which a small group of perhaps 8 to 12 consumers, led by a moderator, discuss and offer opinions about a product, service, or other marketing-related topic. The moderator has a specific agenda and guides the discussion in order to accomplish the study's objectives, but participants are also encouraged to respond

CASE IN POINT 10.1
Smile—The Mannequin May Be Watching You

It's not at all uncommon for a store owner or sales associate to observe customers as they browse, hoping to gain valuable insight into their needs and preferences. But what if it's a mannequin that's conducting the observational research?

That may sound like something out of science fiction, but several dozen EyeSee mannequins, sold by Italian mannequin maker Almax SpA, are already being employed by a handful of luxury retailers with the goal of helping them better understand their customers, as well as enhance their product assortment and customers' shopping experience.

The EyeSee mannequin looks like a normal mannequin, and can be adorned in the latest fashions, just like any other mannequin. However, the EyeSee is equipped with a special camera in one eye, which is able to "observe" customers in the vicinity and provide valuable information to the retailer, such as the number of people passing a display window at certain times of day, how many stop to look at a particular display and for how long, how many people enter the store, and at what times there is a greater influx of customers.

But that's not all. The camera feeds information about what it sees into facial-recognition software, revealing details about customers including their age, gender, and race. This gives retailers even more data they can analyze and use to improve everything from their merchandise assortment to their staffing requirements. For example, Almax reports that one clothing store that purchased the $5,130 device decided to introduce a children's apparel line when the mannequin's keen eye determined that more than half the customers in the store in the middle of the afternoon were kids. And another retailer changed out its window displays to appeal better to men after discovering that male customers spent more than women did during the first two days of a sale. To address privacy concerns, the mannequin doesn't store or transmit any of the images it records, and retailers must have a closed-circuit television license to use the EyeSee technology.

Sound spooky to know that a mannequin could be spying on you? Watch out, because it could get even more so. Almax is also testing word-recognition technology that would let retailers listen in on customers' comments about what the mannequin is wearing!

Sources: Almax, "Beautiful and Smart: From the Combination of Craftsmanship and Technology Comes a New Concept of Mannequin," News release; and Andrew Roberts, "Bionic Mannequins Spy on Shoppers to Boost Luxury Sales," *Bloomberg*, November 21, 2012, http://www.bloomberg.com/news/2012-11-19/bionic-mannequins-spy-on-shoppers-to-boost-luxury-sales.html.

to each other's comments and elaborate on their thoughts and beliefs.

Focus groups traditionally take place in special conference rooms that are equipped with one-way mirrors, allowing researchers or representatives from the client company to observe without being intrusive or influencing the discussion. Video and/or audio recording equipment may also be hidden behind the glass so that participants will not be distracted or intimidated by it; this enables the session to be streamed in real time to others at a remote location, or simply recorded for review at a later time. With wide availability of high-speed Internet, many focus groups are now taking place online, saving researchers the time and cost of gathering participants together in one physical location. These online focus groups take place in a chat room–like venue, with participants typing in their responses to the moderator and to others in the group. In cases where participants have access to devices with built-in webcams and microphones, online sessions may include two-way video and audio, bringing the online version closer to recreating a face-to-face focus group session. Whether in person or online, actual products or product prototypes may be used for participants to react to and evaluate, or the discussion may focus on intangible concepts to help marketers judge the viability of a new idea or direction.

Based on the objectives of the research, focus group researchers carefully select the participants for each study, screening potential respondents

FIGURE 10.4 Focus groups, whether conducted in person or online, are designed to encourage free discussion of ideas and opinions about a product or service.

according to specific criteria defined by the marketer. A study about a new style of backpacks designed with pockets to charge an MP3 player and speakers to play music without earphones might be restricted to teenagers, identified as the maker's main target market. Research regarding a new anti-wrinkle cosmetic formula might require participants to be women between the ages of 35 and 55, and already users of a particular brand of cosmetics. Because a focus group session takes an average of two hours to conduct, participants are usually paid for their time.

LET'S TALK

Think of a new product that has recently reached the stores in your area. Do you think its manufacturer could have benefited from focus group research about the product? What types of consumers might have been involved? What specific features of the product might they have been asked about?

Depth interviews are similar to focus groups but involve just one participant offering thoughts and opinions to a researcher. The interview, which typically runs between a half hour and an hour, also generally takes place in a room with a one-way mirror and recording equipment. But since there is only a single respondent, the interviewer can delve more deeply into the person's feelings, or present several products or concepts about which the subject's responses can be compared.

For example, a depth interview might be used to test several different advertising approaches.

Perhaps a retailer is ready to launch a new campaign and needs to know whether a fast-moving, flashy, hip-hop style of TV commercial will draw a better response than one with a whimsical, humorous tone. A skilled interviewer can show examples of commercials in each style and then draw out the respondent's conscious, and sometimes unconscious, reactions to each and reasons why the person liked one better than another.

Because quantitative and qualitative research provide different types of data, a research project will often combine both methods, providing marketers with more comprehensive results. One example is a Nickelodeon/Youth Intelligence Tween Report that investigated whether and to what extent the 9- to 14-year-old age group influences family purchasing decisions. The report combined results from a quantitative telephone survey and a separate series of focus groups, and found that while tweens rely on their parents to pay for "necessities" such as clothing, food, and room décor, nearly three out of four tweens have "a lot of say" when buying clothes for themselves.[7]

Analyzing and Reporting Research Data

Once the data for a research project has been collected, the information is organized, processed, and analyzed to determine the results. Responses to each quantitative research question are tabulated, usually through a computer program, and the numbers can be categorized according to the study's objectives. For qualitative research, the person or persons conducting the study generally review and analyze their own results.

Once the research has been analyzed, the researchers create a report, which often begins with a brief executive summary of the findings and then provides full details of the results, including charts, graphs, and other supporting information and illustrations (Table 10.2). The report also describes the methodology that was used, along with a copy of any questionnaire used in the research. Perhaps most important, the research report may suggest a plan of action based on the findings. Suggestions to the marketer might consist of broad recommendations or specific marketing tactics that the research indicates might be successful.

Putting Marketing Research to Work

Market and marketing research can be used in numerous ways by designers, manufacturers, and retailers, both to improve their products and to enhance their relationship with consumers—and thereby influence consumer behavior. Design elements of products (for example, a special jacket pocket designed specifically to hold a smartphone)

Table 10.2 The results of a research study are often presented in charts or tables.

How often do you shop for clothing for yourself, whether or not you actually intend to buy anything?				
	All Shoppers	**Down Market**	**Middle Market**	**Up Market**
At least once a week	7%	5%	7%	9%
Two to three times a month	19%	13%	21%	21%
Once a month	19%	16%	18%	22%
Once every 2-3 months	25%	23%	24%	27%
Once every 4-6 months	21%	24%	22%	17%
Once a year	5%	9%	4%	3%
Less often than once a year	4%	10%	3%	2%
Never	1%	1%	1%	0%

Source: Retail Forward Shopper Scape™.

Marketers Tap into Advanced Social Intelligence for Goldmine of Consumer Data

Social media continues to grow exponentially—and it's creating a deluge of information about what consumers like, don't like, share, talk about, and buy. Literally billions of daily consumer posts from tens of millions of individuals across social networks and other online channels have the potential to deliver extraordinary insight to businesses that are savvy enough to take advantage of what has been termed "advanced social intelligence." It is a 21st-century tool that offers marketers unprecedented access to data that can lead to better understanding of the market, the consumer, and the competition.

Aside from its immediacy and scope, what makes advanced social intelligence different from traditional market research is that it provides a rich source of data about people, their experiences, and their opinions, all offered spontaneously and without the filter of a formal survey or focus group. As one marketing executive put it: "Essentially, the ability to understand the billions of social comments broadcasted by consumers daily provides smart companies access to the world's largest focus group without having to ever ask a consumer a specific question."

There are a number of ways in which advanced social intelligence is already having a positive impact on marketing:

- It provides a better understanding of the path consumers take to reach their buying decision, as well as better understanding of the decisions themselves.
- It offers a deeper insight into customers' personas and what motivates them, allowing marketers to pinpoint how and where to best communicate with these consumers, as well as to identify new potential target customers.
- It helps companies develop products with clearer knowledge of the competitive landscape, consumer attitudes and behaviors, and consumer needs that remain unfilled.

Sources: Kevin Glacken, "The Enterprise-Wide Advantage of Advanced Social Intelligence," *Social Media Today*, April 13, 2013, http://socialmediatoday.com/kglacken/1373466/enterprise-wide-advanced-social-intelligence; Michael Cohn, "The Impact of Advanced Social Intelligence on Marketing," *Social Media Today*, June 27, 2013, http://socialmediatoday.com/compukol/1563266/impact-advanced-social-intelligence-marketing; and Mark Harrington, "Five Ways that Advanced Social Intelligence Helps Marketers," *MarketingProfs*, April 26, 2013, http://www.mpdailyfix.com/five-ways-that-advanced-social-intelligence-helps-marketers/.

can be tested for consumer reaction; so too can new categories of merchandise a company might be introducing. Research is equally important in helping marketers shape their message to consumers, as well as in pinpointing the best vehicles for conveying the message. As we'll explore in the following section, communication between marketers and consumers is increasingly a "two-way street," providing marketers with even more information that they can collect and use.

ELEMENTS OF FASHION COMMUNICATION

The opportunities for reaching fashion consumers are as great or greater than with virtually any other type of product. In addition to standard advertising, fashion marketers can stage fashion shows or hold a **trunk show,** where a designer or representative of a manufacturer brings an entire line to a store for customers to see and buy. Brand-name apparel companies or designers can dress characters in movies and on popular TV shows, putting their products and names prominently in the public eye. They can also capitalize on celebrities who wear their label in real life (Figure 10.5); think of Lululemon, for one, whose trendy, technical athletic apparel has been spotted on Katy Perry, Allison Williams, Sandra Bullock, Emily Blunt, even First Lady Michelle Obama, and others in the rich-and-famous set, drawing the attention of the public and the media to the clothing brand.

In today's digital world, the avenues of communication for fashion marketers are far more plentiful than in the past, with consumers turning to websites, blogs, social networks, YouTube, and even text messages on their mobile phones for all types

FIGURE 10.5 When a famous person appears in public wearing a particular brand or designer label, it can have a strong influence on the celebrity's fans who want to emulate the look.

of information. The explosion of "new" media has obviously created more ways for marketers to reach consumers. But it has also created new challenges for marketers, who must not only try to stand out in the crowd, but who must also determine which of the many media their target consumers are most likely to use. For these reasons, marketing research is an increasingly important tool to help designers and fashion companies stay in tune with their consumers' lifestyles and preferences.

Traditional Media

Clearly, fashion marketers still communicate with consumers through traditional channels, including print media (newspapers, magazines, catalogs, etc.), broadcast media (television and radio), fashion shows, and in-store displays and promotions. But with changing technology——and consumers' attraction to it—the lines between those traditional channels and newer types of media are blurring ever more rapidly.

For example, fashion magazines continue to be important for disseminating fashion news, and because they track key demographic information about their readers and subscribers, marketers know exactly what audience they are reaching with their ads. The difference today is that, in addition to their print versions, most publications, including *Vogue* and *Elle,* also offer digital editions of their magazines that consumers can read on their iPad or other tablet computer. In addition, fashion magazines feature some content on their websites, enabling marketers to reach an online audience that might not go out and buy a magazine. Publishers in recent years have also created a new genre of magazine/catalog hybrids called **magalogs**—shopping magazines that feature an array of "editors' choice" products, complete with details on how to buy them, meeting the need of time-starved consumers for merchandise that is easy to buy and has been preselected for its quality and style. Like standard fashion magazines, shopping magazines use websites in addition to their print publications, and further extend their reach to consumers through social media. Two of the best-known are *Lucky,* which translates trends into "must-have" purchases across fashion, beauty, and design; and *Domino,* which showcases stylish home décor and was relaunched in 2013 as an e-commerce site coupled with a quarterly print magazine (Figure 10.6).

FIGURE 10.6 Traditional fashion magazines, and their newer cousin, magalogs, are still an effective medium that marketers use to communicate with their target consumers, whether they are reading a print edition or an online or tablet version.

Shopping Magazines Revamp to Regain Success

When it was launched in 2000, *Lucky,* the Conde Nast shopping magazine, was unlike any fashion magazine that came before, blurring the line between editorial and advertising and openly offering product recommendations to its readers, as if they were coming from a best friend. And the formula was a big success—until the economy tanked and consumers pulled back on discretionary spending, resulting in a drop in advertising revenue that is the lifeblood of any publication. Enter Eva Chen, who was promoted to editor in chief in mid-2013. Chen is a 33-year-old social media whiz, who can often be found taking photos of her accessories to post later for her followers on Instagram or Twitter. ("Accessories of the day: comfortable @ chloefashion Susannas & a @LouisVuitton Sofia for 5837 pre-fashion-month errands," read one recent tweet.) Why is that significant? Because many industry observers believe her promotion may represent a whole new era not just for *Lucky,* but for the fashion magazine business as a whole, whose editorial leadership has been dominated by women in their late 40s to 60s. Said Leah Chernikoff, the editorial director of Fashionista.com, "If Eva turns *Lucky* around, that will be a sign to publishers to have someone young and connected digitally at the helm."

Being social-media savvy does not mean that Chen doesn't appreciate the printed page— only that she, like a growing number of people, consumes media "in a lot of different ways." Said Chen, "Nothing will replicate the feeling of ripping out something from a magazine. Maybe I'll go online and stalk that item and look at the tear sheet again." But she is definitely bringing a fresh eye to *Lucky's* look and coverage. Among the early changes Chen made to the magazine were replacing grid layouts that had typically shown dozens of pairs of shoes with less rigid page designs highlighting a few select styles, and adding first-person essays on style, along with an editor's letter highlighting Chen wearing current fashion looks.

Taking a different path is *Domino,* another shopping magazine that had also faced low advertising revenues and actually folded in 2009. *Domino* was relaunched, however, as a quarterly magazine under a new ownership banner in October 2013—and additionally reborn as an e-commerce site that combines traditional editorial content with online shopping. Full articles from the print magazine appear on the *Domino* website, but the website offers a variety of ways for readers to interact with the content. For example, buttons at the top of each article let

(continued)

visitors choose whether to read the story, shop it, or view its photos. More than 30,000 home décor products are available for sale on the site, which means a reader could fall in love with the total look of a room photographed for the magazine and conceivably purchase every item shown with just a few clicks.

What's more, since Domino is actually selling the products to consumers, it will have a wealth of data at its fingertips to provide powerful insight into what its readers are looking for— and what they're buying.

Sources: Marisa Meltzer, "Eva Chen, Trending Now at Lucky Magazine," *New York Times,* August 14, 2013, http://www.nytimes.com/2013/08/15/fashion/eva-chen-trending-now-at-lucky-magazine.html; Christina Chaey, "How Domino Magazine Resurrected Itself as an E-Commerce Startup," *Fast Company,* October 9, 2013, http://www.fastcompany.com/3019162/buyology/how-domino-magazine-resurrected-itself-as-an-e-commerce-startup; Domino.com.

The use of television by fashion and other marketers is also evolving to match new realities—for instance, that consumers (especially young people) are spending more time online and less time watching TV (or may be watching their favorite shows online), and that digital recording technology lets consumers easily fast-forward through commercials. Some marketers have been successful at developing offbeat or edgy commercials to catch consumers' attention and draw them into stores; Target did this with its hip, fast-paced montages that blended from one product to the next, all to the beat of popular songs. Fashion marketers have also recognized the popularity of reality TV shows, and are using that vehicle to communicate fashion messages to consumers who may skip commercials. Among recent fashion-related programs is *Project Runway,* an elimination contest for aspiring fashion designers who are mentored by Tim Gunn, chief creative officer of Kate Spade & Co. (formerly Liz Claiborne Inc.), with judges that have included Heidi Klum, Michael Kors, Vera Wang, Zac Posen, and others. The show creates buzz and publicity for the young designers, who may have garments featured in print media, integrated into a limited edition look for a particular clothing brand, sold at an online fashion store such as Blue Fly.com, or, in the case of the finalists, presented at New York Fashion Week.

Another tactic marketers are employing more frequently is product placement, also called embedded marketing, where their merchandise is being used by characters or is visible on the set of a TV show or film. (Remember the *American Idol* judges conspicuously drinking Coca-Cola?) Marketers in the United States spend more than $5 billion a year on product placement, with the largest portion going to television and movies, and a small but growing share going to webisodes and social media.[8] Recently, the technique has expanded to include "digital product integration," in which products are digitally inserted into scenes of TV episodes after they've been filmed.

LeT'S Talk

What is your opinion of product placement in TV shows and movies? Do you think this an acceptable way to get exposure for a product, or do you feel that marketers are trying to "trick" the audience?

In-store marketing is also constantly evolving, and new technologies are playing a role there as well. The use of interactive displays is still relatively limited, but units such as those in Niketown stores allow marketers to create two-way communication with consumers—in this case, letting shoppers order custom shoes that are delivered in two weeks by mail.[9] Other marketers, addressing an aspect of shopping they've learned their customers want, have redesigned their stores to create "environments," complete with cozy fireplaces (at Timberland) or afternoon tea (American Girl Store).[10] Even fashion shows have been updated for today's experience-hungry and tech-savvy consumers. Target, for example, once created a "vertical" fashion show, with suspended models "walking" a runway down the side of a building at Rockefeller Center in New York City.[11] And virtually all designer runway shows are now being streamed live to the computers, tablets, and smartphones of eager consumers around the world.

"New" Media

Even as marketers update their use of traditional media, they are also actively seeking ways to reach target consumers, particularly the younger generation, through newer channels. As a 2006 *New York Times* article stated, "The number of vehicles through which young people find entertainment and information (and one another) makes them a moving target for anyone hoping to capture their attention."[12] If anything, that statement is even more true today, thanks to the explosive growth of mobile media. And it is not only young people, either. Marketers had already begun actively pursuing the attention (and dollars) of women via the Web vs. the more customary media used to reach them after surveys found that the number of women online and the amount of time they spend online was outpacing men.[13] More recent trends have spurred marketers to focus greater attention on reaching women through even broader digital means. Consider Rue La La, which offers exclusive flash sales of designer goods to a members-only customer base. The retailer realized that more than 40 percent of its sales were stemming from smartphones and tablets, particularly the iPhone and iPad—and also discovered that a consumer using all three screens (desktop, tablet, and smartphone) was 540 percent more likely to make a purchase than someone who shops only by computer. So it quickly updated its apps to make shopping easier and more enjoyable for customers, no matter what device they were using.[14]

Some online communications tools that were still relatively new to marketers just a decade ago are today considered established and even old hat. E-mail, for example, has become a routine method for sending customers newsletters, notices about special sales or events, and even personalized messages based on information the marketer has about their product preferences or shopping habits. Some companies find success reaching target customers by advertising in e-zines, such as DailyCandy, which are online magazines covering a range of topics that deliver daily e-mail updates on what's hot to consumers who register for the free service. Apparel retailer Scoop NYC, which operates stores in four states, once found that just being mentioned in an e-zine boosted sales at its website.[15]

Marketers are also using richer content and interactive content, such as blogs, on their own websites to communicate better with consumers online. Blogs are appealing to many people and businesses because they feature two-way communication; marketers also appreciate this aspect because it lets them have a dialog with consumers. Even more opportunity for dialog comes from marketers' presence on a range of social media sites their customers frequent, including Facebook, Twitter, Pinterest, Instagram, and others, and many companies have staff dedicated to updating content on those sites and responding to consumer questions or comments (Figure 10.7).

FIGURE 10.7 The fashion world increasingly reaches target consumers online through social media, blogs, and mobile devices.

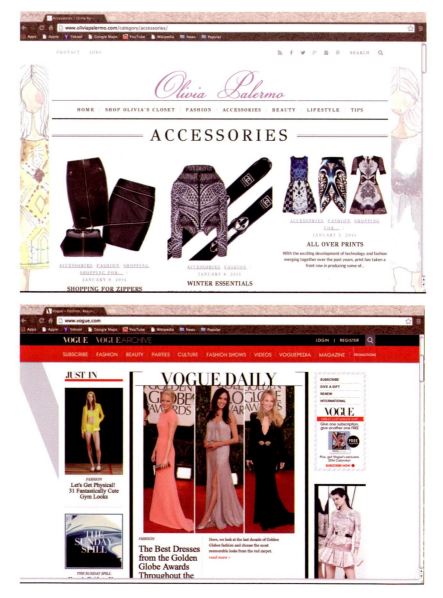

Even video games have become a channel for marketing communications. Knowing that video games are a $14 billion-plus market in the United States, activewear companies such as Nike, Adidas, Reebok, and Puma have entered agreements with game companies to feature their apparel on characters in the games. L'Oréal has even gotten into the action. Armed with the knowledge that 40 percent of the Microsoft Xbox's 20 million users are female, the cosmetics giant created "The Next Level" app for the game console, designed to be a one-stop beauty and style hub on which women can watch how-to videos and gain more information on products.[16]

Other Communication Vehicles

There are many other methods that marketers use to communicate with consumers today. For example, some companies know they can reach their target audience through sporting events, and may advertise during televised games and matches, or they might even sponsor certain events. A growing number are also using buzz marketing (discussed in Chapter 1), the technique designed to generate excitement among a key group of consumers so that they will start a word-of-mouth campaign to spread news about the product or service. In some cases, companies will even hire "brand ambassadors" from among their target consumer group. These people receive money and/or merchandise not only to get the buzz going but to gather feedback from other consumers and perhaps steer them to the company's website to participate in surveys.[17] With all the different communication channels—and technology that seems to change on a weekly basis—you can see how important ongoing marketing research is for companies so they can understand who their target consumers are, *and* how best to reach them!

Because social media play such a key and growing role in marketers' understanding of and communication with their customers, we'll examine that topic in depth in the next chapter.

Summary

Marketers use research to better understand the needs and wants of their target customers. If the information that marketers are gathering relates to general size and trends of a market or industry, they use market research. If the information is needed to analyze a marketing opportunity or problem in order to find a solution, they use marketing research.

Before research begins, the objectives of the study are defined. The objectives help determine whether to conduct secondary research (gathering data from existing sources) or primary research (designing an original research study). Among the many sources of secondary research are government agencies and market research firms.

There are two types of research methodologies. Quantitative research is objective and focuses on numbers and facts that can be analyzed statistically. It is generally done through surveys (given either in writing or by an interviewer), or by observation (which can be done by people or mechanically/electronically). Attitude scales are used in quantitative research to determine respondents' level of opinion about a subject. Qualitative research is subjective and focuses on people's feelings and opinions about a product or service. The two most common forms of qualitative research are focus groups and depth interviews.

Marketers can use research results to focus their marketing message to their target consumers and to determine the best way to reach them. New media and changing technologies, including rapid growth in mobile communications, are creating new avenues and opportunities for communication with consumers.

KEY TERMS

Attitude scales

Count

Depth interview

Focus group

Likert scale

Magalog

Marketing research

Objectives (for research)

Primary research

Qualitative research

Quantitative research

Secondary research

Trunk show

QUESTIONS FOR REVIEW

1. Explain the difference between market research and marketing research, and give an example of information that each might be used to collect.

2. What are some sources of secondary research data? What are the advantages of doing secondary research over primary research?

3. What is the difference between quantitative research and qualitative research? Name two methods of conducting each type of research.

4. What is an attitude scale? Give an example of a question that might be used on one.

5. Why is marketing research important to marketers' communication with consumers?

ACTIVITIES

1. Read through a recent newspaper or magazine, and see how many articles you can find that report or include the results of research. Decide whether each is an example of secondary research or primary research, and explain how you know.

2. Look online for research related to a fashion category of your choice. Provide a summary of what you find, including the research source, whether the study involved quantitative or qualitative research or both, what types of consumers were targeted for the study, key results, and any other details.

3. Pick a fashion trend to track (for example, a specific color, skirt length, shoe style, etc.), and spend at least half an hour at a mall or shopping center conducting your own observational research. Be prepared to explain how you conducted the study and share your results with the class.

4. Imagine you are a marketing executive for a company making women's dress shoes and are considering adding a line of coordinating handbags. Create an attitude scale with five questions you would ask your current shoe customers that would help you make marketing decisions regarding handbags.

5. List a variety of traditional and "new" media and conduct an informal survey of ten other students to determine which they use to learn about fashion products. Do the same survey with a group of older adults. How do answers from the two groups differ? Are there media that both groups rely on?

MINI-PROJECT

Working with one or two other students, choose a fashion product or category and create a mock research study about it. Define the objectives of the research, and determine whether it would be qualitative or quantitative (or both), what research methods you would use, and what types of consumers you would survey. Create a sample questionnaire that reflects your objectives and methods.

REFERENCES

1. Jennifer Overstreet, "How Crocs Is Building a Brand Bigger than the Clog," *Retail's BIG Blog,* August 29, 2012, http://blog.nrf.com/2012/08/29/how-crocs-is-building-a-brand-bigger-than-the-clog/.

2. ACNielsen, "Our History," http://acnielsen.com/company/history.shtml.

3. Whipple, Sargent & Associates, "Market Research Guidelines," Corporate brochure, www.whipplesargent.com/mrguide.pdf.

4. "State of the Hispanic Consumer: The Hispanic Market Imperative Report," The Nielsen Company, Quarter 2, 2012, http://nielsen.com/content/dam/corporate/us/en/reports-downloads/2012-Reports/State-of-the-Hispanic-Consumer.pdf.

5. "Santa Fe New Mexico Household Income" and "Albuquerque New Mexico Household Income," Department of Numbers, www.deptofnumbers.com/income.

6. The NPD Group, "NPD Expects Positive Back-to-School Season for E-Commerce," News release, July 10, 2013.

7. The Intelligence Group/Youth Intelligence, "Money Savvy Tweens Have a Big Say in Spending," News release, August 10, 2005.

8. Kortney Stringer, "Advertising: Pop-In Products," *Detroit Free Press,* February 16, 2006, www.marathondigital.com/news_ad_pop_up.html.

9. Research and Markets, "Global Product Placement Spending Forecast 2012-2016," News release, December 20, 2012.

10. Wendy Mendes, "Showcasing Brands," *GlobeSt.com,* June 6, 2005, www.globest.com/retail/advisor/1_35/advisor/15173-1.html.

11. Emily Kaiser, "Retailers Shift Ad Strategies in Digital Age," *Reuters,* February 12, 2006, http://today.reuters.com/news/articlebusiness.aspx?type=media&storyID=nN10184324&imageid=&cap=&from=business.

12. Tom Zeller Jr. "A Generation Serves Notice: It's a Moving Target," *New York Times,* January 22, 2006, www.nytimes.com/2006/01/22/business/yourmoney/22youth.html?ex=1295586000&en=d23bc480d739c911&ei=5088&partner=rssnyt&emc=rss.

13. Theresa Howard, "Marketers Go Fishing for Female Web Surfers," *USA Today,* March 19, 2006, www.usatoday.com/money/advertising/2006-03-19-webwomen_x.htm?CFID=507767&CFTOKEN=39368927.

14. Bill Siwicki, "With 40% of Sales Coming through Mobile Devices, Rue La La Updates Its Apps," *Internet Retailer,* October 2, 2012, http://www.internetretailer.com/2012/10/02/40-sales-coming-through-mobile-rue-la-la-updates.

15. Elizabeth Weinstein, "Retailers Tap E-Zines to Reach Niche Audiences," *Wall Street Journal*, April 28, 2005, http://online.wsj.com/article/SB111411501158013598.html?apl=y.

16. Jeanine Poggi, "L'Oreal Seeks Women in Unlikely Place: On Xbox," *Advertising Age*, October 3, 2012, http://adage.com/article/digital/l-al-seeks-women-place-xbox/237556/.

17. Kathleen Kiley, " 'Brand Ambassadors' Representing Consumer Products in Teen Nation," *KPMG Consumer Markets Insider*, July 28, 2005, www.kpmginsiders.com/display_analysis_print_nobuttons.asp?strType=&cs_id=138056.

CHAPTER 11

Social Media and the Fashion Consumer

WHAT DO I NEED TO KNOW ABOUT SOCIAL MEDIA AND THE FASHION CONSUMER?

✔ The origin and different types of social media

✔ How the use of social media influences consumers' buying behavior

✔ How marketers use social media to learn about and communicate with their customers

✔ The ethical issues that can arise with use of social media

When you got up this morning, how long was it before you checked in with your friends . . . not in person or by phone, but on Facebook or Twitter? Perhaps you sat down to read the latest entry on your favorite fashion blog—or to write an observation about a new trend on your own blog. Maybe you shared a photo on Instagram of the jacket you just bought, or pinned your original design for an appliquéd tote bag on your Pinterest board, or watched a YouTube video in which someone demonstrated how to emulate the hairstyle of an actor you like.

Every day, hundreds of millions of people log in to social networking sites, making connections with everyone from best friends to favorite celebrities, and sharing their thoughts and feelings about everything from the new cereal they tried for break-fast to why they're volunteering at a cancer walk. So it's no wonder that marketers of fashion goods are paying attention. For example:

- A Samsung smartphone commercial showed customers commenting on features of the latest iPhone as they waited in line for an Apple store to open—such as one customer saying, "I heard that you have to have an adapter to use the dock on the new one," to which another replied, "Yeah, yeah, but they make the coolest adapters." According to Samsung, those lines and others in the ad's script were based on hundreds of thousands of real customer comments on Twitter complaining or poking fun at specific features of the iPhone 5. The commercial drew more than 32 million YouTube views in two weeks.[1]

- J. Crew offered Pinterest followers a sneak peek at some head-to-toe looks from its upcoming catalog before the catalog hit the mail. Each pin was accompanied by an invitation to contact the retailer's stylist team for help in pre-ordering the look before it became available through the print catalog and on the company's website. Although the company did not disclose specific results of the Pinterest tactic, its overall revenues increased 6 percent and its direct sales increased 13 percent for that calendar quarter.[2]

- After JCPenney realized it had gone down the wrong path (see Chapter 5) and wanted to regain customers' trust, it used Facebook and Twitter to apologize to customers and assure them that the company was listening to them. A Facebook post stated, "It's no secret. We've made some changes. Some you've liked and others you didn't. We've heard you—and we're listening. Let us know what

you think." The post received nearly 57,000 "likes" and more than 19,400 comments, and was shared by more than 3,700 followers.[3]

What is it about social networking that appeals so much to consumers, young and old? What influence do social media sites have on consumer buying behavior? How do consumers use social media to form or reinforce their opinions about fashion goods—and how can fashion marketers use these media to improve their visibility, target their audience more precisely, and interact with customers in a way that builds sales and loyalty? Those are all questions we'll examine in this chapter.

What Is Social Media?

The term social media encompasses a broad swath of Internet communications, and those communications channels are in an almost constant state of flux and evolution. But in essence, we can define **social media** as the collection of online spaces and tools that allow individuals and groups to generate content and engage in interactive, peer-to-peer conversations and content exchange. Just as traditional media span a variety of types and categories (see Chapter 10), the same is true of social media, which include social networking sites like Facebook, social bookmarking sites like Delicious, microblogging sites like Twitter, social news sites like Digg, video sharing sites like YouTube, social shopping sites like Wanelo, and many others, all centered on user participation and interaction.

Engaging with other people is clearly not a new human activity. Social interaction not only satisfies our primary human needs but also helps us find meaning, a sense of belonging, and even pure pleasure. What has changed throughout different historical periods is the means for socializing. Here's the parallel: People used to gather in a common location—whether the courtyard of a castle, the town square, or the neighborhood mall—to interact in person. Now they can get together using any computer, tablet, or smartphone with an Internet connection. So, instead of having to physically go somewhere to meet, we can interact, share, and communicate with others in the digital world no matter where we are, and at any hour of the day or night (Figure 11.1).

LET'S TALK

How do you use social media? To share news, display your fashion preferences, shop, communicate with friends? Have you used social media to find a job, conduct research, or establish new personal or business relationships?

Studies have found that people post on social media primarily to share interesting things, important things, or funny things—just as they would do if they were seeing friends or others face to face. Other key reasons include to share a personal belief or philosophy, to recommend a product or

FIGURE 11.1 Social media lets us communicate and interact with others without being in the same physical location.

service, and to support a worthwhile social cause (Figure 11.2).[4] In addition to posting their own thoughts, consumers also use social media for reasons that can vary by their age and family situation, among other demographic factors—and those demographics even influence which specific sites they prefer to use. Moms, for instance, use the gamut of social media platforms, and particularly Facebook, more than the general population does, and rely on parenting-related social media to learn about which brands and products to buy.[5] Many teens, on the other hand, prefer Twitter and Instagram to Facebook, and cite Twitter as having the most influence on their purchases.[6] Of course, those

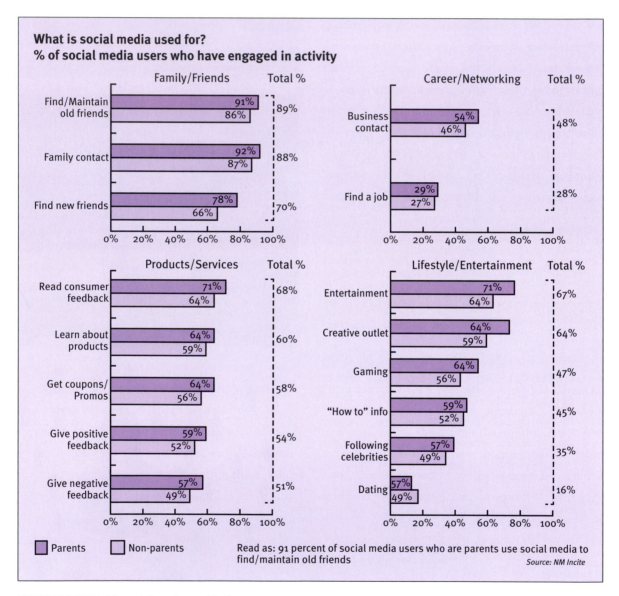

FIGURE 11.2 What is social media used for?

preferences could change next week or next year (or by the time you're reading this) because social media change so rapidly, with once-popular sites falling by the wayside and new ones popping up to fill a new niche. It's clear that marketers have their work cut out for them both to harvest customer data from the wealth of online and mobile media, and then strategically incorporate the right mix of social media into their marketing strategy to best reach their goals and meet their customers' needs.

EVOLUTION OF THE WEB

What's the difference between the Web (short for World Wide Web) and the Internet? In simple terms, the Internet is a huge network of networks, the infrastructure that connects millions of computers together globally and enables them to communicate. The Web, on the other hand, is one specific means of accessing information over the medium of the Internet. Utilizing browsers, such as Internet Explorer or Firefox, users enter Web addresses known as URLs (uniform resource locators) to access Web pages, and then can jump to other sections or pages by clicking on embedded hyperlinks within a Web page or document. Most, but not all, of consumers' online activity takes place on the Web; e-mail and instant messages, for instance, are disseminated over the Internet but not on the Web.

Web 1.0 and Web 2.0 are technical terms that explain different stages in the development of the Web. Web 1.0 was the early stage during which companies presented information and users could just access and view this information. It was static, authoritative, and controlled. It was a one-way communication and for that reason less interesting and

engaging. Web 2.0 emerged not long after Web 1.0, allowing users to interact and generate their own content through blogs, message boards, videos, podcasts, and so on; in short, Web 2.0 enabled the birth of social media.

The evolution of the Web has brought us from the Internet period, where consumers were only able to receive companies' messages, to the information period, where consumers could actively search for material, to the connected period of Web 2.0, where consumers can generate their own content, have two-way communication with others, and stream information through a growing variety of social media platforms (Figure 11.3). (See Table 11.1.)

And it doesn't stop there. The next step may be dubbed the "personalization period," if (but more likely *when*) the vision of Web 3.0 becomes reality. What is Web 3.0? It has been referred to as the "intelligent Web," since it is expected to introduce

FIGURE 11.3 The social media landscape is vast—and evolves almost daily.

Table 11.1 Evolution of the Web

	Internet Period	**Information Period**	**Connectivity Period**
Activity	Consumer *receives* information.	Consumer *searches* for information.	Consumer *interacts/streams* information.
Method	Use an Internet provider.	Use a search engine.	Use a social media platform.

new techniques for organizing content, as well as new tools that will make it possible to collect, interpret, and use data in ways that can add meaning and structure to information where it didn't exist before—in other words, to make the Web even easier to use, more efficient, and more valuable to its users. In concept, Web 3.0 will enable services that can sort through vast amounts of data from a variety of digital sources, from Web content to e-mail to files on a PC's hard drive, to pinpoint the most pertinent information and deliver more relevant search results. This highly targeted data could in turn pave the way for marketers to provide never-before-seen levels of customization to consumers.[7] Can you imagine your own "personal brand"? That is one of the tantalizing possibilities of Web 3.0.

TYPES OF SOCIAL MEDIA

Under the banner of social media, there are many different types of social platforms—and those categories tend to shift and blur on an ongoing basis as consumers find new ways to connect and share, and as site developers introduce new features or adapt existing functions to generate new consumer interest or meet new demand. Among the primary types of social media are social networking sites, blogs and microblogs, video and photo sharing sites, and social shopping sites, along with other categories such as social news and bookmarking sites, Wikis, podcasts, and more. Let's look at those that have the most relevance for consumers of fashion.

Social networking refers to websites and services that allow users to share ideas, activities, events, interests, photos, and so on with other people in the network, and may include mechanisms for e-mail and instant messaging among users. Users generally create a personal profile that others can view, enabling members to find friends and choose the people or organizations with whom they want to connect. Social networks often involve people who have the same interests, activities, or backgrounds, and may allow for members to create their own smaller groups within the network based on a common theme (such as members of a particular high school class). Examples of social networking sites are Facebook, Google+, MySpace, LinkedIn, and Tagged.

Facebook is by far the biggest social networking platform today, with more than a billion members worldwide reaching across almost all demographics. Although Facebook started as a social directory for college students, it quickly expanded to welcome anyone and everyone, encouraging members to share and comment on each other's news, photos, videos, and links, eventually adding the option for businesses to create their own presence on the site. More than 15 million companies and organizations now maintain a Facebook page,[8] enabling them to communicate with current and prospective customers and increase awareness of their brand. Consumers follow brands for updates and special offers, and may interact with a company by posting comments and/or sharing information about the brand with others in their network. A recent CMB Consumer Pulse study found that more than a third of consumers interact with their favorite brands on Facebook, and after "liking" a brand, 56 percent are more likely to recommend the brand to friends and 51 percent are more likely to buy a product (Figure 11.4).[9]

Other well-known social networking platforms include Google+, the second largest social networking service, described by Google as a "social layer" accessible across a range of sites; MySpace, an early pioneer that fell out of favor but was reinvented with a greater music orientation by singer/actor Justin Timberlake, who has an ownership stake; Tagged, a social discovery site that allows members to browse other members' profiles, play games, and share tags and personal gifts; and LinkedIn, used primarily for business and professional networking.

A **blog** (shortened from "web log") is an online journal in which an individual, group, or corporation presents a record of observations, opinions, experiences, and other thoughts for readers. To keep the sites fresh, most bloggers add new entries frequently, sometimes daily. The introduction of Web 2.0 technology and software tools that enable individuals to publish blogs without having to learn Internet coding led to a surge in the number of

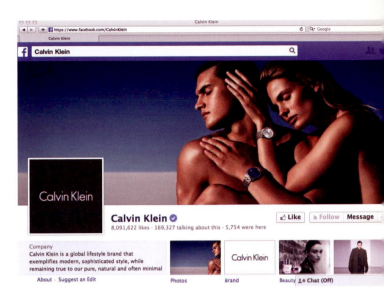

FIGURE 11.4 More than half of consumers are more likely to recommend a brand to friends after they "like" it on Facebook.

blogs, estimated to be more than 160 million worldwide. Early on, blogs were primarily the work of a single individual publishing his or her thoughts and ideas about a single subject, but over time, the platform expanded to include multi-author blogs and corporate blogs, among others.

Blogs in general are ranked by consumers as the third most influential digital resource and the top social media influence when they're deciding what to buy.[10] Fashion blogs, which represent a large subset of the blogosphere (totality of online blogging), play an increasingly important role in the realm of fashion, apparel, and personal style, with top fashion bloggers now wielding as much influence as magazine editors in shaping trends and sharing the latest news and images from the runways. Among the most-followed independent fashion blogs are Girls Off Fifth, On the Racks, Bag Snob, The Curvy Fashionista, and Citizen Couture.[11]

A **microblog** is also a social platform for sharing thoughts, ideas, or opinions but the entries are condensed to a much shorter format than a standard blog. Two prominent examples of microblogging sites are Twitter and Tumblr.

The most popular is Twitter, with more than 500 million registered users. Twitter users choose other members of the network to "follow," and any new posts appear in the user's main Twitter feed. Each post, or "tweet," is limited to 140 characters, but users can also incorporate links, photos, and video into their tweets, as well as "retweet" items of those they follow—a capability that often helps generate buzz or cause a marketing message or news item to go viral. Twitter also popularized the use of the **hashtag,** a word or phrase preceded by the symbol "#" that enables users to easily retrieve a grouping of all messages that contain that word or phrase. Designers and other fashion brands have become avid users of Twitter as a marketing tool. (See Case in Point 1.4 in Chapter 1 about Kenneth Cole's controversial tweets.) The site has also been growing in popularity among teens, with 26 percent calling it the most important social network to them, versus 23 percent who cited Facebook as their favorite.[12]

Video and photo sharing platforms are a form of social networking that allows users to post personal photographs and videos for their friends and others to view online or via a mobile device. YouTube is the biggest video sharing site, attracting 1 billion unique viewers each month and receiving 100 hours of uploaded video every minute. The site displays a wide variety of user-generated video content, including movie and TV clips and music videos, and amateur content such as video blogging and educational or instructional videos. Rising quickly in popularity is Instagram, which grew to 150 million active users within just three years of its launch. Instagram enables users to take pictures and videos, apply digital filters to them, and share them on a variety of social networking services.

Pinterest is another rapidly growing site for photo sharing and social networking, with an estimated 70 million users. The pinboard-style website allows users to create and manage theme-based collections of images, such as events, interests, and hobbies. Users can browse other pinboards for images, re-pin images to their own boards, or "like" photos. In addition, there are a number of "micro-sharing" platforms like Vine, which lets users take very short (6-second) videos to share on social networks with the capability of "revining" them (similar to the retweets of Vine's parent, Twitter); and Snapchat, with which users can send photos or videos to a controlled group of recipients and set the length of viewing time, from 1 to 10 seconds, before the images are deleted from the device and the service. Along with consumers, fashion marketers are increasingly taking advantage of the various photo and video sharing services to reach customers with visual images that promote their brand—and with good reason. A study by ROI Research found that almost half of respondents were more likely to engage with a brand on social media when it posted an image.[13]

Yet another form of social media that influences fashion consumption is the category of **social shopping,** a method of commerce that uses technology to mimic the social interactions found in physical malls and stores. Unlike a standard retail website that consumers browse on their own in an isolated shopping experience, at a social shopping site they can browse through product feeds that are curated specifically for them and filled with items posted or made popular by other users. The idea is to help reaffirm and guide consumers' purchase decisions in a virtually collaborative buying experience. Among the top fashion-related social shopping sites is Wanelo (taken from "want-need-love"), which brings together products from a wide array of stores into one pinboard-style platform. Users can browse, save, and buy items, post new products from around the Web, and follow members, stores, or product collections. Members can also create collections—similar to Pinterest boards—from items onsite or external links, and an added social aspect enables users to tag Wanelo and Facebook friends to specific products (Figure 11.5).[14]

As you can tell, despite the broad classifications of social media, it's not always easy to pigeonhole a particular site in just one category, since many combine aspects of social networking, photo and video sharing, microblogging, and even shopping all through one site or service. But the overriding commonality is that all these types of social media allow and encourage users to communicate and interact—with each other, with the broader network, and often with their favorite brands.

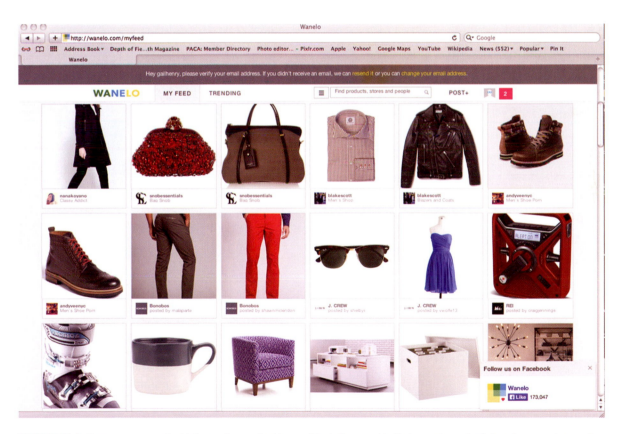

FIGURE 11.5 Consumers can find information on fashion and be influenced in their purchase decisions by many types of social media, including social shopping sites.

Fashion Shoppers Go Social for Inspiration

It's clear that consumers of all stripes increasingly turn to social media for all kinds of information and interaction. But what about that key target audience of female fashion consumers? How do they use social media when they want inspiration for a fashion purchase?

That is precisely what NetBase, which provides social intelligence data to clients, set out to discover, commissioning Edison Research to conduct a study of 1,005 women who have profiles on at least one social network. When the results were in, two particular segments of consumers stood out—based not on traditional demographics but rather on the women's fashion attitudes: "Fashionistas," women who strongly agree with the statement, "Fashion and beauty are extremely important to me," representing 28 percent of respondents; and

(continued)

How Consumers Use Social Media

It may be impossible to put an exact number on how many consumers use social media, but we know the number is enormous. What is sometimes easy to forget is how quickly the phenomenon has grown. As recently as 2008, only 29 percent of adult Internet users were also social media users. By 2013, that number had more than doubled to 72 percent.[15]

LET'S TALK

Do you think it's probably safe to say that among teenage Internet users, the use of social media climbs to near 100 percent? Do you know anyone who does not use social media at all?

The question is, what role do social media play in consumer behavior? A very big role, as it turns out.

For one thing, research has confirmed that consumers are influenced by social media when deciding what to buy. One study showed that nearly a third of consumers are influenced by blogs (31.1 percent) and Facebook (30.8 percent), followed closely by groups/forums (28 percent) and YouTube (27 percent).[16] The level of social media influence is even higher for key groups of fashion consumers. According to a survey of "fashionistas" and "social shoppers," nearly two-thirds are influenced in their purchase decisions by fashion blogs and message boards, and Facebook inspires fashion decisions for over half of fashionistas and nearly three-quarters of social shoppers.[17] (See Case in Point 11.1.)

There are multiple reasons why fashion consumers turn to social media, but four key areas are to seek information on a product or brand; to get recommendations about a potential purchase; to interact with a brand; and to receive discounts or special offers.

"Social shoppers," women who strongly agree with the statement, "The brands and products my friends use influence my own purchase decisions," comprising 15 percent of survey respondents.

The study found that both fashionistas and social shoppers are in sync with the total sample of women surveyed in terms of having a profile on Facebook, with close to 100 percent penetration for that platform. More important, because simply having a profile on a social network doesn't automatically mean it influences a consumer's fashion purchases, the study delved into the degree of influence of different social media. The findings? Facebook does inspire fashion decisions in at least one product category for 72 percent of social shoppers and for 56 percent of fashionistas.

Digging deeper, the survey asked the women about the influence of social media in their quest for inspiration regarding specific categories of apparel, accessories, and beauty products. Across the board, the influence of Facebook on social shoppers was stronger than with any other social platform, with the top five categories influenced being casual clothing (47 percent), cosmetics (43 percent), special occasion clothing (42 percent), costume jewelry (41 percent), and active/fitness clothing (40 percent).

Fashionistas, on the other hand, while also finding influence on Facebook, tend to turn more to fashion blogs and message boards for their inspiration. Blogs are most influential to this group in the categories of cosmetics (37 percent), special occasion clothing (36 percent), costume jewelry (35 percent), casual clothing (34 percent), and special occasion footwear (30 percent). The only two categories in which Facebook is slightly more influential to fashionistas than fashion blogs/message boards are active/fitness clothing and active/fitness footwear.

Twitter does not rank among the top five social media platforms in terms of influence on fashion decisions, according to the study, even though most social shoppers and fashionistas maintain a Twitter profile. But Pinterest and Instagram do wield influence, undoubtedly due to the visual nature of fashion and those sites' core function as photo and video sharing platforms. Approximately half of both fashionistas and social shoppers find inspiration on Pinterest, with a somewhat lower percentage for Instagram. However, Instagram users tend to be a younger demographic—and looking specifically at the 18 to 29 age group, the study found that Instagram does inspire decisions in at least one fashion category for 42 percent of those women.

Source: "Social Channels of Influence in the Fashion Industry: A Consumer Study," NetBase Solutions, Inc., 2013.

SEEKING PRODUCT/BRAND INFORMATION

According to research, the primary reasons that consumers engage with a brand on social media are to find out more about its products or services or to keep up with its activities. Twitter and Facebook are the preferred sites for more than half of consumers who say they follow brands to stay up-to-date on the companies' activities, with YouTube, Instagram, and Pinterest also each used by more than a third of consumers. To learn about a product or service, more than 6 out of 10 consumers turn to YouTube, while more than half look to Facebook and Pinterest, and slightly fewer use Twitter and Instagram.[18] (See Figure 11.6.)

In addition, 45 percent of consumers say they regularly check out brands' social networking pages—a number that rises to 54 percent for consumers under age 35, as you can see in Table 11.2. What does this tell marketers? Consumers want easy access to product and brand information and convenience to help them make informed decisions.

SEEKING RECOMMENDATIONS

One of the most remarkable changes the use of social media has brought in marketing and consumer behavior is the enhanced interaction among consumers themselves regarding a brand. Consumers have always tended to buy something that was recommended to them, especially by someone they trust, more frequently than buying something simply being marketed to them. When your parents and grandparents were your age (or even older) and were considering a purchase, they probably asked the opinion of family and friends in a conversation conducted face to face or maybe over the telephone. With the use of social media, consumers can instantly access opinions from an extended circle of friends and acquaintances, the marketplace, and

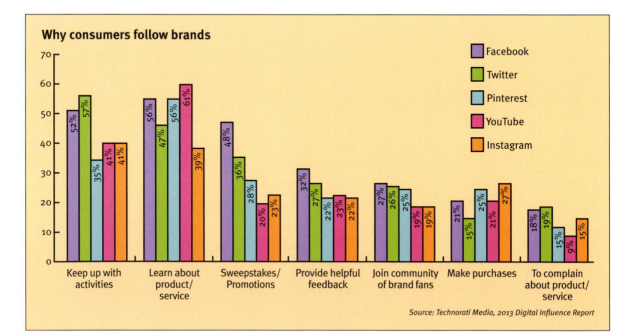

FIGURE 11.6 Why consumers follow brands.

Table 11.2 Consumers Follow Brands on Social Media

I regularly check out brands' social networking pages, such as Facebook.

		Gender		Age		
	Total	**Male**	**Female**	**Under 35**	**35 to 49**	**50 to 64**
Agree very much	16%	14%	18%	21%	15%	9%
Agree somewhat	29%	28%	30%	34%	28%	22%
Disagree somewhat	25%	26%	25%	25%	25%	26%
Disagree very much	29%	31%	27%	20%	32%	43%
(Agree)	45%	43%	48%	54%	43%	31%
(Disagree)	55%	57%	52%	46%	57%	69%

Source: Ipsos and Ipsos Global @dvisor, January 2013.

a huge network of people potentially anywhere in the world; social channels work as the new word-of-mouth advertising. In fact, social media sites are influencing consumer purchases much more than conventional advertising.[19]

One key consumer segment that relies on social media for recommendations is women ages 18 to 34 who have kids. As a group, moms are 20 percent more likely to use social media than the general population, and 91 percent use social media regularly. What's more, moms report that posts from a friend recommending a product or brand are 16 percent more influential than posts from a brand—and posts from another mom are 55 percent more influential than posts from a brand.[20]

Taking it a step further, some consumers and businesses have begun to use **crowdsourcing,**

gathering information or feedback from a wide variety of people to help understand and resolve issues, make purchase decisions, or get answers to specific questions.

PROVIDING CUSTOMER FEEDBACK

Because social media enable two-way conversation between customers and brands, consumers have an unprecedented ability to offer feedback—whether positive or negative—to companies with which they engage. More than one in five consumers say that they follow brands to provide helpful feedback, while fewer than one in five use social media to complain about a product or service, according to research.[21]

Leaving a Facebook comment or posting a tweet presents a quick and convenient way for consumers to ask a question or share their opinion with a brand about anything from the way a product performs to the way a company operates. For example, when JCPenney was criticized by a small but vocal group of conservative customers who didn't like the retailer's choice of openly gay Ellen DeGeneres as its spokesperson, thousands of other consumers took to social media to voice their support for the choice and the company. By contrast, Gap was the target of a negative social media campaign when it initially hesitated in signing an accord to improve safety and working conditions in Bangladesh clothing factories following a devastating fire; the company did join the pact after certain provisions were tweaked. (See Chapter 15 for further discussion.)

LET'S TALK

Why do you think consumers might tend to leave more positive feedback than negative comments about a brand on social media? Have you ever offered your feedback to a brand? Was it positive or negative? Did you get a reply?

OBTAINING COUPONS/DISCOUNTS

Another key motivation for consumers to follow brands on social media is to obtain coupons, discounts, or other special offers. Nearly half of consumers (48 percent) "like" a brand on Facebook in order to qualify for sweepstakes and promotions; more than a third follow companies on Twitter for the same reason, according to one research study.[22]

How Marketers Use Social Media

Understanding customers' needs and meeting them better than the competition is the foundation of the marketing concept, and social media offers marketers a whole new way to learn about current and potential customers—based on information volunteered by the customers themselves. (See Chapter 9, Case in Point 9.2.) To tap into that data, marketers have implemented systems to monitor the vast numbers of comments and posts for information pertinent to their brand. They have also adapted their strategies to incorporate the social media platforms most used by their target market. These platforms allow marketers to "listen" to what customers like and don't like, to gauge the level of consumer response to their products or brand, to communicate directly with large numbers of customers and

Table 11.3 Because of social media, I am more likely to

Try new things based on friends' suggestions	80%
Encourage my friends to try new products	74%
Stay more engaged with the brands I like	72%
Share any negative experiences with brands or products	42%
Not buy certain products because I learned of a negative customer experience	32%

Source: CMO Council and Lithium, "Variance in the Social Brand Experience" study.

potential customers, and to engage those customers in real-time (or near real-time) dialogue.

Social media has clearly become a standard element in the marketing mix. The vast majority of companies now use at least some **social media marketing (SMM)**—the process of garnering consumer attention and sales through use of social media platforms—to complement their traditional marketing strategies by sharing content, videos, and images to reach more customers, and by creating relationships with customers to increase sales and brand awareness. In 2013, 77 percent of Fortune 500 companies had an active Twitter account, 70 percent had a Facebook page, and 69 percent had a YouTube account.[23] As journalist Antony Young wrote in *Ad Age,* "The top marketers are demonstrating that the future of our industry is not about social marketing. It's about marketing in a social era."[24]

It's no wonder that virtually all fashion marketers, including American Eagle, Gap, Victoria's Secret, Macy's, and Nike, have organically incorporated the use of social media into their marketing strategies to promote their brands. Furthermore, social media, through its capability for two-way conversation, creates a new kind of intimacy between consumers and companies, so the companies no longer appear distant and faceless. This interaction allows consumers to get more relevant and timely data about the brands they like, while marketers develop information for more directed marketing campaigns, which ultimately drive sales (Figure 11.7).

Social media's benefits to marketers fall into a number of areas. Let's examine a few of particular importance, including collecting data about target customers, communicating product and brand information to consumers, interacting with customers to enhance loyalty, and driving sales.

COLLECTING DATA TO BETTER UNDERSTAND CUSTOMERS

You'll recall from Chapter 10 that marketers rely on research to identify their target customers and to understand those customers' needs and wants. Social media provide an abundance of current, sometimes deeply personal data about consumers' lifestyles, preferences, beliefs, friends, interests, and shopping habits, which marketers can harvest, process, and then incorporate into their marketing messages far more quickly, and in a more customized way, than they could in the past.

FIGURE 11.7 Different consumers use different social media to connect with their favorite brands, so most marketers invite customers to "follow them" on a range of social platforms.

Macy's Stars in YouTube Videos

Founded in 1858, Macy's may have its roots in the nineteenth century—but it also has two feet planted firmly in the twenty-first. If there were any doubt, it only takes a look at how the iconic department store is not only embracing social media but also innovating ways to better communicate with customers on a range of social platforms.

In a recent interview, Macy's group vice president of digital/new media and multicultural marketing, Jennifer Kasper, explained that social media is growing in importance to the retailer because it is important to its customer. "It's where the hub of her relationships are being managed and where's she's learning about new things and what's trending in general in her life—whether it's a fashion trend or entertainment news," Kasper said. "It's important for us to be there as a brand—to be chiming in as much as it's appropriate and facilitating ways that she can share information."

Macy's has already expanded its presence across the range of social media but continues to seek new ways to engage customers. Take YouTube, for example. While the retailer had previously posted its own videos on the site, it took a whole new approach to the medium when it decided to enlist four outside YouTube personalities to create videos that would feature Macy's apparel, accessories, and beauty products. Among them, the four boast nearly 2.6 million subscribers and their videos have logged some 303 million hits. As Kasper explained, the goal was to allow these independent video bloggers leeway to share with their fans their own impressions of Macy's, "with the hope that their individual fan bases will be more excited about shopping at Macy's when they hear one of the vloggers they follow had a great experience with us."

Macy's partnered with StyleHaul, a YouTube fashion and beauty network, to create the videos, which were designed to target Millennial customers. The YouTubers selected encompassed different style profiles, including a polished, put-together type; a free-spirited, casual mom personality; a preppy, girl-next-door persona; and a style maven with the knack for being able to pull off virtually any outfit. Even before the YouTube launch, tweets and Instagram posts that the four shared from the video shoots had already started a buzz, generating more than 4 million impressions and inspiring comments or shares from almost 100,000 followers.

Although Macy's did not set specific sales goals that it wanted the videos to achieve, the retailer did incorporate e-commerce tools that would make it easy for viewers to purchase any featured items. And one of the four YouTubers set her own goal of having products she mentioned actually sell out for Macy's!

Sources: Rachel Brown, "Macy's Millennial Push Hits YouTube," *WWD*, September 13, 2013, www.wwd.com/retail-news/department-stores/macys-millennial-push-hits-youtube-7150752; "Macy's Says Social Media Strategy Begins with Good Content," *eMarketer*, November 1, 2013, www.emarketer.com/Article/Macys-Says-Social-Media-Strategy-Begins-with-Good-Content/1010351.

COMMUNICATING PRODUCT/ BRAND INFORMATION

As mentioned earlier in the chapter, consumers turn to social media to keep up with favorite brands and to learn about products and services. So communicating that information is a key aspect of marketers' social media strategy. For example, when Saks Fifth Avenue revamped its shoe department, the high-end retailer supplemented announcements made via e-mail and on its website with a mix of social media tactics, including a contest in which a pair of shoes was awarded to a winner each day for 30 days. To enter the contest, users had to take a photograph of their favorite shoes and tag them with a special caption on Instagram; Saks' Facebook app was used to showcase contest entries and winners. In addition, much of the retailer's blog and other social media content centered on the remodeled shoe floor.[25]

Fashion brands increasingly rely on social media when they introduce new products or collections, sometimes offering customers and fans minute-by-minute coverage of runway shows from around the world. For its February 2013 fashion show, for instance, Topshop live-streamed the show over the Internet and garnered 4 million viewers. Not to stop there, for the September debut of its Spring 2014 collection, the retailer once again live-streamed its show but added features that allowed viewers to see color options for products as they appeared on the runway, as well as to capture and share their favorite looks on Facebook and Twitter through a "shoot the show" tool. Going even further, Topshop incorporated Chirp, a mobile app that sends images and links to handheld devices via sound, to distribute

FIGURE 11.8 Fashion marketers continually seek new and innovative ways to incorporate social media into their strategy. Topshop, for instance, created a series of interactive social media experiences around a recent London fashion show.

images of its new looks along with prep and backstage shots (Figure 11.8).[26]

INTERACTING WITH CUSTOMERS

Just as customers use social media to communicate with brands, brands must reciprocate by responding to consumer questions and concerns when necessary and appropriate, and by addressing existing or potential problems before they become worse or spread through cyberspace, impacting the brand's image and reputation. A survey by American Express found that customers on average are willing to spend 21 percent more with companies that provide great service, and that one in five consumers have used social media for customer service, expecting more than a simple "canned" response. In other words, just getting a customer's "like" does not guarantee that a company is winning the customer's loyalty. The like has to be reinforced by responsive communications and customer service.[27]

A perfect example involved the chief blogger for Dell Computer, who immediately started blogging and tweeting to customers when it was discovered that some batteries in the company's laptops could explode. Customers were surprised—and very pleased—that the company quickly addressed the issues with such personal care. The result was a terrific public relations boost![28]

DRIVING SALES

Of course, sales are the lifeblood of any business, so driving sales is another key aspect of the way businesses use social media. This can involve a variety of tools including special deals, coupons, and promotions to generate consumer interest and buzz, and to inspire consumers to make a buy. One study regarding Pinterest, for example, found that nearly a quarter of users headed to the store to buy an item they liked or pinned on their own board.[29]

Marketers of fashion goods are increasingly looking for ways to use the power of social media to drive sales and increase traffic to their store or website. Sony, for instance, ran a Twitter campaign that offered followers the opportunity to build a customized Vaio laptop and get a 10 percent discount; more than 1,600 Twitter followers jumped at the chance. Department store chain Bloomingdale's tapped into the "selfie" craze (of consumers snapping their own photos on a mobile device) for its #Bloomie-Selfie Instagram contest, in which fans were asked to submit a selfie that highlighted a favorite beauty or styling tip they used to enhance their snapshot. As submissions were received, Bloomingdale's placed them on a board so that fans could vote for their favorite—which meant that some entrants shared the contest on their own social media pages in order to accrue more votes, thereby spreading further word of mouth for the promotion. The ultimate winner received a $1,000 Bloomies gift card; and the retailer had the opportunity to gain new insights into its customers, based on the products and beauty tips that were featured in the entries.[30]

The bottom line is that with social media, consumers' buying cycle is becoming: See a product

Table 11.4 Consumer Digital Purchasing Steps

Consumer Steps	Awareness	Interest	Evaluation	Decision
Consumer Action	See a visual. (Notice a product on a company website, in an ad, on YouTube, shared by a friend on Pinterest, etc.)	Click on it. (Get information and more details.)	Shop. (Compare alternatives.)	Buy. (Choose the product and where to purchase it.)

or service recommended on a social media platform, click on it for more information, shop online for alternatives, and buy. Marketers that position themselves on the social media their customers are frequenting, and that are most adept at providing the tools that make those steps easy and convenient, gain a competitive advantage and the opportunity to reach the greatest possible universe of new and established consumers.

Challenges of Social Media Use

There are clearly enormous benefits to both consumers and marketers in using social media. But there are also some challenges. One of those challenges is the scope and fluid nature of the social media platforms. Among the hundreds (or thousands) of different sites and services, consumers and marketers must not only make choices about which to support and use, but must also stay alert to new media that join the mix, offering new functions or features, and perhaps supplanting a site that had been considered *the* place to be. It can take significant time and effort to build a presence and a network or following on a social site, and neither companies nor individuals are eager to lose that investment.

Another big issue for marketers is making sure they have a social media strategy that not only effectively reaches target customers but communicates their message with clarity and consistency. If consumers have a perception of a brand based on their experience and what they've seen through traditional media, the brand's social media image and messages need to be in sync, or else customers could become confused or alienated.

The use of social media can also raise issues regarding copyright and intellectual property ownership. In the past, it would have been inconsequential for consumers to tear a photo out of a fashion magazine and stick it on their bedroom wall or bulletin board. Today, if consumers re-pin a photo onto their Pinterest board, for example, it could be an infringement on the copyright of whoever took or owns the photo. This is an area for which clear rules and enforcement mechanisms are being debated among all the parties involved.

Perhaps the biggest issue surrounding social media is the ethical issue of privacy and security. When consumers share personal information on a social media site, they do so trusting that their information will not be compromised, sold to other entities, or hijacked by third parties for uses that the consumers did not intend. Unfortunately, the digital online world has expanded with such speed that adequate privacy controls have not been able to keep pace. A growing number of groups and individuals are advocating for stricter privacy rules, and the concern is justified, although few would want regulations to put a damper on the open access and freedom of information the Internet provides. Some solutions will most likely be developed in coming years, since it is highly doubtful that social media will disappear anytime soon.

In the meantime, the Ethics Resource Center (ERC), a nonprofit organization that researches

Monetizing Word of Mouth—at the Expense of Privacy

A wealth of research has underscored the fact that consumers are more likely to buy something based on the recommendations of friends on social media. So it shouldn't be too surprising that marketers would like to capitalize on those recommendations and find ways to turn consumers' word-of-mouth sharing into actual advertising endorsements—potentially starring: You.

Few would dispute that the use of "real people" (as opposed to skinny, air-brushed-to-perfection models) in advertising is a good thing, removing some of the pressure consumers (and particularly young girls) may feel to achieve an impossibly ideal image. But what happens when those real people are indeed *real people* who have simply engaged in the standard social media practice of "liking" a product or posting a positive comment about a brand?

That is the issue that jumped to the forefront when Google announced that it would place some Google+ users' photos and comments in advertising endorsements across the Web. Google's updated terms of service informed users that "your friends, family, and others may see your (Google+) profile name and photo, and content like the reviews you share or the ads you +1'd." The move permits sharing of member endorsements in a similar manner to that of Facebook, which already enabled members' "likes" to be seen on other websites visited by friends in their network.

In its announcement, Google stressed that the change was meant to help consumers make better choices, saying, "We want to give you—and your friends and connections—the most useful information. Recommendations from people you know can really help." And the company did provide an "opt-out" mechanism for consumers who pay attention and choose not to unwittingly have their endorsements spread across the Web.

Nonetheless, Google's decision set off a new round of alarm bells for privacy advocates, who urged the Federal Trade Commission to ensure that consumers are given enough capability to protect their privacy online. In the meantime, consumers might want to be a little more circumspect with their "+1s" and "likes."

Sources: Cecilia Kang, "Google to Put User Photos, Comments in Online Ad Endorsements," *Washington Post,* October 11, 2013, http://articles.washingtonpost.com/2013-10-11/business/42926754_1_google-and-facebook-google-user-google-policy; and Larry Magid, "Google May Feature You in an Ad with 'Shared Endorsements' (Unless You Opt-Out)," *Forbes,* October 11, 2013, www.forbes.com/sites/larrymagid/2013/10/11/google_feature_you_in_ad/.

ethical standards and practices in both public and private institutions, recently produced a National Business Ethics Survey (NBES) to explore the connection between ethics and social media. One troubling result from this survey is that "active social networkers show a higher tolerance for activities that could be considered unethical." (See Figure 11.9.)

The point is that social media provide opportunities to quickly and widely communicate information, whether it's true or false, impacting both brands and consumers. As messages get reposted, the trickle-up or -down effect may alter the perceptions of information, assumptions, and conclusions.

One can imagine that the challenges Nike faced in the 1990s, with scandals about sourcing products from providers that used child labor, would have been exponentially greater if those events had unfolded in today's social media world! These communications and engagements can alter relationships between companies and consumers and companies and society at large.

With knowledge of how social media influence consumers when they are looking to buy, let's turn next to how consumers actually make their purchase decisions—the topic of Chapter 12.

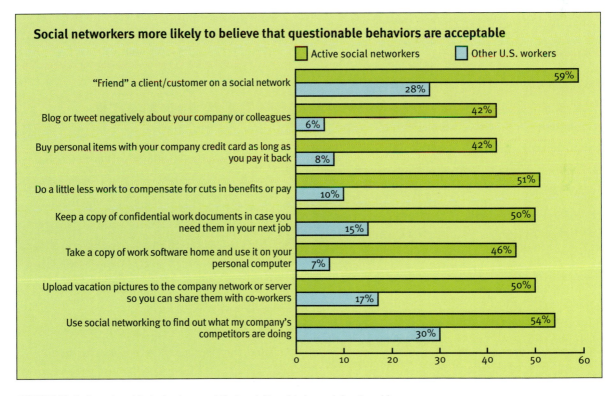

FIGURE 11.9 Questionable behaviors and their relationship to social networking.

Summary

The term social media refers to the collection of online spaces and tools that enable users to generate content and engage in peer-to-peer conversation and interaction. The concepts and technology of social media change at seismic rates, but all are enabled by the evolution of the Web and the development of Web 2.0. Consumers have a variety of different platforms on which to engage, including social networking, blogs, microblogs, video and photo sharing sites, social shopping sites, and others. The lines among the classifications are often blurred, with many social media sites incorporating more than one aspect of content and interaction.

Social media play a key role in consumer behavior; research confirms that consumers are influenced by social media when deciding what to buy. Fashion consumers turn to social media to seek product and brand information, to find recommendations, to provide customer feedback, and to obtain special deals and discounts, among other reasons. As a result, marketers have incorporated social media marketing into their total marketing strategy. Among the uses are to collect data to better understand target customers, to communicate product and brand information to consumers, to interact with customers, and to drive sales.

Along with the many benefits of social media to both consumers and marketers, there are several areas that present challenges or potential problems. Keeping pace with the rapidly changing social media landscape is one challenging aspect, which for marketers includes the need to present a consistent brand message across all media, whether traditional or social. Privacy and security of consumers' personal information is perhaps the most serious ethical issue facing consumers and marketers who use social media.

KEY TERMS

Blog

Crowdsourcing

Hashtag

Microblog

Social media

Social media marketing (SMM)

Social networking

Social shopping

QUESTIONS FOR REVIEW

1. In what ways did the development of Web 2.0 enable the birth and growth of social media?

2. What are four types of social media that have an influence on fashion consumers' behavior?

3. Name three ways in which consumers use social media to help them make a purchase decision.

4. Why is it important for marketers to have a presence on social media?

5. What is the biggest concern for consumers who share their information on social media?

ACTIVITIES

1. Select one product or service that you purchased recently, and exemplify consumer activities that relate to each of the periods shown in Table 11.1, Evolution of the Web.

2. Explain how the concept of crowdsourcing works and how you could apply this process to either something that relates directly to you or to a marketer's planned activities.

3. Select two social media sites you have used, and explain how content on those sites influenced you to buy or not to buy a product.

4. Refer to Table 11.4, Consumer Digital Purchasing Steps. Think of two purchases you would like to make, one costing between $10 and $15 and one between $100 and $500. Describe how you might go through each of the steps shown in the table, and which would be most important to you when purchasing an item in each of the price ranges.

5. Identify a brand that you follow and discuss how its social media communications keep you loyal to the brand.

MINI-PROJECT

Select a fashion-oriented blog and choose a post that tries to influence readers to consider purchasing a particular product. Describe the overall focus of the blog, then cite three reasons why the persuasive message of the post you chose appeals to you. Then state any drawbacks or areas the blog does not cover that might cause you to lose interest in its message. What might you do to correct that drawback? How would you write the post to be more influential?

REFERENCES

1. Suzanne Vranica, "Tweets Spawn Ad Campaigns," *Wall Street Journal,* October 22, 2012, p. B5.

2. Susan Reda, "J. Crew's Pinterest First," *Stores,* October 2013, http://www.stores.org/content /jcrew%E2%80%99s-pinterest-first.

3. www.facebook.com, JCPenney home page.

4. Ayaz Nanji, "Why People Share on Social Media," *MarketingProfs,* September 6, 2013, www .marketingprofs.com/charts/2013/11564 /why-people-share-on-social-media.

5. Ayaz Nanji, "Moms More Likely to Use Social Media and Mobile, and to Shop Online," *MarketingProfs,* May 6, 2013, www.marketing profs.com/charts/2013/10704/moms-more- likely-to-use-social-media-and-mobile-and-to- shop-online.

6. Zoe Fox, "Twitter Dethrones Facebook as Teens' Favorite Social Network for Shopping," *Mashable,* October 23, 2013, www.mashable .com/2013/10/23/teens-favorite-social- network/.

7. Verizon, "Web 3.0: Its Promise and Implications for Consumers and Business," White paper, 2010.

8. John Koetsier, "Facebook: 15 Million Businesses, Companies, and Organizations Now Have a Facebook Page," *Venture Beat,* March 5, 2013, http://venturebeat.com/2013 /03/05/facebook-15-million-businesses- companies-and-organizations-now-have-a- facebook-page/.

9. "10 Facts about Consumer Behavior on Facebook," *Social Media Quickstarter,* http:// www.socialquickstarter.com/content/103-10 _facts_about_consumer_behavior_on _facebook.

10. Lenna Garibian, "Digital Influence: Blogs Beat Social Networks for Driving Purchases," *MarketingProfs,* March 18, 2013, www.marketingprofs.com/charts/2013/10336/digital-influence-blogs-beat-social-networks-for-driving-purchases.

11. Emanuella Grinberg, "Style Bloggers to Follow in Any Season," *CNN,* February 20, 2013, http://www.cnn.com/2013/02/20/living/nyfw-fashion-bloggers/.

12. Zoe Fox, "Twitter Dethrones . . ."

13. David K. Williams, "How the Smartest Companies Leverage Visual Social Media," *Forbes,* October 27, 2012, http://www.forbes.com/sites/davidkwilliams/2012/10/27/how-the-smartest-companies-leverage-visual-social-media/.

14. Kara Kamenec, "10 Best Social Shopping Sites Right Now," *PCMag.com,* September 27, 2013, http://www.pcmag.com/article2/0,2817,2424709,00.asp.

15. Maeve Duggan, "It's a Woman's (Social Media) World," *Pew Research Center,* September 12, 2013, www.pewresearch.org/fact-tank/2013/09/12/its-a-womans-social-media-world/.

16. Lenna Garibian, "Digital Influence . . ."

17. NetBase Solutions Inc., "Social Channels of Influence in the Fashion Industry: A Consumer Study."

18. Lenna Garibian, "Digital Influence . . ."

19. Michelle B. Kunz, Brittany Hackworth, Peggy Osborne, and J. Dustin High, "Fans, Friends, and Followers: Social Media in the Retailers' Marketing Mix," *The Journal of Applied Business and Economics, 12*(3), 61-68, http://www.na-businesspress.com/JABE/KunzWeb.pdf.

20. Ayaz Nanji, "Moms More Likely . . ."

21. Lenna Garibian, "Digital Influence . . ."

22. Ibid.

23. Dara Kerr, "Fortune 500 Companies Give Social Media a Thumbs-Up," *CNET,* July 24, 2013, http://news.cnet.com/8301-1023_3-57595401-93/fortune-500-companies-give-social-media-a-thumbs-up/.

24. Antony Young, "ANA Meeting Takeaway: Social Is Now a Core Driver of Strategy," *Ad Age,* October 8, 2013, http://adage.com/article/special-report-ana-annual-meeting-2013/ana-takeaway-social-a-core-driver-strategy/244626/.

25. Tricia Carr, "Saks Calls Attention to Revamped Shoe Floor Via All-Encompassing Digital Efforts," *Luxury Daily,* August 31, 2012, www.luxurydaily.com/saks-calls-attention-to-revamped-shoe-floor-via-all-encompassing-digital-efforts/.

26. Lauren Indvik, "Topshop to Use Chirp App to Distribute Runway Looks via Sound," *Mashable,* September 12, 2013, http://mashable.com/2013/09/12/topshop-show-chirp/.

27. Adam Broitman, "Get Ready for the Loyalty Marketing Renaissance of 2013," *Ad Age,* September 4, 2012, http://adage.com/article/digitalnext/ready-loyalty-marketing-renaissance-2013/236999/.

28. Lon Safko, *The Social Media Bible: Tactics, Tools and Strategies for Business Success,* 2nd ed. (Hoboken, NJ: John Wiley & Sons, Inc).

29. Lydia Dishman, "J. Crew's Smart Pinterest Play: Move Beyond Inspiration to Make a Sale," *Forbes,* August 20, 2013, www.forbes.com/siteslydiadishman/2013/08/20/j-crews-

smart-pinterest-play-move-beyond-
inspiration-to-make-a-sale/.

30. Joe McCarthy, "Bloomingdale's Balances Selfies
with Beauty Tips in Instagram Contest," *Luxury
Daily,* October 31, 2013, www.luxurydaily.com
/bloomingdales-balances-selfies-with-beauty-
tips-in-instagram-contest/.

ADDITIONAL RESOURCES

Baird, H. C., and G. Parasnis. "From Social Media to
Social Customer Relationship Management."
Strategy & Leadership 39(5), 30–37. doi: http://
dx.doi.org/10.1108/10878571111161507.

Banda, T. "7 Popular Types of Social Media Fans."
Reach Local. http://blog.reachlocal.com/699691
/2013/05/17/7-popular-types-of-social-media-
fans-infographic.html.

Bard, M. "15 Categories of Social Media." *Mirna
Bard.* http://www.mirnabard.com/2010/02/15-
categories-of-social-media.

Bloch, E.. "Social Media Demographics: Who's Using
Which Sites." *Flow Town,* April 9, 2010.http://
www.flowtown.com/blog/social-media-
demographics-whos-using-which-sites.

Bower, K. "Marketing Sherpa 2012 Search
Marketing Benchmark Report-SEO Edition."
Marketing Sherpa. http://www.marketingsherpa
.com/2012SearchMBRSEOExcerpt.pdf.

Breur, T. Data "Analysis across Various Media: Data
Fusion, Direct Marketing, Clickstream Data and
Social Media." *Journal of Direct, Data and Digital
Marketing Practice.* 2011. 13(2), 95–105. doi:
http://dx.doi.org/10.1057/dddmp.2011.32.

Carmichael, M.. "The Demographics of Social Media."
Ad Age, May 16, 2011, http://adage.com/article

/adagestat/demographics-facebook-linkedin-
myspace-twitter/227569/.

Cavico, F. J., B. G. Mujtaba, S. C. Muffler, and
M. Samuel. "Social Media and the Workplace:
Legal, Ethical, and Practical Considerations for
Management." *Journal of Law, Policy and
Globalization* 12 (2013). http://iiste.org/Journals
/index.php/JLPG/article/viewFile/5261/5265.

Cooper, M. "Unlocking the Power of Social Data."
Chief Executive, December 20, 2012. http://chief
executive.net/unlocking-the-power-of-social-
data.

Cora, I. D., V. Tomita, D. Stuparu, and M. Stanciu.
"The Mechanisms of the Influence of Viral
Marketing in Social Media." *Economics,
Management and Financial Markets,* 2010. 5(3),
278–282. http://search.proquest.com/docview
/815240043?accountid=130772.

Dash, R. "The 10 Social Media Metrics Your
Company Should Monitor." *Social Times,* May 22,
2013. http://socialtimes.com/social-media-
metrics_b2950.

Dave, R. "Global Marketing via Social Media and
E-commerce." 2010. *Dell Report.*

Edosomwan, S., K. P. Sitalaskshmi, D. Kouame,
J. Watson, and T. Seymour. "The History of Social
Media and Its Impact on Business." *Journal of
Applied Management and Entrepreneurship,* 16(3),
79-91. Retrieved from http://search.proquest
.com/docview/889143980?accountid=130772

Flew, T. *New Media: An Introduction.* 3rd ed. Australia
and New Zealand: Oxford University Press,
2007.

Gaebler. "How Much Do Television Ads Cost?"
Resources for Entrepreneurs. http://www.gaebler
.com/Television-Advertising-Costs.htm.

Garibian, L. "Social Networking: 45% Check Out Brands' Pages." *Marketing Profs,* 2013. http://www.marketingprofs.com/charts/2013/9944/social-networking-45-check-out-brands-pages?adref=nlt012913.

Guglielmo, C. "Facebook Facts, Stats, and Trivia for Future Jeopardy Contestants." *Forbes,* May 17, 2012. http://www.forbes.com/sites/connie guglielmo/2012/05/17/facebook-facts-stats-and-trivia-for-future-jeopardy-contestants/.

"Italy's Finest Fashion in Social Media." *Social Bakers*. http://www.socialbakers.com/storage /www/italian-fashion-final.pdf.

Kaushik, A. "Best Social Media Metrics: Conversation, Amplification, Applause, Economic Value." *Occam's Razor,* 2011. http://www.kaushik.net/avinash/best-social-media-metrics-conversation-amplification-applause-economic-value/.

Kim, A. J., and E. Ko. "Do Social Media Marketing Activities Enhance Customer Equity? An Empirical Study of Luxury Fashion Brand." *Journal of Business Research* 65 (2012): 1480–1486. doi: 10.1016/j.busres.2011.10.014.

Larson, D. "Spring 2012 Social Media User Statistics." *Infographic,* May 15, 2012. http://blog.tweetsmarter.com/social-media/spring-2012-social-media-user-statistics/.

Lauby, S. "Ethics and Social Media: Where Should You Draw the Line?" *Open Forum,* March 17, 2012. https://www.openforum.com/articles /ethics-and-social-media-where-should-you-draw-the-line/.

Merrill, T., K. Latham, R. Santalesa, and D. Navetta. "Social Media: The Business Benefits May Be Enormous, but Can the Risks—Reputational, Legal, Operational—Be Mitigated?" *Ace Group Progress Report,* 2011. http://www.acegroup .com/us-en/assets/ace-progress-report-social-media.pdf.

Mershon, P. "How B2B Marketers Use Social Media: New Research." *Social Media Examiner,* April 24, 2012. http://www.socialmediaexaminer.com /b2b-social-media-marketing-research/.

Metscher, R. "Ensure that Strategy, Not Tactics, Drives Your Social Media." *Marketing Profs,* May 31, 2013. http://www.marketingprofs.com /articles/2013/10784/ensure-that-strategy-not-tactics-drives-your-social-media?adref=nlt053113.

Michaels, A. "Social Media Study: Why Consumers Engage With Brands." *Social Media Management*. Ann Michaels & Associates, January 9, 2012, http://www.socialmediamanagement.net /blog/2012/01/09/social-media-study-why-consumers-engage-with-brands/.

Moorman, C. "Measuring Social Media ROI: Companies Emphasize Voice Metrics." *Forbes,* May 21, 2013. http://www.forbes.com/sites /christinemoorman/2013/05/21/measuring-social-media-roi-companies-emphasize-voice-metrics/.

Olenski, S., "When It Comes to Brands, Consumers Use Social Media for This More Than Anything Else." *Social Media Today,* October 4, 2011. http://socialmediatoday.com/steve-olenski /370277/when-it-comes-brands-consumers-use-social-media-more-anything-else.

Patrick, R. G., and J. Dangelo. 2012. "The Evolution of Social Media as a Marketing Tool for Entrepreneurs." *The Entrepreneurial Executive* 17: 61–68. http://search.proquest.com/docview/10 37409443?accountid=130772.

Rao, L., "How Social Media Drives New Business: Six Case Studies." *Tech Crunch,* July 17, 2010. http://techcrunch.com/2010/07/17/how-social-media-drives-new-business-six-case-studies/.

Redsicker, P. "9 Consumer Social Media Trends That Could Impact Marketers." *Social Media Examiner,* February 6, 2013. http://www.socialmedia examiner.com/9-consumer-social-media-trends-that-could-impact-marketers/.

Shin, N. "7 Steps for a Successful Social Media Strategy." *Social Media Examiner,* July 21, 2010. http://www.socialmediaexaminer.com/7-steps-for-a-successful-social-media-strategy/.

"Social media." *Dictionary.com Unabridged.* http://dictionary.reference.com/browse/Social media.

Solis, B. "ROI: How to Measure Return on Investment in Social Media." *Brian Solis,* 2010. http://www.briansolis.com/2010/02/roi-how-to-measure-return-on-investment-in-social-media/.

Stacy, M. P. S., and L. R. David. "Social Media: More Available Marketing Tools." *The Business Review, Cambridge* 18.2 (December 2011): 37–43. http://search.proquest.com/docview/925638744?accountid=130772.

Sterne, J. *Social Media Metrics: How to Measure and Optimize Your Marketing Investment.* Hoboken, NJ: John Wiley & Sons, 2010.

CHAPTER 12

Consumer Decision Making

WHAT DO I NEED TO KNOW ABOUT CONSUMER DECISION MAKING?

✔ The five basic steps most consumers take in making a purchase decision

✔ How perceived risk influences consumers' purchase decisions

✔ What methods of comparison shopping consumers use and why

✔ The three types of decision making

✔ How market habits influence an individual's decision-making process

On the way to his part-time job, Peter had dropped his cell phone (again) and the screen cracked, so he knew that he really had to get himself a new one this time. But what should he get? He'd been slower to upgrade than many of his friends, and he knew that he'd have a lot of choices to make. Right off the bat, he'd need to decide whether to stay loyal to his wireless carrier or switch to a different company if he could get a better deal or better service that way. And should he stick with a more basic feature phone to keep his costs low or splurge on one of the latest smartphones with a full data plan for accessing the Internet—and if he did that, which brand and operating system would be best? He'd seen a couple of people whose phones had screens almost as big as a tablet computer, but did he really want one that large? Some had built-in GPS navigation, he knew, and front-facing cameras, good for taking "selfies"; some had wireless charging, which might be nice. One of his friends even had a phone with HD playback so he could watch streaming movies when he was traveling. No matter what other features he might decide on, Peter knew he must have one with scratch-resistant glass! The rest of the decisions would have to wait until he could poke around online, talk to some friends, and check out some phones in person at the store.

Like every consumer, Peter must go through a number of steps before making a decision. He may consciously or unconsciously consider alternatives, and also evaluate those alternatives logically or emotionally. This chapter addresses common issues that surface in the course of making a buying decision. We will discuss the components of the decision-making process, the effort involved in making different choices, and some considerations that may arise before, during, or after the selection.

How Consumers Make Their Choice

You'll remember from Chapter 4 that consumers are motivated to make a purchase after they recognize some type of need. We don't have what we'd like or need to have, so we make the decision to buy. Decisions are required because we have options. If we didn't have options (and ones that might lead to favorable results), we'd probably live very simplified lives. Imagine having just one possible shirt or a single pair of shoes available for you to buy when you needed them. Shopping would be very quick and easy, but also very boring!

In marketing jargon, a consumer who's making a decision is actually trying to "solve a problem." According to psychologist Lars Perner, Ph.D., a problem is "a discrepancy between a desired state and an ideal state, which is sufficient to arouse and activate a decision process."[1] So, when there are choices, people must generally think about and evaluate alternatives, move forward with a selection, then review the benefits to see if the final decision was a good one.

THE DECISION-MAKING PROCESS

While they may not realize it, most people go through five basic steps when making a decision, as shown in Figure 12.1: (1) recognize or identify the problem, (2) collect information about alternative solutions, (3) evaluate the alternatives, (4) choose the best alternative, and (5) evaluate the decision. Let's look at each of those steps in detail.

1. Recognize/Identify the Problem or Lack of Something

Problem awareness occurs when someone perceives an imbalance between his or her current situation ("as is") and an ideal ("should be") situation. If this gap (the distance between these two opposites) is large and important to the person, and potential solutions are available, the person becomes aware that there must be a change. If, on

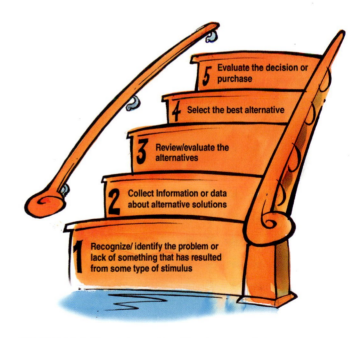

FIGURE 12.1 The staircase identifies the steps that go into making a decision.

Choosing the Right Fragrance: The Nose Knows

It's safe to say most people would agree that certain smells are truly unpleasant; think skunk, dead animals, and rotten sauerkraut, to name a few. But there is much more room for personal opinion when it comes to what smells really wonderful—a fact that suits the fragrance industry just fine, as perfume marketers develop thousands of different scents and market them in ways designed to entice consumers into a decision to buy.

Those thousands of different scents, however, can make it very difficult to choose which one is right for you as your own "signature" scent (or which one will please a friend or loved one as a gift). Whether you've never worn perfume or you're simply ready to try something new, the decision obviously rests on your personal preferences. You may know that you prefer a fruity fragrance to a spicy one. Or maybe you simply hate scents that seem "heavy" and know you'd like something lighter. Perhaps you aren't even sure of that much and simply know that you'll recognize the right scent when you smell it!

Because there is such an abundance of options found everywhere from the discount store shelf to the upscale department store beauty counter, knowing the basics can help you start to narrow your choices, since perfumes tend to fall into a number of specific categories of scent—although fragrance chemists mix and match among those to create each unique formula. That said, the basic categories include: *Floral,* the most popular, containing the fragrance of one specific flower or a bouquet of several varieties; *Oriental,* offering a richer, spicier, muskier aroma; *Chypre,* with an earthy, woodsy, mossy scent; *Green,* imbued with fresh, grassy, outdoorsy scents; and *Fougere,* characterized by mossy ferns and fresh herbs, and often used in men's fragrances.

Ready to make your decision? Not just yet, since almost every perfume contains layers of scents, referred to as "notes," to create its unique bouquet. When you first apply a perfume, what you smell right away are the top notes, and these evaporate quickly, usually within 15 minutes. As the top notes begin to dissipate, the heart or middle notes emerge; these are what make up the majority of the scent. Base notes, on the other hand, are what linger on the skin, and may not be detectable until you've been wearing the fragrance for a while. The base notes enhance the middle notes to create the fragrance's dominant theme.

Think you're all set now? Think again. There are also different formulations of fragrances that represent the concentration of perfume oil in what is usually an alcohol base, ranging from the highest 20 to 30 percent concentration in perfume (also called parfum), and working down through eau

(continued)

de parfum, eau de toilette, eau de cologne, to eau fraiche (1 to 3 percent concentration). You can also choose between sprays and splash versions.

Didn't realize it would be so complicated? It doesn't have to be if you understand that it really boils down to thinking of your favorite smells in everyday life and using those to choose a perfume with similar notes. And don't hesitate to ask your friends and family what they think of a fragrance. The choice is ultimately yours, but a second (or third) opinion on whether others think it suits you never hurts!

Sources: Jessica Padykula, "Types of Perfume: Finding the Right Fragrance for You," *SheKnows.com,* March 7, 2011, www.sheknows.com /beauty-and-style/articles/825299/how-to-choose-a-fragrance; Susan Fenton, "Common Scents: 6 Basic Fragrance Types," *Bankrate,* February 6, 2006, http://www.bankrate.com/brm/news/advice/20040213b1.asp; The Fragrance Shop, "Fragrance Guide," http://www.thefragranceshop .co.uk/fragrance-guide.aspx

the other hand, the gap is not large enough to cause some level of discomfort, the person is not likely to make a change (see Figure 12.2). We become aware of a "problem" because of a stimulus, something that attracts or directs our attention and opens our eyes to a possible lack of something, causing a state of discomfort brought about by an unsatisfied want or need. (These internal factors are discussed in Chapters 3 and 4.) In turn, this stimulus motivates a response, some kind of reaction to the stimulus (Figure 12.3).

For example, if Rachel looks at herself in the mirror when she puts on her new pair of jeans and thinks she looks OK or pretty good, she probably will not be very concerned about purchasing a gym membership to work on slimming down—in other words, there is a *small gap* between the "as is" and "should be" situation. However, if she doesn't like the way she looks and feels as if the jeans had fit her better when she bought them last month, there's a very good chance that she will seriously consider doing something that will result in her looking and feeling better—that is, there is a *large gap* between the "as is" and "should be" situations. (See Section A of Figure 12.2.)

Recognition of these gaps can occur either *internally,* from within the individual herself, or *externally,* as a result of marketing influences. Here are some examples of the kind of situations that would cause **internal recognition,** defined as awareness of a need or problem that originates within the individual: (1) Don runs out of breakfast cereal, or realizes the heels on his shoes are badly worn; (2) Lynette uses up her eyeliner or finds nothing in her closet that's suitable to wear to an upcoming party; (3) Nicole colors her hair and then realizes she also needs a deep conditioning shampoo.

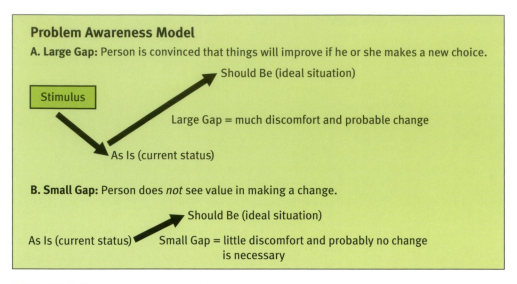

Problem Awareness Model

A. Large Gap: Person is convinced that things will improve if he or she makes a new choice.

Stimulus

Should Be (ideal situation)

Large Gap = much discomfort and probable change

As Is (current status)

B. Small Gap: Person does *not* see value in making a change.

Should Be (ideal situation)

As Is (current status)   Small Gap = little discomfort and probably no change
is necessary

FIGURE 12.2 Problem-awareness model.

FIGURE 12.3 A stimulus leads to a response.

On the other hand, it is the job of marketers to create **external recognition**—awareness of a need or "problem" that is stimulated by an outside source and that might be solved with a new or different product or service. Marketers work to create external recognition by using various advertising, sales, promotional, or public relations initiatives. For example, Rachel sees an ad on her iPad for jeans with new details that she loves. The ad has caught her attention and

touched her emotionally; she feels the desire to buy the jeans because she thinks her wardrobe needs a little more "spice" and the jeans will add it.

2. Collect Information or Data about Alternative Solutions

After identifying a problem, the next step involves collecting information about ways to eliminate the problem, thereby easing the discomfort. **Information**

collection includes the search for and selection of information that provides alternative foundations for making good decisions. Therefore, we identify some alternatives and determine which ones are suitable. A person considering an expensive purchase usually devotes fairly significant time to thinking about the purchase and collecting information (high involvement), whereas someone making an inexpensive choice may spend little time and effort (low involvement).

The search for information takes place both internally and externally. An internal search is simply thinking about prior purchase experiences to remind ourselves what was good or bad about each. Consumers today also rely heavily on external information sources such as the Internet, product reviews on social media or other sites, product testing organizations, reference guides, friends, expert sources, or just shopping at various stores (Table 12.1). We collect data whether we actively look for information, consider our past experiences, or remember advertising we previously heard or saw when we weren't really looking for a particular product or service (marketers refer to this last type as "low-dose" advertising[2]).

What happens next? **Information filtering**—sorting through all the collected data, then prioritizing and selecting that which is most useful to us in our decision making. For example, Rachel does not find information about the specific jeans she's considering on YouTube or Pinterest, but she does get helpful tips from a couple of fashion blogs and magazine photos before she talks to her most trusted friends for their advice on which jeans to buy. Note that consumers are influenced in their information search as well as in their ultimate decision by the same social influencers discussed in Chapter 8.

Another factor that plays a role in the decision-making process is the element of risk (the chance of loss). People handle risk—or the perception of risk—differently. Some people have personalities that process risk more comfortably; others struggle with it constantly.

Perceived risk is the risk a customer believes exists in the purchase of goods or services from a specific retailer, whether or not a risk actually exists.[3] The following five risk areas are of particular concern to consumers in relation to the purchase of goods and services:

- *Functional.* Does it work/perform as expected?
- *Monetary.* Is there a higher value than cost to me for using this product or service?
- *Physical.* Are there any potential issues of comfort or safety related to using this?
- *Psychological.* How accurately does this product or service reflect my self-image?
- *Social.* Will friends and others view me in a positive light if I use this?

TABLE 12.1 External Information Sources

Traditional	Internet-based
Coworkers	www.google.com
Doctors	www.webmd.com
Family	www.bing.com
Friends	www.facebook.com
Libraries	www.wikipedia.com
Media	www.lycos.com
Schools	www.census.gov

Perceived risk is generally low when a consumer doesn't really know too much about potential problems that might arise when using a product or service. Conversely, when consumers mentally exaggerate potential problems, the associated risk is perceived to be high.

Effective marketing campaigns address consumer perceptions of potential problems. Marketers may highlight specific customer benefits that minimize risk (no-questions return policy if not satisfied) or demonstrate how their brand provides a better solution than another brand, perhaps through positive testimonials from actual consumers. Marketers help us "see" the logical and emotional benefits associated with a specific product or service as a way of reducing the perception of risk. For example, before buying a pair of stilettos, Eleshia considers the potential foot problems (physical) associated with wearing them, but goes ahead with the purchase because the designer shoes are only for special occasions and will definitely impress her friends more than the chunkier-heeled pair (social). Guo decides to buy a high-end watch that is a little out of his price range (monetary) because it matches his desired self-image for his new job much better than the lower-priced models he looked at

(psychological). Lindsey selects a fabric purse over a leather one because it has more features she likes but wonders if it will hold up to the wear-and-tear during her typical day (functional); she doesn't worry too much, however, since the store accepts returns for any defect for up to a year. (See Figure 12.4.)

3. Review/Evaluate the Alternatives

How did Eleshia, Guo, and Lindsey work through their respective concerns? They first identified some alternatives, and then weighed the benefits associated with the various choices before making their decision. By collecting and filtering sufficient information, we can usually identify a number of viable alternatives to bridge the gap between what we have (our "as is") and what we want (our "should be"). If we then take the time to consider the pros (why it will work well) and cons (why it won't work well) of each possible choice, we'll make a more informed and probably successful selection. The review and evaluation process consists of three steps:

1. Figuring out the standards or guidelines on which to base a decision
2. Determining the importance of each standard or guideline
3. Prioritizing (ranking) the alternatives

FIGURE 12.4 Perceived risk: "Should I really experiment with some new or untried product or service?"

For example, you want to go to dinner with your significant other, and you have to decide where to go. You have already suggested four or five places. Using the three-step process mentioned above, your conversation might sound like this:

"How are we going to decide which restaurant we should go to tonight?" (The standards or guidelines under consideration might include ambience, convenience, dress code, entertainment, type of food, location, price, promotional coupons, and service.)

"OK, how important are each of these to you?" (The guidelines are then ranked as very important, not so important, completely unimportant.)

"Let's figure out our top two choices and then discuss them." (The alternatives are prioritized.)

If it's too difficult to evaluate the importance of each standard or guideline (the second of the three-step process mentioned above), consumers might revert to brand equity, the "added value a brand name/identity brings to a product or service beyond the functional benefits provided."[4] And if none of the alternatives meets or exceeds expectations, consumers might decide to not purchase the product or service at that time; for instance, if all the restaurants you and your boyfriend/girlfriend were considering turn out to be either too pricey or too far away to suit you, you might simply choose to cook dinner at home instead. What role do marketers play in this process? They try to educate consumers about which standards or guidelines should be used, guide them in the ranking or prioritizing of these guidelines—and sometimes adapt their own strategies and operations if that's necessary for capturing or keeping consumers' purchasing dollars and loyalty. (See Case in Point 12.1.)

In order to fully weigh the pros and cons of their alternatives, many people undertake **comparison shopping,** a process whereby a consumer gathers as much information as possible about similar products and services in order to compare their features, pricing, and other details before deciding which to purchase. This activity consists of doing the necessary research, which nowadays may well begin online with an initial search for possible product options, and perhaps a look at several manufacturer or retailer websites. Comparison shopping might also include going to one or more stores to examine the merchandise first-hand, and to read more detailed information on the product's packaging or labels, or on point-of-purchase displays (store fixtures that hold merchandise and often feature additional product information).

Comparison shopping today could be considered easier or more complicated, depending on a consumer's tolerance for stimulation, desire for information, and ability to process the information. While the wealth of information that's available on the Internet can be overwhelming, there are tools that can make the comparison process organized and efficient. Search engines, such as Google and Bing, can provide consumers with an initial foundation for what's

When Consumers Choose Online Alternatives to Stores, the Emporium Strikes Back

When Jessops, a British camera store that went out of business after 78 years, closed its doors for the final time, a sarcastic note on the door said: "The staff at Jessops would like to thank you for shopping with Amazon." The explosion of online shopping had taken its toll on the retailer—just as changes in technology and the marketplace have pushed out once-prominent U.S. retailers, too, such as Borders, whose book selection couldn't keep pace with the emergence of e-books, and Tower Records, one of a number of music megastores that were doomed when consumers shifted focus from CDs to digital tracks they could download straight to their MP3 players.

The sad truth for many traditional retailers is that shoppers are increasingly choosing to go online to browse and to purchase. And the simple retail formula that worked so successfully for so many years—find a concept that resonates with customers, open additional branches and draw more shoppers to existing ones, then use that growing sales volume to negotiate better prices from suppliers—just doesn't cut it anymore. So do we sound the death knell for brick-and-mortar retailers? Are these stores out of options and ready to lie down and play dead?

On the contrary, the smartest stores are adapting to the new landscape and finding ways to influence consumers' decisions about where to shop. For one thing, retailers understand that shopping is about entertainment, not just purchasing. When consumers shop, they are exploring and discovering new things to want, not just fulfilling a need. Plus, unlike a computer screen that may be visually appealing only, a successful shop will enthrall all the senses, making the experience immersive. A perfect example is Apple, whose showrooms encourage customers to play with the merchandise—and in terms of sales per square foot, its stores surpass all other American retailers.

In other words, consumers evaluate their shopping alternatives and may revisit the brick and mortar stores when those retailers offer the right blend of merchandise, price, convenience, and entertainment to sway consumers in their decision making. In a physical store, retailers can guide customers in their evaluation of purchase alternatives—such as explaining how buying certain accessories, like a computer bag or cables, will complement their purchase of a laptop. Marketers can also influence consumers' decision to shop in-store by offering rewards, such as shopping points or a gift-with-purchase goodie bag.

So, will you buy more or fewer things online or go into stores to enjoy the experience? What factors that marketers bring to your attention will help you evaluate the alternatives?

Source: "The Emporium Strikes Back," *The Economist,* July 13, 2013, http://www.economist.com/news/briefing/21581755-retailers-rich-world-are-suffering-people-buy-more-things-online-they-are-finding.

available; and there is also a multitude of comparison shopping websites (also known as comparison shopping engines)—such as PriceGrabber, Woot, NexTag, and ShopLocal—that provide instant data on where a product is sold and how much it costs at different retailers. A rapidly growing number of consumers are also turning to their smartphones and mobile apps to comparison shop, making use of technology that enables them to be looking at a product in one store and simultaneously check it out or look for other alternatives at another store or online. Aside from the technology-related tools that make the evaluation process work more smoothly, there are also simple mental rules of thumb (methods based on common sense) that help people make decisions more quickly. Because we don't always make decisions rationally or objectively, we use these rules of thumb or mental generalizations, termed **heuristics,** to help in weighing our choices and alternatives.

For example, Kourtney, who wants to buy a car, tells her friend that she will not buy one from a used car lot because her past experiences lead her to believe that it's really better to go directly to an authorized pre-owned dealer or to buy one through the Internet. Or Graham, who wants to buy a single-family house, remembers how difficult it was for a friend of his to buy a condo on his own instead of using the services of a real estate agent. After three months, the friend finally hired a real estate agent, who reduced the stress associated with making an offer, keeping the deal together, and finally closing and taking possession of the property.

4. Choose the Best Alternative

The next step in the decision-making process is the evaluation of key points—the pros and cons—that differentiate the choices. But how do we actually choose the best alternative? What kind of guidelines, technological tools, or influences from others direct us to select one item over another as being the best choice? In many cases, marketers, understanding their target customers' needs and wants, provide those guidelines and influences to consumers. Michael Solomon, a well-known consumer behavior scholar and author, calls the features that differentiate our choices *determinant attributes* and suggests that a marketer's job done well will frequently result in the successful education of consumers to select key factors to be used in the decision-making process.[5] Once we select the major criteria or features we think will provide the greatest benefits, we can move forward with the best alternative choice.

Marketers create advertising and promotional campaigns designed to emphasize the existence of a large gap between the customer's "as is" situation (what is currently owned or used) and the "should be" status (the ideal—the total benefits when using the product or service), as illustrated in Figure 12.5. If the marketer has done a good job of convincing customers of their need and persuading them that its product solves their problem, the consumer's best alternative is to buy the marketer's product or service.

Consumers generally select the alternative that has made the strongest impression; that is, the marketer has created the widest distance between the "as is" and the "should be." When the marketer makes it easy for the consumer to (1) understand the differences among competing brands, (2) relate to and visualize the sizable improvements gained, and (3) minimize the difficulty in decision making, the consumer can select much more easily and confidently, and then make the decision to buy

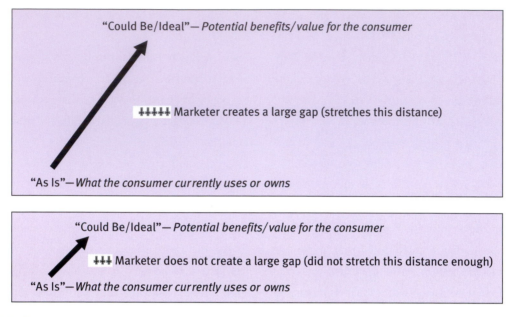

FIGURE 12.5
Marketers strive to create a large gap between the "as is" and "could be/ideal."

the product or service. (This last step is referred to as "purchase behavior.") For example, a computer salesperson demonstrates added features that significantly improve productivity, efficiency, and the "fun factor" between a customer's current computer and a new one.

5. Evaluate the Decision or Purchase

Obviously, both consumers and marketers want the end result of the purchase behavior and post-purchase evaluation to be very positive. Have you ever had good or bad feelings about a purchase you just made, or decided you needed to buy something else to go with your initial purchase? For example, you buy a pair of boots and then realize how well a particular belt would go with them, or that you really need a thicker pair of socks to wear with them. Or perhaps you're buying a new flat-screen, wall-mounted HDTV for your living room and feel

that a cabinet to hold your Blu-ray player and Xbox would work nicely underneath. And then there's the experience of feeling guilty or having second thoughts about what you just bought and thinking that maybe you should not have purchased it. This sense of uneasiness is known as buyer's remorse or post-purchase dissonance (also discussed in Chapter 4).

During post-purchase evaluation, consumers judge whether the product or service they bought has met, exceeded, or not met their expectations (Figure 12.6). Situations such as the ones described above can lead to either additional purchases or reconsideration of the original purchase decision. The marketer's objective in either scenario is to anticipate and address these common kinds of thoughts after the purchase. This is done to increase the purchaser's long-term satisfaction and customer loyalty and to reduce product

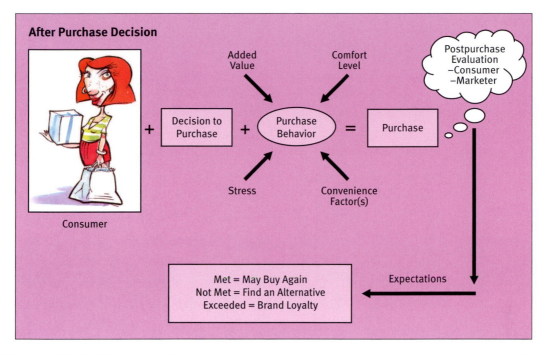

After Purchase Decision

Consumer

Added Value → Comfort Level →

Decision to Purchase + **Purchase Behavior** = **Purchase**

Stress ↗ Convenience Factor(s) ↖

Postpurchase Evaluation —Consumer —Marketer

Met = May Buy Again
Not Met = Find an Alternative
Exceeded = Brand Loyalty

← Expectations

FIGURE 12.6 Decision making continues through post-purchase evaluation, which helps consumers decide whether or not the product or brand met their expectations.

returns. Repeat purchases signal that the customers' experiences have been positive. Savvy marketers address potential post-purchase issues by finding ways to positively reinforce the value and benefits attached to their products. For example, a sales associate forwards an article to a client who just purchased an item; the article reinforces how others are enjoying and benefiting from a similar purchase. Or an online retailer might ask customers to share a review of their purchase on the website. These customer reviews not only provide invaluable feedback to the retailer and the product's manufacturer, letting them know what customers liked and didn't like about the goods and the purchasing experience, but can also help other consumers who might be starting their own decision-making process and collecting information about alternative solutions.

Types of Decision Making

Although this chapter has presented a common method for decision making, there is really no single way to make decisions. If you use more logically based, left-brain thinking to process information and carefully review the pros and cons, you are using what researchers call the **rational perspective.** Marketers who understand how rational perspective consumers learn, retrieve, collect, analyze, and process information can implement strategies into marketing campaigns that appropriately target this type of analytical consumer. Stanford University marketing professor Itamar Simonson suggests that consumers who consciously choose specific store environments and experiences are more likely to consciously process a marketer's strategy—in other words, it is not lost in the "noise" of a typical store.[6]

Customer Reviews Gain Clout

In the age of Web 2.0 and social media, consumers have at their fingertips an enormous volume of online information that can assist them in weighing alternatives and making a purchase decision. And among the most powerful tools they can access are customer reviews.

According to one study, nearly two thirds of consumers (63 percent) said they are more likely to purchase from an e-commerce site that has user reviews, in essence because their level of trust increases when they're able to learn what other customers thought about a product. Even negative reviews can actually have a positive influence on consumer buying behavior—and can also help decrease product returns at the same time. For example, if a potential customer is considering a particular dress on a retail website, and several reviews mention that the dress seems to run one size too large, she will be more likely to choose the correct size for herself before ordering, assuming everything else about the dress is acceptable.

For marketers, monitoring reviews, both good and bad, has become a critical element of doing business. Particularly when a consumer is unhappy with something, being on top of the discussion allows a marketer to address the problem and rectify it before the complaint goes viral.

Best Buy is one retailer that is paying close attention and taking its customer reviews very seriously, initiating a variety of actions to address issues that are raised in reviews, including sharing feedback with applicable vendors. In fact, the retailer places such high value on the tool that it openly encourages customers to review their purchases, sometimes offering a reward such as points that can be used toward future purchases. And going forward, the retailer plans to expand the program by presenting not just individual customer reviews, but a range of different types, including product reviews by experts in a category, crowdsourced reviews from the entire Best Buy customer community, and even reviews written by friends in the customers' social media sphere.

Sources: Stephanie Landsman, "Love It or Leave It—Growing Power of Customer Reviews," *CNBC.com,* June 9, 2013, www.cnbc.com /id/100792646; and Natalie Beigel, "Why Every Online Merchant Should Use Product Reviews," *Prestashop,* August 1, 2013, www.prestashop .com/blog/en/why-every-online-merchant-should-use-product-reviews/.

On the other hand, actions consumers have learned in response to specific stimuli are collectively called the **behavioral perspective.** (See the discussions in Chapter 3 about behavioral learning conditions and Chapter 4 about rational versus emotional motives.) Study of decision-making behaviors at Duke University and Stanford University, among others, suggests that this type of specific learned response to stimuli provides the framework of habitual or automatic responses that people use to make or improve judgments or choices.

Low-involvement decision making in fashion-oriented purchases is sometimes referred to as "impulse buying." Marketers use store design, product placement, even scents to trigger impulse purchases. Richard L. Petersen, M.D., a Stanford University neuroeconomics research scientist, noted that "when someone views a potential gain in the environment, the brain's cycle of reward approach motivation is set into action." This all leads to the choice selection.[7]

Finally, someone using the **experiential perspective** (explained by gestalt psychology, discussed in Chapter 3, and the ABCs of attitude covered in Chapter 5) considers the overall experience, not just a particular point or the "how" of the situation.[8] These are the metaphorical "lenses" in the consumer's glasses that incorporate the values, beliefs, behaviors, and domestic and global views that influence that person's decisions. (See TORA described in Chapter 5.)

Technology also provides solution alternatives. For example, you may have price-compared a potential purchase item by scanning it with your mobile device, had an e-receipt with a thank-you sent to you after a purchase, viewed a selection of products related to your current search that appeared on a retail website, gotten an e-mail from a retailer about a new product arrival that reflects your preferences based on prior purchases, or paid for a product or service by strategically tapping your smart card at the checkout counter.

Consumers can also use technology to preprogram their own decisions; examples of this include using a DVR to record television programs for later viewing; using e-mail filters to automatically sort messages into folders for more efficient reviewing; using e-mail and browser features that can help detect and eliminate spam (unsolicited and unwanted commercial messages) and phishing (e-mail scam conducted for the purposes of information or identity theft); and the re-programming of your home security and thermostat systems from a remote location.

Consumers' Effort Level in Decision Making

How much effort do we put into making a decision—not much, a moderate amount, or a lot? Consumer behaviorists use the terms "routine," "limited," and "extensive," respectively, to describe the various levels of effort expended by consumers in decision making.

Naturally, each category is relative to the individual's situation and personality; for example, a person buying his or her first car may see it as a very significant decision-making process, while another person who trades in a car every couple of years might view it as requiring limited effort. We can characterize **routine** or **habitual decision making** as an autopilot mechanism, a low-involvement situation in which not much thought is needed to make a decision (for

TABLE 12.2 Effort Exerted in Making Purchase Decisions

Type of Effort	Purchase Time Line	Cost	Search Effort	Example
Routine	Frequent	Low	Minimal	Fast food Breakfast cereal Disposable pen Lip gloss
Limited	Periodic	Moderate	Moderate	Prescription sunglasses Brand name handbag Bridge jewelry
Extensive	Not very often	High	High	Graduate school Furniture Car

example, buying the daily newspaper). **Limited decision making** is a process that involves some thought, but frequently involves general rules of thumb we've learned or borrowed from others (for example, buying winter boots that are waterproof and have a non-slip sole). With **extensive decision making,** necessary for high-involvement situations, we take more time to weigh the pros and cons, along with the perceived risks and benefits (for example, selecting a college or signing a lease on an apartment). (See Table 12.2.)

MARKET HABITS

Consumers often behave in certain patterns with regard to their purchases; these are known as "market habits." In addition to heuristics (previously defined as mental generalizations that help us make decisions more quickly), people also use other decision-making methods (Table 12.3) that are considered less sophisticated than the models discussed earlier in the chapter. Customers with

an **inertia habit** frequently buy the same brand because it takes little or no energy; thus any competitor that makes the purchase of a similar product even easier may win over a customer. A *brand-loyal* person sticks with the same brand of product or service, frequently due to both logical and emotional rewards (benefits received) learned through past experiences. For example, a brand-loyal consumer repeatedly buys a specific make of athletic gear or the same brand of underwear because the products have consistently met all the criteria for satisfaction. And finally, another group of consumers with a distinguishable market habit are those who prefer to keep consumption choices that belong and relate specifically to their own culture; this is called **ethnocentrism.** (See discussions of culture as it relates to consumer behavior in Chapters 1, 9, and 14.)

Because the decision-making process is so complex, it's very important that marketers understand not only the steps consumers go through to make a decision, but all the factors that can influence them

TABLE 12.3 Market Habits that Affect Consumer Purchase Decisions

Consumer Pattern	Description	Example of customer response
Brand loyal	Choice based on logical and emotional benefits learned through past experience	"I'll never switch because the product always works great and I like that the company supports good causes."
Ethnocentric	Choice that specifically relates to one's own culture	"I buy American-made products whenever I can."
Heuristics	Choice based on rules of thumb, or mental generalizations and shortcuts	"I didn't know Company X made this product, but I like their other products, so this should be good, too."
Inertia	Choice made out of habit or laziness	"This is the toothpaste my mom always bought and I don't need to try another brand."

before, during, and after a purchase is made. That means that ongoing communication with customers, and feedback from both those who bought and those who didn't buy, is important to marketers in ensuring they understand and are meeting their customers' needs.

The next question is, where and how do consumers buy fashion products? Chapter 13 explores these issues.

LET'S TALK

Have you ever written an online review of a product you bought? If yes, did you leave positive or negative feedback? When you're researching a potential purchase, do you give more weight or less weight to positive reviews versus negative ones, or do you consider them equally? Explain your answer.

Summary

Decision making is a multistep process that is influenced by both internal and external forces. These forces can play a role before, during, or after the decision is made. The five-step decision-making process helps consumers identify, evaluate, and feel satisfied about the results of their decision. The process begins with problem awareness, a consumer's response to a stimulus that leads to recognition of a gap (distance) between the current "as is" and ideal "should be" situations. Marketers try to stretch this gap when it is small and use various media to alert, educate, and persuade consumers to accept their particular product or service as a solution to the problem. When consumers perceive this added value (that is, when the gap is large and the product or service will help close that gap) and judge a perceived risk to be manageable, the decision to buy is usually the result. Online tools enable consumers to collect and filter abundant information about alternative solutions; consumers may also use simple, mental rules of thumb (heuristics) to help make them evaluate the pros and cons of different alternatives.

Some important decision-making factors that marketers try to address in advance are (1) the amount of energy consumers will expend in making a decision, (2) how consumers perceive the benefits expected from a purchase, and (3) the level of stress associated with the decision. If a customer's expectations are met, a repeat purchase might happen; if expectations are not met, consumers might decide to consider a substitute product or service. Marketers who anticipate and exceed customer expectations often create brand loyalty, whereby customers continue to make positive buying decisions about specific products or services.

KEY TERMS

Behavioral perspective

Comparison shopping

Ethnocentrism

Experiential perspective

Extensive decision making

External recognition

Heuristics

Inertia habit

Information collection

Information filtering

Internal recognition

Limited decision making

Perceived risk

Problem awareness

Rational perspective

Routine/habitual decision making

QUESTIONS FOR REVIEW

1. Why are marketers thought of as problem solvers, and how can marketers create wants?

2. What are the five steps in the decision-making process? Which of these steps is the most important?

3. How does the problem awareness model relate a large gap versus small gap to the probability of success in a marketer's attempt to influence a consumer decision?

4. What are the differences between actual and perceived risk, and why are these ideas important to consumers and marketers?

5. How do the rational, behavioral, and experiential perspectives in decision making differ?

ACTIVITIES

1. Name a product and a service you are going to purchase in the next three to ten weeks. Use each of the terms noted in the Problem Awareness Model, Figure 12.2, (for example, "as is," "should be," "stimulus"), and specifically identify and relate them to your actions and thoughts as you become aware of your "problem."

2. Identify two fashion products or services and two different media stimuli sources that guided you to recognize a "problem."

3. Illustrate the concept of information filtering, and relate it to your purchase of a fashion product or service you have bought during the last 12 months.

4. Create and explain a table of data that identifies two positive and two negative reasons that someone would consider after purchasing an item that was clearly more expensive than originally anticipated.

5. Interview several consumers who recently purchased a product or service primarily based on choices that related specifically to their own culture.

MINI-PROJECTS

Teaming with two other class members, identify a product or service that each team member recently purchased using either routine, limited, or extensive decision making. (Note: Each team member should select a different decision-making category so that each one is discussed.) Then:

1. Describe your purchase and explain the type, purchase time line, cost, and search effort used (that is, how you got your information).

2. Discuss the major factor(s) that influenced your decision making (for example, value, comfort level, convenience, and/or stress issues). Rank these factors in order of importance.

REFERENCES

1. Lars Perner, "Decision Making," *The Psychology of Consumers: Consumer Behavior and Marketing,* accessed August 31, 2007, www .consumerpsychologist.com/#Decision.

2. Girish Punj, "Presearch Decision Making in Consumer Durable Purchases," *Journal of Consumer Marketing* 4 (Winter 1987).

3. Melody Vargas, *Retail Glossary of Terminology,* accessed August 31, 2007, http://retailindustry .about.com/library/terms/p/bld_perceivedrisk .htm.

4. Jacob Jacoby and Leon B. Kaplan, "The Components of Perceived Risk," *Advances in Consumer Research* 3 (1972): 6–10 and 382–83.

5. Michael Solomon, *Consumer Behavior: Buying, Having and Being* (Upper Saddle River, NJ: Prentice Hall, 2007), 321.

6. Itamar Simonson, "In Defense of Consciousness: The Role of Conscious and Unconscious Inputs in Consumer Choice," *Journal of Consumer Psychology* 5, no.3 (2005).

7. Howard Greenfield, "Neuromarketing: Unlocking the Decision-Making Process," accessed September 7, 2004, www .marketingprofs.com/4/greenfield1.asp.

8. Clare Torrans and Dr. Nada Dabbagh, "Gestalt and Instructional Design," George Mason University, March 8, 1999.

ADDITIONAL RESOURCES

Berman, Barry, and Joel R. Evans. *Retail Management A Strategic Approach,* 10th ed. Upper Saddle River, NJ: Prentice Hall, 2007.

BPlans.com. Glossary of Business Terms. www .bplans.com/site_search/?q=glossary+of+ business+terms

SearchSecurity.com. Glossary. http://whatis.tech target.com

Wolff, David. "Exactly What Is 'Experiential Marketing'?" *Ageless Marketing Blog.* January 12, 2005. Accessed August 31, 2007. http:// agelessmarketing.typepad.com/ageless _marketing/2005/01/exactly_what_is.html.

CHAPTER 13

How Fashion Consumers Buy

WHAT DO I NEED TO KNOW ABOUT HOW FASHION CONSUMERS BUY?

✔ The influence of the fashion life cycle on consumer purchasing

✔ What is meant by fast fashion and how it has changed the fashion life cycle

✔ What omnichannel retailing is and how it is being driven by consumer buying behavior

✔ The variety of places consumers can shop for fashion and how they differ

✔ How the shopping environment and level of service influence fashion consumers

Once upon a time, when your grandparents and probably your parents were your age, if they needed or wanted to purchase a product, they had to leave their home, travel to a retailer during normal store hours, and hope that the store had the item they were looking for. Yes, they could shop from a catalog from the comfort of their couch. But they'd likely have to wait two or three weeks for the order to arrive (especially if they mailed an order form versus ordering over the phone)—plus, they might not be able to order at all if they didn't have the desired catalog in hand.

Fast forward to today, and those constraints on purchasing seem almost as quaint and old-fashioned as townsfolk gathering in the square to await the arrival of mail and packages on the Wells Fargo wagon. In fact, for today's consumers (maybe even your grandparents), the idea of not being able to shop at virtually any retailer and buy virtually any product on any day, at any hour, and from anywhere, is unthinkable. Yes, consumers can and still do visit nearby stores to shop and purchase on the spot. But thanks to the Internet and the increased capabilities of digital devices, they can also browse the merchandise of retailers across town, across the country, or across oceans, and purchase goods with a few clicks or taps on their computer, tablet, or smartphone. And forget about waiting weeks to have an item in their possession. The promise of quick deliveries, often within a day or two, is now the norm for many sellers eager to solidify customer satisfaction and loyalty. Or if consumers don't want to wait even that long, there are many products they can order digitally and then pick up in person within minutes at a brick-and-mortar location.

Changes in Fashion and Fashion Consumption

Where and how people buy products is as much a part of consumer behavior as what they buy and why, especially with the wealth of shopping options made possible by today's technology. No longer are consumers willing to settle for the selection of goods they can find at the local mall—and retailers know it. In 2013, the National Retail Federation's NRF Foundation released a report, entitled "Retail Insight: Spotlight on Modern Retail," to highlight the transformational shift taking place this decade. The report gathered examples from research as well as facts from government resources, the media, and retail industry reports, and one of the key takeaways was that the consumer is not only in charge, but is driving innovation in the retail industry. "From finding an item online, to checking customer reviews in an app, to finding it in the store, consumers expect—if not demand—a seamless experience," the report stated.[1] In other words, consumers want to be able to shop in a manner that is most convenient for them at any given time, using online, in-store, catalog, and mobile shopping interchangeably. We'll examine this concept of "omnichannel" retailing a little later in this chapter. But first, let's look at how different consumers make different purchase decisions based on the newness of a fashion, or its stage in the fashion life cycle.

FASHION LEADERS AND FOLLOWERS

As we've seen in previous chapters, many factors come into play whenever consumers need (or want) to purchase something. Similarly, how they go about shopping and buying can depend on everything from what item they're seeking, to how much time they have, and even what mood they're in on a given day. When it comes to fashion merchandise, the purchasing process also depends on what kind of fashion consumer a person is—that is, how the individual relates to products within the fashion life cycle.

As you can tell from observing people, both in your own surroundings and on television and in other media, some people are fashion leaders and some are fashion followers. As discussed in Chapter 6, fashion leaders—also known as fashion innovators—are those people who seek out new fashion and wear it before it becomes generally accepted. The evolution of style seems to come so naturally to fashion innovators that they often simply trust their instincts and buy clothing on impulse.

The majority of people are **fashion followers,** those who adopt a look only after they are sure of a fashion trend. There are several reasons why consumers might be fashion followers. They may not have the time, money, or interest to spend on fashion pursuits; or they may be insecure about their own tastes, so they look to others to determine what is acceptable and appropriate, including imitating people they admire. They might follow to keep pace with neighbors or to be accepted by their peer group, or they might simply need to be exposed to new styles for a while before accepting them.[2] Whatever their reason, fashion followers are crucial to the fashion industry because they, as much as fashion leaders, contribute greatly to the ebb and flow of styles known as the fashion life cycle.

THE FASHION LIFE CYCLE

All products have a life cycle, and fashions are no different. A **fashion life cycle** is the length of time that a given look or style is popular. Whether a fashion look begins in a designer's runway show or on the streets of a city, its life cycle consists of five stages: introduction, rise, peak, decline, and obsolescence or rejection. That cycle is generally represented by a bell-shaped curve, as shown in Figure 13.1.

Introduction

The **introduction phase** of the fashion life cycle is when a new style first appears. Many times, that

will be at the launch of a new designer collection for the coming season, where only a few garments are produced and their prices are at a high level. Only a small number of consumers can afford this couture apparel, and its availability is limited to a handful of exclusive ateliers. Some styles are rejected outright by the public, which may include retailers and the media, and never make it past the introduction stage. But if a style catches on and is wanted by consumers, it enters the next phase.

Rise

The **rise phase** is the period when a look is growing in popularity. Early in this stage, a style that started at the couture level will generally spread first to the higher-end department and specialty stores, such as Neiman Marcus or Saks Fifth Avenue. In time, the style will be copied at a wider range of price levels and appear in mainstream department and specialty stores such as Macy's and The Limited.

The rise phase of the fashion life cycle is dependent on **knock-offs,** the industry term for copies

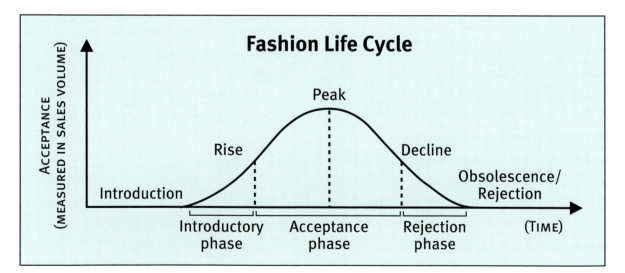

FIGURE 13.1 Fashion life cycle.

of the original styles. Some apparel makers specialize in copying high-fashion apparel; one of the best known is designer Victor Costa, who at one time was called the "Copy-Cat King." Knock-offs can be exact duplicates of an original designer garment (minus the designer label), referred to as "line-for-line copies." At other times, knock-offs modify or reinterpret the style, incorporating certain key features of the original such as a specific neckline or sleeve treatment; these are known as "adaptations."

You might think that apparel knock-offs would be illegal, but under current U.S. copyright law, they are not. A rule within the law states that copyright does not protect the design of "useful" articles like clothing, since their aesthetic features are not separable from their utilitarian function—in this case, covering the body. However, fashion accessories such as handbags are protected by copyright law, so knock-offs of those items are considered counterfeit and are illegal to produce or sell. (Counterfeits are discussed in greater detail in Chapters 15 and 16.)

Some people in the fashion industry are pushing to extend copyright protection to apparel designs, and several pieces of legislation have been proposed in the U.S. Senate but not enacted, the most recent being the Innovative Design Protection Act of 2012 (also known as the "Fashion Bill"). Others in the fashion business, however, believe that copying is actually good for the industry, accelerating the fashion life cycle and stimulating greater interest in and development of new fashions.[3] Even renowned designer Karl Lagerfeld said, about being imitated, "[Coco] Chanel called it flattery. For me, it's good because it pushes me to things they can't copy."[4]

Peak

A style that is in the **peak phase** of its life cycle is at the height of its acceptance and popularity (Figure 13.2). At this stage, it is widely available at all price ranges and may be found in a wide variety of store types, including popularly priced department and chain stores such as JCPenney and Kohl's, and discount retailers such as Target and Ross Stores.

Decline

Once a style has saturated the market, people begin to tire of it and the most fashion-conscious

FIGURE 13.2 At the peak phase of the fashion life cycle, a style—such as this woman's yoga pants—can be seen seemingly everywhere.

consumers have already turned their attention to newer looks. At that point, the style is in the **decline phase,** experiencing decreasing sales and availability only in the lower price ranges. Retailers will not order any new garments in the style and will try to sell any leftover inventory at sale or clearance prices.

Obsolescence or Rejection

The **obsolescence** or **rejection phase** marks the end of a style's life cycle, indicating that the look is out-of-date and no longer being sold, except perhaps in thrift stores. From time to time, an obsolete style will be revived and reintroduced in an updated version. For example, bell-bottom pants (first popular in the 1960s) were reborn in the late 1990s as boot-cut or flare-leg trousers.

LENGTH OF FASHION CYCLES

The basic progression of a fashion life cycle is the same for all looks and styles, although the length of time from introduction to rejection can vary dramatically and a certain style may drop out of the fashion life cycle at any time or remain in vogue for decades. A **classic style,** for example, is one that is characterized by a simplicity of design that keeps it from becoming easily dated, and therefore it has an extended life cycle that may last many years, with occasional modifications to keep it fresh and current. Examples of fashion classics include the Chanel jacket, Keds sneakers, button-down shirts, and trench coats (Figure 13.3a).

A **fad,** on the other hand, is a short-lived fashion that bursts onto the scene, is wildly popular among a target group of consumers, then disappears, sometimes in a year or two, sometimes in a single season (Figure 13.3b). A fad may reflect some cultural phenomenon of its time, and in general, either its concept is too extreme or it does not have strong enough design elements to ensure long-term acceptance. Some fads over the years have included poodle skirts in the 1950s, pet rocks in the 1970s, and stirrup pants in the 1990s. Recent fads that you might remember are Snuggie blankets with sleeves, platform shoes (repeating a 1970s fad), low-rise jeans, the DanceDanceRevolution videogame, and cause-related plastic wristbands.

FAST FASHION

The twenty-first century has seen a dramatic acceleration of the fashion life cycle, made possible in part by advanced technology and instant global communications, which can give consumers immediate exposure to new fashion looks from anywhere in the world. The use of digital photography, streaming Internet video, text and picture messaging, and other mobile communications tools means that a new style seen on a fashion show runway can be transmitted almost immediately to a knock-off producer's factory—and the knock-off might actually arrive in stores *before* the original! This rapid dissemination of fashion information, along with the development of computerized equipment enabling speedier production, has spawned a new breed of retailers that practice "fast fashion." **Fast fashion**

FIGURE 13.3 Classic styles, like the Chanel jacket (left), can be in style for many years. Fads (right), however, are popular for only a short time.

is the term for offering consumers the latest fashions as quickly as possible. Because the apparel is also designed to be very affordable, it has sometimes been called "disposable chic" or "cheap chic" (a phrase that some people have also used to describe Target's trendy, inexpensive apparel).

One of the best-known fast-fashion retailers in the United States is Sweden-based H&M, which, because of its direct relationship with hundreds of manufacturers worldwide, can move a trendy new design from the studio to the store in a matter of weeks (Figure 13.4a). Zara, a fast-fashion retail chain based in Spain, moves even more quickly: Because the company maintains its own production facilities near its design and distribution headquarters, it is able to take the hottest current designs from the drawing board to the store shelf in as little as two weeks (Figure 13.4b). Other retailers taking a

fast-fashion approach include Forever 21, Charlotte Russe, Japan-based Uniqlo, and British chain Topshop, which opened its first U.S. stores in 2007.

In addition to its speed to market, another aspect of fast-fashion apparel is that it is generally produced in small quantities, so that some of the most popular items might arrive in stores and be sold out less than a week later. That perceived scarcity of hot items contributes to the stores' appeal to their target customers, since consumers who are eager for the latest look feel the need to grab a new style quickly before it's gone.

The growth of fast fashion has had an impact on the entire fashion field, forcing the industry out of its traditional two-season calendar in which retailers committed to the bulk of their inventory at least six months in advance and assortments were swapped out based more on dates than

FIGURE 13.4 Retailers such as H&M and Zara take a "fast fashion" approach to get new looks to consumers within weeks of their introduction.

on timeliness. (You may remember shopping as a kid for bulky back-to-school clothes in the heat of August, since by winter, the store would already be putting spring apparel on display.) Now, even non-fast fashion stores tend to introduce new apparel on a year-round basis, meeting consumers' appetite for the latest trends and for styles they can wear right away. There is a downside to fast fashion, however. Because it is produced so rapidly, the apparel's quality and longevity have come under scrutiny, and some question the environmental responsibility of creating massive amounts of what some consider disposable fashion. (See Point of View 13.1.) Whatever direction the concept moves in coming years, however, its impact on the fashion business and its appeal to fashion-seeking consumers will remain.

RETAIL MARKETING OF FASHION

The emergence and growth of fast fashion is a current illustration of the fact that retailers have always sought ways to provide consumers with the products they want and need, when they want and need them. From the first enterprising pioneer who set up a general store to sell necessities to frontier farmers and homesteaders, to the first Internet entrepreneur who saw a way to sell products through cyberspace, the retail industry has continually adapted to meet constantly shifting consumer lifestyles, desires, and behaviors.

Today's fashion retailers face an even greater necessity to adapt, as digital technologies continue to turn traditional shopping behavior on its head. When Internet shopping proved its viability more than a decade ago, marketers began to realize that the model of separate and distinct channels for buying goods—physical stores, catalogs, the Internet, and direct selling—was no longer workable; customers might still want to buy from a given retailer, but they liked having a choice of whether to buy in person, at home on their computer, or whatever way was most convenient for them at the moment. That recognition led to the birth of **multichannel retailing**—the use of catalogs, stores, and the Internet in a coordinated marketing plan— as stores rushed to create websites, catalog and online retailers looked to open stores, and the lines between channels began to blur.

Consumers Like Their Fashion Fast—
But Do They Also Want It to Last?

In fashion, styles have always come and gone as consumers tired of one look and fell in love with the next. But never before has the speed of that change been as quick—and consumers' hunger for the latest trends as obvious—as it has since the appearance of fast fashion retailing. Indeed, the proof comes from the stunning growth and success of the leading fast fashion chains: H&M is now the second largest apparel retailer in the world, surpassed only by Inditex SA, parent company of Zara—not to mention that the chief executive officer of Uniqlo's parent company, Fast Retailing, is the wealthiest man in Japan.

While each of those retail chains has its own distinct model for sourcing, production, and merchandise assortment, what they have in common is a deep understanding of what their customers want and need. Far from simply guessing about what the next hot style will be, the retailers have developed sophisticated systems for identifying consumer preferences and desires. H&M, in particular, is renowned for its focus on researching and predicting emerging trends.

That said, the very core of fast fashion is dependent not only on speed to market of current styles, but also affordability, enabling consumers of average means to purchase new apparel frequently. As a result, the quality of the clothing can suffer, with some items reported to survive only a few washings before falling apart.

Compounding the quality issue, some people have begun taking fast fashion retailers to task for environmental reasons. Critics cite a waste of resources, such as fuel and water, used to produce so much cheap apparel—as well as the fact that clothing may be thrown away as opposed to donated or sold to consignment shops due to its poor construction. That has led some people to call the goods "landfill fashion."

The perception of poor quality has imbued negative connotations to the very term "fast fashion"—to the point where Uniqlo and H&M choose not to identify themselves by that label. Uniqlo, in fact, takes pride in keeping its quality high and its prices low by locking in factory time in advance and creating garments at a steady pace all year long, rather than chasing the latest trend and rushing shoddy garments through at specialty factories.

What does this mean for the future of fast fashion? As with all retailing, companies will likely adapt, perhaps slowing their pace slightly, perhaps raising their prices a little, perhaps adjusting in

(continued)

other ways. But in the end, it is doubtful that the concept of getting current fashion to eager consumers on a timely basis will go away; consumers have overwhelmingly voted with their wallets that they want new styles while they're still new.

Sources: Jim Zarroli, "In Trendy World of Fast Fashion, Styles Aren't Made to Last," *NPR.org,* March 11, 2013, www.npr.org/2013/03/11/174013774/in-trendy-world-of-fast-fashion-styles-arent-made-to-last; Greg Petro, "The Future of Fashion Retailing: Part 1 – Uniqlo," *Forbes,* October 23, 2012, www.forbes.com/sites/gregpetro/2012/10/23/the-future-of-fashion-retailing-part-1-uniqlo/; Greg Petro, "The Future of Fashion Retailing: The Zara Approach (Part 2 of 3)," *Forbes,* October 25, 2012, www.forbes.com/sites/gregpetro/2012/10/25/the-future-of-fashion-retailing-the-zara-approach-part-2-of-3/; Greg Petro, "The Future of Fashion Retailing—The H&M Approach (Part 3 of 3)," *Forbes,* November 5, 2012, www.forbes.com/sites/gregpetro/2012/11/05/the-future-of-fashion-retailing-the-hm-approach-part-3-of-3/; Seth Stevenson, "Polka Dots Are In? Polka Dots It Is! How Zara Gets Fresh Styles to Stores Insanely Fast—Within Weeks," *Slate.com,* June 21, 2012, www.slate.com/articles/arts/operations/2012/06/zara_s_fast_fashion_how_the_company_gets_new_styles_to_stores_so_quickly_.html.

But change did not end with multichannel retailing. Consumers quickly became frustrated if an item found on a retailer's website was not available in the store, or if an item that was ordered and didn't fit could not be returned to a store location for credit or exchange. They also, as you learned in Chapter 11, began turning increasingly to social media for information and recommendations on what to buy and where. What's more, a growing number of consumers began using smartphones and other mobile devices to access the Internet from anywhere they found themselves, taking advantage of the ability to research products, compare prices, download coupons from retail apps, and make purchase decisions based on information literally at their fingertips. In some cases, consumers started engaging in **showrooming,** or visiting a physical store to examine goods first-hand but then looking for a lower price and purchasing online.

The end result is that modern retail is adapting once more and becoming **omnichannel retailing,** a structure in which merchants focus on engaging and serving their customers in a seamless manner regardless of the method, online or offline, those customers are using to shop. Whereas multichannel retailing enabled consumers to complete transactions through multiple connected channels, such as in a brick-and-mortar store as well as a retail website, omnichannel retailing goes further, with the goal of offering consumers the same experience across any and all channels. The approach may vary somewhat among individual retail companies. Some, such as Staples, for instance, are featuring in-store kiosks that, in essence, recreate an online shopping experience within the store, allowing consumers to find more information on products or purchase goods for later pick-up. Others, such as Best Buy, enable consumers to purchase an item online but pick it up, usually within the hour, at a local store location. Still others are using mobile apps to enhance consumers' shopping experience; Sephora's mobile app, for instance, lets customers view their past purchases, read or write product reviews, create a shopping list, and more, and can be used in-store (thanks to free WiFi) to scan products or find special offers.

Of course, as pointed out above, one of the biggest constants in retailing is change, and what works for fashion retailers and consumers today may not be as effective in years to come. Considering the seismic shifts in technology and consumer behavior already taking place this century, a 2013 report by the Shop.org Think Tank views omnichannel as simply a bridge to the retail organization of the future, noting: "Growth retail companies in 2023 will bear little resemblance to today's organization. . . . The successful retailer in 2023 will be driven by and designed around a consumer who demands a holistic, customer-focused shopping experience."[5]

WHERE CONSUMERS BUY FASHION

Even with the strong trend to omnichannel retailing, there are still broad categories that define different types of fashion merchants today. Some retail classifications are based on price, some on breadth of product assortment or level of service, and some on the method by which consumers purchase. Let's look at the key categories of store retailing, e-commerce, catalogs, and television shopping, as well as some other important ways in which consumers obtain fashion.

Store Retailing

Despite the fact that consumers' options regarding where to spend their shopping dollars have dramatically increased, as much as 90 percent of purchases in recent years were still made in "brick-and-mortar" retail venues—that is, in physical stores (Figure 13.5).[6] Within that overall category, consumers' shopping options range from large department stores, to specialty shops, to discount stores, boutiques, designer outlets, and more.

Department stores, with their broad assortments of styles and brands for women, men, and children, remain a top choice for fashion purchases.

FIGURE 13.5 Department stores are still a favorite place for women consumers to shop for apparel.

Burberry Brings Digital Shopping to Life

With consumers clamoring for the conveniences of omnichannel shopping, retailers of all stripes have been revamping their design strategies and incorporating technology to weave their online and offline entities into one seamless whole. Among those retailers is the iconic Burberry. When customers enter the renovated Burberry store on London's historic Regent Street, it's like no store they've ever seen before. As the retailer's then chief executive officer said at the store's September 2012 unveiling, "Burberry Regent Street brings our digital world to life in a physical space for the first time, where customers can experience every facet of the brand through immersive multimedia content exactly as they do online."

Among its highlights, the store features 100 video screens and 500 speakers, all synchronized to disseminate information and brand content to shoppers as they browse. Apparel is tagged with RFID devices, so when a customer picks up a jacket, for instance, the tag sends a signal that causes multimedia content related to the product to appear on a nearby screen or mirror, such as information about the item's construction, or a video of the piece as it was worn on the runway. Pop-ups can even appear on a mirror that let the customer know what others have bought after looking at the item being examined, much in the way online retailers offer suggestions for additional or alternate purchases. In addition, store associates are equipped with iPads that enable them to call up a customer's purchase history and preferences—yet one more way that the store is erasing the lines between online and store.

What about U.S. consumers? Are they left out of this high-tech shopping experience? Not at all. Burberry opened a similarly outfitted store in Chicago, complete with digitally enhanced architecture, interactive environment, iPad-equipped sales associates, a new "collect-in-store" service, and more omnichannel shopping touches.

Sources: Fred Minnick, "Burberry's New Look," *Stores,* January 2013, http://www.stores.org/stores%20magazine%20january%202013/burberry%E2%80%99s-new-look; *Burberry website,* www.burberry.com.

While the number of individual department store companies has shrunk over the past two decades (and particularly after a major merger in 2005 that converted a number of other retail names to Macy's), department stores still attract shoppers who want a wide selection of better-quality fashion merchandise. At the higher price levels are retailers such as Neiman Marcus, Nordstrom, Saks Fifth Avenue, and Bloomingdale's, which cater to an upscale clientele, carry designer and upper-tier labels, and tend to offer more customer service. Mid- and lower-price department stores are less known for service than they used to be, but offer a strong assortment of national brand, designer, and their own private label fashions. Among the most prominent department store names in this category are Macy's, JCPenney, Kohl's, Dillard's, and Sears. In addition, some higher-end chains have launched or expanded their own lower-priced stores to target customers who want the look and taste level of the brand but who cannot or do not wish to pay top dollar for the goods found in the original store. Nordstrom Rack, Saks Off Fifth, and Last Call Studio by Neiman Marcus are examples.

Discount stores have taken a bigger portion of consumers' fashion dollars in recent years, as they have raised the fashion level of their merchandise while maintaining prices that are affordable to most consumers. Leading the pack of discounters is Target, whose on-trend assortment of "cheap chic" apparel became so popular that it led other discounters to try adding more upscale fashions to their merchandise mix. While discount stores generally carry a mixture of national brands and private label apparel, Target has differentiated itself by offering a number of exclusive apparel collections by designers such as Isaac Mizrahi, Missoni, Phillip Lim, and Peter Pilotto.

Specialty stores are another important channel for consumers shopping for fashion goods. As the name implies, specialty stores focus on a relatively narrow segment of apparel or other goods to attract a specific target consumer. Within the apparel category, there are specialty stores that carry clothing for children, for teens, for men, for plus sizes, and many other target groups (Figure 13.6). Some stores limit their offerings to a lifestyle category such as active sportswear or career wear, or to a particular price range. There are also specialty stores that focus on non-apparel fashion goods, such as jewelry, accessories, home furnishings, footwear, and luggage and leather goods. Talbot's, Casual Male, Victoria's Secret, Foot Locker, Claire's, and Bed Bath & Beyond are all examples of specialty stores.

On occasion, an existing specialty store company sees an opportunity to target a different consumer segment and launches a new retail venture, a strategy that may or may not prove to be successful. Ann Taylor Stores, known for career wear, created Ann Taylor Loft to sell lower-priced casual clothes, and the concept—now called simply LOFT—has become one of the leading women's specialty fashion brands in North America. American Eagle Outfitters, on the other hand, launched Martin + Osa to offer sportswear for men and women ages 25 to 40, an older demographic than the typical American Eagle customer, but sales were not as robust as hoped and the stores closed after four years. The company's

FIGURE 13.6 Specialty stores focus on a limited range of merchandise. Apparel specialty stores, such as Old Navy, may also target certain size ranges within their selection of apparel.

Aerie chain, however, which sells intimate apparel and sleepwear targeted to 15- to 21-year-old girls, has grown to more than 140 stand-alone stores, as well as having merchandise sold within the American Eagle stores.

In addition, a growing number of apparel brands and designers have established their own full-price retail stores, giving consumers an opportunity to buy a complete range of merchandise under a single label. Among the companies operating their own retail locations are Ralph Lauren, Coach, Kate Spade, and Lacoste.

E-Commerce

Shopping done on the Internet by means of a computer, tablet, smartphone, or any other electronic device is known as **e-commerce,** sometimes called e-tailing. It might be hard to believe, but in the year 2000, many people thought Internet retailing—which was still in its infancy—was already dying. Some thought that consumers would only buy products they could touch first or see in person, or wouldn't want to wait for their purchases to arrive; others believed concerns about the security of personal information and credit card details would keep consumers away. Clearly, that was not the case, and as retailers got better at their presentation and logistics, consumers became more comfortable with the idea of clicking to buy. According to Forrester Research, by 2003, online sales in the United States (not including travel) had passed the $100 billion mark, and between 2003 and 2006, they more than doubled, to nearly $220 billion.[7] By 2013, that number had climbed to $262 billion, representing about 8 percent of all retail sales, and was predicted to skyrocket to $370 billion by 2017.[8] To borrow from

Mark Twain, it's clear that those early reports of the death of online shopping were greatly exaggerated!

Helping propel the growth of e-commerce is the dramatic rise in the use of mobile devices. At the end of 2013, nearly two thirds of U.S. consumers owned a smartphone and more than a third owned a tablet, meaning that they could take the Internet with them almost anywhere they went. The ease of accessing websites or using mobile apps to check product availability, read user reviews, compare prices, and click to purchase, even while browsing a physical store, has given consumers a new set of tools in deciding what to buy and where. As a result, the sub-category of **m-commerce,** or shopping using a mobile device, is growing rapidly. One study estimated that American consumers used mobile devices to make purchases of more than $25 billion in 2013;[9] another research company put that figure at over $41 billion—and projected that by 2017, retail sales made on mobile devices would climb to well over $100 billion.[10]

Online retailing was initially dominated by "dot-coms," or retailers that sold only on the Internet, and there are still numerous "pure-play" e-tailers (as Internet retailers without a physical store are called). Amazon.com, Zappos.com, and Bluefly.com are three examples. Today, however, most brick-and-mortar retailers are also using the Internet as an additional outlet to supplement their in-store business; this two-pronged approach has been nicknamed "click-and-mortar." Most of these retailers feature full online sales and support of their merchandise offerings—in fact, retailers frequently offer a wider selection of products on their websites than they can physically stock in their stores. Sometimes the extended selection includes a greater breadth of items from a particular brand or designer, or it may include sizes outside the most common range, for which there is less in-store demand. Even luxury goods are increasingly being sold online, both by upscale retailers such as Nordstrom and Bergdorf Goodman, and by Internet-only companies like Net-a-porter.com and Yoox.com.

For fashion consumers, shopping online offers both advantages and disadvantages. On the negative side, consumers can't touch and examine the products before buying, and in the case of apparel, they obviously can't try on the clothes before purchasing them. The social aspect and face-to-face interaction of shopping in a store is also missing—although some consumers enjoy a virtual interaction with other consumers via social shopping sites (see Chapter 11). Some consumers are still uncomfortable using a credit card over the Internet, and others don't like to pay the shipping costs. On the positive side, shopping online gives fashion consumers access to a far wider selection of retailers and merchandise than is available in their local shopping area. Online tools such as product search, price comparisons, and reviews by other consumers can also help them to find the right item at the best price. In addition, to address consumer resistance to paying extra to receive goods, many retailers offer free shipping, sometimes tied to a minimum order amount; and some, particularly footwear e-tailers such as Zappos.com and Shoebuy.com, also offer free return shipping for items that the customer decides not to keep due to poor fit or any other reason. Many click-and-mortar retailers also allow customers to return online purchases to a physical store, saving the hassle of return shipping. Consumers frequently double-check the return policy of a retail website before placing an order, and may look for a product elsewhere if they know returning it could be inconvenient or costly.

LET'S TALK

What products would you consider purchasing online or via mobile app? Are there any items you'd prefer to buy in a physical store? Why or why not?

Catalogs

With the growth of the Internet and online shopping, many people thought printed catalogs would become obsolete. But that has hardly been the case. For one thing, the growing use of tablet computers has meant an increase in the number of catalogs that shoppers can browse on their tablet screen, replicating the page-turning of a print catalog and reacquainting consumers with that form of shopping. That said, more than 12.5 billion printed catalogs are still sent to U.S. homes every year, according to the Direct Marketing Association; and nearly three in ten Americans made a catalog purchase in 2011.[11]

Catalog shopping has some of the same advantages and disadvantages of online shopping, including the benefit of being able to purchase from a retailer without a nearby location, as well as the downside of not being able to try on apparel before buying. Catalogs, however, may be preferred by those remaining consumers who are not computer-savvy or who feel uneasy about giving credit card information online—or who simply like the personal contact of speaking to someone on the phone to place their order. A printed catalog also offers the benefit of being tactile and able to be marked up, put down, and returned to later to browse further, without the need to type or search on a screen. Increasingly, many consumers may use a printed catalog to make their decision about what to buy, but then go online to place the order on the retailer's website or to the store to see the item in person.

Some companies that began their business as catalog-only, such as Norm Thompson (which sells men's and women's apparel, home décor, and gourmet foods), have translated their catalog to a complementary website sales operation. Others, such as J. Crew and upscale women's apparel retailer Coldwater Creek (which filed for bankruptcy in 2014), have gone online and also added physical stores to expand on their catalog sales. On the other hand, illustrating the continued viability of catalogs, some traditional store retailers have added catalogs to their mix or reinforced their use of catalogs in recent years. Bath & Body Works, for example, followed the launch of its retail website a few years ago with the launch of a print catalog;[12] and Victoria's Secret continues to send catalogs on a regular basis, reaching more than 390 million customers each year.

Television Shopping

Television shopping, via networks such as QVC and HSN, has been a favorite consumer pastime for more than three decades, enabling pajama-clad consumers to go on day or night shopping sprees long before PCs and the Internet were an everyday part of most households. But with advances in interactive technology, a new incarnation called "t-commerce"—combining television with e-commerce—is poised to take off. This updated version of television shopping allows consumers to use their TV's remote control to order products they see on the screen on a range of networks and within regular (not just shopping channel) programming.

Imagine: press a few buttons on the remote and the Gap shirt you're admiring on the *American Idol* contestant is on its way to your home!

Among the major companies that have jumped on the t-commerce bandwagon is American Express, which is partnering with Fox and NBC Universal to enable consumers to purchase certain products they see on shows such as *New Girl* and *Fashion Police*.[13] Another is consumer electronics giant Samsung, which has pre-loaded a t-commerce app created by Delivery Agent, Inc., on some of its Smart TVs. The app is built on a platform that maps more than a million products across more than 500 shows by network, program, episode, character, scene, or ad, and then makes those products available for sale via consumers' remote control.[14]

Other Ways Consumers Buy Fashion Goods

Department, discount, and specialty stores, along with the Internet, catalogs, and television, may be the primary places where consumers shop for fashion, but they are not the only places. In the brick-and-mortar world, many consumers delight in finding bargains on top brand merchandise at outlet stores, which have increased in number as some companies seek ways to enhance awareness and sales of their brand. While outlet stores originated as a means for marketers to sell their discontinued or defective merchandise, that is no longer strictly the case, since many brands saw a greater opportunity to market to the consumers flocking to the stores in search of value and a great deal. Some fashion companies now use these stores to test new designs before introducing them on a wider basis; and some, like Brooks Brothers and Gap, even design some merchandise exclusively for their factory and outlet stores.[15]

Consumers can also shop for fashion merchandise via the direct sales method, such as through Avon Products, which sells apparel and accessories in addition to its signature cosmetics and skin care products; and via house parties, where consumers can socialize while buying products ranging from lingerie, to cosmetics, to shoes, and more. And for fashion consumers whose pocketbook can't keep up with their tastes, there are a number of retailers, both online and off, that will let customers rent luxury products (from a Chanel handbag, to a Vera Wang necklace, to a Zac Posen gown) for a fraction of the price of buying them. One of the best known is Bag Borrow or Steal, a website through which consumers can rent the handbag or jewelry of their dreams for a one-month period, and then exchange it for another when they're ready for a new look. Le Tote, on the other hand, offers a fashion rental model similar to Netflix's DVD rental program. For a modest monthly fee, consumers can borrow a choice of either jewelry only or full outfits and accessories, keeping them for as long as they'd like or returning them for a new look at any time. Yet another approach is offered by Rent the Runway (Figure 13.7), which does not require a membership fee but enables consumers to rent dresses from more than 170 designers, paying just a fraction of what it would cost to purchase them. (See Case in Point 13.2.)

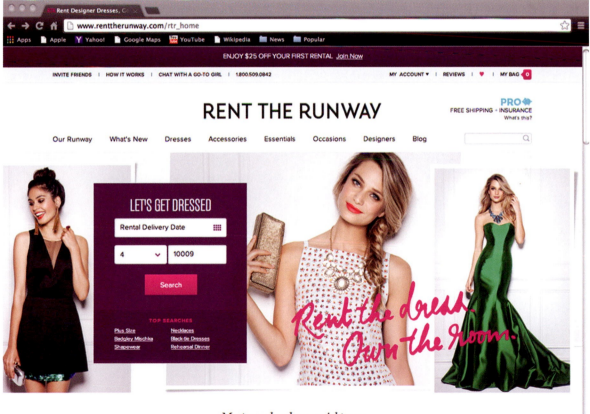

Most popular dresses right now

FIGURE 13.7 Some retailers, such as Rent the Runway, allow consumers to rent designer or luxury fashions for far less than it would cost to purchase the goods.

Renting Glamour

Until a few years ago, when a woman needed a dress for a special occasion, she could re-wear something already in her closet (which might not be an up-to-date style); spend hundreds or even thousands of dollars on a chic new dress at a high-end retailer (which she might not be able to afford); or buy something more reasonably priced (which probably wouldn't make her feel as fabulously fashionable).

Then along came Rent the Runway—and now any woman can be decked out in a designer frock for a big event, without shelling out big bucks. With more than three million members, the website boasts partnerships with 170 designer brands and offers 35,000 dresses, all available for a four-day or eight-day rental period for as little as $30 (and up to about $500).

One aspect making Rent the Runway unique is that customers do not have to choose a dress based solely on how it looks on a professional model. The site is chock-full of photos that actual renters have uploaded of themselves wearing the clothing, with the option to provide their height, weight, and chest size along with a review. New renters are able to search for women of a certain age, shape, or size (including plus-size, recently added to the selection), to see how a dress looks on someone similar to themselves before ordering. That consumer data, including where the renters live and what occasion they're renting the dress for, provides a wealth of built-in marketing information that Rent the Runway can then use to adjust its assortment or services going forward.

Understanding the market and consumer behavior is actually a big key to the company's success, according to Candace Corlett, president of WSL Strategic Retail, who attributes acceptance of the rental model to the Millennial generation. Millennials, she said, "are part of a generation that has grown up buying and selling things on eBay. Reselling and buying pre-owned is part of their mindset, so it makes perfect sense that they would be receptive to renting a designer dress. This generation wants the best, but they're also more cognizant of excess and of the need to live within their means."

To reach even more consumers with more options, Rent the Runway has begun a push into brick-and-mortar, with its first venture being a showroom at the Henri Bendel flagship store on New York's Fifth Avenue. Consumers can try on and rent a selection of dresses available on-site; staff in the showroom lend assistance and can scan each dress a customer tries on with an iPad, adding it to the consumer's virtual closet for later reference. A second showroom opened in early 2014 at the Cosmopolitan of Las Vegas, offering more than 1,000 dresses for consumers to rent on the spot and return the next day.

Sources: Susan Reda, "Leasing the Latest Looks," *Stores,* May 2013, http://www.stores.org/STORES%20Magazine%20May%202013/leasing-latest-looks; Lauren Walker, "Rent the Runway Teams Up with Henri Bendel for Brick-and-Mortar Experience," *FashionMag.com,* October 18, 2013, http://us.fashionmag.com/news/Rent-the-Runway-teams-up-with-Henri-Bendel-for-brick-and-mortar-experience,362897.html#.UtW_Y7SFf8k; and Renttherunway.com.

Some fashion consumers also enjoy bidding for items in online auctions, such as at eBay, or grabbing goods offered in a **flash sale**—an online, limited-time discount on branded, sometimes high-end merchandise, such as through sites including Gilt Groupe, RueLaLa, and Groupon, or offered by retailers such as upscale Neiman Marcus. Others choose to browse in thrift shops, consignment shops, and vintage clothing stores, perhaps searching for a bargain on a gently used designer item or hunting for a one-of-a-kind treasure to enhance their wardrobe or their home décor. Those shopping venues can also become a source for consumers who are ready to part with fashion items. Unless an item is ripped, stained, or otherwise too worn to be reused, many consumers donate their clothing or home fashions to a charity or thrift shop. For better items in good condition, they might decide to resell them online or through a consignment shop, where the shop takes a percentage of the sale price. Another growing trend, made possible by mobile technology, is a clothing swap, in which consumers use an app to find and list apparel or accessories they can trade with other fashionistas, enabling both parties to freshen their wardrobes at minimal expense.

INFLUENCE OF SHOPPING ENVIRONMENTS

As discussed in Chapter 12, a variety of conscious and unconscious techniques are involved in consumers' decision making, including the choice of where to shop for a particular product. Rational aspects, such as a retailer's general price range or a store's proximity to the consumer, will enter into the decision, as will emotional aspects, such as how previous purchases there made the shopper feel or how prestigious the retailer is with the consumer's peer group. The retailer's services and product mix are also important, as is the atmosphere of a brick-and-mortar store, and retailers focus heavily on these areas in their planning and marketing in order to win consumers' interest and loyalty.

Physical Surroundings

A survey conducted by IBM found that 46 percent of shoppers said they tend to stay away from retailers that look and feel the same as other retailers, and about a third avoid stores that are disorganized.[16] What do those numbers tell us? They confirm that the appearance and ambience of a store are very important to consumers in deciding where they want to shop when they shop in person.

The physical features of a store are often what give consumers their first impression of a retailer, so most stores devote considerable effort to designing a look and atmosphere that will create a favorable impression as well as differentiate them from other stores. That mind-set applies to the store's exterior as well as its interior. Architectural details and meticulously designed display windows are frequently used to capture the style and essence of a store's merchandise—and catch the eye of target consumers. But a few mall-based stores have taken another approach, differentiating themselves by doing away with the traditional floor-to-ceiling glass storefront. For example, the storefronts of Hollister, an Abercrombie & Fitch lifestyle fashion brand aimed at high schoolers, have an exterior that mimics a beach shack with wooden shuttered windows.

A store's interior is designed to both accentuate the merchandise and appeal to the store's target consumers. Retailers scrutinize everything from color schemes and lighting, to the genre and volume of background music, to the size and comfort of dressing rooms when planning a store's layout and ambiance (Figure 13.8). When Barneys New York opened a new Boston store, it was designed to reflect the retailer's luxe image, with décor that includes an elegant staircase, huge skylight, and a women's shoe department with chic sofas and banquettes and a fireplace.[17] At its New York flagship store, Macy's recently undertook a $400 million renovation meant to help capture a bigger portion of the booming luxury goods market, as well as to enhance the store experience for customers, including some six million tourists who visit the Herald Square landmark each year. The makeover includes a street-level grand hall dotted with top designers' wares and luxury goods showcases, set off by white marble floors, high ceilings, and a wraparound mezzanine overlooking the cosmetics and luxury handbag counters.[18] By contrast, big-box stores such as Home Depot and Costco use a purposely spartan décor to emphasize their extensive selection and low prices.

Retailers that target a younger, hipper consumer also design their stores to reflect the likes and lifestyles of those customers. For example,

FIGURE 13.8 Retailers devote much effort to creating a store ambience that will appeal to their target consumers and give them a reason to come to the brick-and-mortar store. Burberry's renovated Regent Street store in London, for instance, incorporates video screens and other high-tech amenities.

Hointer Gives Consumers a Glimpse of the Store of the Future

Imagine combining the things you like best about shopping in a brick-and-mortar store (touching, feeling, trying on, walking out with your selection) with the things you like best about shopping online (efficiency, easy selection, unlimited inventory) . . . and you might be imagining Hointer, which opened its first shop in 2012 in Seattle—not with the goal of becoming the next big retail chain, but rather to provide an innovation and learning incubator to take retailing into the future.

Initially targeting shopping-averse men, the Hointer store is divided into a showroom and a micro-warehouse in back. The showroom, featuring primarily jeans, looks sparse but offers about ten times the selection of a typical store—just not piled and scattered on shelves, tables, or traditional racks. Instead, a single pair of each style of pants hangs from a bar, attached by carabiners to be easily viewed from all angles. Customers can download a Hointer app to their smartphone or use a store-supplied tablet to scan or tap an item's tag, and up pops what looks like the product page of an e-commerce site, complete with description, Instagram photos, and even competing prices. To try on a pair, consumers enter a size and color and head to the dressing room. Within 30 seconds, an automated robotic system plucks the clothing from the micro-warehouse and delivers it right to the customer. If the jeans fit, customers can swipe a credit card right then and there and be on their way. If not, they place the unwanted items in a return chute and they're automatically removed from the app's shopping cart; or they can use the app to request that a different size or color be whisked to them automatically, all without leaving the dressing room.

While Hointer's founder Nadia Shouraboura, a former Amazon supply chain and fulfillment tech exec, expected customers to quickly select jeans and be "in and out in a minute," she was surprised to find that wasn't the case at all. "Men were coming in and actually enjoying it. They were spending more time in a store than they had ever spent before. First it was all about how fast it could be. But it turned into something much more about allowing people to discover, to try things on, to learn more about the different brands. Men come in now and might try on 10 different pairs, 20 different pairs, and we hear them laughing, having fun."

Sources: Fiona Soltes, "Automatic for the People," *Stores,* March 2013, http://www.stores.org/STORES%20Magazine%20March%202013 /automatic-people; Dan Berthiaume, "Hands-On Shopping," *Chain Store Age,* November 2013, p. 21; Carol Spieckerman, "Hointer's New Tricks for Bricks," *RetailWire,* August 29, 2013, www.retailwire.com/new-article/16991/hointers-new-tricks-for-bricks; "Innovation Watch: Hointer Uses Robotic Technology to Pull in Male Shoppers," *RetailWeek,* October 21, 2013, www.retail-week.com/home/innovation-watch-hointer-uses-robotic-technology-to-pull-in-male-shoppers/5054126.article; "Hointer—Bringing Together the Best of In-Store and Online Shopping," *Retailsedge,* June 7, 2013, http://retailsedge.com/2013/06/07/hointer-bringing-together-the-best-of-in-store-and-online-shopping/.

when Aeropostale created a new prototype store in Garden City, New York, a couple of years ago, the chain traded in its usual sleek, clean design for a moodier, more textured look, meant to be more in line with today's teen personality, with touches including exposed brick walls, fixtures made from reclaimed wood, and murals featuring iconic New York landmarks and neighborhoods. Along with the visual changes, the store added a high-tech note to the design with in-store iPad kiosks that not only let customers scan products to read reviews or access a "build your own outfit" guide, but that personalize the music playing while they shop. Tablets in the fitting rooms allow customers to choose the tunes they're listening to while trying on clothes; but even more captivating is a crowdsourcing iPad jukebox that lets shoppers choose songs they'd like to hear played store-wide—inspiring them to stick around and shop while they wait for their song to come on.[19]

Service and Amenities

As retail consultant Anthony Stokan, author of *Naked Consumption: Retail Trends Uncovered,* pointed out, modern consumers expect more than mere satisfaction from retailers. They want to be delighted, so that they will feel passionate about the retailer.[20] In many cases, that means retailers, both online and offline, must go above and beyond providing the right merchandise in the right setting by also offering exceptional service—and sometimes additional "extras."

Obviously, good customer service means different things to different shoppers, but it is at least somewhat important to a whopping 99 percent of consumers when deciding to make a purchase, according to a national survey conducted by the NRF Foundation and American Express. In the survey, two-thirds of shoppers said it was extremely important for retail employees to be courteous, and 61 percent found it important that employees be available to ask for help. For online shoppers, good customer service translated to on-time deliveries for 73 percent of respondents, while 74 percent wanted the retailer to handle questions and requests quickly.[21]

Some retailers have turned to technology to help improve their customer service, such as installing in-store computer kiosks that let shoppers instantly order an item or size that might not be in stock, or providing GPS-type functionality in their apps that helps guide consumers more quickly to the aisle with the goods they're seeking (Figure 13.9). Online retailers have also stepped up their service levels, such as with enhancements to the "live chat" options that allow consumers to ask for help in real time. Designer clothing e-tailer Bluefly, for instance, introduced a chat service in which, if a customer searches for more than three items in five minutes (which presumably indicates more than just casual browsing), a pop-up window appears featuring a friendly face offering help.[22]

As brick-and-mortar retailers face ever-stiffer competition for consumers' time and money, both from other retailers and from the Internet, many are focusing on ways to enhance the shopping experience in ways that customers can't enjoy online—a tactic also meant to reduce consumers' showrooming tendencies. Some have expanded their services and implemented customer amenities that range from play areas for children, to Wi-Fi access, to special events and entertainment. Nordstrom, one of numerous retailers to recognize and address the distinct shopping preferences of men in recent years,

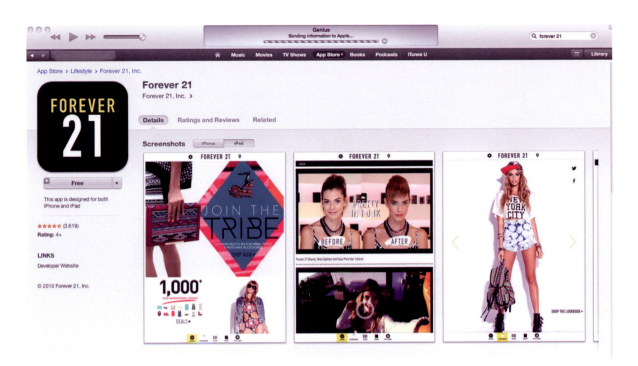

FIGURE 13.9 The concept of customer service extends to the convenience of being able to get merchandise information whenever and wherever consumers want it—in store, online, or via mobile apps.

included a coffee bar, complimentary shaves, and lots of gadgets when it opened a temporary men's store in New York's SoHo neighborhood.[23] On the other hand, boutique-style clothing store White House Black Market taps into the social tendencies of its female clientele by encouraging shoppers to model apparel in front of a large mirror placed in the center of the store.[24]

Malls and shopping centers are equally involved in trying to give consumers added reason to leave their couch and spend time shopping or browsing by staging concerts and art shows, hosting farmers markets and community events, and incorporating destination tenants such as restaurants, movie theaters, health clubs, and more. In many cases, stores are also focusing not just on products but on presenting solutions that their products can offer customers, perhaps grouping items that complement each other within a single display. Bed Bath & Beyond and The Container Store, for example, have both created model dorm rooms at college campuses to give students (and their parents) ideas on how to make their own room more comfortable and organized.[25]

LET'S TALK

What service do you expect to receive from stores where you shop? Do you expect more attention from a clothing store than a drug store? Does the level of service influence whether you'll shop there again?

Product Mix

Even the most wonderful store ambience, spectacular website, or outstanding service will not satisfy consumers if they can't find the products they want at a given retailer. So retailers must continually adjust their merchandise to meet the needs and expectations of their target customers, as well as work closely with manufacturers to make sure that products are available when consumers want them.

Despite the fact that all retailers have a defined group of target consumers, offering the right mix of merchandise requires constant attention to what customers are looking for, since needs can change. Plus-size consumers, for instance, have told retailers that they are interested in more fashion-forward apparel and, as a result, stores including Ann Taylor and Banana Republic, as well as designers including Eileen Fisher, are offering fashions in larger sizes.[26] Similarly, Gap recently introduced its women's products in petite and tall sizing, although the sizes are available only on the retailer's website.[27]

Shopping Up and Shopping Down

One of the big differences in the way consumers buy today is that their income does not automatically translate to where they decide to shop or how much they spend. A consumer might shop at a high-end boutique and splurge on a designer dress for an important occasion, but then go to a discount store for a bargain on sheets. Lois Huff, senior vice president at research and consulting firm Retail Forward, referred to this phenomenon as "bipolar purchasing," in which shoppers "can go down and get some great fashions at the lower prices, but then they also go up and get something that really satisfies the ego."[28]

This new-millennium trend is also documented in *Treasure Hunt: Inside the Mind of the New Consumer,* whose authors see the end of only the rich buying expensive goods, the middle class buying mid-priced products, and the poor buying cheap merchandise. Instead, consumers at all income levels are shopping at lower-priced stores such as Wal-Mart, Target, and Costco—partly because they don't want to overpay for an item, but also because getting a bargain on one purchase gives them more money to splurge on a luxury or indulgence.[29] That growing tendency of consumers to cross-shop is even changing the tenant mix in many malls, which are rethinking the conventional formula of department store anchors supporting a blend of smaller specialty stores. Some malls now feature discounters such as Target next to high-end department stores such as Neiman Marcus, along with other stores, such as Best Buy and Bed Bath & Beyond, which were not traditionally found in malls.

In the next chapter, we'll look at the global consumption of fashion, and explore the ways in which various nationalities and ethnicities exhibit different buying behaviors while sharing certain universal fashion traits.

Summary

Where and how consumers buy fashion products is an important aspect of consumer behavior. Consumers are either fashion leaders or fashion followers, depending on how they relate to products within the fashion life cycle. All fashion products follow the same cycle of introduction, rise, peak, decline, and rejection or obsolescence, although the length of time from introduction to rejection can vary tremendously. The rise phase of the cycle is characterized by knock-offs, which are lower-priced copies of an original style. Getting the latest fashions to consumers as quickly as possible is termed "fast fashion," and practiced by retailers including H&M and Zara. The popularity of fast fashion, which meets consumers' desire for having on-trend merchandise available in a timely manner, has influenced other retailers to new merchandise on a year-round basis, instead of on a more traditional two-season schedule.

Consumers have many choices for purchasing fashion, and their desire to be able to buy offline or online equally easily has led to the growth of omnichannel retailing, in which retailers seamlessly blend the purchase process among store, online, catalog, and mobile. Despite the growth of e-commerce, about 90 percent of apparel purchases in recent years were still made in brick-and-mortar stores. Fashion consumers shop most frequently in department stores, followed by discount stores and specialty stores. Specialty retailers target a narrow consumer group or specific style or price range, and sometimes create new retail concepts to address a different target market. A growing number of consumers are shopping for fashion goods on the Internet, and "pure-play" e-tailers have been joined online by brick-and-mortar retailers adding Web sales to their operations. Catalogs remain another important shopping source for fashion consumers, who have additional shopping options including outlet stores, television shopping, and even luxury rental stores.

Consumers are influenced in their shopping choices by a store's physical features and atmosphere, which retailers design to enhance their merchandise and to attract their target consumers. Service is also important to shoppers, who increasingly expect additional amenities from retailers, such as entertainment or personalized assistance. Other factors affecting where consumers shop are the retailer's assortment of merchandise and the availability of products consumers are seeking. A trend in shopping behavior that has emerged in recent years is the tendency of consumers to shop either up or down from their traditional income level.

KEY TERMS

Classic style

Decline phase

E-commerce

Fad

Fashion followers

Fashion life cycle

Fast fashion

Flash sale

Introduction phase

Knock-offs

M-commerce

Multichannel retailing

Obsolescence or rejection phase

Omnichannel retailing

Peak phase

Rise phase

Showrooming

QUESTIONS FOR REVIEW

1. What are the five phases of a fashion life cycle? Describe what occurs in each phase.
2. Describe what omnichannel retailing is and explain the changes in consumer behavior that helped push retailers to adopt the omnichannel model.
3. Name three types of stores where consumers can make fashion purchases, and give an example of each.
4. What are some of the advantages of shopping for fashion goods on the Internet or from a catalog? What are some of the disadvantages?
5. What are three key aspects of a shopping environment that influence consumers' desire to shop at a particular store?

ACTIVITIES

1. Look through a variety of magazines or store circulars, or browse online, and find an example of a style at each phase of the fashion life cycle. Make a note of where you found each example. How does the source help you determine whether the style is in the first half or second half of its cycle? Can you find multiple examples of a peaking style at different prices or offered by retailers at different price tiers?
2. Think of a fashion product or style that is currently or has recently been a fad. List the attributes of the item, including the gender(s) and age group(s) it appeals to, where or how it began (for example, from a movie or celebrity, etc.), and how long it was or has been popular. In your opinion, why do you think the item caught on? Why do you think it won't remain popular? Survey your classmates for their views.
3. Pick two different specialty stores to visit and compare how their store environments are designed to appeal to their target customer. Make note of elements, including the storefront, the style of merchandise sold and the way it is displayed, the lighting and music, the appearance of the sales associates, and so on, and how those elements contribute to the total ambience. How successful are the stores in conveying an immediate image? If they are targeting a similar consumer, how do their approaches differ? How are they similar? Present your findings to the class.
4. Pretend you are planning to buy a particular item of clothing. Choose three different retailers that sell apparel online, and browse their websites. How easy or difficult is it to search each site? Can you find size and color information easily? What tools does each e-tailer provide to help you find your item and/or any similar styles? Do any of the sites pop up suggestions for complementary or alternative items? Do they let you know whether the item is available in your size, or whether it's available for pick up at a nearby bricks-and-mortar store? Do they provide clear information on how merchandise can be returned? Make a chart comparing the features and ease of use of the three sites.
5. Visit a local thrift store or consignment shop or go to an online auction site (such as eBay) and browse through a selection of the clothing

for sale. How much appears to be recently at the end of its fashion life cycle, and how much would be considered vintage styles? Do you see any current styles? If you're looking online, find two or three items that are drawing multiple bids, and see how they are described, whether new or used, vintage, and so on. If you're in a shop, see if you can speak to the owner or manager, and find out what criteria he or she has for accepting items for sale and what types of items seem to sell fastest.

MINI-PROJECT

Imagine you are going to open your own apparel store. Remembering all the factors that influence consumers as they shop and buy, write a full description of what your store would be like, including customers you'd target, types of merchandise you'd carry, price ranges of the merchandise (low, medium, high), features of the store ambience (for example, styles of lighting, displays, music, etc.), level of customer service you'd offer, how you would incorporate online and/or mobile sales, and so forth. Present your "store" to the class.

REFERENCES

1. NRF Foundation, "Retail Insight: Spotlight on Modern Retail," October 2013, http://research .nrffoundation.com/Default.aspx?pg=9001 #.UsmsgbSFf8k.

2. Gini Stephens Frings, *Fashion from Concept to Consumer*. 4th ed. (Englewood Cliffs, NJ: Prentice Hall, 1994), 61.

3. Chris Sprigman, "Fashion's Piracy Paradox," *University of Chicago Law School Faculty Blog,* November 13, 2006. http://uchicagolaw .typepad.com/faculty/2006/11/fashions _piracy.html

4. Marion Hume, "If You've Got It, Flaunt It," *Time,* March 20, 2005, www.time.com/time /magazine/article/0,9171,1039713,00.html.

5. Shop.org Think Tank, "The Retail Organization of 2023: The Customer Is King (For Real)," *NRF.com,* October 2013, https://nrf.com /resources/retail-library/the-retail- organization-of-2023-the-customer-is-king- real

6. Christopher Matthews, "Future of Retail: How Companies Can Employ Big Data to Create a Better Shopping Experience," *Time,* August 31, 2012, http://business.time.com/2012/08 /31/future-of-retail-how-companies-can- employ-big-data-to-create-a-better-shopping- experience/?id=gs-main-mostpop2.

7. *National Retail Federation and Forrester Research, Inc.,* "Online Clothing Sales Surpass Computers, According to Shop.Org/Forrester Research Study," News release, May 14, 2007.

8. Forrester Research, "U.S. Online Retail Sales to Reach $370 Billion by 2017," News release, March 13, 2013.

9. Morgan Sims, "What Effect Do Smartphones Have on E-Commerce?," *iMediaConnection,* September 10, 2013, http://blogs.imedia connection.com/blog/2013/09/10/what-effect- do-smartphones-have-on-ecommerce/.

10. eMarketer, "Mobile Devices to Boost US Holiday Ecommerce Sales Growth," News release, September 5, 2013.

11. Katie Little, "Not Your Grandma's Catalog—A Retail Mainstay's Reinvention," *CNBC.com,* October 12, 2012, www.cnbc.com/id/49387775/.

12. Melissa Dowling, "Bath & Body Works Goes Direct," *Multichannel Merchant,* May 1, 2006, http://multichannelmerchant.com/mag/bath _body_works_05012–n6/.

13. Bill Hardekopf, "American Express Dives into 'T-Commerce,'" *Forbes,* November 28, 2012, http://www.forbes.com/sites/moneybuilder /2012/11/28/american-express-dives-into-t-commerce/.

14. Delivery Agent, Inc., "Samsung Electronics and Delivery Agent Launch T-Commerce Shopping," News release, July 16, 2013.

15. "Retailers Eye Outlet Stores for Growth," *Reuters,* January 28, 2006, http://asia.news .yahoo.com/060127/3/2eu3z.html.

16. IBM, "Retailers Offering a 'One Size Fits All' Shopping Experience Will Lose Customer Loyalty," News release, May 24, 2005.

17. "Barneys' Luxe Brand of Hip Balances Cool with Commerce," *Boston Globe,* April 9, 2006, www .boston.com/business/globe/articles/2006/04 /09/barneys_luxe_brand_of_hip_balances _cool_with_commerce/.

18. Julie Satow, "Macy's Splurges on a Makeover on 34th Street," *New York Times,* November 5, 2013, www.nytimes.com/2013/11/06/real estate/commercial/macys-splurges-on-a-makeover-on-34th-street.html?adxnnl=1& adxnnlx=1383924448-x6yKZYVN3g7UpjKQe /2XxQ.

19. Janet Groeber, "Mood Swing," *Design:Retail,* March 25, 2013, http://www.designretailonline .com/displayanddesignideas/magazine/Mood-swing-9075.shtml.

20. David Graham, "Tuning in to Teens," *Toronto Star,* May 1, 2006, http://pqasb.pqarchiver .com/thestar/access/1029517821.html?dids=1 029517821:1029517821&FMT=ABS&FMTS= ABS:FT&date—ay+1%2C+2006&author=David +Graham&pub=Toronto+Star&edition=&start page=E.01&desc=Tuning+in+to+teens+Tuning +in+to+%27+the+dark+side%27.

21. National Retail Federation, "Importance of Customer Service Reinforced in NRF Foundation/American Express Study," News release, November 23, 2004.

22. Bob Tedeschi, "Salesmanship Comes to the Online Stores, but Please Call It a Chat," *New York Times,* August 7, 2006, www.nytimes .com/2006/08/07/technology/07ecom.html ?ex=1184558400&en=6122c9b16afa8281& ei=5070.

23. Eric Wilson, "New Wrinkle in Men's Wear: Shops Just for Men," *New York Times,* September 5, 2012, www.nytimes.com/2012 /09/06/fashion/new-york-fashion-week-new-wrinkle-in-mens-wear-shops-for-men-only .html?_r=0.

24. Sanette Tanaka, "His and Hers Shopping Rules," *Wall Street Journal,* September 5, 2012, http://online.wsj.com/news/articles/SB10000 8723963904442737045776334724447 77942.

25. Zachary A. Goldfarb, "Retailers Seize Dorm-Decorating Moment," *Wall Street Journal,* August 16, 2005, http://online.wsj.com/article /0,,SB112415052745013871,00.html.

26. Susan Chandler, "Retailers Are Sizing Up an Overlooked Market," *Chicago Tribune,* May 28,

2006, www.redorbit.com/news/science
/525673/retailers_are_sizing_up_an
_overlooked_market_department_stores_and
/index.html.

27. Gap Inc., "Gap Introduces Petite & Tall Sizes for
Women," News release, January 18, 2006.

28. "Attention Shoppers: Great Deals in Retail
Mergers." *Knowledge@Wharton,* March 30,

2005, http://knowledge.wharton.upenn.edu
/article.cfm?articleid=1158&CFID=2866161&
CFTOKEN=53701311.

29. Laura Landro, "When Luxury Meets
Parsimony," *Wall Street Journal,* June 22, 2006,
http://online.wsj.com/article/SB115092941
682786837.html.

CHAPTER 14

Global Consumers of Fashion and Design

WHAT DO I NEED TO KNOW ABOUT GLOBAL CONSUMERS OF FASHION AND DESIGN?

✔ The influence of culture on the kinds of products and marketing strategies to which consumers around the globe respond

✔ The importance of understanding the various subcultures in the United States and how their distinct values affect purchasing behavior

✔ Why mistakes are made by marketers who are insensitive to the customs and symbols that are important to consumers of other cultures

✔ How fashion and design unify the world despite cultural differences among nations and societies

✔ The vital roles that importing and exporting play in the global economy and dissemination of fashion trends

From Japan to Jakarta and from Nevada to North Carolina, consumers' purchasing habits appear to be quite similar—and at the same time, quite different. What human beings need, what we desire, and what we value definitely vary from country to country and culture to culture; yet many of the things we all want and enjoy, including in the realm of fashion, are actually universal.

Are We All Alike?

To be successful, marketers need to understand how people differ from place to place, especially in today's interconnected world. In the United States alone, people of different nationalities, religions, locations, political parties, and social classes have beliefs and customs that are unique. Can they all want the same products among the dizzying array of goods available? (see Figure 14.1.)

Subcultural Differences Influence American Buying Habits

The United States is composed of a multitude of subcultures, smaller groups within the larger society/culture, such as persons of the same age, political ideology, ethnicity, social class, sexual orientation, and so on, that possess distinct beliefs, goals, interests, and values that differentiate them from the dominant culture. Hispanic, Italian, Irish, Polish, Indian, and Arab people compose some of the many ethnic subcultural groups that are living, working, and raising families in the United States. However, while they all might call this country "home," look

forward to fireworks on the Fourth of July, favor democracy, and love Superman and Mickey Mouse, researchers have learned that members of these groups do not necessarily share all the same preferences when it comes to consumer goods. Additionally, these differing preferences are much more complex than simply favoring Thai food over Chinese or straight-leg jeans over boot-cut jeans, and they must be studied and understood if marketers are to address and appeal to the varied interests and desires of U.S. shoppers. Read Case in Point 14.1 and you'll get a glimpse of how consumers in three important ethnic groups differ from one another and the U.S. population as a whole.

Let's Talk

Are subcultural behaviors passed down from generation to generation, or are they transmitted in other ways? Do you think we inherit them, learn them, or adopt them? Are you a member of a subculture? If you think you are, how did you come to understand the behaviors that are expected of you?

MARKETING TO DIVERSITY

Diversity is a concept that is of great interest to the modern businessperson. **Diversity** is that which makes us dissimilar or different from one another. Americans are a diverse bunch, made up of people who've come to the United States from all over the world and who live their day-to-day lives in very different ways. Although we may have in common our respect for the ideals of freedom and independence (even though exactly *what* those ideals mean to each

FIGURE 14.1 Do consumers the world over want the same things? The answer is yes . . . and also, no.

A Look at Three Key American Subcultural Groups

The buying power of African Americans, already at the $1 trillion mark, is expected to reach $1.3 trillion by 2017—which clearly makes this segment of the population a critical consumer market in the United States. What's more, African Americans, who number some 43 million, have distinct shopping characteristics from other consumer groups, according to research conducted by the Nielsen Company.

For one thing, Nielson finds, African Americans are more aggressive consumers of media, watching more television, reading more financial magazines, and spending more than twice the time at personal hosted websites as any other group. In addition, they shop more frequently than all other groups, making an average of 156 shopping trips per year, compared to 146 for the total market. Smaller retailers generally have the most appeal to blacks, with drug stores, convenience stores, dollar stores, and beauty supply stores among the outlets most frequently visited.

The Nielsen research also found that African Americans have unique digital and mobile habits. More than 7 in 10 own a smartphone, compared with just 62 percent for the total U.S. population; and they spend 44 percent more time on education and career websites. Contributing further to the market impact of the group is the fact that a higher percentage of African Americans are attending college; and the number of African American households earning $75,000 or more has grown by 63.9 percent in the last decade, a greater rate than for the overall population.

Sources: The Nielsen Company, "African-American Consumers Are More Relevant then Ever," News release, September 19, 2013; Kunbi Tinuoye, "Shopping Habits of African-Americans Revealed by Nielsen Research," The Grio, January 7, 2012, http://thegrio.com/2012/01/07 /shopping-habits-of-african-americans-revealed-by-nielsen-research/.

✳ ✳ ✳ ✳ ✳ ✳

At 52 million strong, the U.S. Hispanic population has a buying power of $1.2 trillion—and the consumers holding the purse strings for the group are the women. According to a study by Nielsen, 86 percent of Latinas consider themselves to be the decision makers in household spending. And with that spending expected to pass $1.5 trillion by mid-decade, spread across a range of product categories including groceries, beauty products, technology, and cars, marketers are paying very close attention.

Making this group even more intriguing is that the modern Latina is "ambicultural"; in other words, she can pivot effortlessly back and forth between the English and Spanish languages and cultures. She is more likely to have children—63 percent of Latinas have kids under 18 years old, compared to just 40 percent

(continued)

of non-Hispanic white females—but she is also better educated than ever before: According to Nielsen, for the first time, more Latinas are enrolling in college than non-Hispanic females.

What's more, because U.S. Census data estimate that Hispanic women will comprise 30 percent of the total female population by 2060, closing the gap with the non-Hispanic white female population (expected to drop to 43 percent), Latinas' tastes, values, and preferences will become a larger part of the mainstream market, with the lines between what is considered "American" and what is considered "Latino" becoming increasingly blurred.

Sources: The Nielsen Company, "Latinas Are a Driving Force Behind Hispanic Purchasing Power in the U.S.," News release, August 1, 2013; Nina Terrero, "How Latinas Are Increasingly Influencing What Products You Will Be Buying," *NBC Latino,* August 2, 2013, http://nbclatino.com /2013/08/02/how-latinas-are-increasingly-influencing-what-products-you-will-be-buying/.

✳ ✳ ✳ ✳ ✳ ✳

Asian Americans number more than 19 million, and they are one of the fastest-growing multicultural demographics in the country, surging in number by 58 percent between 2000 and 2013. A more staggering statistic, however, relates to the group's buying power: It has grown more than 520 percent, to some $720 billion, since 1990 and is expected to top $1 trillion within a few years, according to research by the Nielsen Company. Contributing to that buying power is the fact that Asian-American households are 54 percent more likely than U.S. households overall to have annual incomes greater than $100,000.

Asian Americans tend to shop more often than their white counterparts, particularly in the categories of food, apparel, housing, and transportation. Name brands matter to these shoppers, about 35 percent of whom told Nielsen they were "swayable shopaholics," indicating they take pleasure in the act of buying, may buy on impulse, and are willing to pay extra for products they want. Asian Americans also do more online shopping than the general population, with 77 percent noting they'd bought something online in the past year, compared with 61 percent of other consumer groups.

In addition, Asian Americans are tech-savvy and well-educated, with half of those over age 25 holding a bachelor's degree; only 28 percent of the general population can say the same. And although 61 percent say they speak English very well, more than 75 percent speak another language when they're at home, which means marketers might want to consider a multi-lingual strategy to reach this powerful consumer group.

Sources: The Nielsen Company, "Significant, Sophisticated and Savvy: The Profile of the Asian American Shopper," News release, December 3, 2013; Tiffany Hsu, "Asian American Consumers: Nearing $1 Trillion in Buying Power," *Los Angeles Times,* November 20, 2012, http://articles .latimes.com/2012/nov/20/business/la-fi-mo-asian-americans-nielsen-consumers-20121120.

of us probably differs), our unique orientations can't help but influence our behavioral (including consumer) patterns.

Adding to the issue of diversity are the regional consumption behaviors and preferences that exist in various geographic locations in the United States. People living on the far northeastern coast need cold-weather clothes for at least half the year, while those living in the deserts of the Southwest might not even own coats. Marketers need to recognize such differences (in this example, weather-influenced behavior) so they can tailor strategies to meet the needs of the marketplace, whatever they might be.

Diverse lifestyles also have a place in the subcultural mix. A lifestyle (discussed in Chapter 9) is an individual's distinctive way of living—a pattern that influences a person's choices in all areas of life, from how one spends his or her time to how one spends his or her money. Consumer researchers continuously identify, track, and study emerging and alternative lifestyles, knowing that distinctive lifestyles often produce new kinds of buyers with new and specific needs. And, as we know, new needs create new opportunities for products and the marketing of those products.

Clearly, as much as Americans share in terms of certain beliefs and behaviors, there are many kinds of people who are part of this country; this makes the United States a **multicultural** society, with a dominant culture that includes many subcultures. We all consume goods, but do so in different ways.

As varied as our buying behavior is, however, there are certain products and consumption activities that not only communicate connectedness, but function as symbols that tell observers we all belong to the same culture, even though we may not have been born into it. Eating turkey on Thanksgiving, sporting baseball caps with our favorite team's name, wearing denim with everything, and preferring Nike to other shoe brands are all signals that some degree of acculturation has occurred. **Acculturation** is the process of adapting to a new primary or mainstream culture. Those who are born into a culture go through the much easier process of **enculturation,** whereby humans learn about and act according to the expectations of their own culture from birth on. Although most people living in the Unites States identify, at least somewhat, with the ethnic and religious groups into which they were born, or the countries where their relatives came from, many make at least some effort to adapt to the predominating culture in an attempt to identify with those around them (an example could be learning to speak and read English). Such adaptation allows for a certain degree of comfort, security, and convenience.

CONSUMPTION MIRRORS CULTURAL VALUES

As discussed in Chapter 9, values are ideas we consider important, principles for behavior that matter to us. A **value system** is "a learned organization of principles and rules to help one choose between alternatives, resolve conflicts, and make decisions."[1] Every culture has certain values that its members share, and although it seems that some values change over time, it's probably more accurate to say that the methods or symbols used to express the values are what actually change. Therefore, marketers must be careful not to misuse these methods and/or symbols, since misinterpretation can lead to misunderstanding. For example, Jean Paul Gaultier,

A British View of American Consumers

The following tongue-in-cheek opinions from a British observer focus on the American lifestyle and consumption habits, as excerpted from a guide meant to help transplants from other countries adapt to U.S. life. The observations reveal some of the ways Americans are viewed by others—admittedly with exaggerations. Some are favorable, others unflattering, but are they accurate?

The United States is one of the most cosmopolitan countries in the world and primarily a nation of foreigners who have as much in common with one other as Africans have with Australians or Asians with Europeans. However, despite its diverse mix, the U.S. isn't necessarily the popularly depicted melting pot, but a potpourri of ethnic splinter groups often living entirely separate lives with their own neighborhoods, shops, clubs, newspapers, and even television and radio stations.

If there's one single motivation uniting all Americans, it's their desire to be rich and famous (I want it all NOW!). Americans not only believe that you can have everything, but that you owe it to yourself to have it all: beauty, education, fame, health, intelligence, love, money, etc., but if they cannot have it all, most Americans will settle for money. To be considered seriously rich in the U.S., you must be fabulously wealthy with a fleet of gold-plated Cadillacs, luxury yacht, private jet, and a mansion "on the hill" with scores of servants. The best of everything is every American's birthright, and they will borrow themselves into bankruptcy if they have to in order to provide it for themselves and their families.

Americans are the greatest consumers in the history of the world and their primary occupation is spending money—when not spending money they're thinking about spending it. Displaying the correct "labels" is vital, as your status is determined by what you wear, drive, inhabit, or own. Status is everything to Americans, who buy more status symbols than any other nation and believe there's no point in buying anything expensive if it isn't instantly recognizable and desirable. Ostentatious consumption is the order of the day (if you've got it, flaunt it!).

Size is everything and bigger is always better; big cars, big homes, big breasts, big pay checks, big cities, big football players, big Macs, big stores—everything is big (most things in the US come in three sizes: big, huge and gigantic!). To Americans, size and quality are inextricably linked and your success in life is illustrated by the size of your office and the number of zeros on the end of your salary. Likewise new, which always equates to improved, and is infinitely better than old in the American throwaway society. Americans are continually "trashing" or trading in last year's model, whether it's their car, home, or spouse.

(continued)

the avant-garde French couturier, is famous for what is referred to as **cultural borrowing,** the use of symbols that are meaningful to other cultures. But borrowing these symbols does not necessarily mean they are truly understood by the users, or are properly used. Why not? For the simple reason that they've been taken out of their original context. In one of Gaultier's collections, he created clothing based on the traditional dress of Hasidim, the ultra-orthodox sect of the Jewish religion, which included dark gray or black gabardine suits, oversized long suit jackets, and wide-brimmed, fur-trimmed hats. This caused numerous debates and articles about whether Gaultier went "too far" or showed a lack of respect for the religion he used as his inspiration.

Marketers agree that in most situations, it's best not to use certain religious or cultural images or symbols unless their exact meanings and proper usages are understood, in order to avoid misinter-pretations. Another factor marketers must acknowledge when targeting multiple cultures is that in each value system, the values are ranked differently. For example, speed and efficiency are high priorities in some cultures, while in others it is patience that's considered crucial. Additionally, some values are culture-specific. Individualism for example, is one of the most prized American values, whereas in Japan, the focus is on fulfilling one's obligations to others, which is viewed as a far greater achievement than serving the self.[2] Obtaining a state of self-assurance and independence would not be something to aim for in Japanese culture; instead, one's efforts should go toward the creation of harmony and consideration for what is in the best interest of the group to which one belongs. Japanese-Americans also tend to rank obligation and harmony high, but convey them in a way that is "acceptable" in the United States.

Belonging and achievement are important goals for members of cultures that value individualism (see Maslow's Hierarchy of Needs, Chapter 4). One way for cultures and subcultures to attain these goals is through the purchase of similar items, especially those that are fashion and/or design related. This is because the possession of designed goods is largely symbolic; owning/wearing certain products is a way of conveying social status, letting others know you understand what a given culture values, and clarifying your own position in that culture. Thus, when Japanese people become part of American culture, they are likely to choose products that help them express a combination of values from both countries. For example, a Japanese-American might serve dinner to his guests on red lacquer plates with antique chopsticks, but have the guests sit at his chrome-and-glass dining room table, rather than on floor cushions.

In the 1970s, researcher Jonathan Gutman explored the role that cultural values play in influencing purchase behavior. His **means-end chain** is a structure that links a consumer's knowledge about a product's attributes (benefits or risks) with the desired cultural value state the person wants to achieve. In other words, the means = the product, the end = the desired value/outcome.[3] Thus, an impeccably tailored suit by Ralph Lauren (an example of a highly symbolic product) would be a means by which a consumer could enjoy a positive consequence, be it status, a feeling of belonging, or any positive experience (Figure 14.2). When marketers are trying to attract the attention of multicultural consumers, they must be continuously aware that

FIGURE 14.2 The symbolic value of a tailored Ralph Lauren Purple Label suit, worn here by Jay-Z on the Academy Awards red carpet, goes far beyond the cost of the suit itself.

the portrayal of a product and how it's presented and positioned is frequently more important than its functionality or utility.

Marketers have a challenging task in today's mobile and global world, where so many cultural influences must be studied and understood. How do marketers determine which product attributes (product properties and the benefits they provide) are most meaningful to so many consumers in so many cultural groups? They identify the beliefs (values) that are important to the society/group that's being targeted, focus on the ones that are most

Cultural Anthropology Plays a Role in Cross-Cultural Marketing

Looking at the world today, one would be safe in saying that globalization is an inevitable process. Does it follow then that cross-culturalization will also be inevitable?

There is no question that the world is becoming more homogeneous. Numerous studies conducted by cultural anthropologists investigating how culture impacts human behavior show that there are fewer and less pronounced distinctions between the markets of various nations; and for some products, those distinctions no longer exist at all, meaning that marketers do not always need to adapt their goods for consumers in different countries.

But at the same time, there are some cultural differences between nations, regions, and ethnic groups that are actually becoming stronger. This means that a true understanding of cultural differences on a national, local, and ethnic level is one of the most significant skills for firms to develop in order to have a competitive advantage in international business.

One clear example of how using cultural anthropology helped one group of marketers succeed while another did not relates to the marketing of color televisions in Asia. Back in the early 1980s, both Japanese and European TV manufacturers were considering entering the Chinese market, so they conducted comprehensive studies to determine the market's viability for their products. Based on their research, European marketers concluded that, because of China's low GDP (gross domestic product—the total dollar value of all goods and services produced over a specific time period, which indicates the size and growth of a country's economy), it was not likely that Chinese consumers would have the means to buy luxuries like color televisions. So they decided not to try to sell their products in China.

On the other hand, the Japanese TV marketers' research looked beyond just the economics. Their studies showed that the Chinese have a strong cultural tradition of saving that is passed down from one generation to the next. What's more, unlike Western culture, in which people spend money they don't yet have to buy goods immediately, the Chinese save money with the goal of buying something in the future. The Japanese research discovered that almost every family in China had been saving for two to three years for the express purpose of owning a color TV. In addition, even though there were Chinese companies that manufactured TVs, Chinese consumers expressed more confidence in products imported from another country.

As a result, the Japanese marketers came to the conclusion that Chinese families would indeed buy high-quality Japanese color televisions, and they were right. Throughout the late 1980s and 1990s, Japanese-made color TVs dominated the imported television market in China, and those marketers profited greatly—because they made the effort to understand a facet of Chinese culture that their European competitors did not.

Source: Kathy Tian and Luis Borges, "Cross-Cultural Issues in Marketing Communications: An Anthropological Perspective of International Business," *Journal of China Marketing*, Vol. 2(1) 2011, http://www.na-businesspress.com/IJCM/TianKWeb2_1_.pdf.

heavily weighted, develop products that are innovative and well designed (while continuously referring to those beliefs), and devise the marketing stimuli most likely to appeal to each group. To do this, modern marketers have turned to revisit an old field of study. **Anthropology,** the study of human cultural characteristics that include habits, customs, and relationships, is no longer only about studying the artifacts left behind by past peoples; rather, in its newer incarnation, it has become an aid to the understanding of what members of varying cultures want today. **Cultural anthropology** focuses on the common symbols, values, and beliefs of social groups and institutions.

Marketers consider the importance of all of these factors in their development of sound marketing strategies. Marketers also use ongoing research about emerging design trends in the multicultural marketplace compiled by **trend forecasting services,** which provide advisories formulated by professional observers of cultural shifts that contain calculated predictions about the likely direction in which design preferences are moving. (See Chapter 1 for additional information about trends and forecasting.)

Awareness of the direction in which trends are moving is crucial to the efforts of anyone planning a marketing strategy, whether it's for a global or local audience. Award-winning journalist and multimedia entrepreneur Guy Garcia offers some astute observations in his book, *The New Mainstream: How the Buying Habits of Ethnic Groups Are Creating a New American Identity,* pointing out that products today are endorsed by a variety of individuals who, not that long ago, would have been considered "outsiders" rather than the celebrities they are now. Chinese basketball players,

African-American golf champions, and Latino film stars, all of whom demonstrate the new kind of socioeconomic power in the United States, are reflecting the changing demographic and consumer makeup of the country. The United States has evolved from a "melting pot" to a "salad bowl" of all kinds of people with different interests, experiences, and orientations, and these groups have become a new and influential multiethnic block of tastemakers and trendsetters.[4]

Fashion and Design as Unifying Forces

In addition to studying the differences among the members of our diverse population, marketers also have discovered that the purchase and ownership of fashion-related goods can bring people together in many ways. Many people interested in fashion and design are curious about how others around the world view, wear, and create designed goods. The designed items we choose are regarded by many researchers as an unspoken language that can communicate information about our universal similarities and function as a unifying device (see Case in Point 14.2).

WE ARE THE WORLD

A dominant issue for many companies in the modern marketplace is **globalization,** the ability to offer and market a product any place in the world where a demand for it exists. Continuing to grow and increase profits is a common business objective, and today many businesses do that by entering foreign markets and expanding their customer bases.

What Do Fashionistas in Los Angeles, Paris, and Shanghai Have in Common?

As more and more consumers around the world are able to connect regularly and instantly with designers, marketers, and other fashion fans via digital communications and social media, fashion preferences are becoming more standardized among countries and cultures. However, although merging preferences have brought us closer to a homogenized global fashion image, there still remain highly differing tastes and cultural preferences across a variety of global markets. That is what led Martine Leherpeur Conseil (MLC), a strategy and consultancy agency based in Paris, to study the similar and dissimilar tastes of 25- to 35-year-old female fashion consumers living in cities the agency identified as three "aspirational fashion hot spots": Los Angeles, Shanghai, and Paris.

MLC presented its findings at a Who's Next trade show highlighting fashion trends and innovations, and according to reporting from the presentation, the L.A. fashionista is "far from the cliché 'bimbo' stereotype" but neither is she one to blend into the crowd; rather, noted Jean-Philippe Evrard, MLC's managing director, "There is certainly a slight 'look-at-me' factor, but nothing too ostentatious." In Los Angeles, "effortless glam" is the name of the game. This could mean a pair of shorts (L.A.'s favorite clothing item) worn with boots or simple, low-key pieces paired with statement-making jewelry, shoes, and handbags. Since Los Angeles is primarily a beach culture, "legs are constantly on show, hair is blonde from the sun, and make-up is kept very minimal," the agency found. In addition, sub-cultural touches are often integrated into the L.A. look, such as the popular boho and new-age trends.

Chinese women, on the other hand, particularly those in Shanghai, exude flawless sophistication and are quite willing to embrace lengthy beauty regimens to achieve a desired outcome. Noted Laetitia Orlandi, head of MLC's Shanghai branch, "Very much reflecting the image of the city, the Shanghai woman is somewhere between the East and the West," she strives for elegant style, but adds a dash of confidence and independence. Her stylishness is often established by her outerwear, such as a structured coat, leather jacket, or fur, along with the all-important handbag, which is an important signifier of status. As in southern California, the weather in Shanghai is warm much of the year, so Chinese fashionistas also like to flaunt bare legs.

Unlike the Shanghai women who pursue perfection, Parisian fashionistas strive for "effortless chic." A look considered quite voguish is the definitive trench coat worn with ballet flats and a chignon in slight disarray, representing "a penchant for classic looks with a modern twist." Sneakers, vintage bags, and buttoned-to-the-top

(continued)

shirts are a few of the newer trends that fashionable French women are sporting.

Despite the differences in attitude and approach to style among these global fashion centers, MLC identified some items that are important in all three locales: Celine handbags, skinny jeans, ankle boots, stilettos, and nail polish, among them—all interpreted in ways distinct to each location, of course.

As Evrard concluded, "Global fashion is dotted with local trends and differing personalities." Hmmmm. So, is there really such a thing as a "global image"? Clearly, establishing a single personality for an international brand is not as easy as it may seem—at least not without a bit of local adaptation.

Source: Anais Lereverend, "What Do LA, Paris and Shanghai Fashionistas Have in Common?", *FashionMag,* July 12, 2013, http://us.fashionmag .com/news/What-do-LA-Paris-and-Shanghai-fashionistas-have-in-common-,341678.html#.UhojAT88Xae.

The United States is one of the biggest *importers* of fashion-related goods. **Imports** are those goods and services provided by foreign producers that are purchased and brought into a country. **Exports** are any goods or commodities produced in one country and transported to another country in a legitimate fashion, typically for use in trade. Exported goods or services are provided to foreign consumers by domestic producers. To be considered legitimate, all trading must be done in accordance with the receiving country's regulations, including **tariffs** or **duties,** additional monies or taxes on imports imposed by the country receiving those goods, and **quotas,** limits on the quantities of certain goods that can be brought into a country. Both are ways a country can protect its own producers since both, referred to as *trade barriers,* usually result in decreased demand for foreign goods and increased demand for similar products made in the home country.

LET'S TALK

If you were to look through your closet, how much of your wardrobe do you guess was made in another country? Do you pay attention to where something was produced when you're shopping? Has that ever influenced your decision to buy or not buy?

When a country imports more than it exports, it creates a **trade deficit.** Conversely, when a country exports more than it imports, it creates a **trade surplus.** At the start of the new millennium, a combination of factors (including expired trade agreements and lower prices offered to American companies by overseas manufacturers of a variety of goods) left the United States with a significant trade deficit. The deficit shrank somewhat as the world struggled to recover from the economic crisis

Asos.com Conquers the World with Fashion

If you've ever shopped at Asos.com, you're not alone. In fact, you would be one of the nearly *8 million* active customers that Asos boasts—and also one of the *20 million* unique visits the online-only retailer receives on its website each day, from fashion consumers all around the world.

That global customer base is precisely what Nick Robertson, co-founder and chief executive officer, has aimed for, based on his belief that what consumers buy should not have to be dictated by where they live. So the British-based retailer targets primarily twenty-something consumers, an age group that spends about 40 percent of its fashion budget online—and a group that Robertson wants to enable to buy anything it desires, regardless of language or geography.

That philosophy is the heart and soul of the company's focus, and it is what has propelled Asos into the enviable position of being the fastest-growing online fashion retailer in the world. Contributing heavily to the company's success are its country-specific websites that speak customers' language whether they live in France, Germany, Russia, Australia, the United States, Spain, the United Kingdom, Italy, or China.

Asos sells its own brand of apparel but also partners with other retailers to sell their products, making it a one-stop shop for target consumers. Its platform gives those partners a global reach they wouldn't otherwise have without taking it upon themselves to open their own physical stores around the world or introduce their own multi-language websites—either of which would involve far more investment of time and finances than piggybacking on Asos's established framework.

What exactly does that global reach translate to? For one thing, the almost 8 million active customers is a huge increase from the retailer's less than half a million customers in 2006, and more than double the 3.2 million it tallied in 2011. And looking at the barometer of social media, its numbers continue to grow, as well: Asos has garnered well over 3 million Facebook "likes," and has more than half a million followers on Twitter and 2.3 million on Google+.

Sources: Asos website, www.asos.com; Vicki M. Young, "WWD CEO Summit: Asos.com's Nick Robertson Looks to the Future," *WWD*, October 30, 2013, http://www.wwd.com/retail-news/direct-internet-catalogue/asoscoms-nick-robertson-looks-to-the-future-7255134?navSection=package&navId=7253694&module=Retail-hero.

and recession late in the decade, but remains a topic of discussion among the government, industry, and economists to ensure that the U.S. economy is not negatively impacted.

These factors, plus many more, have combined to make marketing U.S. products globally a critical issue for many companies. World trade has exploded, fueled by peoples' frequent exposure to other cultures and their practices. Exchanging information about lifestyles, products, and events through travel, television, social media, music, movies, mobile communications, and the Internet has become the norm, resulting in widespread interest in foreign products by people around the world. There are obviously tremendous opportunities beyond our borders, and as consumers from overseas market segments have shown, they are just as interested in acquiring international products as Americans are.

Global business expansion continues to grow at a remarkable pace. Estée Lauder products are sold in Russia, Nike is popular in Vietnam, and Starbucks has opened coffeehouses in India. Similarly, merchandise from European companies such as Sephora, Mango, and French Connection are now in many American homes. Becoming active and competitive in the global marketplace has become the key to ongoing success for many companies. And maintaining a more equal balance between a country's imports and exports, referred to as a **balance of trade,** would appear to be advantageous, although there is some disagreement among experts as to whether or not this is actually true.

The United States has posted a trade deficit since the 1970s, and it rapidly increased after 1997. Some evidence suggests this is because ours is a dominant economy, and global business profits are high, indicating that a trade deficit increases during times of economic expansion, and slows during times of contraction. Certainly part of the trade imbalance can be traced to the outsourcing of manufacturing jobs by many U.S. companies, resulting in fewer goods actually produced in the United States, and therefore fewer to export. However, in 2012 the total U.S. trade deficit decreased slightly from 2011, a good sign to those who see it as an indication that the economy is strengthening. A lower deficit means exports are starting to gain on imports, and this is good for business, since it will eventually create more U.S. jobs.[5]

So, is a trade deficit good or bad? Many economists, including the late Milton Friedman, highly respected winner of the Nobel Prize in Economics, have taken the position that a large trade deficit (importation of goods) actually signals that the currency of the recipient country is strong and desirable. To them, a trade deficit simply means that consumers get to purchase and enjoy more goods at lower prices; conversely, a trade surplus implies that a country exported goods that its own citizens did not get to consume and enjoy, and that they paid higher prices for the goods that were consumed. According to Friedman, "A fallacy seldom contradicted is that exports are good, imports bad. The truth is very different. Our gain from foreign trade is what we import. Exports are the price we pay to get imports; the citizens of a nation benefit from getting as large a volume of imports as possible in return for its exports or, equivalently, from exporting as little as possible to pay for its imports."[6] While a widely accepted premise for many years, economists have recently started to rethink Friedman's contentions.

For instance, others, like *New York Times* columnist Paul Krugman, himself a Nobel laureate, have said that a trade deficit indicates that America is living beyond its means, spending far more than it earns. Several years ago, Krugman suggested that the trade deficit would eventually have to become smaller or a decline in the foreign exchange value of the dollar would result. If that happened, he said, consumers would be unable to continue buying as many products from other countries. Furthermore, Krugman predicted that American workers, especially those with less formal educations, would see their jobs shipped overseas, or find their wages decreased, as others with similar qualifications crowd into their industries looking for employment to replace the jobs they lost to foreign competitors[7] who charge lower prices to produce many items. How many of these predictions have actually come to pass?

Regardless what school of economic thought one subscribes to, one trend is clearly emerging—consumers everywhere are more interested than ever in goods from outside their own countries, while at the same time questioning the wisdom of continuing to send jobs overseas. In the United States, there is a growing movement among consumers to buy "Made in USA" merchandise, as one means to help the job market and improve the overall economy. A current rise in labor costs for some overseas manufacturers means that certain goods will become less economically advantageous to produce in foreign countries, which could also help revive U.S. manufacturing.

That hardly means that international trade will slow down—particularly when it comes to fashion, since consumers around the world are continually looking for the latest products and trends, wherever they may have originated. So we can expect to see global companies continuing to make their way to the U.S. marketplace, both by supplying us with products we desire (Uniqlo, Zara, L'Occitane) and by purchasing companies we think of as irrefutably

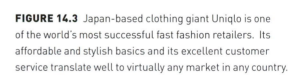

FIGURE 14.3 Japan-based clothing giant Uniqlo is one of the world's most successful fast fashion retailers. Its affordable and stylish basics and its excellent customer service translate well to virtually any market in any country.

American (Barneys New York, Ben & Jerry's, Columbia Pictures). Like it or not, no one disagrees that business is now an international activity conducted in a connected and complicated international environment (Figure 14.3).

UNDERSTANDING AND ACCOMMODATING THE GLOBAL CONSUMER

More and more, companies are incorporating global thinking into the design of their marketing strategies (Figure 14.4). But how does one think globally when accustomed to only "thinking locally"? After all, thought processes are influenced by experiences, and those processes are based on a one-country experience or what's been called a "domestic mind-set."[8]

For marketers, developing a global way of thinking involves closely examining and analyzing the forces at play within the targeted country—physical forces (location, natural resources, climate), financial/economic forces (banking practices, currency stability), sociocultural forces, historic and political forces, labor and production capabilities, and access to technology. Those wishing to successfully compete in the global market must also assess competitive forces, determine the amount of investment required, and gauge the company's ability and willingness to adapt products and marketing strategies to the needs and demands of customers with different orientations.

Obviously, the global marketplace is both large and complex. So, how can a marketer determine where specific opportunities are?

FIGURE 14.4 The opulent BurJuman shopping mall in Dubai is known for its beautiful architecture, stunning décor, and elegant high-end retail shops, designed to appeal to affluent customers from all over the world.

Going "Glocal": How Smart Brands Adapt to Foreign Markets

Imagine walking into McDonald's and ordering a shrimp burger and fragrant tea for dinner instead of a Big Mac and a Coke. Or maybe you prefer KFC. How would you like a Peking duck burger instead of fried chicken and biscuits? Those alternate items certainly wouldn't be on the menu in any of the chains' U.S. restaurants. But the brands, which are as American as apple pie (or Big Macs or buckets of chicken), have expanded their businesses on a global scale—and have done so by understanding that they can only be successful in foreign markets by adapting to local tastes, attitudes, and values . . . hence the shrimp burgers offered in Tokyo and the Peking duck in Shanghai.

It's a concept that Sylvia Vorhauser-Smith, a contributor to *Forbes,* dubs "glocalization." The word may not be in any dictionary (yet!), but the concept of a "hybrid of global and local" certainly has merit, she says, noting, "Ten years ago, we might have seen global and local as the two ends of a dichotomous spectrum, but today we are appreciating that we can be both, we can be glocal."

The reason, according to Vorhauser-Smith, is that despite the enormous globalization that has taken place in recent decades, people still tend to find comfort in the familiarity of their local environment—including the language, the music, the food, the atmosphere of the neighborhood. At the same time, through the reach of television, the Internet, and social media, people are exposed to other cultures far more than ever in the past. A more mobile society means that immigrants bring their customs to new locales, opening shops and restaurants, and giving their new neighbors both the desire and the opportunity to sample some of the unique offerings of cultures other than their own.

As Vorhauser-Smith points out, your own tastes in food are probably "much more diverse than those of your grandparents. Chances are you have traveled abroad to experience a different culture. Chances are your work colleagues come from at least half a dozen different ethnic backgrounds. You're already a glocal!"

So, how does a marketer tap into the glocal qualities of target market and use them successfully? As Vorhauser-Smith says, it requires new skills that reflect cultural awareness, flexibility, and the ability to adjust to behaviors different from one's own. "Studies show that successful cross-cultural leaders can combine general intelligence IQ with emotional intelligence EQ and provide the appropriate context via cultural intelligence CQ," she states. "These are high order, strategic, new-generation abilities that will distinguish real global citizens from those with a one-dimensional mindset."

Source: Sylvia Vorhauser-Smith, "Going 'Glocal': How Smart Brands Adapt To Foreign Markets," *Forbes,* June 22, 2012, http://www.forbes.com/sites/sylviavorhausersmith/2012/06/22/cultural-homogeneity-is-not-an-automatic-by-product-of-globalization/.

CASE IN POINT 14.4
Asia Goes "Cheap Chic"

Attention Chanel, Louis Vuitton, Gucci, and other ultra-high-end retailers. The statistics are in. In China and throughout Asia, luxury brands are taking a backseat to inexpensive fast fashion chains. Known for their cheap and chic fashions (most items are priced at considerably less than $100), retailers such as Uniqlo, Zara, and H&M have been stirring up increasing interest in markets around the world—and now that Chinese consumers have jumped on the bandwagon as well, the growth of fast fashion in Asian countries is outpacing that of luxury for the first time.

This trend comes at a time when Asia is a more significant consumer market in general than it ever was in the past. In fact, according to market research firm Canadean, Asia recently zoomed past the United States to become the world's biggest retail market, with sales that climbed to $3.8 trillion in 2011—a full 41 percent of the global total—from $3.2 trillion (31 percent) just five years earlier.

Until recently in China, the luxury sector had accounted for a large chunk of the boom in consumer purchasing, as wealthy businessmen and government officials eagerly snapped up expensive goods for themselves or as gifts. Now, however, several high-end brands that had enjoyed tremendous success in China have slowed their expansion plans, recognizing that a change is occurring.

What's causing this change? A new and even larger group of shoppers—members of China's growing middle class—want brands that match their more modest budgets. Chen Jing, for instance, a 20-year-old living in Beijing, would be hard-pressed to buy many luxury items on her restaurant salary of 3,000 yuan ($485) a month. But she said she loves to shop frequently for stylish clothes at H&M and Zara.

Also, younger Chinese consumers have more disposable income than their parents did at their age, and are eager to spend it on the latest fashions. As 24-year old Shao Wenbi noted, "We're all looking for what's new. No one wants to look out-of-date." He tends to frequent H&M to find casual outfits or clothing to wear to his job as a market researcher.

The growth of a number of "local" fashion brands based in Japan and Korea is yet another factor contributing to Asia's changing shopping habits. Japan-based Uniqlo, for instance, has been opening two stores a week, on average, throughout Asia, and is now the continent's largest apparel chain. In addition, fueled by a burgeoning global interest in Korean pop culture (think Psy and "Gangnam Style"), a number of brands and clothing retailers from South Korea are expanding in China, Singapore, and throughout Asia.

The end result of all these trends is that apparel sales in China are on a huge upward trajectory. The Boston Consulting Group projects that those sales will exceed 800 billion yuan, or about $130 billion, by 2015, nearly

(continued)

doubling from 460 billion yuan in 2011. The firm also estimates that within the total global fashion market, China alone will account for 30 percent of the growth in the next five years.

Those numbers have other fashion marketers paying serious attention. German sportswear company Adidas, for example, has upped the roster of fashion options it is offering in China, spanning everything from high-heeled sneakers and fur-trimmed leather coats to its lower-end NEO brand skinny jeans and gingham shirts. And Gap Inc. recently announced plans to expand further into the Chinese market, with 35 new Gap stores set to join the 47 already in place. The company was also considering opening Old Navy and Banana Republic stores, recognizing that Chinese consumers are hungry for both global brands and American style.

Source: Mariko Sanchanta and Laurie Burkitt, "Asia Gravitates to Cheap Chic," *The Wall Street Journal*, April 13, 2013, http://online.wsj.com /article/SB10001424127887324874204578438343105661244.html?mod=dist_smartbrief.

Research and experience show that the largest markets for U.S. goods are in countries with the following:

- A sophisticated infrastructure
- A large industrial base
- A stable financial base
- A transportation network

Another positive indicator is that the country is already doing its own importing and exporting of products.

Developing countries present different kinds of opportunities, including specific demand patterns and economic needs that have to be met in accordance with their limited financial resources. However, the marketplace of each nation is fluid, and the possibility exists that interest in fashion goods could develop anywhere. (See Case in Point 14.4.) Therefore, in-depth examination and assessment of a country's market attractiveness is a prerequisite to sound selection of potential trading partners.[9]

Although the ever-changing dynamics of today's marketplace are providing a wealth of exciting opportunities, it's essential for all global marketers to remember that when a company does decide to expand globally, it's not enough to simply transfer to another country a product that's been well received in the home country, no matter how many consumers have responded favorably to it. Although that's certainly a solid reason to begin exploring expansion options, it's not a guarantee of success. As previously stated, the keys to success in the global business world are evaluating the environment (cultural, economic, political) and designing strategies that will connect with people in the host culture. Adaptation is key.

Finally, it's essential that global marketers not only develop global information systems but that they also develop *themselves,* personally, by learning a language other than English and by making genuine efforts to consider non-judgmentally the practices of people from countries with which they're unfamiliar. Traveling abroad can be both educational and helpful in developing personal connections with people from other countries. To successfully reach and service consumers, understanding and addressing both universal and diverse human values and needs is at the core of the process. Only then can marketers begin to create business relationships that truly span the globe.

Today, successful businesspeople have to surmount many challenges, whether marketing products locally or abroad. Demonstrating social responsibility, adhering to quality standards, and supporting fair treatment of workers are just some of the ethical issues that we will address next in Chapter 15.

Summary

Although people from different parts of the world differ in many ways, research and observation have shown that, despite these differences, we are all very interested in goods and services from other countries. Additionally, sharing products and practices tends to foster relationship building and increase acceptance, both of which grow from recognizing our similarities and appreciating our differences.

Whether targeting subcultural groups within the United States or those in foreign countries, consumer behaviorists know that understanding and respecting diverse cultures, lifestyles, and values are key factors in the growth of any business, no matter who the customers are or where they live. Entering any new market requires the assessment of needs, preferences, and potential buying power of that culture prior to expansion. It's also imperative that

marketers consider the meanings of cultural symbols in order to avoid their misuse. Using cultural anthropology as a basis for analysis of preferences can be helpful, as can information from trend forecasting services and research firms that track the needs and wants of diverse market segments.

Globalization efforts must be carefully planned and conducted. As long as accurate information is obtained, trade agreements are understood and enforced, and appropriate marketing strategies are used, the import and export of goods and services can be beneficial and rewarding.

KEY TERMS

Acculturation

Anthropology

Balance of trade

Cultural anthropology

Cultural borrowing

Diversity

Duties

Enculturation

Exports

Globalization

Imports

Means-end chain

Multicultural

Quotas

Tariffs

Trade deficit

Trade surplus

Trend forecasting service

Value system

QUESTIONS FOR REVIEW

1. Define "subculture." How can subcultural differences affect consumer purchases?

2. What is a lifestyle? How are subculture and lifestyle related? Make a list of specific products that could be termed "lifestyle products," and explain your reasons for choosing those products.

3. Explain cultural borrowing and how it might be misinterpreted if used without sufficient research. Discuss the importance of understanding cultural values when using this technique.

4. How can marketers use trend forecasts to meet consumer needs? Give examples that relate to marketing designed goods.

5. Define "globalization." List three specific considerations that should be addressed by any business seeking to introduce a new product to another country.

ACTIVITIES

1. Watch the film *Monsoon Wedding* with a classmate. Discuss how the buying behavior of the bride's father reflects both the Indian culture and the universal desires of fathers of brides everywhere. Submit a written summary of your conclusions.

2. Interview a student from another country. Ask him or her to describe the shopping habits, product preferences, and availability of designed goods in his or her culture. How do they differ from those of Americans? Do the marketing practices also differ? Present your findings in a three- to five-minute report to the class.

3. Choose a group within the United States that practices an alternative lifestyle. Investigate the value system, customs, shopping habits, and product preferences of its members, and discuss your findings with classmates and their implications for marketers.

4. Choose an American product that is currently being sold in another country, and determine how it and/or the accompanying marketing strategies have been modified for the host culture. Discuss possible reasons for the modifications with classmates.

5. The majority of fashion goods in the United States are now made outside of this country. Choose an American apparel designer/manufacturer that has its goods produced overseas. In class, lead a discussion about the fashion industry's reasons for using foreign labor rather than keeping jobs within the United States.

MINI-PROJECTS

1. The North American Free Trade Agreement virtually eliminates tariffs and quotas on imports and exports among Canada, Mexico, and the United States. In a well-organized two- to three-page paper, cite and discuss three ways this agreement is intended to benefit consumers in all three countries and whether or not expectations are being met.

2. Many people in the United States endorse an *increase* in trade barriers such as quotas and tariffs, believing that buying fewer goods from other countries will protect the jobs of U.S. citizens and avoid dependence on foreigners. "Buy American" is the basic premise of this theory, known as *protectionism.* Investigate the origins, strategies, and proposed policies behind protectionism, and in a well-organized two- to three-page paper, discuss how this policy could be beneficial and/or harmful to the United States.

REFERENCES

1. Milton Rokeach. *The Nature of Human Values,* New York: The Free Press, 1973, 10.

2. Marieke K. de Mooij, *Global Marketing and Advertising,* "Values and Marketing," http://www.sagepub.com/upm-data/5314_De_Mooij_chap_5.pdf. accessed 12/12/13

3. Jonathan Gutman. "A Means-End Chain Model Based on Consumer Categorization Processes," *Journal of Marketing* 46, no. 2, Spring 1982.

4. Knowledge@Wharton, Review of Guy Garcia's *The New Mainstream: How the Buying Habits of Ethnic Groups Are Creating a New American Identity,* November 21, 2005, http://knowledge.wharton.upenn.edu/article.cfm?articleid=1270.

5. Kimberly Amadeo. "The U.S. Trade Deficit," updated March 8, 2013, http://useconomy.about.com/od/tradepolicy/p/Trade_Deficit.htm.

6. Milton Friedman and Rose Friedman, "The Case for Free Trade," *Hoover Digest,* October 30, 1997, http://www.hoover.org/publications/hoover-digest/article/7125.

7. Paul Krugman, "Trouble with Trade," The *New York Times,* December 28, 2007.

8. Jean-Pierre Jeannet and H. David Hennessey, *Global Marketing Strategies,* 6th ed. (Boston: Houghton Mifflin Company, 2004), 217–18.

9. Ibid., 267.

ADDITIONAL RESOURCES

Assael, Henry. *Consumer Behavior: A Strategic Approach.* Boston: Houghton Mifflin Company, 2004.

Butler, Sara. "M&S to Contact Workers in Asia by Mobile to Check Factory Conditions." *The Guardian,* September 17, 2013, http://www.theguardian.com/business/2013/sep/17/marks-spencer-factory-workers-asia-mobile.

Chaney, Lillian H., and Jeannette S. Martin. *Intercultural Business Communication,* 3rd ed. Upper Saddle River, NJ: Pearson Prentice Hall, 2004.

Ferraro, Gary P. *The Cultural Dimension of International Business,* 3rd ed. Upper Saddle River, NJ: Prentice Hall, 1990.

Harrell, Gilbert D. *Marketing: Connecting with Customers,* 2nd ed. Upper Saddle River, NJ: Prentice Hall, 2002.

Hoyer, Wayne D., and Deborah J. MacInnis. *Consumer Behavior,* 4th ed. Boston: Houghton Mifflin Company, 2007.

Morse, David. "As People, and as Consumers, Many Asian-Americans Must Balance the Demands of Two Cultures." *Quirks,* June 2008, http://www.quirks.com/articles/2008/20080604.aspx?searchID=623124179&sort=5&pg=1.

Taborda, Joana. "United States Balance of Trade." *U.S. Census Bureau.* September 4, 2013, http://www.tradingeconomics.com/united-states/balance-of-trade.

"The American Style: Culture, Politic, Mentality and Lifestyle," *Just Landed.* January 15, 2009. http://www.justlanded.com/english/USA/USA-Guide/Culture/The-American-style.

Sherwood, Seth. "The Oz of the Middle East." *New York Times,* May 8, 2005.

Weil, Eric. "Study Looks at Habits of African-American Students as Consumers." *Target Market News,* September 8, 2006. http://targetmarketnews.com/storyid07210602.htm.

Wilson, Eric, and Michael Barbaro. "Basic Chic from Japan. But Will It Sell?" *New York Times.* November 10, 2006. http://www.nytimes.com/2006/11/10/business/worldbusiness/10retailhtml?pagewanted=all&_r=0.

Part V
FASHION CONSUMERS AND RESPONSIBLE CITIZENSHIP

JUST like any other industry, the fashion business functions within the greater framework of society, subject to the rules and standards of behavior that govern both individual and corporate entities—some of which are examined in Part V.

How ethical issues shape consumer behavior and fashion buying decisions is explored in Chapter 15, along with a look at some of the ways fashion businesses address their social and environmental responsibilities, often earning customer loyalty at the same time. Chapter 16 describes the role of the government and other organizations in developing laws or programs to help protect consumers of fashion from harm, as well as to help them make more informed purchase decisions.

CHAPTER 15

How Ethics and Social Responsibility Impact Consumer Behavior

WHAT DO I NEED TO KNOW ABOUT THE IMPACT OF ETHICS AND SOCIAL RESPONSIBILITY ON CONSUMER BEHAVIOR?

✔ What the concepts of ethics and social responsibility encompass

✔ How specific ethical and social issues can influence consumer buying decisions

✔ Why consumer theft and counterfeiting affect consumers as well as fashion marketers

✔ Why consumer privacy is a growing ethical issue for businesses and their customers

✔ How fashion marketers incorporate social responsibility into their businesses and why

Imagine what you would do in each of these situations:

- You're browsing in a store's accessories department with two friends and one dares the other to throw a scarf around his neck when no one is looking and walk out without paying for it.
- You're sightseeing with friends in New York City's Chinatown and a smiling woman invites you through a nondescript doorway to show you a Kate Spade bag you can have "very cheap."
- Your best friend is dying to show you the great vintage coat she thinks you should buy at the consignment shop, and when she leads you to the rack, you love the style but see that it's made of real fur.
- You read a news update about a fire that killed a dozen workers in an overseas factory after the owners ignored repeated safety warnings, and learn that your favorite brand of jeans was producing some of its apparel there.
- You notice several friends tweeting about a designer you'd never cared for, mentioning that his brand would be donating $2 million to an environmental cause you hold near and dear.

What do you think you would say or do in each of these situations? How would these situations influence your future behavior? Your responses depend on a number of factors, but the most fundamental of those is your ingrained sense of moral values and principles, which can be powerful forces in consumer behavior.

Defining Ethics

As you've learned throughout this book, many conscious and unconscious factors go into every purchase decision a consumer makes. For a growing number of consumers in the 21st century, those factors include ethical considerations. **Ethics** is a system of moral values, or a set of principles that define right and wrong. In some cases, ethical standards are established for an entire culture or profession; medical ethics, for example, prescribe that physicians shall provide competent medical care, with compassion and respect for human dignity and rights, and shall support access to medical care for all people. Individuals also have their own personal ethical standards, formed by a combination of upbringing, experiences, and beliefs, such as the "golden rule" of treating others as you would want to be treated. Consumers' personal ethics might lead them to reject apparel made out of animal fur, or to bypass a street vendor hawking $30 "Louis Vuitton" bags. Laws are generally based on ethics—for example, in the United States, it is both illegal and unethical to plagiarize someone else's work. Other ethical standards are not actually law, even if they are commonly accepted as being wrong, and may even carry some form of punishment. For instance, most people would agree that it is unethical to cheat on a test, and that act can have consequences specific to a school's set of rules, even though it is not a crime in the eyes of the law.

Going hand in hand with ethics is social responsibility. **Social responsibility** refers to the principle that everyone is responsible for making the world a better place for all its inhabitants. In business, the concept means that companies, for the privilege of conducting their business, should contribute to the welfare of society and not be solely devoted to maximizing profits. When a company provides free child care to its employees, or organizes a recycling program for its used products, it is being socially responsible. On an individual consumer level, social responsibility can take the form of a charitable act, such as donating a still-good winter coat to a homeless shelter to benefit someone less fortunate, or volunteering a weekend to help build a house for Habitat for Humanity. Individual social responsibility also extends to consumers' choice of products, such as the conscious decision to buy clothing made of bamboo—which is renewable and grown in an environmentally friendly way—or to buy goods from a company that donates a portion of its sales to help save the rainforests.

In this chapter, we will explore how ethics and social responsibility come into play in the fashion world, examining the way consumers incorporate these concepts into their buying behavior, as well as the way marketers use them not only to do what's right, but to help influence customer loyalty.

Consumer Theft

One of the most obvious breaches of ethics is stealing; and it is a crime in every country in the world. Yet, as you know, not everyone obeys the law, and **inventory shrinkage**—a term that includes employee theft, shoplifting, vendor fraud, and administrative error—is an enormous problem, costing U.S. retailers more than $35 billion a year, according to an annual survey conducted by the University of Florida. That number represents about 1.4 percent of retailers' total annual sales, with employee theft, known as "pilferage," accounting for the largest losses, or about 44 percent.[1] One of the boldest examples of employee theft in recent years involved a former vice president of product development for Tiffany & Company, who pled guilty to

stealing more than $2.1 million in jewels from her then-employer.

SHOPLIFTING

Shoplifting has actually declined slightly in recent years, and accounts for just over one-quarter of retail losses.[2] Shoplifting is not only a crime, but a consumer behavior that is often not based on need. The action of a desperate Hurricane Katrina victim stealing bread to feed a child is understandable; but what about the celebrity caught shoplifting a mascara from a local CVS? There have been quite a few instances over the years of famous and presumably wealthy people stealing from stores, perhaps simply for the "thrill" of it. Notably, actress Lindsey Lohan added more negative headlines to her resume when she was accused in 2011 of taking a $2,500 necklace from a Venice, California, jewelry shop. Most shoplifting is on a smaller scale, and some people might try to rationalize the theft of a candy bar or lipstick as being inconsequential. But even those "small" crimes contribute to an overall problem that hurts both retailers and other consumers. In an effort to thwart both employee theft and shoplifters, retailers have to spend millions of dollars on security, ranging from uniformed or undercover security guards to often cumbersome security systems, such as bulky plastic tags that have to be removed from apparel and accessories once consumers pay for them (Figure 15.1). That expense gets built into the prices retailers charge consumers for their goods, and even then, since no security system is foolproof, stores may be forced to raise their prices to make up for sales lost to theft—a solution that affects the store's entire customer base.

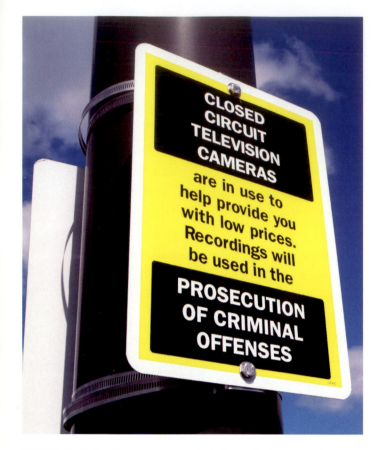

FIGURE 15.1 Retailers employ a variety of security measures to combat theft by both employees and shoplifters.

LET'S TALK

What would you do if you were in a store and noticed someone shoplifting? Would you notify store personnel? Discuss why or why not.

In recent years, a new breed of thieves has compounded the problem. Their crime is called **organized retail theft**, also known as "boosting," and it usually involves multiple shoplifters working together to steal larger quantities of products, which are stolen not for personal use, but to resell through fencing operations (individuals or groups that receive and dispose of stolen goods) or perhaps at flea markets or on the Internet. Industry experts estimate that losses due to organized retail theft cost the United States $30 billion a year, and the problem has grown so significantly in the past decade that retail industry groups, government, and law enforcement are all looking at ways to specifically address the problem. In 2004, retailers formed the National Retail Federation (NRF)/FBI Intelligence Network in an effort to better share information and identify active criminal operations around the country. In addition, legislation passed in 2006 established an Organized Retail Theft Task Force at the FBI. Thanks to the increased law enforcement efforts, several crime rings around the country have been caught and dismantled in recent years, including one in Texas that was responsible for stealing some $10 million in merchandise each year from 2008 to 2012.[3]

FRAUDULENT RETURNS

A related issue involves people who make dishonest returns to stores. Have you ever known someone who bought an expensive dress, wore it to a party or other event with the tags tucked inside, and then returned it to the store as new? Retailers call this practice of returning used merchandise that is not defective "wardrobing," and not only is it unethical, it is just one type of return fraud that costs U.S. retailers nearly $9 billion each year.[4]

Other examples of fraudulent returns include people returning an item to a store using a counterfeit receipt or an altered e-receipt from an online purchase, or shoplifting merchandise and then returning it for cash or store credit. In some cases, individuals sell actual store receipts that have not expired, and the buyers shoplift identical merchandise that they then "return" to the store with the receipt and obtain credit in the form of a gift card. Taking it a step further, some thieves who have obtained store gift cards for fraudulent returns then try to sell the cards online, a tactic that led eBay to begin limiting sellers to one gift card auction per week, with a maximum value per card of $500.

The problem of return fraud has forced many stores to adopt stricter return policies that affect all customers. Because retailers estimate that some 13 percent of returns made without a receipt are fraudulent, nearly three-quarters now require customers returning items with no receipt to show identification. Some, including Victoria's Secret and Bath & Body Works, employ database services to track return patterns and identify customers whose return activity is suspicious. Those customers may then be refused future return privileges. Other stores have shortened the time period during which customers can return goods to the store. REI, for instance, recently placed a one-year limit on returns of its outdoor clothing and gear after years of accepting returned merchandise no matter how long ago it had been purchased.[5] Bloomingdale's has adopted yet another tactic, as you'll see in Case in Point 15.1.

Whether we're talking about outright theft or fraudulent returns, it is difficult to know what combination of internal and external factors and personality traits may motivate a specific individual to commit illegal or unethical acts—and why another person surrounded by similar influences chooses to act in a more ethical manner.

Counterfeiting

When you hear the word "counterfeit," your first thought may be of fake $20 bills. But counterfeiting is actually a much larger issue—and one that today represents a sophisticated, worldwide operation costing the global economy as much as $250 billion a year.[6] We're talking about **counterfeit goods,** unauthorized copies of designer or branded products designed to mimic the authentic goods (down to the detailing, logo, and even the label). Their appeal to consumers is clearly that they look like the real thing, yet are sold for only a fraction of the price of the original. While apparel and fashion accessories make up the largest category of products being targeted by counterfeiters, it's important to note that counterfeit apparel is not the same as apparel knockoffs, which do not pretend to be an original brand and which are considered an integral part of the fashion life cycle (see Chapter 12). Popular jeans and sports jerseys are among the most common counterfeit clothing items seized by U.S. authorities, valued at nearly $15 million in one recent year. Shoes rank even higher, with more than $25 million worth of counterfeit seizures that same year; and while they used to comprise mostly athletic footwear, the fake shoes now include popular brands like Ugg and luxury brands like Christian Louboutin and Jimmy Choo. In addition to mimicking the style down to the smallest detail (like the Louboutin signature red sole), a clever counterfeit will include a replica shoebox, dust bag, and even minor

Retailers Change Tactics to Combat "Wardrobing"

Until businesses like Rent the Runway came along a few years ago, there was no legitimate way for fashionistas of limited means to wear a fancy frock to a gala event and then return the dress afterward. But that didn't stop some consumers from trying. High-end retailers have long been plagued with the problem of wardrobing, where customers purchase a pricey dress for a special occasion and then return it to the store the next day—without admitting it was worn, of course. And while retailers are well within their rights to refuse a return, some feel the risk of alienating a loyal customer is not worth it, so they bite the bullet and offer the refund. Says Richard Mellor, vice president of loss prevention at the National Retail Federation, "It is a delicate balance of loss prevention and good customer service, and the relationship has to be handled with appropriate finesse."

Clearly, it's a tricky situation. But because of an uptick of wardrobing activity in recent years, many merchants have decided it's time to take a firmer stance regarding the practice. Among them: Bloomingdale's and Nordstrom.

In early 2013, Bloomingdale's started placing three-inch black plastic tags, nicknamed "b-tags," on dresses that cost more than $150. The tags, along with a paper tag explaining the devices' purpose and how to remove them, are placed conspicuously—such as in the front along the hemline—to make it impossible for the dress to be worn in public without the tag being seen. Store associates are tasked with explaining to consumers that they can take the garment home without removing the tag, until they're sure they want to keep it; and shoppers on the Bloomingdale's website are alerted to the presence of the tag on a dress's product page details, so they aren't taken by surprise when the order arrives. After that, once the tag is snapped off, the apparel cannot be returned.

Taking a more subtle tack is Nordstrom, which is not using chunky plastic anti-wardrobing devices but instead is affixing silver-colored paper tags under the arm or sleeve of its expensive special-occasion dresses. The tags must still be attached to a dress in order for it to be returned.

After Bloomingdale's began using the black tags, some complaints quickly began to appear on social media—such as one Twitter user who said the tags tore some items when she removed them at home—and other retailers will surely be paying close attention to how the policy plays out. But Bloomies stood by the tags' use, saying they reinforce that the company "will be unable to accept return merchandise that has been worn, washed, damaged, used, and/or altered." And noted one retail consultant, "They [Bloomingdale's] are going to alienate customers that abuse the policy. And I don't think that is so bad."

Sources: Cotton Timberlake, "Don't Even Think about Returning that Dress," *Businessweek*, September 26, 2013, http://www.businessweek.com/articles/2013-09-26/return-fraud-clothing-and-electronics-retailers-fight-back; Cotten Timberlake and Renee Dudley, "Bloomingdale's Black Tags End Party for Next-Day Returns," *Bloomberg Businessweek*, September 17, 2013, www.businessweek.com/news/2013-09-17/bloomingdale-s-black-tags-end-party-for-next-day-returns; Eun Kyung Kim, "Bloomingdale's New B-tags Block Used Clothing Returns," *Today*, September 19, 2013, http://www.today.com/money/bloomingdales-new-b-tags-block-used-clothing-returns-4B11199683.

FIGURE 15.2 Street vendors are one potential source of counterfeit goods, but even reputable retailers have been accused of selling fakes.

Table 15.1a Top Nine Counterfeited Products in the US in 2013

1. Handbags/wallets
2. Watches/jewelry
3. Consumer electronics/parts
4. Wearing apparel/accessories
5. Pharmaceuticals/personal care
6. Footwear
7. Computers/accessories
8. Labels/tags
9. Optical media

*based on retail value of seizures by U.S. Customs and Border Protection

Source: 24/7 Wall St.

Table 15.1b Some of the Most Frequently Counterfeited Fashion Brands

1. Louis Vuitton	6. Adidas
2. Christian Louboutin	7. Gucci
3. Tiffany	8. Uggs
4. Rolex	9. Chanel
5. Nike	10. Coach

Source: CocoKouture.com

packaging details like the little moisture-absorbing micro-tech insert. Perfume, watches, and handbags (Figure 15.2) are other products found on lists of most counterfeited fashion goods.[7] (See Table 15.1.)

Selling counterfeit merchandise is against the law; and while it is not illegal to purchase fake goods, it is unethical to knowingly do so. In some cases, consumers may truly believe (or want to believe) that they've found an exceptional deal on a normally high-priced item. (Point of View 15.1 describes how to spot a fake product.) In other cases, they may be aware that they're buying a counterfeit but other motivations (social acceptance, limited finances, need for self-esteem, and others) override ethical considerations.

Because counterfeiting has become such a huge issue in the marketplace—worldwide, the manufacture and sale of fake goods is estimated to be a $650 billion-a-year industry—businesses are taking unprecedented steps to combat it. Brands such as Fendi, Gucci, Yves Saint Laurent, and Bottega Veneta sew holograms into the lining of their handbags, boots, and even mink coats, with encrypted codes that allow police and customs officials to authenticate the products with a special magnifying

How to Spot a Fake

OK, so it's not illegal to knowingly buy a counterfeit Rolex watch or Coach handbag . . . and those companies have tons of money anyway, so what can it hurt? Well, for one thing, it might be hurting women or children somewhere in the world who are working in unsafe conditions, being paid next to nothing, to churn out the fake goods.

If that argument gives you pause, your next question might be: How can I tell if I'm buying a fake? It's actually pretty simple if you follow these tips from the International AntiCounterfeiting Coalition.

Does the price seem too good to be true? It helps to be familiar with the normal price range for a product you're considering, and if the vendor is selling it for a fraction of what you know it should be, chances are it's not the real deal.

Is this the type of retail venue where the product would normally be sold? It's a safe bet that brands you would find in high-end department stores or designer boutiques are not going to expand their distribution to street vendors in New York's Chinatown or Los Angeles' Santee Alley.

Does the product, labeling, and packaging look the way it should? If the seller wants to attach a designer label or brand logo to the product, or you notice that "Calvin Klein" is spelled "Calvin Kline," you'd do best to walk away.

Source: The International AntiCounterfeiting Coalition.

---

device.[8] Some companies hire private investigators to track down counterfeit merchandise and the people making or selling it. A number of well-known brands have also taken successful legal action to stop copy-cats, such as:

- Versace SpA was awarded $20 million in damages for counterfeiting and trademark violations in a case against 72 retail stores in Southern California and Arizona that were selling counterfeit products including Versace, Gianni Versace, Versace Jeans Couture, and V2.[9]

- Coach Inc. was awarded a $257 million judgment in a lawsuit against 573 online vendors that were selling counterfeit merchandise with the Coach trademark.[10]

- LVMH Moet Hennessy Louis Vuitton settled a lawsuit against Walmart for selling counterfeit Fendi brand bags and wallets in its Sam's Club stores.[11] The giant retailer had previously settled similar lawsuits brought against it by Tommy Hilfiger, Nike, Nautica, Polo, and the Fubu group at Inter Parfums.[12]

In addition to businesses' efforts to fight back against counterfeiters, government and law enforcement are playing a stronger role by passing tougher laws and cracking down on sellers, shippers, and even landlords who rent to businesses marketing fake goods. For example, as part of an operation dubbed Project Copy Cat, federal law enforcement agencies recently seized 70 websites that were illegally selling counterfeit merchandise ranging from baby carriers and professional sports jerseys to jewelry and luxury goods. All the sites closely mimicked legitimate websites selling authentic merchandise, duping consumers into unknowingly buying counterfeit goods.[13] (See Chapter 16 for more on the role of government.)

The concern regarding counterfeiting is not only that the legitimate companies stand to lose business and sales, but also that manufacturers of counterfeit products do not pay taxes, which hurts the economy for everyone, and they likely do not pay fair wages or benefits to workers, who might even be children if the goods originate in countries without strict labor laws. Designers and manufacturers hope that by making the public more aware of all those factors, consumers will choose to act ethically and pass up the next "great deal" they see on a branded or designer product, thereby making it less profitable for counterfeiters to stay in business.

Let's Talk

Have you ever bought something you knew was a counterfeit? Knowing all the negative effects that counterfeits have on legitimate businesses and the economy, would you buy one in the future? Why might you discourage a friend from buying one? Discuss your reasons.

Business Ethics

While counterfeiting is a clear-cut violation of the law, there are many decisions that legitimate businesses make every day that involve ethical considerations. In some cases, making a decision that is unethical leads to committing an illegal act. News headlines in the early 2000s were dominated by ethics scandals at corporate giants Enron, Tyco, and Adelphia, to name some of the most prominent, in which business and accounting rules were bent and/or broken, resulting in enormous losses for the companies' employees and shareholders, as well as prison terms for key executives involved in the criminal actions. A few years later, the actions and activities of a number of major banks and financial institutions were considered responsible for the economic crisis and recession that dealt an enormous blow to the job market, the housing market, and virtually all areas of the economy around the world. Yet, for the most part, those actions did not lead to prosecutions, despite the fact that most of the general public felt that ethical, and perhaps legal, boundaries had been crossed. In other words, the line between unethical and illegal is not always clearly defined, and company executives must often rely on their own sense of right and wrong to reach a decision.

Sometimes, listening to customers can help a business determine the best course of action, particularly when dealing with an issue about which consumers feel strongly and make their opinions known. Monitoring comments and feedback on social media (see Chapter 11) makes it much easier than in the past for marketers to keep a finger on the pulse of what customers are thinking, and by extension, to adjust their strategies to meet customer expectations. The penalty for ignoring customers' opinion in matters of ethics may well be the loss of their business and loyalty. A recent study on global corporate social responsibility found that 91 percent of respondents believe companies must go beyond the minimum standards required by law to operate responsibly—and 90 percent of consumers would stop buying a company's products if they learned that company had engaged in irresponsible or deceptive business practices.[14] Let's examine a few of the ethical areas that affect the fashion industry.

CONSUMER PRIVACY

Consumers have always viewed certain personal information—for example, their tax returns and medical records—as being private. With modern technology, however, those and other personal records are no longer primarily stored on paper in a filing cabinet, but instead are recorded digitally on computers and other electronic media that are potentially vulnerable to theft or to hacking (unauthorized computer access). In recent years, prominent retailers including Target and Michaels had their data security breached, and private information of tens of millions of customers was compromised. If key information, such as a person's social security number, falls into the wrong hands, it can lead to identity theft, in which a criminal obtains credit and spends sometimes massive amounts of money using another person's identity, leaving the innocent person responsible for clearing his or her name. As a result, protecting consumers' privacy has become a serious ethical issue

for marketers who gather and retain customers' personal data.

For example, like many consumers, you may belong to one or more retail **loyalty programs,** which offer a reward or an incentive to keep shoppers returning to the store. One of the most common forms of loyalty programs is the "frequent shopper card" that enables you to get discounted prices at your local supermarket or drugstore. Other retailers may use their store credit card as a "reward" card, tracking the dollar amount of your purchases and offering special sale prices, exclusive sale days, and other perks to keep you coming back to their store (Figure 15.3).

While loyalty programs offer benefits for consumers, they also benefit retailers, enabling them to collect purchasing information that can help them

FIGURE 15.3 Store credit cards provide benefits to consumers through their loyalty programs, but they also gather personal information that raises privacy issues.

identify trends and fine-tune their merchandise assortment. In some cases, retailers use knowledge of a customer's previous purchases in order to personalize offers with other products that the store thinks might be of interest to that consumer. (The concept of marketing customization was introduced in Chapter 2.) While receiving personalized messages about products targeting their needs can be useful, some consumers fear that the amount of information retailers gather about them could become intrusive or be misused; or they worry that the retailer might sell the information to another company that in turn might misuse it or not keep it safe. One study found that the information shoppers find most acceptable to give retailers includes their name (89.8 percent), e-mail address (78.1 percent), and street address (60.7 percent). Less than half (46.8 percent) found it acceptable for retailers to collect information on past transactions.[15]

Online activity, whether it's shopping or social networking, raises additional privacy issues and concerns. With the rapid growth of e-commerce, online marketers looked for ways to better understand and serve customers in cyberspace, and began using cookies to record and store information about consumers who visited their site. As discussed in Chapter 10, cookies are tiny pieces of software that websites download onto consumers' computers so they can document how often consumers visit their site, what they look at or buy, and, with the development of tracking cookies, what they do before and after visiting the site. Some sites, including social media sites, require users to register with certain personal information and then log in with a password each time they return, as a way of authenticating the user's identity but also to enable better

tracking. Because of privacy concerns, however—and particularly after revelations that the federal government's National Security Administration was engaged in widespread monitoring of Internet activity—more consumers started deleting cookies stored on their computer, or blocking cookies from being installed to begin with, making them less useful for marketers. While still widely used, cookies may be replaced in coming years by other, more sophisticated methods that are already being developed, deployed, and improved upon, such as authenticated tracking, browser fingerprinting, cross-device tracking, and others.[16] Some of these newer methods have the added benefit for marketers of being able to glean information from consumers' mobile devices, which cookies cannot. Whatever technologies are implemented, it seems certain that there will be new or continuing concerns regarding how much or how little they protect consumers' privacy when using a digital device. (See Point of View 15.2.)

There are also privacy concerns that surround the growing use of RFID (radio-frequency identification) tags on merchandise. Considered a boon to manufacturers and retailers, the inexpensive chips, which are often smaller than a grain of sand, can be embedded in virtually any merchandise—from a piece of apparel to a pack of gum—and read by a wireless device from several yards away, providing a cost-effective way to automate inventory levels and track merchandise all the way from factory to store checkout. But because each chip has a unique ID code, some people worry that they could also be used to track consumers themselves as they carry or wear products with embedded chips. That is an ethical issue that privacy watchdogs and some

Connecting the Dots on Consumers' Private Data

Smartphones are remarkable devices that offer consumers communication, entertainment, and information, at any time and in (almost) any place. But what you might not think about when you're sending a text, making a call, or using an app is the fact that your smartphone contains a lot of information about *you*—such as where you are at any given time, what you've searched for online, what you may have bought . . . information that advertisers and tech companies like Google and Facebook would just love to be able to tap into. Why? Because just as they use cookies to follow people with tracking ads as they browse various websites, these companies are eager to translate that capability to the mobile universe, and to be able to reach smartphone users with the same type of personalized, ultra-targeted advertising that's used online.

The challenge up to now has been that cookies don't work on mobile devices. But leave it to the wizards of technology at a number of start-up companies, including one called Drawbridge, to find another solution—and even more significantly, one that uses complex statistical algorithms in order to link various unconnected devices to one user. Previously, there was no way to determine that a single consumer was using a particular home computer, work computer, cell phone, and tablet if those devices were not digitally connected. With the Drawbridge technology, however, a user's behavior can be triangulated among devices using anonymous, relatively non-invasive data, such as the browser client, site accessed, and time stamp; then a "bridging" algorithm assesses the probability of two different devices being associated with the same person. When a specified level of probability is reached, the company calls it a match.

More than 1.5 billion devices have been linked in this way by Drawbridge. So what does that really mean? It could mean that if Ted browses a retail website one evening on his laptop at home, he might see an ad for that retailer on his smartphone the next day on the train to work. Or if Felice uses her lunch break to research a vacation in Puerto Rico on her work computer, an ad for a resort in San Juan might pop up on her tablet that evening. What's more, the technology pinpoints users so accurately that it could actually show different, personalized ads to two different family members on a single tablet they share.

This advanced technology could be the beginning of a whole new era for customized marketing; but it could also be ushering in a slew of new privacy concerns. Privacy advocates have already expressed concern that consumers do not have a clue about the extent of their private information

(continued)

residing on their phone, or how vulnerable it might be when they perform even everyday functions like downloading and using apps. Drawbridge is quick to point out that it is not using direct tracking or geolocation tools, which could set off all kinds of privacy alarm bells. But others are skeptical that personal information will remain truly anonymous—and the debate over this and other aspects of digital privacy will likely continue for many years to come.

Sources: Claire Cain Miller and Somini Sengupta, "Selling Secrets of Phone Users to Advertisers," *New York Times*, October 5, 2013; "Tracking Adverts Set to Jump across Gadgets," BBC, December 7, 2012, http://www.bbc.co.uk/news/technology-20638132; and Jessica Leber, "Get Ready for Ads that Follow You from One Device to the Next," *Technology Review*, December 5, 2012, http://www.technologyreview.com/news/508176/get-ready-for-ads-that-follow-you-from-one-device-to-the-next/.

lawmakers are urging industry to address as use of RFID tags becomes more widespread. Already, amusement parks have begun using RFID tags to help lost children get back to their parents, and marathon runners can wear RFID-equipped bracelets so friends and relatives can follow their progress in a race, among other applications of the technology.[17]

ETHICAL ADVERTISING

Advertising is a critical tool by which fashion marketers communicate with their target customers, but there are aspects of advertising that can raise questions of ethics. One of the most basic is the long-standing question of whether advertisers try to create a need where none exists. In the fashion world, one could argue that clothes generally do not wear out after one season, and therefore trying to convince consumers that they need to buy a new wardrobe that reflects the newest styles could

be considered unethical. Today's consumers, however, have grown up surrounded by advertising and, for the most part, understand its intent; in general, they are not easily manipulated by an ad's pitch. In addition, advertisers who make outright false or misleading claims are subject to prosecution under the truth in advertising laws enforced by the Federal Trade Commission (FTC). (See Chapter 16.)

Of greater concern to some consumers is the content of certain advertising. Obviously, the purpose of advertising is to get a product or brand noticed. But what if it is attracting attention by featuring scantily clad models (Figure 15.4), subtle or not-so-subtle sexual innuendoes, or other elements that push the envelope of good taste? Because marketers are competing for consumers' attention amid an increasing array of media and messages, they may sometimes use questionable taste to try to break through the "clutter." What's more, since taste is subjective, advertising content that one audience

FIGURE 15.4 Victoria's Secret has pushed the boundaries with its sexy ads, which entice some consumers but may offend others.

even from those who like the clothing, the company did not change its risqué ad strategy.

There are occasions when advertisers themselves take the initiative to counteract what some consider objectionable content or images, as Dove did when it began using "real" women with real-life shapes in ad campaigns for its body-care products. (See Chapter 6, Case in Point 6.1.) At other times, if an ad is offensive to enough people, it can cause a consumer backlash against the company. That is especially true if the advertising is directed at children or teenagers. A Macy's store in Portland, Oregon, for example, came under fire for a back-to-school ad that featured T-shirts emblazoned with "Beer Pong" and other beer-related slogans on display in the store's teen section. After complaints from a local substance-abuse prevention group and a TV news report spotlighting the controversy, Macy's removed the shirts from all its stores across the country.[19]

finds acceptable may be offensive to another audience. Some fans of American Apparel's hip clothing, for example, may enjoy the company's racy ads, while others might find them sexist and in bad taste. Two recent ads (one picturing a woman in nothing but an oversized sweater, lounging with her legs in the air) were actually banned by the British Advertising Standards Authority, based on at least one complaint it received about the ads being "overtly sexual." American Apparel decided to post the ads on Facebook and Twitter and ask its followers what they thought[18]—perhaps more as a way to stir up buzz than to actually gain insight for future ads, since despite a good number of negative comments,

FUR AND ANIMAL TESTING

One of the most emotional topics for those discussing ethics in fashion involves the use of animal fur in apparel. People who oppose cruelty to animals believe that using fur in clothing and accessories is both unethical and immoral; some particularly aggressive anti-fur activists have been known to throw red paint (symbolizing blood) on women wearing fur coats, although the ethics of such behavior could certainly themselves be called questionable. Less violent protests have been organized by various groups, notably People for the Ethical Treatment of Animals (PETA), a global animal rights group, which often enlists celebrities to help raise the visibility of the anti-fur message. Among those who have appeared in PETA ads are actors Charlize Theron, Jamie Bamber, and Alyssa Milano, and Olympic gold medalist Amanda Beard; actress Pamela Anderson even stripped down to a G-string in a London shop window on behalf of PETA, under a banner that read "Rather bare skin than wear skin."[20] In 2013, West Hollywood, California, became the first city in the United States to actually ban the sale of fur used in wearing apparel, although some small retailers were fighting the ban.

Because many consumers oppose the use of fur in fashion, and because there are many alternatives, including high-quality fake fur, a growing number of designers and apparel marketers have made the decision not to use real fur in their lines or sell it in their stores. Among them are J. Crew, Stella McCartney, Polo Ralph Lauren, Calvin Klein, Tommy Hilfiger, Ann Taylor, Uniqlo, and many more. Others, however, continue to incorporate fur into their apparel (Figure 15.5). One of those is Carolina Herrera, whose fall and winter 2013 collection featured a variety of pieces using fur, some of it dyed in deep violet and rich green hues.[21]

FIGURE 15.5 Some designers and apparel manufacturers still use real fur in their lines, despite the fact that many consumers find it unethical.

LET'S TALK

Do you think that Carolina Herrera incorporated fur into her collection because she thought it worked best for her design concepts or because she thought her customers would want to buy it—or both? Do you think she did marketing research first to gauge customer opinion on the topic? Why or why not?

A related ethical issue involves the use of animals in testing the safety of cosmetics and cosmetics ingredients. Many consumers believe it is wrong to deliberately harm animals in the development of new beauty and personal care products, and go out of their way to purchase from companies that maintain a no-animal-testing policy. Some individuals or groups even **boycott** companies that test on animals; that is, consumers make the conscious decision not to purchase any of the companies' products as a protest and moral statement.

A growing number of beauty companies have listened to consumers' views and tailor their marketing message to that audience by promoting their products as "not tested on animals." The Leaping Bunny program of the Coalition for Consumer Information on Cosmetics, a group of animal-protection organizations that encourages consumers to purchase non-animal-tested products, has developed a cruelty-free standard for companies producing cosmetic, personal care, and household products. Its website, leapingbunny.org, also offers a list of companies that comply with the standard (such as Burt's Bees, The Body Shop, and Kiss My Face), helping consumers find and choose products from manufacturers that share their belief. Consumers in Europe seeking cruelty-free cosmetics have it even easier: As of 2013, the use of animal testing for personal products was banned by the European Union for all member countries.

LABOR PRACTICES

Over the past several decades, American manufacturers—including fashion companies—have moved an increasing proportion of their production to countries where it costs less to manufacture the goods. In some cases, those countries may not have or enforce laws to protect workers from unsafe conditions or to ensure they are paid a living wage. Such workplaces are often referred to as **sweatshops,** or factories where workers are obliged to work long hours, under poor conditions, for very little pay. Most Americans probably think of such factories as strictly a third-world problem and a long-gone relic of the 19th and early 20th centuries in their own country. But in fact, despite

numerous labor laws, the prevalence of sweatshops in the United States has been growing since the 1970s, according to *Slaves to Fashion* author Robert Ross, who estimates that there were still some 255,000 workers toiling in U.S. sweatshops in 2000, primarily in New York City, Texas, and California.[22] Between 2008 and 2012, the U.S. Department of Labor investigated more than 1,500 garment industry employers in Los Angeles, San Diego, and surrounding areas, and found labor law violations, primarily involving wages, in 93 percent of the cases; most of the workers involved were Latin American and Asian immigrants.[23]

Examples of poor working conditions in the United States persist despite the fact that less than 20 years ago, actress and TV celebrity Kathie Lee Gifford made front-page news when it was discovered that her Kathie Lee clothing line, sold by Walmart, was made by sweatshop workers in Honduras and in New York City. The publicity from this case did help raise awareness of the prevalence of sweatshops and harsh working conditions in the global fashion industry, which in turn led to public pressure on companies to verify that the products they sell have been manufactured according to ethical labor practices, wherever in the world they are produced. Some companies are actively addressing the issue. In 2004, the Fair Factories Clearinghouse (FFC) was formed through a partnership of Reebok International Ltd., the National Retail Federation, Retail Council of Canada, and World Monitors Inc., with the mission of creating a global database of information on factories and workplace conditions. The information can be easily shared among members—which include Burberry, Cole Hahn, L.L. Bean, Levi's, Nike, and many more—enabling manufacturers and retailers to make informed decisions as they source (find suppliers for) merchandise and to improve factory workplace conditions around the world.[24]

The problem is hardly solved, however, and the issue of safe working conditions leapt to the forefront again in 2013, when an eight-story factory complex in Bangladesh collapsed, killing more than 1,100 workers in one of the world's worst industrial accidents. A fire in another Bangladesh factory six months earlier killed more than 100 workers. The workers who died in the collapse were reportedly earning only $38 a month, and were producing clothing for American and European marketers. Among the U.S. companies known to have used factories in Bangladesh (although not necessarily at the time) include Walmart, JCPenney, Benetton, Children's Place, Dress Barn, and the Walt Disney Company. The tragedy quickly led to heightened efforts to improve and ensure safe working conditions, with European companies banding together to take action, and a separate alliance of nearly 20 North American retailers (including Walmart, Gap, Target, and Macy's) creating a five-year safety plan for Bangladesh garment factories. The plan committed $42 million for worker safety, including inspecting every factory within a year, along with more than $100 million in loans and other financing to help owners of Bangladeshi facilities correct safety problems.[25]

The movement toward ethical labor practices has also spread to other companies in the apparel industry. For example, manufacturers including Nike and Tommy Hilfiger have formalized codes of conduct for their factories, prohibiting child labor and requiring that legal minimum wages be paid.[26] Walmart increased its inspections of thousands of foreign factories from which it buys clothes, shoes, toys, and other products, although critics maintained that the chain was still not doing enough;[27] in fact, the retailer has been fined for repeat violations of workplace safety and health standards at some of its U.S. stores.[28] Yet other companies have been founded specifically for the purpose of creating apparel according to **fair-trade practices,** or standards for working conditions, environmental responsibility, and fair pricing that are based not only on ethical labor practices but also on the intent to provide opportunity to disadvantaged workers and help alleviate poverty.[29] Originally limited to commodities such as coffee, tea, fruits, and cotton, the concept of fair trade has gotten a strong toehold in the clothing marketplace, some of it inspired by U2 lead singer and activist, Bono. In 2005, Bono introduced Edun, a fair-trade line of apparel made from organic materials, which has been sold through high-end stores including Saks and Nordstrom (Figure 15.6). More recently, a group of former Lands' End executives launched Fair Indigo, offering its own line of fair-trade apparel.[30] The selection is designed for mainstream consumers and includes men's and women's apparel, as well as accessories, jewelry, and gift items.

SOCIAL ISSUES

Anyone who reads or watches the news cannot help but be aware of challenges that affect the entire planet, from environmental issues such as climate change and dependency on fossil fuels, to societal issues such as poverty and disease. Individuals and companies that work to address some of those challenges—whether or not the hardships directly

FIGURE 15.6 A growing fair-trade movement has spawned new apparel companies, such as Edun, that operate with ethical labor practices and use organic materials in their clothing.

affect them—are taking social responsibility and acting in an ethical manner. While many actions on the part of businesses come from a true sense of wanting to "do good," for marketers it can also make good business sense: According to the same global study on corporate social responsibility mentioned earlier in this chapter, 91 percent of consumers, if offered comparable price and quality, would switch brands to one associated with a good cause. The study also found that 92 percent of consumers would buy a product with a social or environmental benefit if given the opportunity, and 84 percent would tell their friends and family about a company's corporate social responsibility efforts.[31] (See Figure 15.7 for other data from the study.)

ENVIRONMENT

Some people consider protecting and preserving the environment to be one of the most serious issues of our time. Countless scientific studies have demonstrated the toll that modern human activities are taking on the earth and its atmosphere, and an increasing number of people are looking for ways to lessen their own impact on the environment. As a result, numerous companies in the fashion industry have been exploring ways of doing business that are more environmentally friendly.

For example, Timberland, the outdoor clothing manufacturer, has long been committed to lessening the environmental impact of its manufacturing, including efforts to reduce its use of harmful chemicals and increase its use of more-sustainable natural resources. More than a decade ago, the company began exploring ways to reduce its carbon emissions and developed a multifaceted plan that included building a wind farm in the Dominican Republic, installing solar panels at one of its distribution centers in California, and purchasing power generated by renewable resources. By 2006, the company had cut its emission of greenhouse gases by 17 percent;[32] and in 2009, it shrank the carbon footprint of its U.S. stores another 11 percent by switching more than two thirds of its North American stores to LED lighting.[33] Among the company's other environmental initiatives, it pioneered eco-labels on its apparel, modeling

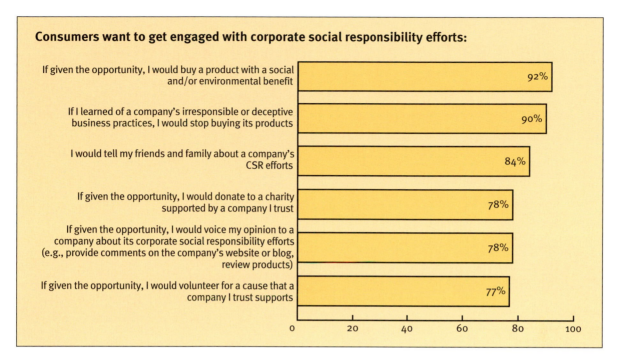

Consumers want to get engaged with corporate social responsibility efforts:

Statement	Percentage
If given the opportunity, I would buy a product with a social and/or environmental benefit	92%
If I learned of a company's irresponsible or deceptive business practices, I would stop buying its products	90%
I would tell my friends and family about a company's CSR efforts	84%
If given the opportunity, I would donate to a charity supported by a company I trust	78%
If given the opportunity, I would voice my opinion to a company about its corporate social responsibility efforts (e.g., provide comments on the company's website or blog, review products)	78%
If given the opportunity, I would volunteer for a cause that a company I trust supports	77%

FIGURE 15.7 How important is corporate social responsibility to consumers?

Source: Cone Communications/Echo, 2013 Global CSR Study

them after nutrition labels on food packaging and giving consumers a way to instantly measure a potential purchase for its level of climate impact, resource consumption, and eco-conscious materials.[34]

Companies across the spectrum of fashion industries have joined the "green" movement—not only to demonstrate concern for the environment, but also because they recognize that it's good business. In addition to the potential cost savings they can gain from reducing the materials and energy their operations consume, marketers stand to benefit from increased sales and customer loyalty, since consumers who feel strongly about doing their part tend to seek out products that they feel do the least harm to the planet. As a result, recent years have seen manufacturers and retailers implement programs ranging from printing catalogs and other materials on recycled paper to reducing excess packaging, converting facilities to wind and solar energy, cutting pollution by eliminating vehicle idling, and more (Figure 15.8). Providing a showcase example of environmental commitment is Destiny USA, a super-regional shopping center in Syracuse, New York, built on a former landfill on Lake Onondaga. Not only did the developers take responsibility for clearing oil tanks and other environmental clean-up, but in a recent expansion of the mall, they worked in cooperation with the United States Green Building Council to earn its Leadership in Energy and Environmental Design (LEED) certification, becoming the largest LEED Gold Certified commercial retail structure in the United States and third largest in the world. Retail tenants are also required to adhere to LEED specifications in areas including

Here Comes the Sun—and It's Lighting Up Retail Stores

Shop in almost any retail store today and you're sure to see environmentally friendly merchandise—maybe T-shirts made with organic cotton, furniture made from recycled plastic or reclaimed wood, or hairbrushes with handles fashioned out of highly renewable bamboo. But going beyond the products being sold, U.S. retailers, and particularly large chain stores, are leading the environmental charge in even more critical ways.

Whether it's installing solar panels on the roof or a wind turbine in the parking lot, big-box retailers are going green to save green—and to help save the planet while they're at it. Said Rhone Resch, chief executive of the Solar Energy Industries Association and the Vote Solar Initiative, "Five or six years ago, you probably would have read about a pledge in an annual report about what they're doing for the environment. Now what you're seeing is it's a smart investment that they're making for their shareholders, and this is a standard business practice."

Whatever their motivation, major retailers are seeing the (sun)light: Nearly half of the top 20 commercial solar power customers are retail chains. And those retailers are exploring other forms of renewable energy, as well. For example:

- Drugstore chain Walgreens had installed 134 solar systems across the country by mid-2012, with plans for many more.
- IKEA planned to have solar arrays on virtually all its furniture stores and distribution centers by the end of 2012, and also incorporated a geothermal power system at a new store it built in Colorado.
- Kohl's already had more than 150 solar locations by the end of 2012, and was also testing wind energy, along with adding more electric vehicle charging stations at its stores.
- And Walmart was on track to have 1,000 solar installations in place by 2020, while also testing out wind power. Not only did the giant retailer install a huge one-megawatt wind turbine at a distribution center in California, but it has also placed smaller wind turbines on the tops of lamp posts in some of its stores' parking lots.

Source: Diane Cardwell, "Chain Stores Said to Lead Firms in Use of Sun Power," *New York Times*, September 12, 2012.

FIGURE 15.8 Many fashion retailers and manufacturers are addressing environmental issues through the use of renewable energy and other initiatives.

energy efficiency, water efficiency, improved indoor air quality, and construction material initiatives.[35]

LET'S TALK

Have you noticed changes in environmental awareness in any of the retailers you regularly shop or brands you regularly buy—such as stores offering reusable cloth bags or manufacturers reducing their excess packaging? Would changes such as these influence your shopping decisions? Why or why not?

Concern for the environment also extends to fashion products themselves, as an increasing number of consumers choose products that they know are made in an eco-friendly manner. Manufacturers and designers are meeting that demand with apparel made from a variety of sustainable and environmentally sound fabrics, such as organic cotton, soy, corn, and bamboo, and even material made from "repurposed" (recycled) fur, leather, and denim or blended of cotton and recycled plastic soda bottles.

Organic fiber sales in the United States have been growing by double digits in recent years, to over $708 million, according to the Organic Trade Association.[36] Organic cotton, which is grown using no chemical fertilizers, pesticides, or herbicides, is one of the fastest-growing eco-friendly fabrics. Jeans maker Levi's began offering organic cotton versions of its most popular styles in 2006; and organic cotton's use in home textiles has also blossomed, with companies including Welspun and Anna Sova Luxury Organics creating towels, sheets, and blankets from the fabric. Bamboo is also increasingly finding its way into apparel and home textiles products, and is appreciated for the fact that it is highly renewable, can grow a foot or more in a day, and can grow to heights of 80 or 90 feet, making its fiber plentiful. Soy is another renewable fabric source that is increasing in importance in fashion. The company 2(x)ist even offers a line of soybean fiber blend men's underwear, T-shirts, and socks.

CAUSES AND CHARITABLE GIVING

In addition to concern for the environment, social responsibility can encompass a wide variety of direct actions to help people who are sick, hungry,

Patagonia Ups the Ante on Social Responsibility

It's a bold move for an apparel company to encourage consumers not to buy so many clothes—but that's exactly what Patagonia has been doing for a couple of years now. It began with a pre-holidays full page ad in the *New York Times* in 2011 that proclaimed, "Don't buy this jacket." Since then, the outdoor apparel retailer has been beseeching consumers to "buy less" stuff, including via a 28-minute documentary film the company produced, called *Worn Wear.* The film features hard-core customers wearing Patagonia apparel until it is literally falling apart, at which point they slap on some duct tape to hold the clothes together and wear them some more.

The campaign may seem slightly hypocritical for a retailer that's in the business of selling goods—and in fact, in the two years following the jacket ad, the company's sales actually increased by almost 38 percent. Nonetheless, it is very much in keeping with the overriding Patagonia philosophy of taking better care of the planet. For three decades, the company has pledged 1 percent of sales to the preservation and restoration of the natural environment, and has donated more than $46 million to grassroots environmental groups. And it encourages customers to collaborate in efforts to repair, reuse, and recycle its clothing, even adding a "Worn Wear" section to some of its stores, where it sells reconditioned garments that customers have traded in for store credit.

What's more, Patagonia is taking its social responsibility efforts beyond just the environment. For one thing, the company announced the 2014 introduction of a line of "Fair Trade certified" clothing, produced in factories that are monitored and certified by the nonprofit Fair Trade USA organization using social and environmental standards for fair wages and safe conditions. The initial offering includes nine yoga styles, and for every piece of clothing sold, Patagonia will pay a premium into a workers' fund that can be used for scholarships, medical care, disaster relief, or whatever the workers themselves collectively decide.

Going even further, Patagonia recently launched a corporate campaign that is meant to address more than just new technologies that can help protect the planet by reducing resource use and waste. Its "Responsible Economy" project goes deeper to the core of what it identifies as a greater societal issue: namely, growth-based capitalism, and the assumption that a growth economy equals prosperity and a healthy society. The goal is to inspire other businesses to reexamine their business models that rely strictly on compound annual growth, and start a conversation that might lead to a more sustainable future for everyone on the planet.

Sources: Kyle Stock, "Why Patagonia Wants to Sell You Ratty Old Swim Trunks," *Bloomberg Businessweek,* September 25, 2013, www.business week.com/articles/2013-09-25/why-patagonia-wants-to-sell-you-ratty-old-swim-trunks; Susanna Kim, "Are Fair Trade Clothes a Fair Deal?," *ABC News,* October 24, 2013, http://abcnews.go.com/Business/major-retailer-signs-sell-fair-trade-clothing-customers/story?id=20660596& singlePage=true; Kyle Stock, "Patagonia's Confusing and Effective Campaign to Grudgingly Sell Stuff," *Bloomberg Businessweek,* November 25, 2013, www.businessweek.com/articles/2013-11-25/patagonias-confusing-and-effective-campaign-to-grudgingly-sell-stuff; Patagonia website, www.patagonia.com.

poor, or homeless. Socially responsible companies often support charitable organizations that work to alleviate problems challenging people and societies. This trend is strong and growing in the fashion business, as in other industries. While there was only a handful of retailers in the 1990s that were socially active—ice cream maker and retailer Ben & Jerry's is a prominent example—the number has grown dramatically since then. As Tracy Mullin, former president and CEO of the National Retail Federation, the world's largest retail trade association, stated, "As our shoppers vote with their wallets, retailers are recognizing that customers want them to make a difference."[37] At upscale women's clothing designer and retailer Eileen Fisher Inc., the corporate commitment to social responsibility is so strong that there is an executive with the title of "Director of Social Consciousness."

One way that companies can express social responsibility is through cause-based or cause-related marketing, in which—you'll recall from Chapter 2—they identify a charity or other cause to which a specified portion of profits from one or more products in their line will be donated. By mentioning the donation in the product's marketing materials, such as in ads and on packaging or hangtags, companies can often influence consumers who support the cause to purchase those items over another product. In some cases, marketers designate an exclusive product or create a limited-time promotion to benefit a cause. Macy's conducts an annual Shop for a Cause event, in which participating nonprofit organizations sell savings passes for $5, for which they keep 100 percent of the proceeds and purchasers receive a discount when they shop at a Macy's store on the designated day. A recent event raised $3.8 million for the March of Dimes and

other local charities across the country.[38] Similarly, through its Kohl's Cares program, Kohl's supports women's health initiatives as well as kids' health and education through the sale of special merchandise, such as an exclusive collection of Tek Gear athletic apparel for which 100 percent of the net profit was donated to support the fight against breast cancer.

In other instances, companies make a longer-term commitment to a cause, aligning themselves with a particular charitable organization and incorporating it into their marketing plans on an ongoing basis. One of the best-known examples is (RED), founded by Bono and Bobby Shriver in 2006 as a method for helping provide a sustainable flow of money from the private sector to fight AIDS. Many iconic brands and organizations—including Gap, Apple, Beats by Dr. Dre, Bed Bath & Beyond, Converse, Starbucks, and Motorola—have partnered with the nonprofit organization to develop (RED)-branded products and services, designating a portion of the profits from those goods for donation to the Global Fund to Fight AIDS.

Natural disasters and other crises also provide manufacturers and retailers with an opportunity to act in a socially responsible manner by donating money and/or products to help people in need. After Hurricane Katrina devastated New Orleans and the Gulf Coast in 2005, as well as following Hurricane Sandy's destruction in parts of the Northeast in 2012, many companies stepped forward to assist with donations of needed supplies and other acts of generosity. In the aftermath of Katrina, for instance, Walmart rushed to reopen stores that had been closed by the storm, enabling victims to buy much-needed supplies, and also gave approximately $5 million in emergency cash to affected employees. Best Buy offered cash advances to its displaced employees and also set up banks of computers with Internet connections in stores so that hurricane victims could contact family members and reach the Red Cross and other assistance agencies.[39]

One of the longest-running charitable programs within the fashion industry is Kids in Distressed Situations (K.I.D.S.), a global charity made up of leading retailers, manufacturers, and licensors of children's and youth products. For more than 25 years, K.I.D.S. has worked in partnership with major foundations to help improve the lives of children and their families who are ill, living in poverty, or the victims of natural disasters, collecting donations of new merchandise from members (and others) to deliver wherever they are needed. After the tsunami disaster in Southeast Asia in December 2004, for instance, K.I.D.S. collected and distributed more than $4 million worth of children's clothing, shoes, and blankets donated by its members. In 2012 alone, the organization distributed $112 million worth of brand-new goods around the world.[40]

Summary

Consumer behavior is sometimes influenced by ethics, a system of moral values or principles of right and wrong. Unethical actions are sometimes, but not always, illegal as well. One aspect of ethics is social responsibility, the principle that everyone is responsible for making the world a better place for all its inhabitants. Individuals as well as companies operate under their own ethical standards.

Consumer theft is both unethical and illegal; shoplifting is a prominent example. Organized retail theft is a growing problem in which teams of shoplifters work together to steal larger quantities of merchandise that is usually then resold. Fraudulent returns are also an issue of concern for retailers, some of which are now using software systems to track returns and try to identify dishonest customers.

Counterfeiting of designer or branded products is a huge, global problem. It is illegal to manufacture or sell counterfeit goods, but knowingly purchasing them is not illegal, only unethical. Businesses, government, and law enforcement are all increasing their efforts to find and stop counterfeiters, who may also break other laws, including labor laws, or help fund terrorist groups.

Businesses face ethical decisions in many aspects of their daily operations. Safeguarding the privacy of consumers is one ethical concern, since the increasing amount of personal information that is being gathered could be vulnerable to theft or computer hacking. Ethical considerations in advertising include the ads' truthfulness, as well as the appropriateness of their content, which can sometimes offend an audience. The use of fur in fashion and product testing on animals are two ethical issues that are highly emotional for many consumers, and a number of designers and manufacturers have eliminated the practices as a show of compassion. Marketers are also making efforts to eliminate the use of sweatshops in the production of their products and are implementing ethical labor practices that include safe workplace conditions and fair wages. A growing number of apparel companies operate under fair-trade principles, incorporating not only ethical labor practices but also the intent to provide opportunity to disadvantaged workers and help alleviate poverty.

Many people see protecting the environment as one of today's most serious ethical issues, and a number of fashion manufacturers and retailers have taken steps to lessen the environmental impact of their operations. Fashion products themselves are increasingly being made with eco-friendly fibers and fabrics, such as organic cotton, bamboo, and soy. Fashion companies also address social responsibility through charitable giving, including cause-based marketing and other donations to charities or victims of disaster.

KEY TERMS

Boycott

Counterfeit goods

Ethics

Fair-trade practices

Inventory shrinkage

Loyalty programs

Organized retail theft

Social responsibility

Sweatshop

QUESTIONS FOR REVIEW

1. What are two common types of consumer theft from retailers? How does organized retail theft differ from regular shoplifting?

2. What are some of the steps fashion marketers are taking to combat counterfeit goods?

3. Name three ways in which marketers might collect information about consumers that could raise concerns about privacy of personal data.

4. What are some of the unethical labor practices that are being addressed by many companies and associations in the fashion industry?

5. Name at least three ways in which some retailers and manufacturers are working to make their operations or products more environmentally friendly.

ACTIVITIES

1. Visit a local store and see how many security measures you can identify that the store is using to prevent theft. Make a list of both the visible deterrents (for example, locked cases, security tags on products, security guard) and more discreet techniques (for example, electronic device at exit, one-way glass from an office area). If you are able to, interview a store manager to learn which of the methods the store finds to be most effective.

2. Do an online search for sellers of "fake handbags" or "replica handbags." Choose a site and compare one of the fake items to a genuine product at that brand's own website. Do you think the differences are distinct enough for the item not to be considered a counterfeit? See if the site selling the fakes has a disclaimer that tells consumers its products are not "the real thing."

3. Find an ad in a fashion magazine that you think some people might consider sexist, indecent, or otherwise offensive in some way. Show it to a variety of people of different ages and genders, and ask them for their reaction. Keep track of the responses and see whether the negative reactions come more from younger or older

people, or more from males or females. Do any people feel so strongly about the ad that they would either boycott the company or, at the other extreme, make a point of buying the product being sold? Present your findings to the class.

4. Select one of your favorite designers or brands and go to the company's website. See if you can find information on causes that the company supports or ways in which it is socially responsible. Does the company give information on its efforts to be more environmentally friendly? Does its website discuss its labor practices or policies? Are you surprised by how much or how little the company is doing, based on its site? Does the information make you feel more or less favorable toward the company than you did before? Discuss your findings and reaction with the class.

MINI-PROJECT

Create a questionnaire with 8 to 10 questions that will let you determine people's opinions on various ethical and social issues as they relate to fashion. For example, you could create attitude scales (see Chapter 10) asking questions such as how likely your respondents would be to shop at a retailer that sells apparel made with fur, how favorably they would view a designer who uses organic fabrics or actively seeks fair trade suppliers, or how likely they would be to purchase an item they knew or suspected was counterfeit. Survey at least 15 different people from different age groups, and write a report of your findings.

REFERENCES

1. Tyco Integrated Security, "National Retail Security Survey Reveals U.S. Retail Industry Lost More Than $35.28 Billion to Theft in 2011," News release, November 27, 2012.

2. ibid.

3. The Federal Bureau of Investigation, "Organized Retail Theft: Major Middle Eastern Crime Ring Dismantled," News release, March 12, 2013.

4. National Retail Federation, "Return Fraud to Cost Retailers $2.9 Billion This Holiday Season, According to NRF Survey Return Fraud Survey 2012," News release, December 4, 2012.

5. Cotton Timberlake, "Don't Even Think about Returning that Dress," *Businessweek,* September 26, 2013, http://www.businessweek.com /articles/2013-09-26/return-fraud-clothing-and-electronics-retailers-fight-back.

6. Thomas C. Frohlich, Alexander E.M. Hess, and Vince Calio, "The Nine Most Counterfeited Products in America," *24/7 Wall St.,* March 27, 2014, http://247wallst.com/special-report/2014/03/27/americas-nine-most-counterfeited-items/.

7. Steve Hargreaves, "Counterfeit Goods Becoming More Dangerous," *CNN Money,* September 27, 2012, http://money.cnn.com /2012/09/27/news/economy/counterfeit-goods/index.html.

8. Christina Passariello, "Holograms Tell Fake from Fendi," *Wall Street Journal,* February 22, 2006, http://online.wsj.com/news/articles /SB114057680060579777.

9. "Versace Awarded $20 Million in Damages," *Daily Front Row,* May 6, 2010, http://www

.fashionweekdaily.com/the-fix/article/versace-awarded-20-million-in-damages.

10. Mark Brohan, "Coach Wins a $257 Million Judgment against Web Counterfeiters," *Internet Retailer,* November 5, 2012, http://www.internetretailer.com/2012/11/05/coach-wins-judgment-against-web-counterfeiters.

11. David Glovin, "Wal-Mart, Fendi Settle Lawsuit Over Knockoff Bags (Update2)," *Bloomberg,* June 6, 2007, http://www.bloomberg.com/apps/news?pid=newsarchive&sid=aoip.LC2na_w.

12. Pallavi Gogoi, "Wal-Mart's Luxury Problem," *BusinessWeek,* June 13, 2006, www.businessweek.com/investor/content/jun2006/pi20060613_187965.htm.

13. U.S. Immigration and Customs Enforcement, "ICE-led IPR Center Seizes 70 Websites Duping Consumers into Buying Counterfeit Merchandise," News release, July 12, 2012.

14. Cone Communications, "2013 Cone Communications/Echo Global CSR Study," http://www.conecomm.com/global-CSR-study.

15. National Retail Federation, "Shoppers Want Loyalty Programs, But Not at the Cost of Privacy, According to New NRF Foundation /Adjoined Consulting Research," News release, January 16, 2006.

16. James Temple, "Stale Cookies: How companies are tracking you online today," *SFGate,* October 2, 2013, http://blog.sfgate.com/techchron/2013/10/02/stale-cookies-how-companies-are-tracking-you-online-today/.

17. Alejandro Martínez-Cabrera, "Privacy Concerns Grow with the Use of RFID Tags," *SFGate,* September 6, 2010, http://www.sfgate.com/business/article/Privacy-concerns-grow-with-the-use-of-RFID-tags-3175330.php.

18. Ellie Krupnick, "American Apparel, ASA On The Outs Again With New Banned Ads," *Huffington Post,* April 12, 2013, http://www.huffingtonpost.com/2013/04/10/american-apparel-asa-banned-ads_n_3051751.html.

19. Andrew A. Newman, "Overage Logos, Underage Market," *New York Times,* October 16, 2006, www.nytimes.com/2006/10/16/business/media/16beer.html.

20. "Pamela Anderson Strips for Anti-Fur Protest," *ExpoSay.com,* June 29, 2006, www.exposay.com/pamela-anderson-strips-for-anti-fur-protest/v/2470/.

21. "Carolina Herrera Plays with Fur at New York Fashion Week," *FashionMag.com,* February 12, 2013, http://us.fashionmag.com/news/Carolina-Herrera-plays-with-fur-at-New-York-Fashion-Week,310894.html#.UllfKxBWiV4.

22. Jessica De Jesus and Tabea Kay, "Ethical Style: There Are Still Sweatshops in America," *Good.Is,* March 29, 2012, http://magazine.good.is/articles/ethical-style-there-are-still-sweatshops-in-america.

23. "Does 'Made in the USA' Mean Not In a Sweatshop?," *Green American,* July/August 2013, http://www.greenamerica.org/pubs/greenamerican/articles/JulyAugust2013/Does-Made-in-the-USA-Mean-Not-In-a-Sweatshop.cfm.

24. Fair Factories Clearinghouse, www.fairfactories.org.

25. Jessica Wohl, "North American Retailers Set 5-Year Bangladesh Factory Plan," Reuters, July 10, 2013, http://www.reuters.com/article

/2013/07/10/bangladesh-factories-northamerica-idUSL1N0FG0HB20130710.

26. Bob Tedeschi, "A Click on Clothes to Support Fair Trade," *New York Times,* September 25, 2006, www.nytimes.com/2006/09/25/technology/25ecom.html?ex=1184558400&en=3f09deab7bbb1840&ei=5070.

27. "Wal-Mart Finds More Foreign Violations at Factories," Associated Press, September 27, 2006, http://www.nbcnews.com/id/15033280/#.Ulq0UBBWiV4.

28. Marcus Baram, "Walmart Fined For 'Unacceptable' Workplace Violations," *Huffington Post,* February 10, 2012, http://www.huffingtonpost.com/2012/02/10/walmart-fined-for-unaccep_n_1268475.html.

29. IFAT: The International Fair Trade Association, "The 10 Standards of Fair Trade," http://ifat.org/ftrinciples.shtml.

30. Susan Chandler, "'Fair-Trade' Label Reaches Retail Market," *Chicago Tribune,* October 8, 2006, http://articles.chicagotribune.com/2006-10-08/business/0610080038_1_fair-trade-wage-lands-end.

31. Cone Communications, "2013 Cone Communications/Echo Global CSR Study," http://www.conecomm.com/global-CSR-study.

32. Jad Mouawad, "The Greener Guys," *New York Times,* May 30, 2006, C1.

33. Corporate Timeline, Timberland, http://www.timberland.com/about-timberland/timeline/.

34. Andrea Newell, "Timberland Eco-labels Go Beyond Green Info," *TriplePundit,* January 26, 2012, http://www.triplepundit.com/2012/01/timberland-ecolabels-beyond-green-info/.

35. Destiny USA's Sustainability Commitment, http://www.destinyusa.com/green.

36. Organic Cotton Facts, Organic Trade Association, http://www.ota.com/organic/fiber/organic-cotton-facts.html.

37. Tracy Mullin, "An Awakened Conscience," *Stores,* August 2006. Retrieved August 22, 2007, from www.stores.org/archives/2006/8/President'sColumn.asp.

38. "About Shop for a Cause," Macy's, http://shopforacause.macysinc.com/About.aspx.

39. H. J. Cummins, "Target, Best Buy Taking Care of Gulf Coast Workers," *Minneapolis Star Tribune,* September 18, 2005. Retrieved August 22, 2007, from www.cebcglobal.org/Newsroom/News/News_092005.htm.

40. Kids in Distressed Situations, http://www.kidsdonations.org/index.htm.

CHAPTER 16

The Role of Government for Fashion Consumers

WHAT DO I NEED TO KNOW ABOUT THE ROLE OF GOVERNMENT FOR FASHION CONSUMERS?

✔ How government plays a part in the way fashion companies produce and market their products

✔ Which federal agencies have oversight of different aspects of the fashion industry

✔ How government rules and standards enable fashion consumers to make informed purchasing decisions

✔ What regulations protect consumers from buying products that could cause them harm

✔ How government and independent agencies work to improve fairness and ethics in the marketplace

Have you ever fallen in love with a great-looking pair of pants at the store, bought them to wear to a party that night, and then when you gathered them up with your other laundry to throw in the washing machine, you happen to notice that the tag says "dry clean only"? You're surely not alone if you've faced that quandary and kicked yourself for not checking the label at the store. But did you ever think about why that label is on the apparel to begin with? If you're a careful shopper, you may well scrutinize all the tags, labels, and packaging for an item before making a purchase, even when it's a relatively low-involvement decision. You might also look closely at a product's advertising, trying to separate the real benefits from the hype. Or you may not worry about any of that and simply choose based on your past experience and perceptions of the brand or type of product.

When shopping for fashion goods, not all consumers do take the time to research their purchases or "read all the fine print." And in many cases, it may not matter. But unfortunately, as discussed in Chapter 15, not all companies follow strict ethical guidelines to ensure that everything about their products, their manufacturing, and their marketing is completely aboveboard, and consumers may unwittingly pay the price. That is where government can play an important role, both in passing and enforcing laws to ensure that products are safe and marketed truthfully, and in giving consumers the tools they need to make an informed purchase. What's more, there are a number of independent organizations that provide resources to help educate consumers and to help businesses better meet the needs of their customers. In this chapter, we'll take a look at some of those agencies, regulations, and organizations to see how they affect the fashion industry and how the work they do can influence consumer behavior.

Federal Agencies

Through the work of various agencies, the federal government provides oversight, creates standards, and enforces regulations designed to protect the public from unsafe products or unfair business practices. Those efforts may be supplemented with additional regulations implemented by individual state governments, and with the programs of industry associations, which sometimes take it upon themselves to adopt voluntary standards for their member companies to follow.

CONSUMER PRODUCT SAFETY COMMISSION

When you think of fashion products, the issue of safety probably doesn't immediately spring to mind. But there are several areas where safety could be a concern if it were not for government oversight. Imagine your jeans bursting into flames if you accidentally dropped a lit match on them, or a small child choking on a decorative teddy bear appliqué that pulled loose too easily from his jacket. Fortunately, those are situations that are very unlikely to occur, thanks to the efforts of the **U.S. Consumer Product Safety Commission (CPSC).**

Created in 1972 by Congress under the Consumer Product Safety Act, the CPSC has as its directive to protect the public "against unreasonable risks of injuries associated with consumer products." An independent agency—meaning it does not report to and is not part of any other department or agency in the federal government—the CPSC's staff of about 500 is responsible for monitoring the safety of more than 15,000 kinds of consumer products sold in the United States, ranging from air fresheners, beds, and carpet to sunglasses, toys, and windows, and much more (Figure 16.1). Since 1972, the work of the CPSC has contributed to a 30 percent decline in the rate of deaths and injuries associated with consumer products.[1]

Despite the CPSC's track record, products that pose a potential hazard can still occasionally find their way into the marketplace. When that happens, and it is brought to the agency's attention, the result is generally a recall. In a **recall,** announcements are issued to the public alerting them to the danger, urging them to stop using the product immediately, and providing them with further information on what to do with the product or how to contact the manufacturer. If the problem is something that can be fixed, the recall notice will provide instructions on how consumers can have the product repaired. If it cannot be fixed, consumers are usually notified of the ways they can get a replacement product or a refund.

Because the year 2007 saw a record number of recalls—many of them involving high lead content in toys and other products—Congress passed the Consumer Product Safety Improvement Act of 2008. The new bill increased funding and staffing for the CPSC, placed stricter limits on lead levels in children's products, restricted certain phthalates in children's toys and child care articles, required mandatory testing and certification of applicable

FIGURE 16.1 More than 15,000 different products, including toys and clothing, are monitored for safety by the Consumer Product Safety Commission.

products, and required the CPSC to create a public database of products.

Flammable Fabrics Act

One of the specific areas the CPSC monitors is the flammability of clothing and household furnishings, using the guidelines set forth in the federal **Flammable Fabrics Act.** Passed in 1953, the Flammable Fabrics Act was written initially to regulate the manufacture of highly flammable clothing, such as brushed rayon sweaters. But Congress amended the act in 1967 and expanded its coverage so that it now regulates the flammability not only of clothing but also of home furnishings, as well as paper, plastic, foam, and other materials used both in apparel and interior furnishings. Responsibility for administering the Flammable Fabrics Act was transferred to the CPSC when that agency was created in 1972.

The CPSC has established mandatory flammability standards for clothing textiles, vinyl plastic film used in clothing, carpets and rugs, children's sleepwear, and mattresses and mattress pads. **Mandatory standards** mean that all manufacturers, retailers, importers, and distributors must ensure that the products they are selling meet specific safety criteria that the agency has set forth. The federal mandatory standards for fabric flammability are based on how quickly and how intensely a given material burns when exposed to a small open flame. Based on the fact that certain fabrics have consistently met the standards, they are exempt from testing and considered safe for use in apparel. Among those are fabrics made entirely of acrylic, modacrylic, nylon, olefin, polyester, and wool. Other fabrics must be guaranteed to have passed the flammability tests before being used in apparel.

Because children can be particularly vulnerable, there are even more stringent safety rules for children's sleepwear. The Standard for the Flammability of Children's Sleepwear: Sizes 0 through 6X became effective in 1972, and the Standard for the Flammability of Children's Sleepwear: Sizes 7 through 14 took effect in 1975. The two standards are nearly identical and prescribe a test requiring that specimens of the fabric, seams, and trim from children's sleepwear garments self-extinguish after exposure to a small open flame. The standards target sleepwear because statistics show that children are most at risk from burn injuries that result from playing with matches, candles, stove burners, and other fire sources just before bedtime and just after rising in the morning.[2]

In 1996, after a review of the circumstances surrounding children's burn injuries, the CPSC amended the flammability standards for children's sleepwear to exclude garments sized for infants nine months of age or younger, and to exclude tight-fitting sleepwear garments. The amendments were based on the premise that those categories do not present an unreasonable risk of burn deaths and injuries, and by revising the rules, the agency would enable consumers to have a greater selection of sleepwear for children while still being protected by safety standards. As a result, children's sleepwear that is not flame-resistant is permitted as long as it fits the child snugly. To alert shoppers to the potential danger of loose-fitting children's sleepwear not made of flame-resistant fabric, the CPSC issued a new requirement in 2000 that children's snug-fitting sleepwear made of cotton or cotton blends must carry a hangtag or permanent label reminding consumers that it must fit snugly for safety (Figure 16.2).

Other Product Hazards

Flammability of clothing and home furnishings is an important safety issue, but there also are many other areas in which the CPSC monitors and regulates safety. The agency frequently issues specific safety alerts when it identifies a potential hazard; alerts in recent years have included such topics as

FIGURE 16.2 The CPSC requires children's sleepwear that is not flame-resistant to carry a yellow hangtag like this one, or to include a permanent label sewn into the neck of the garment that says, "Wear snug-fitting. Not flame resistant."

the danger of strangulation from cords of window coverings and the risk of bunk bed mattresses falling if not properly supported. In many cases, the CPSC works closely with industry to develop voluntary safety standards. To improve the safety of cribs, for instance, the CPSC worked with the Juvenile Products Manufacturers Association, which administers a voluntary program to certify cribs meeting specific standards. The toy industry also actively collaborates with the CPSC and other testing organizations to develop voluntary standards for concerns such as small parts that could become a choking hazard if swallowed by a young child.

In the fashion industries, the volume of product recalls is relatively small, but there have been a number in recent years. Columbia Sportswear Company recalled several models of its Omni-Heat electric heated jackets when it was found that the heated inner wrist cuff could overheat, posing a burn hazard;[3] and Victoria's Secret Direct (the catalog and online division of Victoria's Secret) voluntarily recalled about 500 silk kimono tops because the garments failed to meet mandatory standards for fabric flammability.[4] About 92,000 chamois blankets were voluntarily recalled by Pottery Barn in cooperation with the CPSC because the decorative stitching on the blanket's edge could come loose, allowing a child to become entangled in the yarn, posing a strangulation hazard to young children.[5] Also, thousands of necklaces, bracelets, earrings, and hair accessories were recalled by American Girl Place,[6] and 300,000 children's charm bracelets were recalled by Reebok,[7] both due to the products' high lead content, which would pose a serious health hazard if ingested.

The past decade also saw numerous recalls of certain children's outerwear items, such as jackets and sweatshirts, that included a drawstring at the neck or waist. Those drawstrings had been known to get caught on playground equipment, in bus doors, or on other objects, with sometimes deadly results. In the late 1990s, the CPSC issued guidelines regarding the length of the drawstring, how it is attached to the garment, and other criteria to minimize the danger of injury, and those guidelines were incorporated into a voluntary standard for manufacturers and retailers of children's apparel. After the standard was introduced, fatal incidents involving garments with drawstrings through the neck or hood decreased by 75 percent, and fatalities associated with drawstrings through the waist or bottom

Smokescreen Surrounds Fire Safety Standard for Upholstery

While the Consumer Product Safety Commission has long enforced strict regulations regarding the flammability of clothes and a range of household goods made with fabric, it has yet to issue a comprehensive standard regarding upholstered furniture—despite the fact that, according to the CPSC's own statistics, fires originating in upholstered furniture account for 20 percent of all fire-related deaths in the United States and kill an average of ten people a week. The danger lies in the foam used in a wide range of upholstered furniture, because the petroleum-based material creates a much thicker, blacker smoke than wood or paper. What's more, that smoke is highly toxic, making it particularly deadly to consumers, as well as to firefighters responding to the blaze.

The National Association of State Fire Marshals has repeatedly called for a national fire safety standard for upholstery, and watchdog group Citizens against Government Waste has also pushed for a standard, saying that the CPSC has delayed a decision for years. Even the furniture industry, in an effort to avoid individual states' passing a patchwork of different legislation, supported a 2004 federal proposal to impose a flammability standard covering open-flame ignition sources such as lighters and candles, as well as cigarettes. But despite the CPSC offering preliminary approval, the legislation never went any further.

Nonetheless, the furniture industry has "made great strides in reducing the flammability risks associated with its products," according to the American Home Furnishings Alliance, which noted that most upholstered furniture makers follow a voluntary set of construction guidelines created through an Upholstered Furniture Action Council program. And even though the wheels of government tend to turn slowly, there may still be hope of a CPSC ruling in the not-too-distant future: In April 2013, the commission hosted a public meeting on fire safety technologies to focus on "current and anticipated progress on fire barrier technologies and other options to reduce the fire hazard posed by residential furniture."

Sources: Gary Evans, "CPSC Blasted for Delay on Upholstery Open-Flame Standards," *Furniture Today*, September 20, 2006; Susan M. Andrews, "Fire Marshals Call for Upholstery FR Standard," *Furniture Today*, October 31, 2006; and Jessica Franken and Dawnee Giammittorio, "CPSC Holds Upholstered Furniture Fire Safety Technology Meeting," *Nonwovens Industry*, June 12, 2013, http://www.nonwovens-industry.com /contents/view_capitol-comments/2013-06-12/cpsc-holds-upholstered-furniture-fire-safety-technology-meeting/; Consumer Product Safety Commission, Federal Register Notice: Upholstered Furniture Fire Safety Technology Meeting, http://www.cpsc.gov/en/Regulations-Laws— Standards/Federal-Register-Notices/2013/Upholstered-Furniture-Fire-Safety-Technology-Meeting/.

dropped 100 percent. However, from 2006 through 2010, the agency participated in 115 recalls of non-complying products, leading it to establish in 2011 a mandatory federal safety rule regarding drawstrings in children's apparel.[8]

U.S. Food and Drug Administration

While the CPSC monitors the safety of thousands of types of products, there are other product categories over which the agency has no jurisdiction. One of those categories is cosmetics, which is regulated by the **U.S. Food and Drug Administration (FDA).** The FDA was established in 1930 and is now part of the U.S. Department of Health and Human Services. As described by its mission statement, the FDA "is responsible for protecting the public health by assuring the safety, efficacy, and security of human and veterinary drugs, biological products, medical devices, our nation's food supply, cosmetics, and products that emit radiation."

The need for a government entity to monitor food and drugs became clear in the early part of the twentieth century, when journalists and others began uncovering and publicizing serious problems in the processing of meat and other foods, and exposing the fact that some companies were including dangerous ingredients in their patent medicines (trademarked, nonprescription drugs). That reporting led to the Food and Drug Act of 1906, and later

to the establishment of the FDA, initially to ensure the safety specifically of food and drug products. In 1938, however, the FDA's authority was extended to cover the cosmetics industry when the Federal Food, Drug, and Cosmetic Act was passed.

Federal Food, Drug, and Cosmetic Act

One of the two most important laws covering cosmetics marketed in the United States, the **Federal Food, Drug, and Cosmetic Act (FD&C Act)** prohibits the marketing of adulterated (contaminated) or misbranded cosmetics in interstate commerce (business conducted between parties in different states). As defined by the act, the term "cosmetic" means "articles intended to be rubbed, poured, sprinkled, or sprayed on, introduced into, or otherwise applied to the human body or any part thereof for cleansing, beautifying, promoting attractiveness, or altering the appearance," as well as components of such articles, excluding soap (Figure 16.3). If that sounds like it covers a lot, it does: The FDA estimates that more than 40,000 different cosmetic product formulations are being marketed in the United States, incorporating more than 7,000 different cosmetic ingredients and 4,000 fragrance ingredients.[9] To help manage the vast number and variety of products under its umbrella, the FDA maintains six product-oriented centers that carry out its mission. Cosmetics are monitored by the Center for Food Safety and Applied Nutrition, known as CFSAN.

Although the FDA has legal authority over cosmetics, that authority is somewhat different from other products it regulates. Pharmaceutical drugs, for example, must undergo a stringent and lengthy testing and approval process by the FDA before they're allowed on the market. But with the

FIGURE 16.3 A wide range of personal care products, including skin moisturizers, perfumes, lipsticks, fingernail polishes, face makeup, shampoos, hair colors, toothpastes, and deodorants, are regulated by the Food and Drug Administration.

exception of color additives, the FDA does not test or give approval to cosmetic products or ingredients before they go to market. In other words, it is up to cosmetic firms to substantiate the safety of their products and ingredients before marketing them to the public. That includes not only ensuring that the product and its ingredients are safe but that the product has been prepared, packed, handled, and shipped in a way that prevents it from becoming adulterated.

The FDA can and does, however, inspect cosmetic manufacturing facilities to ensure product safety and accurate branding and, as part of that plant inspection, collects product samples for examination and analysis. The agency may also conduct research on cosmetic products and ingredients to address safety concerns, and as a follow-up to any complaints of adverse reactions from a product. One ingredient that was being studied for safety in recent years, for example, is phthalates (pronounced "thallets"), a group of chemicals found in hundreds of products ranging from toys and wall coverings to personal care products, such as nail polish, hair sprays, soaps, and shampoos. Some research indicates that phthalates might affect sexual development in humans,[10] and in 2008, Congress banned the chemicals from children's products including toys. But despite warnings from a number of medical groups regarding exposure to the chemicals, the FDA had not yet found conclusive evidence that phthalates pose a human health risk to warrant banning them from personal care and beauty products.

Because there remain questions about the safety of some chemicals in everyday beauty products, health research and advocacy groups such as the Environmental Working Group (EWG) have created tools to help consumers research what they are applying to their bodies. For more than a decade, EWG's Skin Deep Cosmetics Database website has allowed consumers to check for potentially hazardous ingredients in their skin care products. More recently, the EWG launched a Skin Deep mobile app, similar to another app called Think Dirty; both enable consumers to scan a product's barcode and receive an instant score on the ingredients, along with suggestions for other products that might have safer ingredients.[11] Some consumers have taken action themselves both to raise awareness of potential dangers lurking in cosmetics and to put pressure on manufacturers and the government to better ensure product safety. (See Point of View 16.1.) In addition, manufacturers are encouraged to register their companies and file Cosmetic Product Ingredient Statements with the FDA's Voluntary Cosmetic Registration Program (VCRP), although there is no requirement to do so.

Fair Packaging and Labeling Act

The FD&C Act goes further in permitting the FDA to take action against companies selling cosmetics that are improperly labeled or deceptively packaged. Under the act, a cosmetic is considered to be misbranded if its labeling is false or misleading in any particular, or its label does not include all the required information, among other stipulations. Those requirements are defined further by the **Fair Packaging and Labeling Act,** which was passed in 1966. Under this act, all cosmetics products must list their ingredients in descending order of predominance (as illustrated by the example

Consumer Advocates Take on the Cosmetics Industry

When women buy cosmetics or other beauty products, they shouldn't have to worry that those creams, lotions, shampoos, gels, and other personal care items might be harmful to their health. But how is the average consumer supposed to know what's really inside those bottles, jars, and tubes? Take a look at a few and you'll see that the lists of ingredients can read like a chemistry book—and even if you could decipher what some of the names are, you still probably wouldn't know what potentially adverse effect they could have on your body and health.

That conundrum is precisely what inspired four San Francisco women to step up to the plate and do something decisive, by founding the Campaign for Safe Cosmetics, a national coalition of environmental, health, and women's groups. The Campaign's mission is to do everything possible to eliminate dangerous chemicals from cosmetics and personal care products, using science and an engaged public not only to pressure companies to make safer products, but to convince the government to pass laws that better protect our health. How has it worked out? Let's just say that observers credit the group for launching the first large-scale grassroots challenge to the $60 billion beauty products industry ever.

It was concern about phthalates that really started the ball rolling. One of the Campaign's co-founders was alarmed after reading research from a number of medical and scientific bodies that indicated the chemicals, even in low doses, may be linked to birth defects and reproductive disorders, among other health issues. She was also concerned by the fact that women are generally exposed to more phthalates than men are, through beauty products. But because chemicals aren't always disclosed on product labels, there was no way to measure the extent of their use—until the Campaign for Safe Cosmetics founders sent dozens of different beauty products to a lab to be tested and analyzed. The results showed that a full three quarters of the products contained phthalates.

Said one of the group's co-founders, "We just felt like this was such a violation of women's trust and human rights. These are chemicals that you are applying directly to your body."

Over the course of its first decade, the Campaign's focus has expanded to include many other chemicals found in personal care products. And in that relatively short time, the group has logged an impressive list of successes. By 2008, more than 1,000 cosmetics companies had signed the Campaign's "Compact for Safe Cosmetics," a pledge to remove phthalates from their products and to replace all hazardous chemicals with safer alternatives. Global giants L'Oreal and Revlon, responding to the Campaign's request, agreed to remove chemicals banned in Europe from their cosmetics sold in the United States and elsewhere around the world. Even Wal-Mart changed its policy at the

(continued)

Campaign's behest and banned some chemicals identified as being harmful from the beauty merchandise it sells in its stores.

Among its other accomplishments, the Campaign for Safe Cosmetics helped push through passage of California's Safe Cosmetics Act in 2005, the first law of its kind in the United States, which requires cosmetic companies to disclose to public health officials the ingredients in the products they sell in California. The group has also been instrumental in promoting federal legislation; with its support, the Safe Cosmetics and Personal Care Products Act of 2013 was introduced in Congress, although passage remains uncertain. Should it or a subsequent effort become law, however, it would mark the first change in legislation governing cosmetics since 1938. And consumers can thank four ordinary women who decided to make a difference.

Sources: The Campaign for Safe Cosmetics, "Campaign Victories and History," www.safecosmetics.org/article.php?id=343; Heather Somerville, "Consumer Advocates Turn Heads in Taking on Cosmetics Industry," *The Seattle Times,* October 14, 2013, http://seattletimes.com/html /businesstechnology/2022044233_cosmeticsafetyxml.html; Amy Westervelt, "New and Improved Safe Cosmetics Act Could Boost Green Chemistry," *Forbes,* June 27, 2011, http://www.forbes.com/sites/amywestervelt/2011/06/27/new-and-improved-safe-cosmetics-act-could-boost-green-chemistry/.

in Figure 16.4) and the packaging must give the net quantity of contents—for example, the actual weight of the face powder without the compact case, or the volume of mascara minus the tube and wand. Cosmetics that do not comply with the Fair Packaging and Labeling Act regulations are considered misbranded under the FD&C Act, and subject to enforcement by the FDA.

Both the Federal Food, Drug, and Cosmetic Act and the Fair Packaging and Labeling Act, along with their related regulations, are intended to protect consumers from health hazards and deceptive practices and to help them make informed purchase decisions. If the FDA has information that a cosmetic product is adulterated or misbranded, it can pursue action through the federal court system to

FIGURE 16.4 FDA labeling rules require ingredients in cosmetics to be listed in order of predominance. How many ingredients do you recognize?

remove that product from the market and/or initiate criminal action against the violator. In the case of a cosmetic product that represents a hazard or is somehow defective, the FDA is not authorized to require a recall, but it does monitor manufacturers or distributors that initiate a voluntary recall of a product. The agency, like the CPSC, also issues alerts, warnings, and informational publications to let the public know about possible safety issues. For instance, one such notice warned consumers of possible allergic reactions to the color additives in temporary decal-type tattoos, and the agency has recommended specific labeling for products containing alpha hydroxy acid (AHA) to make consumers aware that use of the product could increase their skin's sensitivity to the sun and the possibility of sunburn.[12]

FEDERAL TRADE COMMISSION

Another U.S. government agency that helps protect consumers is the **Federal Trade Commission,** or **FTC.** Even if you don't think you know anything about the FTC, you are certainly familiar with some of its work—and it probably influences your behavior and decisions as a consumer, whether you are conscious of it or not. Every time you check the care label on a shirt before throwing it in the wash, or trust a TV ad to be truthful about what a product can do, or enjoy a family dinner without interruptions from telephone sales calls, you are benefiting from some of the rules and laws enforced by the FTC.

The FTC, an independent agency of the U.S. government, was created by the Federal Trade Commission Act of 1914 to prevent unfair methods of competition in commerce, as part of a campaign of "trust-busting." The term **trust** refers to large business entities that succeed in controlling a market, in essence becoming a monopoly. Over the years, Congress has passed additional laws giving the FTC greater authority to police anticompetitive practices beyond just antitrust measures. Among those is the Wheeler-Lea Amendment, passed in 1938, which includes a broad prohibition against "unfair and deceptive acts or practices," and the Magnuson-Moss Act, passed in 1975, which gives the FTC authority to adopt trade regulations that define unfair or deceptive acts in particular industries.

The FTC divides its wide-ranging work among the Bureau of Consumer Protection (whose mandate is to protect consumers against unfair, deceptive, or fraudulent practices), the Bureau of Competition (which is the FTC's antitrust arm, seeking to prevent anticompetitive mergers and other anticompetitive business practices in the marketplace), and the Bureau of Economics (which helps the FTC evaluate the economic impact of its actions). Let's look at some of the specific areas in which the FTC has an impact on the fashion industries and consumer behavior.

Textile Products Labeling

Among the FTC's most visible mandates are the laws that require specific labeling of most clothing as well as textile products commonly used in a household. These labels must include key pieces of information, including the fabric's fiber content, care instructions, manufacturer identification, and country of origin. Depending on what a product is made of, it may be covered by one or more of several different laws and official guidelines.

Textile Fiber Products Identification Act.

The **Textile Fiber Products Identification Act,** also known as the Textile Act, states that any company that advertises or sells clothing or fabric household items must label its products to accurately reflect their fiber content (Figure 16.5). Enforced by the FTC, the Textile Act covers fibers, yarns, and fabrics, as well as an array of household textile products made from them, such as clothing and accessories, draperies, towels and washcloths, bedding, cushions—even ironing board covers and umbrellas. Any product that is covered by the act must include a fiber content statement that lists the generic name of each fiber in order of predominance, and the percentage of the product's weight represented by each fiber. For example, a T-shirt might be labeled "100% Cotton," or a throw "65% Silk, 20% Nylon, 15% Angora." Fibers that represent less than 5 percent of the item's weight must be listed simply as "other fiber(s)." However, if the fiber has a functional significance, even in small amounts, it may be listed. For instance, spandex might be present as only 4 percent of a garment's weight, but without it, the garment would offer no elasticity, so the manufacturer may list it by name on the label.

The Textile Act includes additional stipulations for manufacturers in their fiber content labeling,

FIGURE 16.5 Fiber content labels such as these must be permanently affixed to virtually all clothing and household items made of fabric. Do you check to see what an apparel item is made of before making a purchase?

covering issues such as fiber trademarks, which can be used but only if they appear immediately next to the generic fiber name. Lycra, for instance, is a trademark for a specific type of spandex made by Invista, so its use in a garment cannot be stated on the label simply as "Lycra," but must say "Lycra Spandex." Other requirements are meant to ensure that labeling is not deceptive. For example, if the base fabric of a towel is made of upland cotton and the loops are of pima cotton, a label stating "100% Pima Cotton" would not be acceptable—but the manufacturer could label the towel "100% Cotton, Pima Cotton Loops" or "100% Cotton, 100% Pima Cotton Loops," without misleading consumers. Similarly, if a printed advertisement for a product mentions its fiber content, the ad must also do so in a way that is not false, deceptive, or misleading.

Wool Products Labeling Act. While the Textile Act covers most apparel and fabric home furnishings items, products that contain any amount of wool are subject to the specific requirements of the **Wool Products Labeling Act,** also known as the Wool Act. Under the rules of the Wool Act, even if wool accounts for less than 5 percent of the weight of the product, it must be listed on the label.

The Wool Act addresses the use of specialty wool fibers—such as cashmere, camel hair, mohair, alpaca, llama, and vicuna—as well as the more common sheep or lamb's wool in apparel and home goods. A garment made of any of those fibers individually or in combination may be called simply "100% Wool" or "All Wool," assuming it has no other fiber content; or if it were made only of cashmere, it could be called "100% Cashmere." However, a sweater or blanket made half of wool and half of cashmere would have to be labeled either "100% Wool" or "50% Cashmere, 50% Wool," and to avoid misleading consumers, the product's hangtag or other packaging could not simply say "Fine Cashmere Garment." The same holds true for any printed advertising descriptions, as with the Textile Act rules (Figure 16.6).

◄ Previous   Next ►

Rutherford Park Plaid Blanket
Price: $219.99 - $249.99

A traditional tartan plaid layers beautifully with the romantic florals and heritage prints of our Rutherford Park bed. Woven for a refined hand in plush wool, our throw blanket is finished with a ¼" self-hem. Offered in: full/queen and king. 100% wool. Dry clean. Imported.

Style #2804091

COLOR   Multi-color Large Plaid

SIZE   Select Size ▼

QUANTITY   1 ▼

FIGURE 16.6 Catalogs and websites must give accurate fiber content information, since shoppers cannot look at the products' labels in person. This blanket has been clearly identified by the online seller as "100% wool."

Fur Products Labeling Act. Garments made of fur must follow similar but distinct rules and regulations as set forth in the **Fur Products Labeling Act.** Under this act's rules, garments made either entirely or partly with fur must have a label disclosing, among other things, the type of animal; if the fur is used or damaged; and if the fur product is composed in whole or substantial part of pieces, such as paws, tails, bellies, scraps, heads, and so on. The label must also disclose if the fur is pointed (meaning that separate hairs are inserted into the fur, often either to repair damaged areas or to simulate other furs), dyed, bleached, or artificially colored; or if those treatments don't apply, the fur must be labeled "natural." In addition, the label must provide the textile or wool content of the product.

While the FTC's fur labeling guide provides a list of animals whose fur could be used in a garment, just because an animal name appears on the list does not mean it is necessarily legal to sell that fur in the United States. If the animal is an endangered species, for instance, the sale of its fur is prohibited by the Endangered Species Act of 1973. Similarly, the Dog and Cat Protection Act of 2000 prohibits the distribution, importation, or sale of any products made with dog or cat fur. Under the Fur Products Labeling Act, it is also illegal to label a fur with the name of any animal other than the animal that produced the fur, or to use invented or fictitious animal names. Upscale retailer Neiman Marcus was cited by the FTC twice in recent years over issues of improper fur labeling, including a 2009 investigation involving coats that were labeled "faux fur" when the fur was actually real. In a more recent case, the store allegedly misrepresented that a rabbit fur product had mink fur, as well as advertising garments on its website as being "fake fur" when they were actually real fur. The labels on the garments themselves were correct, but because online shoppers have no way of examining the label until after they've made the purchase, the FTC requires full and accurate information to be given in descriptions on an e-commerce site.[13]

Down, Leather, and Jewelry Products Guidelines. While there is not a separate law regarding the labeling of products made with down or feathers, up until the late 1990s the FTC did have official Down Guides for manufacturers to follow. They were rescinded in 1998, however, since the FTC believed that some of the stipulations were based on outdated manufacturing capabilities, and actually promoted inaccurate labeling and advertising. The International Down and Feather Testing Laboratory and Institute (IDFL) has since published its own labeling standards for the industry.[14] The FTC still offers a brochure of guidelines for manufacturers, since the overall rules of the Textile Act remain applicable to down and feather items, along with general FTC rules regarding deceptive advertising.

General guidelines for the labeling and advertising of leather and simulated leather products are also available from the FTC. In addition, the agency publishes Jewelry Guides that cover advertising claims made for gold, silver, platinum, pewter, diamonds, gemstones, and pearls, and define how certain common terms may be used in ads. For

Is That Fido in Your Fur Coat?

So you're an animal lover who would never under any circumstances buy apparel made with real fur. You find a to-die-for jacket that's trimmed with cozy faux fur and take it home . . . only to hear on the news a week later that the fake fur on your wonderful jacket is not only *not* fake, but is actually fur from a *dog.* How could that be?

Although it's been illegal since 2000 to import domestic dog (and cat) fur—and it's a federal crime to intentionally sell it in the United States—there have still been numerous cases over the past decade in which apparel that was labeled as being faux fur turned out to contain the real thing, and sometimes from man's (and woman's) best friend. Many of these cases were brought to light by the Humane Society of the United States, which frequently conducts undercover investigations to call out offending manufacturers and retailers.

It's hardly just fly-by-night marketers that have been snagged in Humane Society investigations, either. One of the most recent revelations involved Marc by Marc Jacobs jackets that were being sold in-store and online by Century 21 and advertised by the retailer as having faux fur trim. When the Humane Society purchased several of the jackets, however, the actual labels indicated that it was "real raccoon fur," meaning Century 21 had mischaracterized the garments, which is against the law. But it gets worse: Testing found that the fur was not from

raccoons, but from raccoon dogs, an Asian canine breed that looks like an oversized, fluffy raccoon and whose fur is known to be stripped in a particularly cruel and gruesome manner. Because raccoon dogs are not domesticated, importing their fur is not illegal (yet), but misrepresenting and mislabeling it does violate the federal Fur Products Labeling Act.

Many other reputable retailers and designers have been caught up in the fur maelstrom at some point. A few years back, the Humane Society purchased 25 different coats that were labeled as fake fur, only to discover that the fur trim on three of them—one from Nordstrom, one from Tommy Hilfiger, and one from Andrew Marc—came from domestic dogs. How could they tell? Following up on a tip from a consumer who'd bought one of the coats, the Humane Society sent it for testing by mass spectrometry, a technique that measures the mass and sequence of proteins, to determine what species of animal the fur came from. Equally disturbing, out of 25 coats tested, all but one were either mislabeled or misadvertised, most using fur from raccoon dogs.

Snafus with fur can often occur because retailers or designers trust their supplier and are themselves led astray. That doesn't mean they don't take responsibility though. In the above situation, for example, Tommy Hilfiger communicated its concern to customers and eliminated

(continued)

the fur-trimmed garment from its line, while Nordstrom allowed customers who had bought the vests in question to return them, as well as discontinuing its purchases of fur-trimmed products from the vendor that had supplied them.

Yet other fashion companies that have faced issues with mislabeled fur products include JCPenney, Macy's, Burlington Coat Factory, Lord & Taylor, Donna Karan's DKNY, Michael Kors, and Oscar de la Renta. In addition, Sean "Diddy" Combs stopped producing and selling coats from his Sean John line and rapper Jay-Z pulled coats from his Rocawear label, both because the coats featured fur from raccoon dogs.

Sources: Kasie Hunt, "Is Your Fur Fake, or Is It Fido?" The Associated Press, February 23, 2007, http://www.nbcnews.com/id/17298301/# .Ul1jrBDflzo; Larry Mcshane, Glenn Blain, and Tina Moore, "Marc Jacobs' 'Faux Fur' Garments Actually Use the Coats of Chinese Canines: Humane Society Report," *New York Daily News,* March 7, 2013, http://www.nydailynews.com/life-style/fashion/century-21-selling-real-fur-faux-humane-society-article-1.1282382; The Humane Society of the United States, "N.Y. Retailer Sold Marc Jacobs, Other Fur Garments as Faux," News release, March 7, 2013.

example, the guides explain when a product can be called "gold-plated" or when a diamond can be called "flawless."

Country of Origin and Manufacturer Identification. In addition to fiber content and other labeling requirements, products covered by the Textile and Wool Acts, as well as the Fur Products Labeling Act, must include the product's country of origin on the label. A special rule for socks, requiring that the country of origin be placed on the front of the packaging, took effect in March 2006. Imported products must identify the country where they were processed or manufactured; products made entirely in the United States of materials also made in the United States must be labeled "Made in USA" or an equivalent phrase. In some cases, a garment or other product is partially made in another country but finished in the United States, or is manufactured in the United States from imported materials. In either situation, the label must identify the originating country for both the materials and the manufacture. For clothing that is sold online, retailers must state its country of origin in the product description.

Product labels must also include identification of the manufacturer, importer, or other firm that may be marketing, distributing, or otherwise handling the product. This can be either the full company name or the company's Registered Identification Number (RN), as issued by the FTC to U.S. companies.

Care Labeling Rule. Another way in which the FTC helps consumers make informed purchasing decisions is through its **Care Labeling Rule,** which requires manufacturers and importers to attach care instructions to their garments. As the FTC notes in its guide for businesses, "Clothes Captioning: Complying with the Care Labeling Rule," care labels are often a deciding factor when consumers shop for clothing, since many consumers prefer the economy of laundering clothes by machine, while others think that dropping off clothes for dry cleaning is more convenient. Either way, the FTC Care Labeling Rule lets consumers make the choice that is best for them.

The Care Labeling Rule covers all textile apparel with a few exceptions, such as shoes, gloves, hats, belts, and neckties. Piece goods, or lengths of fabric sold for making apparel at home, are also covered. On the label for each garment, manufacturers must provide complete instructions about regular care, or provide warnings if certain procedures would harm the product. For example, consumers would assume that a pair of pants labeled safe for washing would also be able to be ironed; so if ironing could harm the pants, the label should state, "Do not iron." In addition, manufacturers must ensure that the care labels are easily seen or found by consumers at the point of sale, and that they will remain attached and legible throughout the useful life of the product. With both consumers and marketers expressing increased interest in greener ways of caring for clothes, in 2013, the FTC began looking into the possibility of allowing manufacturers and importers to include professional instructions for wet cleaning—an environmentally friendly alternative to dry cleaning—on labels.[15]

Since 1997, the FTC has permitted manufacturers to use specified care symbols instead of written instructions on garment labels (as shown in Figure 16.7). The symbols are intended to allow companies to include the same care labels on garments being sold in Canada or Mexico, as well as the United States. A minimum of four symbols are required for laundering instructions—washing, bleaching, drying, and ironing—with one symbol required for dry-cleaning instructions. Manufacturers may and often do use additional symbols or

FIGURE 16.7 The FTC has permitted the use of these symbols on fabric care labels since 1997. Do you know what they mean without an explanation?

words, or both, to clarify the instructions for consumers; but fortunately for those who cannot decipher the symbols, if there is no clarification on the label, there are numerous websites (including the FTC's) that provide a translation.

Violations of the Care Labeling Rule are subject to enforcement actions by the FTC and penalties of up to $11,000 for each offense. Relatively few cases have been pursued in recent years, but two of the largest in the past involved Tommy Hilfiger and Jones Apparel, each of which paid $300,000 in penalties. In the Hilfiger case, the garments in question were labeled with a washing instruction that, when followed, resulted in dye bleeding from one portion of the garment to another.[16] In the Jones Apparel case, some garments faded when dry-cleaned, while with other garments that featured flocking (a raised design), the flocking disappeared when the garments were dry-cleaned according to instructions. The complaint against Jones Apparel also included some cashmere sweaters that were labeled "dry clean only" but that could actually be safely hand-washed.[17]

Let's Talk

When you're shopping for fashion goods, do you make a point of checking the label for the country of origin? Are you influenced (positively or negatively) in your purchase decision based on where the garment was made? Would you be willing to spend a little more for goods that were made in the USA? Why or why not?

Truth in Advertising

As part of its mandate to protect consumers against unfair, deceptive, or fraudulent practices, the FTC devotes considerable resources to enforcing the nation's **truth-in-advertising laws.** These laws require advertisers—whether in newspapers or magazines, on television or radio, on the Internet or in any other medium—to create advertising that is truthful and to be able to support any claims about a product with reliable, objective evidence (Figure 16.8). The agency is even starting to look at social media to make sure marketers don't slip unsubstantiated or deceptive claims onto their Facebook page or other social media outlet.[18]

According to the FTC's Deception Policy Statement, an ad is deceptive if

- It contains a statement or omits information that is likely to mislead consumers acting reasonably under the circumstances.
- The information is "material"—that is, important to a consumer's decision to buy or use the product.

Similarly, the FTC's Unfairness Policy Statement deems an ad or business practice unfair if

- It causes or is likely to cause substantial consumer injury that a consumer could not reasonably avoid.
- It is not outweighed by the benefit to consumers.

To determine whether an ad is deceptive, the FTC looks at it from the point of view of a "reasonable" or typical consumer, taking the entire ad in context to judge what it conveys to consumers, and what it fails to say that could leave consumers with

FIGURE 16.8 Advertisers must be able to prove any claims they make—whether the claims are express or implied.

a misleading impression about the product. The FTC also looks at both express claims and implied claims in an ad. **Express claims** are those that are made literally; for example, "ABC Mouthwash prevents colds." **Implied claims** are those that are made indirectly or by inference; for example, "ABC Mouthwash kills the germs that cause colds." Although the second example does not literally say the mouthwash will prevent colds, it would be reasonable for a consumer to conclude from the statement, "kills the germs that cause colds," that it will prevent colds. Under the law, advertisers must have proof, such as research results, to support both express and implied claims in their ads.

With increased consumer interest in purchasing green products, the FTC issued Environmental Guides (often referred to as "Green Guides") in 1992, and updated them in 1998, to specifically address environmental advertising and marketing claims within the context of truth in advertising. The guides cover how words like "biodegradable," "recyclable," and "environmentally friendly" can be used in ads, and reinforce the requirement for all claims to be fully substantiated. Because of continuing changes in both green technology and green marketing, the FTC produced another update to the Green Guides in 2012, incorporating newer terms such as "renewable" and "sustainable." Perhaps the most impactful change in the revised guides is that they now expressly prohibit marketers from making "general environmental benefit claims." These include statements such as "green," "eco-friendly," and "environmentally sound," which imply that a product or service is good for the environment without making clear exactly why or how.

LET'S TALK

Can you give an example of advertising that made you wonder about how truthful the advertiser's claims were? Do you think advertisers sometimes try to bend the rules to make their point, without technically breaking the law? Do you think this is a question of ethics? Why or why not?

Price Fixing

As part of its regulation of anticompetitive business practices, the FTC enforces federal laws against price fixing. **Price fixing** occurs when business competitors make an agreement to set the price for which their products will be sold in a given market. The result of price fixing is generally higher prices for the consumer and higher profits for the companies fixing their prices. The laws against price fixing are the reason many products are marked with a "manufacturer's suggested retail price," since by a long-standing law, companies were not permitted to give retailers a minimum or specific price at which they must sell their products. In 2000, women's shoe company Nine West Group agreed to settle charges with the FTC and individual states that it engaged in resale price fixing with certain retailers. The company was accused of fixing retail prices for its shoes as well as restricting when retailers could hold sales and promotions.[19] However, in 2007, a Supreme Court ruling (*Leegin Creative Leather Products, Inc v. PSKS, Inc.*) stated that manufacturers may sometimes set minimum prices for their products. The case was brought by Leegin, manufacturer of Brighton brand women's accessories, which had introduced a marketing initiative designed to provide incentives to retailers that created a separate section for the Brighton brand within their stores. To participate, retailers had to pledge to "follow the Brighton Suggested Pricing Policy at all times." In 2002, Leegin learned that one of its retailers, PSKS, had violated the pricing policy by discounting Brighton merchandise. In response to this violation, Leegin suspended all shipments to PSKS, leading to the lawsuit and eventual Supreme Court ruling. The long-term marketplace impact of the ruling remains to be seen. It has not eliminated all complaints, however, since in 2013, Apple was found guilty of price fixing in a case regarding e-books, a ruling that was being appealed.

Other FTC Regulations

There are many other areas in which the FTC is involved in protecting consumers and enforcing federal rules and regulations. For instance, the agency has developed consumer protection guidelines for use of facial recognition tools, such as those used in virtual makeovers where a consumer uploads a personal photo to a website. The agency gives particular focus to advertising and marketing directed to children, since they are more vulnerable to certain kinds of deception, and reviews those ads from a child's perspective rather than an adult's. For example, in 1998 the FTC oversaw passage of the Children's

Online Privacy Protection Act, a federal law requiring websites to obtain verifiable parental consent before collecting, using, or disclosing personal information from children; and in late 2012, the agency proposed an update to the law to bring it into the twenty-first century. Among other changes, the update acknowledges the massive growth of mobile device usage among kids and the data collection that goes along with it, and categorizes geolocation information, photos, and videos as personal information.[20]

Catalog marketers and online retailers are subject to the FTC's oversight when it enforces laws including the Mail or Telephone Order Merchandise Rule, which requires companies to ship purchases when promised (or within 30 days if no time is specified), or give consumers the option to cancel their order for a refund. Under the conditions of the Do Not Call Registry, established by the FTC in 2003, telemarketers are prohibited from calling consumers who have placed their phone number on the list—although companies with which a consumer has already done business can still call, unless directly requested not to. Cell phones can be added to the registry, but because telemarketers are prohibited from calling cell numbers with auto-dialers, it is generally not necessary.

Consumer credit and financial privacy are also areas where the FTC wields its power. The agency is responsible for enforcing the Truth in Lending Act, which requires creditors to disclose in writing certain cost information, including annual percentage rate, before consumers enter into a credit agreement. The FTC also enforces the Fair Credit Reporting Act, which ensures the accuracy and privacy of information kept by credit bureaus and other consumer reporting agencies, and gives consumers the right to know what information about them is filed in their reports. To further promote informed consumer choice, the FTC maintains the website www.consumer.gov in partnership with the FDA, CPSC, and other agencies; this site features links to many other sources of consumer information.

FEDERAL ANTI-COUNTERFEITING PROGRAMS

As discussed in Chapter 15, counterfeit goods are increasingly prevalent in the marketplace, and the federal government is working to combat that trend on several fronts. The first line of defense is the U.S. Patent and Trademark Office, an agency within the Department of Commerce. By registering trademarks, the agency helps businesses protect their intellectual property investments and promote their goods and services, and helps safeguard consumers against confusion and deception in the marketplace. Those trademarks are further protected by the Lanham Act of 1946, also known as the Trademark Act, which gives trademark users exclusive rights to their marks; as well as by the Trademark Counterfeiting Act of 1984, which makes intentional use of a counterfeit trademark a federal offense.

Other agencies working to stop the marketing of counterfeit goods include Customs and Border Protection, part of the Department of Homeland Security, which devotes substantial resources to intercepting and seizing shipments of counterfeit goods crossing U.S. borders. The Federal Bureau of Investigation (FBI) investigates cases of criminal counterfeiting, and the Department of Justice prosecutes intellectual property crimes on behalf of the United States.

To further coordinate the effort, the **Strategy for Targeting Organized Piracy (STOP!)** initiative was launched in 2004, bringing together all the key agencies in a comprehensive program. In 2006, anti-counterfeiting laws were strengthened even further with the signing of the Stop Counterfeiting in Manufactured Goods Act. While the shipment and sale of counterfeit goods was already illegal, the new legislation closed a loophole that had permitted the shipment of fake labels or packaging, which counterfeiters could then attach to fake products (Figure 16.9).

FIGURE 16.9 Real Louis Vuitton—or fake? Shipment of counterfeit labels, even when not yet attached to a product, is illegal under the Stop Counterfeiting in Manufactured Goods Act.

Other Government Programs

There are many other federal laws and agencies that play a role in the way fashion products are marketed and sold, and that can influence the behavior of consumers. The Equal Employment Opportunity Commission enforces the nation's **Equal Employment Opportunity (EEO)** laws, which prohibit discrimination in hiring based on race, color, religion, sex, national origin, or disability, and which protect men and women who perform substantially equal work in the same establishment from sex-based wage discrimination, among other things. For example, a retailer may break the law in refusing to hire employees based strictly on the fact that they don't have a certain "look" for its sales staff that it believes will attract customers or entice them to buy. In late 2004, a class action suit under the EEO laws was settled by Abercrombie & Fitch for $40 million after a group of black, Asian, and Latino employees alleged that the retailer was hiring a disproportionately white sales force, favoring white employees for the best positions, and discouraging minorities from applying for jobs.[21] More recently, the company faced additional lawsuits over its dress code for employees, as you'll read in Case in Point 16.3.

The **Americans with Disabilities Act (ADA)**, which is enforced by the Department of Justice, further protects the rights of people with disabilities not only in equal employment opportunities but in equal access to public transportation, public buildings, and other places and activities. To comply with the requirements of this law, retailers and other companies must ensure that their places of business have doorways, hallways, and aisles wide enough to accommodate a wheelchair, and that

Courts Dress Down Abercrombie & Fitch for Its Discriminatory Dress Code

There are lots of perks to landing a job in a retail store. The hours can be flexible, there are usually employee discounts, and you're always up to the minute on the latest styles to hit the racks. But for employees of Abercrombie & Fitch—as well as its offshoot brands, Hollister and Abercrombie Kids—there can also be a downside: The retailer has become infamous for its über-strict dress code, to the point where some workers have actually taken the company to court.

While many retailers, particularly in the teen arena, understandably want their sales associates to wear styles that are in keeping with what the store sells, Abercrombie goes far beyond that simple policy approach. The company produces actual style guides that spell out what is acceptable and what is not acceptable, down to the tiniest of details—such as women's jeans being cuffed at precisely seven-eighths of an inch, and the top three buttons of a denim shirt being left undone. Jewelry, hair styles, makeup, manicures, and other personal grooming details come under equal scrutiny, and violations of the dress code, from a single fingernail decal to a five o'clock shadow, can get workers reprimanded, sent home, or fired.

It was when store employees were taken to task for wearing items connected to their religious faith, however, that some decided

to speak out or even push back. For example, on her first day of work at an Olympia, Washington, Hollister store, 17-year-old Anna Zakhlyebayeva—clad in a Hollister tank top, Hollister jeans, and Hollister flip-flops—was stunned when the manager told her she had remove her tiny silver cross pendant because it didn't fit the company's "Look Policy."

And it was not just Zakhlyebayeva's cross. Three other cases, within just a three-year span, were taken to federal court by Muslim women over the wearing of hijabs, or headscarves. The plaintiff in one of those lawsuits was Hani Khan, who was fired from her job at an Abercrombie store in San Mateo, California, for refusing to take off her hijab. According to court documents, Abercrombie argued that its Look Policy goes to the "very heart of [its] business model," and claimed that any deviation from the dress code would threaten the company's success. The judge disagreed—and ruled that Abercrombie had violated federal anti-employment discrimination guidelines.

After paying a combined settlement of $71,000 to two of the Muslim women who had filed lawsuits through the Equal Employment Opportunity Commission (EEOC), Abercrombie agreed to alter its Look Policy, permitting hijabs as an exception to the employee dress code. The retailer also agreed to submit biannual reports

(continued)

to the EEOC for the following three years regarding the new policies.

Said one industry analyst: "It's one thing to say your brand only hires super-skinny females and oddly buff male teenagers. But to show arrogance in disrespecting the religious rights of U.S. citizens is by far the worst thing that has surfaced on the company."

Sources: Kim Bhasin and Caroline Fairchild, "Abercrombie Dress Code Enables Discrimination, Insiders Say," *Huffington Post*, September 18, 2013, http://www.huffingtonpost.com/2013/09/18/abercrombie-dress-code_n_3943131.html?view=screen; and Michael Thrasher, "Abercrombie & Fitch Just Changed Its Infamous Employee Dress Code," *Business Insider*, September 23, 2013, http://www.businessinsider.com/abercrombie-and-fitch-changes-look-policy-2013-9.

wheelchair-accessible ramps or elevators are available in addition to stairs (Figure 16.10). There are also provisions of the ADA that go beyond disabilities per se. In 2012, department store chain Dillard's settled a class action lawsuit for $2 million as a result of its policy and practice of requiring all employees to disclose personal and confidential medical information in order to be approved for sick leave. The settlement also resolved claims that Dillard's terminated a class of employees nationwide for taking sick leave beyond the maximum amount of time allowed, in violation of the ADA.[22]

Many states, counties, and local governments also have their own laws that supplement the federal laws, and state or local agencies that enforce them. All states have a consumer protection or consumer affairs department or agency; sometimes safety rules on the state level are even more strict than the equivalent federal regulations. California, for example, has a flammability requirement for upholstery, even though there is not a federal rule.

FIGURE 16.10 Automatic door openers are one way retailers comply with the Americans with Disabilities Act.

Generally, states also have their own laws regarding advertising, which can impose restrictions above and beyond those of the federal government.

Both federal and state governments provide a wealth of resources for consumers and businesses seeking more information about a particular law, or who want to file a complaint about a safety issue or deceptive business practice. websites for the individual agencies offer extensive information, much of which is also available in print format, often at no charge.

Independent Agencies and Services

Outside of government, there are a number of independent agencies and business groups that work to educate consumers and promote ethical business practices. One of the most widely recognized is the **Better Business Bureau (BBB),** a private, not-for-profit organization. There are local or regional Better Business Bureaus and branches in over 150 locations across the country, all of which fall under the umbrella of the Council of Better Business Bureaus, which was founded in 1912. The umbrella organization is supported by more than 300,000 local business members nationwide, and is "dedicated to fostering fair and honest relationships between businesses and consumers, instilling consumer confidence, and contributing to an ethical business environment."

The BBB is best known for its Reliability Reports on local businesses. These reports, which are accessible to anyone making an inquiry, include information such as whether there are unresolved disputes or consumer complaints against the business. The BBB also offers dispute resolution services, as well as materials and resources for businesses and

consumers on numerous topics, two of which are identity theft and online shopping. It also promotes truth in advertising, encouraging self-regulation of advertising claims by its business members.

Another important organization is the **National Consumers League.** Founded in 1899, the league is a nonprofit membership organization working for health, safety, and fairness in the marketplace and workplace. Among the areas the league monitors are consumer fraud, food and drug safety, fair labor standards, child labor, health care, e-commerce, financial services, and telecommunications. The league promotes consumer education through outreach to high school students and provides information to consumers through publications, media outreach, and multiple websites.

To give the public easy access to the variety of consumer information available, the Federal Citizen Information Center of the U.S. General Services Administration offers a broad listing of national consumer organizations in its free *Consumer Action Handbook;* the information is also available online at the Consumer Action website at http://www.usa.gov/topics/consumer.shtml.

Summary

The federal government plays an important role in creating and enforcing laws that protect the public and help consumers make informed purchase decisions. There are also laws and government agencies on the state and local level that supplement federal regulations, and independent groups that promote consumer education and fair business practices.

The Consumer Product Safety Commission protects the public against unreasonable risk of injury from a wide variety of products. The CPSC administers the Flammable Fabrics Act, which establishes mandatory standards of flammability for textiles used in clothing and many home furnishings. Even more stringent standards apply to the flammability of children's sleepwear. Other safety issues monitored by the CPSC include strangulation and choking hazards and lead content. When unsafe products on the market are identified, the agency works with the company responsible to issue a recall.

The Food and Drug Administration is responsible for protecting the public's health and the safety of products in categories that include food, drugs, and cosmetics. It enforces the Federal Food, Drug, and Cosmetic Act, which prohibits the marketing and sale of adulterated or misbranded cosmetics, as well as the Fair Packaging and Labeling Act, which requires that specific information about ingredients be given on the product labels of cosmetics.

The Federal Trade Commission works to protect consumers from unfair or deceptive practices and to prevent businesses from engaging in anti-competitive practices. The FTC enforces laws regarding labeling of textile products, including the Textile Fiber Products Identification Act, which requires clothing and many textile household products to be labeled with their fiber content, country of origin, manufacturer identification, and directions for proper care. It also upholds the nation's truth-in-advertising laws, as well as regulating mail-order and Internet retailing, consumer credit and financial privacy, and other issues.

Federal agencies involved in the government's anti-counterfeiting efforts include the U.S. Patent and Trademark Office, Customs and Border Protection, and the Federal Bureau of Investigation. Helping to coordinate the work of the various agencies is the Strategy Targeting Organized Piracy (STOP!)

initiative. The Stop Counterfeiting in Manufactured Goods Act recently strengthened the law even further.

Other government regulations affecting fashion commerce and consumer behavior include the Equal Employment Opportunity laws and Americans with Disabilities Act. Outside of government, there are many additional resources for business and consumer information, including the nationwide Better Business Bureau system.

KEY TERMS

Americans with Disabilities Act (ADA)

Better Business Bureau (BBB)

Care Labeling Rule

Consumer Product Safety Commission (CPSC)

Equal Employment Opportunity (EEO) laws

Express claims

Fair Packaging and Labeling Act

Federal Food, Drug, and Cosmetic Act (FD&C Act)

Federal Trade Commission (FTC)

Flammable Fabrics Act

Food and Drug Administration (FDA)

Fur Products Labeling Act

Implied claims

Mandatory standards

National Consumers League

Price fixing

Recall

Standard for the Flammability of Children's Sleepwear

Strategy Targeting Organized Piracy (STOP!)

Textile Fiber Products Identification Act

Trust

Truth-in-advertising laws

Wool Products Labeling Act

QUESTIONS FOR REVIEW

1. Explain the purpose of the Consumer Product Safety Commission, and give three examples of the types of hazards the agency monitors that relate to fashion products.

2. How does the Food and Drug Administration regulate cosmetics, and how does that regulation differ from other products under its jurisdiction, such as drugs?

3. What information must be included on the label of clothing or fabric home furnishings, according to the Textile Fiber Products Identification Act? What does the Care Labeling Rule require?

4. What criteria does the Federal Trade Commission use to judge whether an advertisement is truthful?

5. Name two laws that are designed to protect people from discrimination in either the workplace or in access to public places.

ACTIVITIES

1. Go to the website for the Consumer Product Safety Commission (www.cpsc.gov), and review the product recall announcements for three different months. How many recalls were there in total? How many were related to apparel or fashion? For the fashion-related recalls, make a list of the hazards the products posed, and indicate how many recalls there were for each. What were the remedies for consumers who had bought the products?

2. Go to a drugstore or other retailer that sells cosmetics and toiletries, and choose two brands of a similar item, such as lipstick or toothpaste. Compare the list of ingredients for the two brands. Are there some of the same ingredients in both? Are they in the same relative position in the list of ingredients, indicating their predominance in the formula? Write down the names of two or three ingredients that you are unfamiliar with, and research them to find out what they are and what they do. Share your results with the class.

3. Browse through the apparel in your closet, and find the labels identifying the fiber content. Select five items that have different fiber content from each other, and compare the look and feel of the fabric. Would you have known what the fabric was without looking at the label? Now find the care labels for each and compare how they differ based on the fiber content. Make a chart showing the fabrics and their care, and describe what you think might happen to each garment if you did not follow the care instructions given.

4. Look through a magazine or watch TV to find four or five examples of advertisements for fashion-related products. Write down what the product is and what claim (or claims) the ad is making about the product. Indicate whether the claims are express claims or implied claims.

MINI-PROJECT

Alone or with a group, choose a current fashion item (apparel, accessories, footwear, or personal care/cosmetics), and imagine you are in charge of marketing that item to consumers. Determine the product's key selling points, and create two versions of copy for an advertisement—one version that makes express claims about the product and one that makes implied claims. Describe the kind of proof you think you would need to support each claim.

REFERENCES

1. U.S. Consumer Product Safety Commission, "CPSC Overview," http://cpsc.gov/about/about .html.

2. U.S. Consumer Product Safety Commission, "New Labels on Children's Sleepwear Alert Parents to Fire Dangers," News release, June 26, 2000.

3. U.S. Consumer Product Safety Commission, "Columbia Sportswear Recalls Seven Models of Heated Jackets Due To Burn Hazard," January 29, 2013, http://www.cpsc.gov/en/Recalls /2013/Columbia-Sportswear-Recalls-Seven-Models-of-Heated-Jackets/.

4. U.S. Consumer Product Safety Commission, "CPSC, Victoria's Secret Direct Announce Recall of Silk Kimono Tops," News release, February 23, 2006.

5. U.S. Consumer Product Safety Commission, "CPSC, Pottery Barn Kids Announce Recall of Chamois Blankets," News release, January 24, 2005.

6. Rummana Hussain, "Lead Fears Force Recall of American Girl Jewelry," *Chicago Sun-Times,* March 31, 2006, 20.

7. U.S. Consumer Product Safety Commission, "Reebok Recalls Bracelet Linked to Child's Lead Poisoning Death," News release, March 23, 2006.

8. U.S. Consumer Product Safety Commission, "CPSC Issues New Drawstring Safety Rule for Children's Outerwear Drawstrings at Neck and Waist Present Strangulation Hazard and Other Dangers," News release, July 1, 2011.

9. "FDA Overview," *Medicine Net,* http://www .medterms.com/script/main/art.asp?article key=8468.

10. Peter Waldman, "From an Ingredient in Cosmetics, Toys, A Safety Concern." *Wall Street Journal,* October 4, 2005, http://online.wsj .com/public/article/SB112838975847059205 .html.

11. Natash Baker, "Worried about Chemicals in Cosmetics? Apps May Help," *Reuters,* October 21, 2013, http://www.reuters.com/article /2013/10/21/us-apps-cosmetics-idUSBRE99 K0OV20131021.

12. U.S. Food and Drug Administration, "Labeling for Topically Applied Cosmetic Products Containing Alpha Hydroxy Acids as Ingredients," January 10, 2005, www.cfsan.fda.gov/~dms /ahaguid2.html.

13. "Neiman Marcus Settles with U.S. FTC for Selling Real Fur as Fake," *FashionMag.com,* March 20, 2013, http://us.fashionmag.com /news/Neiman-Marcus-settles-with-U-S-FTC-for-selling-real-fur-as-fake,317517.html.

14. International Down and Feather Testing Laboratory, "USA Labeling Standards—Down and Feather Products," January 2005, www.idfl .com/articles/IDFL%20USA%20Labeling%20 Standards%20(Jan%202005).pdf.

15. Kristi Wolff, "FTC to Host Roundtable on Changes to Care Labeling Rule," *Ad Law Access,* July 26, 2013, http://www.adlawaccess.com /2013/07/articles/federal-trade-commission /ftc-to-host-roundtable-on-changes-to-care-labeling-rule/.

16. Federal Trade Commission, "Tommy Hilfiger U.S.A., Inc., Agrees to Pay $300,000 Civil Penalty to Settle FTC Charges of Violating Care Labeling Rule," News release, March 17, 1999.

17. Federal Trade Commission, "Jones Apparel Group Agrees to Pay $300,000 Civil Penalty to Settle FTC Charges of Violating the Care Labeling Rule," News release, April 2, 2002.

18. Nicole Rose Dion, "Social Media and the Government," *MarketingProfs,* July 31, 2013, http://www.marketingprofs.com/articles/2013/11311/social-media-and-the-government.

19. Federal Trade Commission, "Nine West Settles State and Federal Price Fixing Charges," News release, March 6, 2000.

20. Kate Kaye, "FTC Aims to Bring Child Privacy Law Into 21st Century," *Ad Age,* December 19, 2012, http://adage.com/article/digital/ftc-aims-bring-child-privacy-law-21st-century/238842/.

21. Leung, Rebecca. "The Look of Abercrombie & Fitch. " *60 Minutes,* November 24, 2004, www.cbsnews.com/stories/2003/12/05/60minutes/main587099.shtml.

22. U.S. Equal Employment Opportunity Commission, "Dillard's to Pay $2 Million to Settle Class Action Disability Discrimination Lawsuit by EEOC," News release, December 18, 2012.

GLOSSARY

absolute threshold The lowest level at which our senses can recognize a stimulus (Ch. 3).

acculturation The process of adapting to the primary or mainstream culture (Ch.14).

activation The process by which information can be retrieved in our memory networks (Ch. 3).

actual self In self-concept theory, who we think we are (Ch. 6).

affective element The portion of our attitudes that is made up of our emotions toward an attitude object (Ch. 5).

ambush marketing Strategy of identifying venues where the placement of unique marketing materials is sure to attract consumer and media attention (Ch. 1).

Americans with Disabilities Act (ADA) Law that protects the rights of people with disabilities in equal employment opportunities, as well as in equal access to public transportation, public buildings, and other places and activities (Ch. 16).

anthropology The study of human cultural characteristics that include habits, customs, relationships, and so on (Ch. 14).

approach–approach A motivational conflict in which a choice must be made between two desirable options (Ch. 4).

approach–avoidance A simultaneous desire to engage in a certain behavior and to avoid it (Ch. 4).

archetypes According to Carl Jung, shared memories of the past that become the basis for present culture and are sometimes personified by characters (Ch. 6).

aspirational groups Groups to which we do not actually belong but wish we did (Ch. 8).

associative groups Groups to which we belong and identify, such as a volleyball team or professional association (Ch. 8).

attention The focusing of our thoughts on a certain stimulus (Ch. 3).

attitude Our settled opinion—either positive or negative—about people, ideas, places, or objects (Ch. 5).

attitude objects In consumer behavior, those things about which we form attitudes and opinions (Ch. 5).

attitude scales Research questionnaire tool through which respondents can indicate their level of favorable or unfavorable opinion across a range of answers (Ch. 10).

avoidance–avoidance A motivational conflict in whiich a choice must be made between two undesirable options (Ch. 4).

balance of trade The relationship between a country's imports and exports (Ch. 14).

balance theory Theory stating that people want to maintain harmony or balance in their attitudes (Ch. 5).

behavioral element The portion of our attitudes that determines how we intend to act toward an attitude object (Ch. 5).

behavioral learning Theory that states learning takes place after exposure to external stimuli. Two types of behavioral learning are classical conditioning and instrumental conditioning (Ch. 3).

behavioral perspective The use of actions that consumers have learned in response to specific stimuli as a basis for decision making (Ch. 12).

Better Business Bureau (BBB) Umbrella organization for more than 300,000 local business members nationwide that are dedicated to fostering fair and honest relationships between businesses and consumers, instilling consumer confidence, and contributing to an ethical business environment (Ch. 16).

birthrate The number of babies born in a year (Ch. 9).

blog An online journal in which an individual, group, or corporation presents a record of observations, opinions, experiences, and other thoughts for readers (Ch. 11).

boycott Action in which consumers make the conscious decision not to purchase a product as a protest and moral statement (Ch. 15).

brand The total of all that is known and felt about a product, service, or organization, from its recognizable name, logo, slogan, and packaging to the power it holds in people's minds (Ch. 1).

brand equity The accumulation of brand image and brand loyalty that results in consumer satisfaction, retention, and demand (Ch. 1).

brand image The deliberate, consistent way a product's qualities and essence are communicated to the public (Ch. 1).

brand loyalty Repeat purchase behavior exhibited by customers who have strong connections to a favorite brand (Ch. 1).

brand personification The characteristics, related to human personality traits, that advertisers give to certain brands (Ch. 6).

buyer's market Situation in which there are more sellers than buyers; a consequent excess of supply over demand results in lower prices for consumers (Ch. 2).

buyer's remorse *See* post-purchase dissonance.

buzz The tongue-wagging and word-of-mouth chatter about a product set in motion by marketers, particularly public relations and advertising experts. *See also* ambush marketing; guerilla marketing; viral marketing (Ch. 1).

Care Labeling Rule Law that requires manufacturers and importers to attach care instructions to their garments (Ch. 16).

cause-based marketing or cause-related marketing The public association of a for-profit company with a nonprofit organization, often involving the donation of a specified portion of profits to the nonprofit charity or cause (Ch. 2).

chunking The capacity of our memories to amass large amounts of encoded information on a topic by adding on and linking to what we already know (Ch. 3).

classic style A style or fashion that is characterized by a simplicity of design that keeps it from becoming easily dated (Ch. 13).

classical conditioning Creating change in behavior by teaming an artificial stimulus with a natural one, with the goal of gaining a response from the artificial stimulus alone (Ch. 3).

cognitive element The portion of our attitudes that comes from what we have seen, read, or experienced concerning an attitude object; it forms the basis of our beliefs about that object (Ch. 5).

cognitive learning A problem-solving process where individuals seek out information in order to make an informed decision (Ch. 3).

collective selection A process by which a mass of people formulate certain collective tastes reflected by the goods and services they choose, and their selections illustrate the beliefs and values of the group's social system (Ch. 1).

comparison shopping A process whereby a consumer gathers as much information as possible about similar products and services in order to compare features, pricing, and other details before deciding which to purchase (Ch. 12).

competitive advantage The delivery of benefits that exceed those supplied by the competition, making it the best choice for the customer and the most profitable for an organization (Ch. 1).

compliance Response to social influence that occurs when we choose to do something because someone else asked us to do it (Ch. 8).

compulsive buying behavior Indiscriminate purchasing of goods; a form of neurosis (Ch. 6).

conflict Situation requiring a choice between two actions or behaviors that might result in equally desirable or equally undesirable outcomes (Ch. 4).

conformity A response to social influence that occurs when we behave like others in order to be accepted or feel like "one of the group" (Ch. 8).

conscious motive Reason for an action that we know and understand; we are aware of what we are doing and why (Ch. 4).

consumer behavior The actions and decision-making processes of buyers as they recognize their desire for a product or service, and engage in the search, evaluation, purchase, use, and disposal of that particular commodity (Ch. 1).

consumer confidence How consumers feel about the state of the economy (Ch. 9).

consumer decision-making process Purchase process that includes: need recognition, information search, evaluation of alternatives, purchase, post-purchase evaluation (Ch. 4).

Consumer Product Safety Commission (CPSC) An independent government agency whose directive is to protect the public against unreasonable risks of injuries associated with consumer products (Ch. 16).

consumer socialization The process by which children acquire knowledge about products and services, along with various consumption-related skills needed to function as consumers in the marketplace (Ch. 7).

consumerism (1) The movement protecting consumers by requiring honest packaging and product guarantees. (2) The theory that the greater consumption of economic goods is beneficial. (3) The attachment to materialistic values and possessions (Ch. 9).

consumption The using up of a resource by the person who has selected, adopted, used, and discarded or recycled it (Ch. 1).

consumption roles The expected or prescribed behaviors of consumers within a household; includes information gatherers/influencers, gatekeepers, decision makers, purchasers, and users (Ch. 7).

count Observational research method whereby an observer or team of observers keeps a written tally of the category being studied (Ch. 10).

counterfeit goods Unauthorized, illegal copies of designer or branded products (Ch. 15).

crowdsourcing Gathering information or feedback from a variety of people to help understand and resolve issues, make purchase decisions, or get answers to specific questions (Ch. 11).

cultural anthropology The study of the common symbols, values, and beliefs of social groups and institutions (Ch. 14).

cultural borrowing The use of symbols that are meaningful to other cultures (Ch. 14).

culture All the shared beliefs, values, and traditions learned and practiced by a group of people, who may live close to each other, all of whom are focused on a common quest (Ch. 1).

customization The integration of individual requirements into a product (Ch. 2).

decision maker The person who ultimately determines, with or without input from members of a consumption group, which items will be considered and purchased, and how they will be used and discarded (Ch. 7).

decline phase Stage in a fashion's life cycle when it is experiencing decreasing sales and availability only in the lower price ranges (Ch. 13).

demand The level of desire among consumers for a particular product and the price that people are willing to pay to obtain it (Ch. 4).

demographics The measurable statistics concerning a population, particularly its size, composition, and distribution (Ch. 9).

depth interview A qualitative research method that involves one participant offering thoughts and opinions to a researcher (Ch. 10).

design A creative process, driven by a need, that leads to an invention of some sort, be it practical or artistic, functional or simply attractive, devised to enhance life in some way (Ch. 1).

desire A yearning or longing for something (Ch. 4).

direct (primary) influencers Groups or people with whom we have the most contact, such as family or close friends, and whose opinions are very powerful (Ch. 8).

direction In evaluating the motivation behind a consumer purchase, what the customer wants from a product in terms of features or benefits (Ch. 4).

disassociative groups Groups that do not interest us and of which we may disapprove (Ch. 8).

discretionary income The amount of money consumers have after meeting all expenditures for necessities (Ch. 9).

disposable income The amount of money, after taxes, that people have left for necessities such as food, shelter, utilities, and transportation (Ch. 9).

disposer One who gets rid of a product or discontinues use of a service (Ch. 7).

diversity Variety or variation that which makes us dissimilar or different from one another (Ch. 14).

downward flow (trickle-down theory) Movement of fashion in which styles adopted by upper classes trickle down the social ladder and are later adopted by the mainstream (Ch. 8).

duties Additional monies and taxes on imports imposed by the country receiving those goods (Ch. 14).

e-commerce Shopping done on the Internet by means of a computer, tablet, smartphone, or any other electronic device (Ch. 13).

ego The conscious component of personality, our sense of ourselves; it reacts to reality in a socially acceptable way, serving as a mediator between the desires of the id and the restraint of the superego (Ch. 6).

emotional needs Purchase motivation based on nonrational behavior and reasoning (Ch. 4).

encoding The way we select visual images or words in short-term memory to represent what we want to store in long-term memory (Ch. 3).

enculturation The process through which humans learn about and act according to the expectations of their own culture from birth on (Ch. 14).

Equal Employment Opportunity (EEO) laws Federal laws that prohibit discrimination in hiring based on race, color, religion, sex, national origin, or disability, and which protect men and women who perform substantially equal work in the same establishment from sex-based wage discrimination, among other things (Ch. 16).

ethics A system of moral values, or a set of principles that define right and wrong (Ch. 15).

ethnocentrism Situation in which individuals make consumption choices that relate specifically to their own culture (Ch. 12).

experiential hierarchy An attitude formation during the purchase process by which consumers are interested in enjoying a product, its symbols, and emotional meanings before learning about its features and benefits; the basis for consumption that is hedonic (Ch. 5).

experiential perspective Use of the overall experience as opposed to a particular decision criterion in decision making (Ch. 12).

exports Goods or commodities transported from one country to another country in a legitimate fashion, typically for use in trade (Ch. 14).

exposure Situation that occurs when we encounter a stimulus through our senses: seeing, hearing, smelling, touching, or tasting (Ch. 3).

express claims Advertising assertions about a product's benefits that are made literally (Ch. 16).

extended family Family group that includes grandparents, aunts, uncles, and other relatives beyond the nuclear family (Ch. 7).

extended self Self-identification that represents the relationship between ourselves and our possessions (Ch. 6).

extensive decision making Decision-making process in which the consumer weighs the pros and cons, along with the perceived risks and benefits (Ch. 12).

external recognition Awareness of a need or "problem" that is stimulated by others, such as marketers (Ch. 12).

external (social) factors Elements of motivation derived from outside influences (Ch. 4).

extroverts People who are outgoing and mainly concerned with external matters (Ch. 6).

fad A short-lived fashion that bursts onto the scene, is wildly popular among a target group of consumers, and then disappears (Ch. 13).

Fair Packaging and Labeling Act Law that states all cosmetics products must list their ingredients in descending order of predominance and the packaging must give the net quantity of contents (Ch. 16).

fair-trade practices Standards for working conditions, environmental responsibility, and fair pricing that are based not only on ethical labor practices but also on the intent to provide opportunity to disadvantaged workers and help alleviate poverty (Ch. 15).

false need The desire for something to which we attribute more value than it is actually worth (Ch. 4).

family A group of individuals who live together and are related either by blood, adoption, or marriage; the unit that teaches each member the skills needed to function in society (Ch. 7).

fashion Whatever is of the moment and subject to change; anything that members of a population deem desirable and appropriate at a given time (Ch. 1).

fashion diffusion The spread of a fashion throughout different societal groups (Ch. 8).

fashion followers People who adopt a look only after they are sure of a fashion trend (Ch. 13).

fashion influentials People who recognize and endorse what fashion innovators are wearing and doing (Ch. 6).

fashion innovators (fashion leaders) People who buy the earliest and are the first visual communicators of the season's styles (Ch. 6).

fashion life cycle The length of time a given look or style is popular (Ch. 13).

fast fashion Term for offering consumers the latest fashions as quickly as possible (Ch. 13).

Federal Food, Drug and Cosmetic Act Law that prohibits the marketing of adulterated (contaminated) or misbranded cosmetics in interstate commerce (Ch. 16).

Federal Trade Commission (FTC) Independent agency of the U.S. government created by the Federal Trade Commission Act of 1914 to prevent unfair methods of competition in commerce (Ch. 16).

Flammable Fabrics Act Law that regulates the flammability of clothing and home furnishings, as well as paper, plastic, foam, and other materials used both in apparel and interior furnishings (Ch. 16).

flash sale An online, limited-time discount on branded, sometimes high-end merchandise (Ch. 13).

focus group Qualitative research method that gathers a small group of consumers with a moderator to discuss and offer opinions about a product, service, or other marketing-related topic (Ch. 10).

Food and Drug Administration (FDA) Federal agency that is responsible for protecting the public health by assuring the safety, efficacy, and security of human and veterinary drugs, biological products, medical devices, the nation's food supply, cosmetics, and products that emit radiation (Ch. 16).

forecasting A creative process used by industry professionals to predict future trends (Ch. 1).

functions of attitudes Daniel Katz' theory of the four classifications of attitudes that serve to help us achieve balance in life: (1) utilitarian, (2) value-expressive, (3) ego-defensive, and (4) knowledge (Ch. 5).

Fur Products Labeling Act Law stating that garments made either entirely or partly with fur must have a label disclosing the animal name; if the fur is used or damaged; and if the fur product is composed in whole or substantial part of pieces, among other information (Ch. 16).

gatekeeper A knowledgeable individual who controls access and information flow to followers, and influences them to act in specific ways (Ch. 7).

geodemographic system A consumer-measuring technique combining geography and demographics, first devised by Claritas Corp (Ch. 9).

gestalt psychology The phenomenon of coming to a conclusion after seeing the total picture or pattern; the "aha" experience (Ch. 3).

globalization The ability to market a product anywhere in the world that a demand for it exists (Ch. 14).

goal A particular outcome or end desired by an individual or organization (Ch. 4).

group Two or more people who share similar values and beliefs and communicate interdependently (Ch. 8).

guerilla marketing A term coined by Jay Conrad Levinson to describe unconventional marketing tactics designed to get maximum results from minimal resources (Ch. 1).

habitual or routine decision making Situation in which not much thought is needed to reach a decision (Ch. 12).

hashtag A word or phrase preceded by the symbol "#" that enables users to easily retrieve a grouping of all messages that contain that word or phrase (Ch. 11).

hedonic consumption A part of the emotional aspect of our relationships to products that comes from the ways we respond to stimuli (Ch. 3).

heuristics Simple mental rules of thumb that help us make decisions more quickly (Ch. 12).

hierarchy of effects The series of steps—feelings, beliefs, actions—that we go through in forming our attitudes (Ch. 5).

high-involvement hierarchy An attitude formation problem-solving process consumers use to reach a buying decision about a product that is usually an important purchase (Ch. 5).

horizontal flow (trickle-across theory) Movement of fashion in which influences among peer groups with similar demographic or psychographic profiles are what determine a style's adoption (Ch. 8).

household Any single person or a group of persons who live together in a residential setting, regardless of whether they are related (Ch. 7).

hype A set of activities set in motion prior to the actual introduction of a new product or service that helps create a supportive marketing environment and a spontaneously infectious kind of person-to-person image spinning (Ch. 1).

id (libido) Unconscious personality component that controls our biological drives of hunger, sex, and self-preservation; it is with us from birth, and its impulses require immediate gratification (Ch. 6).

ideal self In self-concept theory, who we would like to be (Ch. 6).

ideal social self-image In self-concept theory, how we would like others to see us (Ch. 6).

immigration The influx of people into a country from another country (Ch. 9).

implied claims Advertising assertions that are made indirectly or by inference (Ch. 16).

imports Goods and services provided by foreign producers that are purchased and brought into a country (Ch. 14).

incentive To move the consumer from an actual state to a desired state; a reason to buy (Ch. 4).

income The money and other assets that people typically receive in a year from their work, property, and other investments (Ch. 9).

indirect (secondary) influencers Groups that are not in our immediate circle of friends and family and therefore do not have a strong influence on our decision making (Ch. 8).

inertia habit Act of completing a consumption activity or buying the same brand because it takes little or no energy (Ch. 12).

information collection The search for and selection of data that provide an adequate foundation for making good decisions (Ch. 12).

information filtering The process of sorting through collected data, then prioritizing and selecting that which best meets our information objectives (Ch. 12).

information gatherer/influencer A person who provides information/guidance to other members of a group about products and services (Ch. 7).

information overload The condition of being bombarded with more information than we can process or store in our memories (Ch. 3).

informational influences Facts, figures, data, and so on from professionals who are familiar with a specific subject or brand that have an effect on our decision making (Ch. 3).

informational social influences Factors that cause us to copy the behavior of others because they directly or indirectly offer information to assist in our decision making (Ch. 8).

innovation Something that is new to the person seeing or experiencing it (Ch. 1).

instinct An innate drive that we are born with and that is largely physiological (Ch. 4).

instrumental conditioning Creating change in behavior by making choices that result in rewards and avoid punishment (Ch. 3).

integrated marketing system (IMS) The continuous, efficient sharing of information and ideas among all participants in an organization, with a goal of organized, effective communication with the desired audience (Ch. 1).

intensity In evaluating the motivation for a consumer purchase, the level of a customer's interest in a product (Ch. 4).

internal (nonsocial) factors Elements of motivation that come from within a person (Ch. 4).

internal recognition Awareness of a need or "problem" that originates within an individual (Ch. 12).

introduction phase Stage of the fashion life cycle when a new style first appears (Ch. 13).

introverts People who choose to turn inward, rather than concern themselves with external matters (Ch. 6).

inventory shrinkage Retail term for losses that includes employee theft, shoplifting, vendor fraud, and administrative error (Ch. 15).

just noticeable difference (j.n.d) The ability of our senses to distinguish between two closely similar stimuli, such as popular music and jazz (Ch. 3).

knockoffs Fashion industry term for copies of the original styles (Ch. 13).

learning The process of changing behavior through experience (Ch. 3).

life expectancy The length of time people will live, and how long they can be productive in an economy and in society (Ch. 9).

lifestyle An individual's distinctive way of living; a pattern that influences a person's choices in all areas of life, from how to spend time to how to spend money (Ch. 9).

Likert scale Quantitative research tool that presents a statement and asks consumers to select a degree of agreement or disagreement with the statement (Ch. 10).

limited decision making Process of decision making that involves some thought, but frequently involves general rules of thumb we've learned or borrowed from others (Ch. 12).

long-term memory The part of memory that stores information we want to keep for permanent use and recall at will (Ch. 3).

low-involvement hierarchy An attitude formation purchase process in which the purchase is insignificant, the consumer does not prefer one brand over another, and does not form a firm like or dislike until after using the product (Ch. 5).

loyalty programs Retail marketing programs that offer customers a reward or an incentive to keep them returning to the store (Ch. 15).

m-commerce Shopping using a mobile device (Ch. 13).

magalogs Shopping magazines, such as *Lucky*, featuring fashion, and *Domino*, showcasing home décor (Ch. 10).

mandatory standards Government rules requiring all manufacturers, retailers, importers, and distributors to ensure that the products they are selling meet specific criteria, usually for safety (Ch. 16).

market research The collecting of information about the marketplace that results in planned marketing activities and that helps generate revenues (Ch. 2).

market segment A homogeneous group of buyers displaying like needs, wants, values, and buying behaviors (Ch. 1).

market segmentation A method for dividing markets into smaller homogeneous units in order to more effectively reach potential customers who reflect similar characteristics, wants, and needs (Ch. 2).

marketing A process that includes the communication of all information sellers want to share with consumers, from the time a product or service is an idea, through its purchase, use, evaluation, and disposal by the customer (Ch. 1).

marketing concept A design that focuses on a company's knowing its clients, satisfying their needs, and doing so more effectively than its competitors at a profit (Ch. 2).

marketing research The process of analyzing a given marketing opportunity or problem, and often finding solutions through understanding the behaviors and preferences of the market's consumers (Ch. 10).

mass marketing The distribution and promotion of the same product to a broad base of all potential customers (Ch. 1).

materialism The importance that we attach to the things we own (Ch. 9).

means-end chain (MEC) A structure that links a consumer's knowledge about a product's attributes (benefits or risks) with the desired cultural value state the person wants to achieve; the means = the product, and the end = the desired value/outcome (Ch. 14).

memory The process of storing and retrieving the knowledge we have learned (Ch. 3).

microblog A social platform for sharing thoughts, ideas, or opinions with entries that are condensed to a much shorter format than a standard blog (Ch. 11).

motivate To impel, incite, or move a person into action (Ch. 4).

motivation The result of forces acting either on or within a person to initiate or activate certain behavior (Ch. 4).

motivational research Field of research that studies the effect of the unconscious id and the superego on motives in purchasing behavior (Ch. 6).

multi-attribute model Fishbein's model stating that a combination of consumers' beliefs, derived from their knowledge of the attributes of a product, reveals their overall attitude toward the product (Ch. 5).

multi-channel retailing The use of catalogs, stores, and the Internet in a coordinated marketing plan (Ch. 13).

multicultural Term used to describe a group of people belonging to a dominant culture but who have diverse cultural backgrounds (Ch. 14).

multiple selves The many roles we each take on in our self-concept (Ch. 6).

National Consumers League A nonprofit membership organization working for health, safety, and fairness in the marketplace and workplace (Ch. 16).

need An internal state of discomfort that calls for a solution. Types include acquired, primary vs. secondary, stability vs. variety (Ch. 4).

need for achievement A personality trait shown by people who want to stand out from the crowd or do better than others (Ch. 6).

need for affiliation A personality trait demonstrated by people who place an emphasis on gaining friends, maintaining close relationships, and belonging to groups (Ch. 6).

need for cognition (NC) A personality trait indicating the desire for knowledge (Ch. 6).

need for power A personality trait shown by people who want to influence or control others (Ch. 6).

need satisfaction The experiencing of pleasure when a need has been addressed (Ch. 4).

negative motivation Impetus for an action that is based more on dissatisfaction with a current situation than on the benefits the action would bring (Ch. 4).

neurosis A mental disorder with emotionally painful symptoms that can surface as anxiety, compulsion, and depression (Ch. 6).

nontraditional family Family group that may include single parents, step-relatives, unmarried partners, and so on (Ch. 7).

normative beliefs The opinions of other people who matter to us (Ch. 5).

normative social influence Form of pressure that requires a person to conform to the expectations of others (Ch. 8).

nuclear family Family group that includes parent(s) and children living together (Ch. 7).

obedience Response to social influence that occurs when one strictly obeys an order from an authoritative person or group (Ch. 8).

objectives (for research) The specific information marketers want to learn through a research study (Ch. 10).

obsolescence or rejection phase Stage that marks the end of a style's fashion life cycle, indicating that the look is out-of-date and no longer being sold (Ch. 13).

omnichannel retailing A retailing structure in which merchants focus on engaging and serving their customers in a seamless manner regardless of the method, online or offline, those customers are using to shop (Ch. 13).

opinion leader Individual who is highly regarded by his peers and serves as a credible source or a liaison, who transmits and translates information from mass media to those seeking advice (Ch. 8).

optimal stimulation level (OSL) Concept that people have different needs for stimulation, most preferring moderate stimulation over high stimulation (Ch. 6).

organized retail theft Multiple shoplifters working together to steal larger quantities of products, which are stolen not for personal use, but to resell (Ch. 15).

peak phase Stage of the fashion life cycle when a style is at the height of its acceptance and popularity (Ch. 13).

per capita personal income Total income of a prescribed area divided by the total population (Ch. 9).

perceived cost The balance between the bundle of benefits received and a competitor's comparable cost (Ch. 2).

perceived risk The risk a customer believes exists in the purchase of goods or services whether or not a risk actually exists (Ch. 12).

perception The process of interpreting our surroundings through our senses (Ch. 3).

perceptual mapping A graphics technique enabling marketers to visualize consumers' attitudes toward their products and those of their competitors (Ch. 5).

personality The individual psychological characteristics that routinely influence the way people react to their surroundings (Ch. 5).

positioning Creating a certain perception or image about a product in the minds of consumers that differentiates it from the competition (Ch. 1).

positive motivation Impetus for an action that is based on recognition of the action's benefits (Ch. 4).

post-purchase dissonance ("buyer's remorse") Situation in which doubt about making a purchase decision follows the actual purchase and creates tension or a state of dissonance; also known as "cognitive dissonance" (Ch. 4).

price fixing Situation in which business competitors make an agreement to set the price for which their products will be sold in a given market (Ch. 16).

primary (basic) needs Basic physiological requirements for all humans, including food, clothing, shelter, sleep, etc. (Ch. 4).

primary data Original information that is collected firsthand via personal interviews, focus groups, and surveys (Ch. 2).

primary research An original study designed to address a company's specific objectives (Ch. 10).

PRIZM A geodemographic method of segmenting markets by ZIP codes, and then combining demographics (such as income and education) with lifestyles, thus identifying areas of similar consumer behavior throughout the United States (Ch. 9).

problem awareness State in which a consumer perceives an imbalance between his or her current ("as is") situation and an ideal ("should be") situation (Ch. 12).

product differentiation Strategy by which companies attempt to make their product seem unique when compared to similar products by competitors (Ch. 1).

psychoanalytic theory Sigmund Freud theory stating that many of our behaviors and dreams come from our unconscious, where thoughts, of which we are largely unaware, are stored (Ch. 6).

psychographics The study of consumer personality and lifestyle (Ch. 9).

psychology The study of individual behavior (Ch. 4).

purchaser One who secures/buys product(s) (Ch. 7).

purchasing power The amount of goods and services the dollar will buy (Ch. 9).

qualitative research Research that is subjective, focusing on people's opinions and attitudes toward a product or service (Ch. 10).

quantifying Measuring and expressing a result as a number equivalent (Ch. 2).

quantitative research Research that is objective, focusing on collecting numbers and facts that can be analyzed statistically (Ch. 10).

quota A limit on the quantity of goods that can be imported into a country (Ch. 14).

rational needs Purchase motivation based on reasoning and logic (Ch. 4).

rational perspective The use of logically based, left-brain thinking to process information and carefully review the pros and cons of a decision (Ch. 12).

recall The removal of an unsafe product from the marketplace, involving public announcements about the danger and providing information on what to do with the product or how to contact its manufacturer (Ch. 16).

reference group Any person or group serving as a point of comparison or frame of reference for an individual when that individual is forming his own beliefs and behaviors (Ch. 7).

retrieval The process we go through to use information stored in our memories (Ch. 3).

rise phase The period in the fashion life cycle when a look is growing in popularity (Ch. 13).

role The behavior expected of a person in a given setting (Ch. 7).

secondary (acquired) needs Needs that are learned in accordance with the values of a person's specific culture and which are met only after primary needs are fulfilled (Ch. 4).

secondary data Information that has been collected from other studies or sources such as textbooks, magazines, the Internet, and other published materials (Ch. 2).

secondary research Locating data from existing sources that meets a study's research objectives (Ch. 10).

selective perception Paying attention to the stimuli that connect to our needs (Ch. 3).

self-concept An individual's perception of his or her own characteristics and attributes (Ch. 6).

self-concept theory Theory stating that in addition to the personality having multiple selves, we envision ourselves both privately and in relation to others (Ch. 6).

self-esteem Our positive and negative opinions of ourselves and our estimate of our self-worth (Ch. 6).

seller's market Situation in which there are more buyers than sellers; increased demand and low supply result in higher prices (Ch. 2).

selling concept Business approach that focuses on trying to sell what a company has already made, not what the customer wants (Ch. 2).

semiotics The study of symbols and their meanings (Ch. 6).

showrooming Visiting a physical store to examine goods first-hand but then looking for a lower price and purchasing online (Ch. 13).

social class Groups of individuals belonging to different levels of society; social classes are hierarchical and, for the most part, depend on levels of prosperity and opportunity, and at times on inheritance (Ch. 8).

social impact theory Theory stating the probability of influence increases depending on the number of people involved and the importance and proximity of the influencers (Ch. 8).

social influence The information or pressure that an individual, group, or type of media presents or exerts on consumers (Ch. 8).

social media The collection of online spaces and tools that allow individuals and groups to generate content and engage in interactive, peer-to-peer conversations and content exchange (Ch. 11).

social media marketing (SMM) The process of garnering consumer attention and sales through use of social media platforms (Ch. 11).

social networking Websites and services that allow users to share ideas, activities, events, interests, photos, and so on with other people in the network, and may include mechanisms for e-mail and instant messaging among users (Ch. 11).

social responsibility The principle that everyone is responsible for making the world a better place for all its inhabitants (Ch. 15).

social self-image In self-concept theory, how others see us (Ch. 6).

social shopping A method of commerce that uses technology to mimic the social interactions found in physical malls and stores (Ch. 11).

socialization Process of preparing children for the future by teaching them the skills, attitudes, and general knowledge necessary to effectively integrate into society (Ch. 7).

societal marketing concept The idea that companies should balance profits with customer wants, competitors' actions, and society's long-term interests (Ch. 2).

sociology The study of group behavior (Ch. 4).

stability Constancy; a need that can motivate people not to take a new action (Ch. 4).

stakeholder A person or persons with an interest in seeing a company succeed (Ch. 2).

Standard for the Flammability of Children's Sleepwear Federal regulations that prescribe a test requiring that specimens of the fabric, seams, and trim from children's sleepwear garments self-extinguish after exposure to a small open flame (Ch. 16).

stealth advertising Devising advertisements in which marketers attempt to conceal the fact that an ad is actually an ad (Ch. 1).

stimulus An energizing force that causes a state of tension or arousal (Ch. 4).

strategic marketing plan A business road map that identifies a specific target market, the preferences of that market's members, and specific ways to connect with and keep them (Ch. 2).

strategy A plan that addresses how to respond to consumers and competitors in the marketplace (Ch. 2).

Strategy Targeting Organized Piracy (STOP!) Government initiative that brings together key agencies in a comprehensive initiative to fight global piracy and counterfeiting (Ch. 16).

subculture A smaller group within a large society/culture (such as persons of the same age, political ideology, ethnicity, social class, sexual orientation) who possesses distinct beliefs, goals, interests, and values that differentiate them from the dominant culture (Ch. 8).

subjective norms Influences on our decision making that include our normative beliefs, plus the extent to which we are motivated to go along with others' opinions (Ch. 5).

subliminal perception The perception of stimuli by our senses below our level of conscious awareness or absolute threshold (Ch. 3).

superego Component of personality that acts as a conscience, promoting acceptable standards of behavior and restraining the impulsive id by creating feelings of guilt to punish misconduct, real or imagined (Ch. 6).

supply chain The organizations and related activities associated with the manufacture and delivery of a service or product. It represents the work flow from supplier to manufacturer to wholesaler to retailer to the end user, the consumer (Ch. 2).

sweatshops Factories where workers are obliged to work long hours, under poor conditions, for very little pay (Ch. 15).

target market Group of potential customers that share similar lifestyles and preferences, on which a company intends to focus its marketing efforts (Ch. 1).

target marketing Defining a specific segment of the market and making it the strategic focus for the business or marketing plan (Ch. 2).

tariffs Taxes on imports imposed by the country receiving those goods (Ch. 14).

Textile Fiber Products Identification Act (Textile Act) Federal law stating that any company that advertises or sells clothing or fabric household items must label its products to accurately reflect their fiber content (Ch. 16).

theory of cognitive dissonance Theory explaining consumers' discomfort due to conflicting attitudes concerning an attitude object, often a recent significant purchase (Ch. 5).

Theory of Reasoned Action (TORA) Theory stating that in addition to the affective, cognitive, and behavioral components of attitude, subjective norms including our normative beliefs (others' opinions) plus the extent to which we're motivated to go along with those opinions play a part in reaching a buying decision (Ch. 5).

trade deficit Situation in which a country imports more than it exports (Ch. 14).

trade surplus Situation in which a country exports more than it imports (Ch. 14).

traditional family life cycle The historically typical stages in relationships through which people pass as they age. Phases include bachelorhood, honeymoon, full nest, empty nest, dissolution (Ch. 7).

traits Distinct characteristics that differentiate us from others and contribute to our behavior (Ch. 6).

trend The direction in which something (such as fashion) is moving (Ch. 1).

trend forecasting services Services that offer advisories formulated by professional observers of cultural shifts that contain calculated predictions about the likely direction in which design preferences are moving (Ch. 14).

trunk show Fashion event in which a designer or representative of a manufacturer brings an entire line to a local store for customers to see and buy (Ch. 10).

trust Large business entities that succeed in controlling a market, in essence becoming a monopoly (Ch. 16).

truth-in-advertising laws Regulations enforced by the Federal Trade Commission that require marketers to create advertising that is truthful and to be able to support any claims about a product with reliable, objective evidence (Ch. 16).

21st-century family life cycle An updated equivalent of the traditional family life cycle, the phases of which include child/teen, single/independent, new couple/partnership, mid-adulthood, empty nest, dissolution (Ch. 7).

unconscious motive Reason for an action in which we are not aware of why we are acting in that particular way (Ch. 4).

unsought goods Products or services that consumers do not actually seek or plan to buy, such as items that are purchased without advance need recognition (e.g., an umbrella for a sudden downpour) (Ch. 4).

upward flow (trickle-up theory) Movement of fashion in which a new fashion idea starts among the lower echelons of society or on the "street" and works its way up (Ch. 8).

user One who consumes/uses a product or service (Ch. 7).

utilitarian influences Factors that cause an individual to yield to another person's or group's influence to gain recognition and reward or avoid punishment (Ch. 8).

VALS A psychographic system developed by SRI International that many marketers employ to find out why customers make certain buying decisions based on psychological traits, motivation, and resources (Ch. 9).

value Tangible or intangible attributes that improve the desirability of a product or service (Ch. 2).

value expressive influences Motivational factors that address core values or the values people believe they should possess, which would enhance their image in the eyes of others (Ch. 8).

value system A learned organization of principles and rules to help one choose between alternatives, resolve conflicts, and make decisions (Ch. 14).

values The ideas one considers important in life; an individual's set of principles for behavior (Ch. 9).

variety Changeability; a need that can motivate people to make a change or do something different (Ch. 4).

viral marketing The passing on of a marketing message to others, much like passing a virus from one person to another (Ch. 1).

wants Desires that are not necessities nor required for survival (Ch. 4).

Weber's Law Theory that states the more intense a first stimulus, the stronger the next stimulus must be in order for people to distinguish it as different (Ch. 3).

Wool Products Labeling Act (Wool Act) Federal rules requiring that, even if wool accounts for less than 5 percent of the weight of a product, it must be listed on the label (Ch. 16).

word-of-mouth marketing (WOM) The passing along from person to person of a marketing message or opinions about a product, which can happen either spontaneously or as a result of a marketer's strategy (Ch. 1).

zeitgeist The spirit of the times, experienced by many people simultaneously (Ch. 1).

FIGURE CREDITS

Chapter 1

Figure 1.1: Per-Anders Pettersson/Corbis

Figure 1.2: Dara Ref.: infusny-05/42|sp|

Figure 1.4: Associated Press

Figure 1.5: Matthew Chattle/Alamy; RICHARD B. LEVINE/ Newscom

Chapter 2

Figure 2.1a and b: Courtesy MY TWINN; ZUMA Press, Inc./ Alamy

Figure 2.2a–f: Andrew Buckin/Shutterstock; Steve Collender/ Shutterstock; dekede/Shutterstock; Shell114/ Shutterstock; Elena Schweitzer/Shutterstock; Courtesy Apple Inc.

Figure 2.4 Courtesy: Fairchild Books

Figure 2.7 Source: Anthony Jenkins for Fairchild Books

Chapter 3

Figures 3.1a, b, and c: Patti McConville/Alamy; VIEW Pictures Ltd/Alamy; VIEW Pictures Ltd/Alamy

Figure 3.2a and b: Joe Schildhorn /BFAnyc/Sipa USA/Newscom

Figure 3.3: The Advertising Archive

Figure 3.4: Yutilova Elena/Shutterstock

Figure 3.5: Courtesy WWW / © Condé Nast

Figure 3.7: Peter Horree/Alamy

Figure 3.8: The Advertising Archive

Chapter 4

Figure 4.1: www.pateo.com/images/maslowmaster4ts.gif. February 6, 2006

Figure 4.2: The Advertising Archive

Figure 4.3: BRAD BARKET/ GETTY IMAGES FOR JC PENNEY

Chapter 5

Figure 5.2: The Advertising Archive

Figure 5.3: BUSINESS WIRE

Figure 5.4: The Advertising Archive

Figures 5.6a, b, and c: The Advertising Archive

Figure 5.7: The Advertising Archive; Courtesy Cotton Inc.

Figure 5.8: Courtesy of L.e.i. Jeans; The Advertising Archive

Figure 5.10: Patti McConville/Alamy

Figure 5.13: The Advertising Archive

Chapter 6

Figure 6.2: Shutterstock

Figure 6.3: The Advertising Archive

Figure 6.4: Courtesy Celestial Seasoning

Figure 6.5: Anthony Jenkins for Fairchild Publications, Inc. Adapted from Atomic Dog

Figure 6.7: The Advertising Archive

Figure 6.8: Eichner/WWD; © Condé Nast

Figure 6.9: The Ford Motor Company

Figure 6.10: Adapted from Schiffman and Kanuk, Fig. 5–7. p. 139. Original source: Jennifer L. Aaker, "Dimensions of Brand Personality," *Journal of Marketing Research* 35, August 1997, p. 352. Permission American Marketing Association

Chapter 7

Figure 7.1a–c: Diego Cervo/Shutterstock (b); Aleph Studio/ Shutterstock (c)

Figure 7.2a–b: BIG CHEESE PHOTO LLC/ALAMY; Jenkins/ WWD; © Condé Nast

Chapter 8

Figures 8.1 and 8.2: Yanes /WWD; © Condé Nast

Figure 8.4a–d: Jenkins /WWD; © Condé Nast (a, b, c); Yanes / WWD; © Condé Nast (d)

Figure 8.5: iQoncept/Shutterstock

Figure 8.6: Pressmaster/Shutterstock 70152043

Figure 8.7: Andresr/Shutterstock

Figures 8.8a–c: Jason Horowitz/zefa/Corbis (a); Tim Pannell/ Corbis (b); Image Source/Corbis (c)

Figure 8.9a–b: Jstone/Shutterstock16415765 (a); s_bukley/ Shutterstock 92668216 (b)

Chapter 9

Figure 9.1: (a) Rathbone/Teen Vogue, © Condé Nast; (b) Hout / Lucky, © Condé Nast; (c) Palmer /WWD, © Condé Nast

Figure 9.2: iStock

Figure 9.3: Chinsee /WWD, © Condé Nast

Figure 9.4: Bill Bachmann/ALAMY

Figure 9.5: Xavier Collin/Celebrity Monitor/Newscom spnphotosfour737024

Figure 9.7: The Advertising Archive

Figure 9.8: Bloomberg/Getty 94829368

Figure 9.9: Andresr/Shutterstock 96816079

Figure 9.10: kali9/iStock

Chapter 10
Figure 10.1: Presselect/Alamy C4FF5A
Figure 10.2: BIG CHEESE LLC/Alamy
Figure 10.4: SPENCER GRANT/PHOTOEDIT INC.COM
Figure 10.5: Ericksen/WWD; © Condé Nast

Chapter 11
Figure 11.1 a–c: Blend Images/Shutterstock 146342387
(a); spirit of america/Shutterstock 132476669 (b); Sylvie
Bouchard / Alamy DJ2D5K
Figure 11.4: Telnov Oleksii/Shutterstock

Chapter 12
Figure 12.3 a BonnieBC/Shutterstock
Figure 12.3 b Bartosz Niedzwiecki/Shutterstock
Figure 12.4 Tommaso Colia/Getty

Chapter 13
Figure 13.2 Survivor, PacificCoastNews/Newscom
Figure 13.3 a Horst P. Horst, 1937
Figure 13.3 b Iannaccone /WWD; © Condé Nast
Figure 13.4 a Martin Good/Shutterstock
Figure 13.4 b Vytautas Kielaitis
Figure 13.5 Justin Sullivan/Getty Images
Figure 13.6 Tim Boyle/Getty Images

Chapter 14
Figure 14.1 c Courtesy Apple Inc.
Figure 14.2 Mazur /WWD, © Condé Nast
Figure 14.3 a and b Courtesy Uniqlo
Figure 14.4 Chris Warde-Jones/Redux

Chapter 15
Figure 15.1 Dennis McDonald/Photoedit Inc.
Figure 15.2 Library of Congress
Figure 15.3 © Royalty-Free/Corbis
Figure 15.4 Advertising Archive
Figure 15.5 Patrick /WWD; © Condé Nast
Figure 15.6 Aquino /WWD; © Condé Nast
Figure 15.7 Cone Communications/Echo, 2013 Global CSR Study
Figure 15.8 zstock/Shutterstock

Chapter 16
Figure 16.1 a John Phillips/PA Wire /Associated Press
Figure 16.1 b PRNEWSFOTO/Carters
Figure 16.3 a Jens /WWD; © Condé Nast
Figure 16.3 b Aquino /WWD; © Condé Nast
Figure 16.3 c Mitra /WWD; © Condé Nast
Figure 16.3 d Crawford /WWD; © Condé Nast
Figure 16.4 © Fairchild Books
Figure 16.5 © Fairchild Books
Figure 16.7 Courtesy of the FEDERAL TRADE COMMISSION
Figure 16.8 Advertising Archive
Figure 16.9 Angelo /WWD; © Condé Nast
Figure 16.10 www.jupiterimages.com

INDEX